corpus leandri spes mea

THE BRILLIANTS
A History of the Leander Club

THE BRILLIANTS

A History of the Leander Club

RICHARD BURNELL AND GEOFFREY PAGE

Leander Club

First published in Great Britain 1997
by the Leander Club
Henley-in-Thames, Oxon
Copyright © 1997 by the estate of Richard Burnell and by Geoffrey Page,
who have asserted their moral rights

ISBN 0 9500061 1 4

Printed and bound in Great Britain
by the Bath Press, Lower Bristol Road,
Bath BA2 3BL

Contents

Acknowledgements	vii
In memoriam Richard Desborough Burnell, 1917–1995	ix
Foreword by Christopher Rodrigues, *Chairman, Leander Club*	xi
Prologue by Geoffrey Page	13

PART ONE by Richard Burnell

1	Cock of the London Water, 1818–1839	21
2	Lean Years, 1840–1855	35
3	Chrysalis Years, 1856–1890	54
4	Metamorphosis, 1891–1899	66

PART TWO by Geoffrey Page

5	The End of an Era, 1900–1914	81
6	Regeneration, 1915–1939	96
7	Revival and Survival, 1940–1953	114
8	New Challenges and a Changing Scene, the 1950s and 1960s	128
9	Moving with the Times, the 1970s	141
10	Renovation and Revolution, the 1980s	153
11	Jürgen Gröbler and the New Order, 1990–1992	175
12	The Greatest of the Brilliants, 1993–1996	186
13	The Way Ahead	197

PART THREE by Geoffrey Page
FACTS AND FIGURES

1	Officers of the Club	204
2	Leander Crews at Henley Royal Regatta	206
3	Leander Members in Olympic, World, European and Commonwealth Championships	246

Index	263

Acknowledgements

Many people have helped me with the preparation of this book and I am greatly indebted to all of them, especially the Club's Chairman, Christopher Rodrigues, who found time in a busy life to write the Foreword.

Special thanks must go also to Ken Hylton-Smith for the considerable time he spent in assisting me to compile the rowing records and in searching the archives and ferreting out illustrations. He was helped in this by his brother Dick, to whom I am also indebted for background information about the river and surroundings in the early years of the Club's existence at Stangate.

I must also thank John Beveridge, the Club's Secretary, for his practical assistance and encouragement; Sam Hall and Dorrien Belson for helping me to untangle the background to the 1985 upheavals; Sir Adrian Cadbury, who provided interesting statistics concerning the relative value of the pound from the last century to the present time; my daughter Fenella, for helping in the preparation of the illustrations; Richard Goddard and his assistants, especially Pam Cole, at the Henley Royal Regatta Headquarters, for help with photographs from the George Bushell negatives in the Henley archives (Nos. 66, 67, 71, 72, 79, 86, 88, 89, 90) as well as others by George Bushell and Sons (Nos. 47, 63, 64, 65, 68, 70, 77); John Shore, who has been especially helpful with photographs (Nos. 11, 12, 14, 16, 19, 22, 23, 24, 26, 28, 29, 32, 34, 41, 42, 43, 45, 46, 53, 54, 55, 56, 57, 61, 82, 83, 84, 93, 94, 95, 101, 102, 103, 104, 105, 106, 111, 112, 113, 115, Plates 9, 16, 19); and the following for kindly supplying others: Allsport (Nos. 51, 58, 59, 60, 78), Maggie Phillips (Nos. 108, 109, Plates 18, 20, 21) and Peter Spurrier (No. 119, Plates 22, 23, 24).

Above all, I am particularly indebted to Tony Pocock, who had previously edited both Richard Burnell's *History of Henley Royal Regatta* and my history of Thames Rowing Club *Hear the Boat Sing*. He not only edited the manuscript of this book with considerable thoroughness but also undertook the task of negotiating with the printers and of sorting out many technical matters to do with the publication of this book.

G.G.H.P.
London, April 1997

1 Richard Burnell (watercolour by Paddy Page)

In Memoriam
RICHARD DESBOROUGH BURNELL
1917–1995

This was to have been Richard's book, and his alone. He was uniquely qualified for this. The son of a distinguished oarsman, he followed in his father's footsteps, rowing for Eton, where he was Captain of Boats, Magdalen College and Oxford University. He was thus bred in the old Orthodox traditions of which Leander was the guardian for so many years. The Second World War delayed his rowing career but afterwards he emulated his father by winning an Olympic gold medal. He twice won the Grand Challenge Cup, as well as the Double Sculls at Henley, always in Leander colours.

His widow, Rosalind, is the daughter of one of his father's great rowing contemporaries, Stanley Garton, while his son Peter became the third generation of Burnells to win an Oxford Blue.

Richard served Leander in many capacities, among them as Captain and President. He was made a Henley Steward in 1965 and was also a member of Berkshire County Council from 1957 to 1967, and Chairman of the Highways and Bridges Committee.

Above all, Richard was rowing's historian, writing *A Short History of Leander* with Harold Rickett in 1968. He also wrote histories of Henley and the Boat Race, as well as, among others, instructional books on sculling. Sometime editor of the *British Rowing Almanack*, he was the Rowing Correspondent of *The Times* from 1946 to 1969, and later of the *Sunday Times* until his retirement in 1990. His knowledge of the history of the Club was without equal in its depth and detail. Who better to record the Club's story than he?

Alas, fate does not take such matters into account. He was well into writing this history when he was struck suddenly with his fatal illness, dying mercifully quickly, but in his last days his wish was that I should complete this book.

Press colleagues for many years, we shared, with his close friend and my predecessor as Rowing Correspondent of the *Daily Telegraph*, the late Desmond Hill, many trips to regattas and championships at home and in many far-flung rowing places in the world. Happy memories of these persist and the pages of this book recall many of these occasions for me, so it was no hardship to accede to his last request. Indeed, it was an honour to be asked. My regret is that Richard did not live to complete a work that was so dear to his heart.

I have left most of what Richard wrote intact, except for some necessary re-writing and editing, which he did not live long enough to do himself. The book therefore appears in two sections, Richard's covering the nineteenth century and mine the twentieth.

I hope the result is a worthy memorial to an old friend and a great Leander man.

G.G.H.P.

Foreword

by Christopher Rodrigues, Chairman, Leander Club

To many, the histories of Leander and Henley are intertwined. Many of the Club's most famous races have taken place over the one mile 550 yards stretch of the River Thames that is the Henley Royal Regatta course, while the Leander clubhouse – regarded by many as the *sanctum sanctorum* of British rowing – sits on the river bank between Henley Bridge and the Regatta finish.

Indeed, it would be easy to regard Leander and its Victorian clubhouse, full of honour boards and one-hundred-year-old trophies, as the home of a quaint anachronism – the amateur sportsman. Surely he and his predecessors – the 'Old Heavies' whose days of competitive rowing are long past – are simply part of a tradition that envelops the Thames Valley for one week a year. A sea of pink, suffused with Pimms and champagne, and even the occasional hippo – that beast which, according to tradition, most closely resembles a Leander member in full flight!

But the essence of Leander lies a lot deeper. It lives in the twists and turns of the Henley Reach, as inhospitable a stretch of training water as you could hope for on a cold, blustery winter morning. It lies buried deep in the cold, dank gym which no self-respecting professional sportsman would use, yet has been the home to a long line of World and Olympic medallists.

It reaches the turbulent swell of the Tideway on the flood where Leander crews have contested so many memorable races and beyond to Los Angeles and Bled, to Xochimilco and Lucerne. The essence of Leander is that first and foremost it is a world-class rowing club. It did not start that way in 1818 but it became true, one race at a time, year after year.

This is the history of that journey and Geoffrey Page is admirably qualified to be our guide. Not only was he a top-level international oarsman himself but he is also the doyen of British rowing journalists. Just as important is Geoffrey's long friendship and professional association with Richard Burnell, the Oxford Blue, Olympic gold medallist and Leander President who started writing this book before his untimely death in 1995.

Their years of working together and their respect for each other's knowledge have melded into a Club history that is both compelling for the insider and engaging to the lay reader.

Now, as Leander approaches the twenty-first century, it looks forward to an era in which, providing the recently announced National Lottery grant is confirmed, the clubhouse will be rebuilt, training facilities will be upgraded and youth and women rowers will flourish alongside their adult male counterparts.

For all the individual effort that will go into every future victory, Leander competitors will go to the start with a unique advantage – the impetus of history.

CORPUS LEANDRI SPES MEA

Prologue

by Geoffrey Page

'Rowing', it has been said, 'is a sport the French rightly reserved for their convicts and the Romans for their slaves.' For neither, however, could rowing correctly be described as a sport, since the unfortunate oarsmen were merely the 'engine-room' for fighting ships or trading vessels, though even from the earliest records of rowing, the sporting element was there. The Egyptians, for example, used boats for both commercial and recreational purposes, a funerary inscription of 1430 BC recording that Amenhotep (Amenophis) II, a famous warrior, was also renowned for his feats of oarsmenship, while the earliest literary reference to rowing as a sport occurs in the *Aeneid*, in which Virgil describes the funeral games arranged by Aeneas in honour of his father.

In Britain, as elsewhere, boats became an essential means of transport when roads, such as they were, were often impassable for carriages and other wheeled vehicles. A notable early example was that of King Edgar, who in 973 AD assembled eight Irish princes, surely one of the most distinguished crews ever, to row him on the River Dee from his palace at Chester to his coronation and back. The value in medieval times of those with a knowledge of the waterways can be gathered from the Domesday Book of 1086, which recorded that steersmen of the royal barges owned many substantial properties.

In the fifteenth century, the Livery Companies and Guilds of the City of London, as well as noblemen and gentlemen of quality, had their own barges with lavish staterooms, rowed by sixteen or twenty watermen in their special liveries. With the great increase in trade from the sixteenth century, London became the centre of commerce for the whole country. The backbone of the trade on the waterways was formed by professional watermen, all of whom, from Gravesend to Teddington, were controlled by the Company of Watermen and Lightermen, founded in 1555. In addition to the several hundred lightermen working the barges, there were literally thousands of licensed watermen providing ferries, the taxis of their day, between the many stairs and landing places on the Thames tideway.

It is hardly surprising that, to augment their meagre earnings, many of these watermen competed against each other for wagers, and money, boats and livery coats and badges were often offered as prizes by the Guilds and Livery Companies, or by the wealthy owners of riverside houses. Few rules governed wager matches, which invariably resulted in fouling and sometimes violence among the competitors.

The oldest surviving race was established in 1715 by the Irish comedian and part-owner of Drury Lane Theatre, Thomas Doggett, for six watermen in the year after they had completed their apprenticeship. The race is no longer for professionals but still takes place annually from London Bridge to Chelsea for Doggett's Coat and Badge under the auspices of the Fishmongers' Company. In 1774 an opera entitled *The Watermen* featured the Doggett's race and included a song *Hero and Leander* which became extremely popular for a number of years, not least by the watermen, who often sang it in public. Perhaps it is not too fanciful to wonder if this may have had something to do with the choice of name for the later Leander Club.

A critical point in the development of amateur rowing on the tideway came with a regatta staged by Ranelagh Gardens in 1775, the Venetian word having been coined a few years previously for an acquatic gathering arranged by the Earl of Lincoln at Walton. The Ranelagh Regatta included a race for twelve pairs of watermen for prizes sponsored by the members of various fashionable clubs, including White's, and attracted a huge assembly of craft as well as large numbers of spectators. Such was the success of the occasion that it led to other proprietors of gardens, theatres and taverns staging aquatic events which included rowing contests. Such activities were not confined to the Thames and in the latter part of the century there were river festivals in many parts of Britain, such as those on the Severn at Shrewsbury, at Newcastle-on-Tyne and Stockton-on-Tees, and even on Lake Windermere. In due course, the Tyne was to become one of the main centres of competitive professional rowing.

Inevitably, gentlemen amateurs began to show an interest in the sport, though documentation of this early development is rare. Among the first amateur boat clubs to be established towards the end of the eighteenth century, initially for recreational purposes, were those of Eton College and Westminster School, named not after the schools but after the boats they used, the Monarch Boat Club of Eton and the Isis Club of Westminster being in existence in the 1790s. Eventually official school boat clubs were formed, at Westminster in 1813 and at Eton in 1816, with watermen as coxes and coaches, and often as strokes of crews, professionals stroking Eton crews until 1828 and steering them until 1837.

Old Etonians formed the Guards and the Funny Clubs, 'funny' being the nickname for a racing single sculler, and funny they must have appeared, because outriggers had not yet been invented and these boats, though as narrow as possible on the waterline, were built with widely flared gunwales, sometimes referred to as 'bat's wings', to increase the leverage. The Star and Arrow Clubs were also in existence by the end of the eighteenth century and were probably established by gentlemen who ate at the Star dining-room in Covent Garden and the Robin Hood coffee house in St James's Square, the latter's sign incorporating a bow and arrow.

Occasional racing at Oxford in hired boats above Iffley Lock had been popular for many years before the first bumping races were organised in 1815. At Cambridge, rowing was not taken up until 1820 and the first recorded races on the Cam were in the Lent term of 1827, the first University Boat Race taking place at Henley in 1829, although the second race did not take place for another six years. The Cambridge University Boat Club was formed in 1828 but Oxford did not follow suit until 1839, the year in which the first Henley Regatta was held and two years after Queen Victoria had ascended the throne.

The development of rowing by gentlemen of leisure and financial security might have happened more rapidly in the closing years of the

2 London, the Thames, with Westminster Bridge, 1746, by Canaletto (detail).

The bridge is nearing completion and the stairs and boatyards at Stangate on the right are on the site of Leander's first premises at Searle's Yard

eighteenth century had not many of them been otherwise engaged in keeping Napoleon Bonaparte on the right side of the English Channel, but the potential was already there. The banks of the Thames, upstream of Old London Bridge, were lined with dozens, if not hundreds, of riverside yards, building, hiring and housing boats, and with countless watermen seeking a livelihood, ready to provide instruction to anyone wanting to learn the aquatic arts. All the facilities were there to enable young men to take to boating, whether for recreation or more serious competition.

It was no accident, therefore, that boating among the leisured classes gained rapidly in popularity after 1815. For years past, rowing had been a sport waiting to be launched and this was the root from which the Leander Club was to grow shortly after the battle of Waterloo.

The end of the war with France meant that, safe from the threat of invasion, the country was at last free to divert some of the wealth generated by the industrial revolution towards recreational activities. Commerce and industry in the rapidly expanding capital city were creating a new monied class, whose young men were seeking outdoor exercise.

It was also no accident that the Oxford and Cambridge Boat Race and Henley Regatta became major sporting events long before Wimbledon and the FA Cup, or that Doggett's Coat and Badge is the oldest event in the English sporting calendar, and the Wingfield

Sculls (1832) the oldest existing individual amateur championship in any sport. The fact is that at the turn of the century the 'popular' sports of today, such as lawn tennis, had either not been invented, or were not yet organised, and certainly not capable of offering recreation to more than a handful of devotees.

This explains why rowing, with all the necessary facilities available, got off to a flying start on the Thames in London. The form which the sport took in its infancy was naturally dictated by what was on offer, which was essentially a choice of boatyards with boats for hire or sale, and tuition from professional watermen. The owners of these establishments quickly responded to the demand by adding changing-rooms, club rooms, and, in some cases, catering facilities which thoughtfully extended to the provision of wines, spirits and cigars.

All this added up to rowing in small units. There was a great deal of sculling and pulling in pair-oars, the boats being the same wherries which the watermen used in their role as water-taxis, but progressively built lighter and handier. Four-oar and six-oar cutters, evolved from the larger craft used for conveying merchandise, and, in the more ornate versions with state cabins, by the owners of riverside mansions, and by the City Livery Companies, for transport and processional purposes.

* * * *

The exact origins of the Leander Club are vague and the date of the foundation of what was to become the world's premier rowing club is also uncertain. Manuscript notes in the Leander archives, unsigned, but, from the handwriting, written by C.M. 'Cherry' Pitman in 1934, contain this passage:

Although Leander Club is the oldest existing society devoted to acquatics, there is no record of the exact date of its foundation. No documents relating to that period are among the archives of the Club. Endeavours have been made from time to time to arrive at exactly when it was founded but they have been universally unsuccessful, though they tended to establish some year in the period between 1816 and 1820 . . . There existed in the last century two clubs of repute. named 'The Star' and 'The Arrow', and it is believed that Leander arose from the ashes of these two, or embodied their members when it was established. The Club's original coat-of-arms consisted of a shield on which was quartered a star and an arrow.

While Pitman was probably correct in suggesting that Leander took on previous members of the Star and Arrow clubs, he was not accurate in saying that Leander arose from the ashes of these two, for the Arrow and Leander at least existed contemporaneously for a number of years. We know from *Bell's Life*, the major source of sporting news in the early years of the nineteenth century, that as late as 1831, Messrs Hunt & Chandler had a new wherry for Mr Lewis of the Arrow Club on stocks, and, that year, the same journal was reporting that 'the Leander and Arrow are about to form one club'.

Pitman went on to quote a letter written in 1905 by H.T. Steward, whom he described as 'undoubtedly the greatest authority of rowing history in his time', to R.C. Lehmann, who was then working on his book *The Complete Oarsman*. In this letter, Steward said that W.L.

Nicholson, who rowed for Cambridge in a race against Leander in 1837, had no knowledge of the foundation of Leander, nor did two members of that Leander crew. Even more surprisingly, one may think, Patrick, later Sir Patrick, Colquhoun, who was to become Secretary of the Club and later still its President, winner of the Wingfield Sculls in 1837 and founder of the Colquhoun Sculls at Cambridge, had also told Steward that he knew nothing of Leander's foundation. Yet he had been a boy at Westminster School and was admitted to The Temple in 1834, so must have been rowing at Westminster at just about the date of Leander's assumed foundation.

In the 1860s, Steward questioned several friends who had been members of the Shark Club, which had been prominent in the early years of the nineteenth century, and they were all emphatic that Leander was 'not going in their day', which Steward reckoned to have ended about 1815. On the other hand, a Cambridge man who joined the Funny Club in 1820 declared that Leander 'was very strong then'.

This gave Steward his bracket of the years 1816–1820. The fine tuning came from an article in *Bell's Life*, which, in describing the 1837 race with Cambridge, referred to 'the long existing and highly respectable Leander Club' and to 'the eighteen or nineteen years which have elapsed since its foundation'. 'This', Pitman decided, 'pretty conclusively proves that the Club was founded in 1818 or 1819'.

Support for the earlier date came from the distinguished Victorian oarsman, Guy Nickalls, who claimed in 1913 in an article in *Fry's Magazine* that he had seen a cutting from a newspaper of 1818 which mentioned the name 'Leander', and today 1818 is generally accepted as the Club's foundation date.

It is possible, of course, that the Club had been in existence for some years before this. Names of boats and clubs in those days were synonymous. Boats have a limited life and a group of oarsmen acquiring a new boat would not necessarily transfer to it the name of the old one. There were no regattas at which to compete and no clubhouses but simply an increasing number of individual oarsmen and groups of oarsmen who hired or purchased boats from local yards for recreational purposes. Sometimes they organised sweepstake events, or wager matches. Sometimes groups became identified with a particular boat which they used or with a particular boatyard which they frequented. So we read of *The Shark*, *The Arrow*, *The Leander*, or *The Gentlemen of the Pearl Cutter* or *The Gentlemen of Lyons*, but the same individual might take an oar in a different boat on different occasions. The same men are known to have been members of more than one group or switched from one to the other.

Many of these groups were small and often ephemeral, frequently merging with each other. The true origins of Leander may lie in an already existing group of oarsmen, rowing from Lambeth, who probably already had their established rules and practices, and who, in 1818 or 1819, acquired a new six-oar cutter, named her 'Leander', and thereafter came to be known by that name. Some of them may indeed have been members of the Star or Arrow clubs, or of other earlier groups which existed prior to 1800.

In his book *Boat Racing* (1876), Edwin Brickwood stated that the Arrow was a six-oar club in the latter part of the eighteenth century, and we know that the Arrow did finally merge with Leander, so at least part of the club did have its roots in the eighteenth century. The Star also merged with Leander, although we do not know when. However, it is a fact that a star appeared on the Waterman's Badge, and on the Club's earliest coat-of-arms which adorned the Goolden Cup of 1854 (see pages 46, 47), while the arrow appeared only on the later Colquhoun Goblets. Moreover, the fact that *Bell's Life* reported the merger of the Arrow with Leander but never mentioned the Star at least suggests that the Star may have predated the Arrow and merged with the Leander before *Bell's Aquatic Register* became a regular feature.

What distinguishes Leander is that it alone has survived to the present day, and what is beyond dispute is that there are no challengers to Leander's claim to be the oldest surviving rowing club.

3 Early gentlemen amateurs on the river, c. 1830

PART ONE
1818–1899
by
Richard Burnell

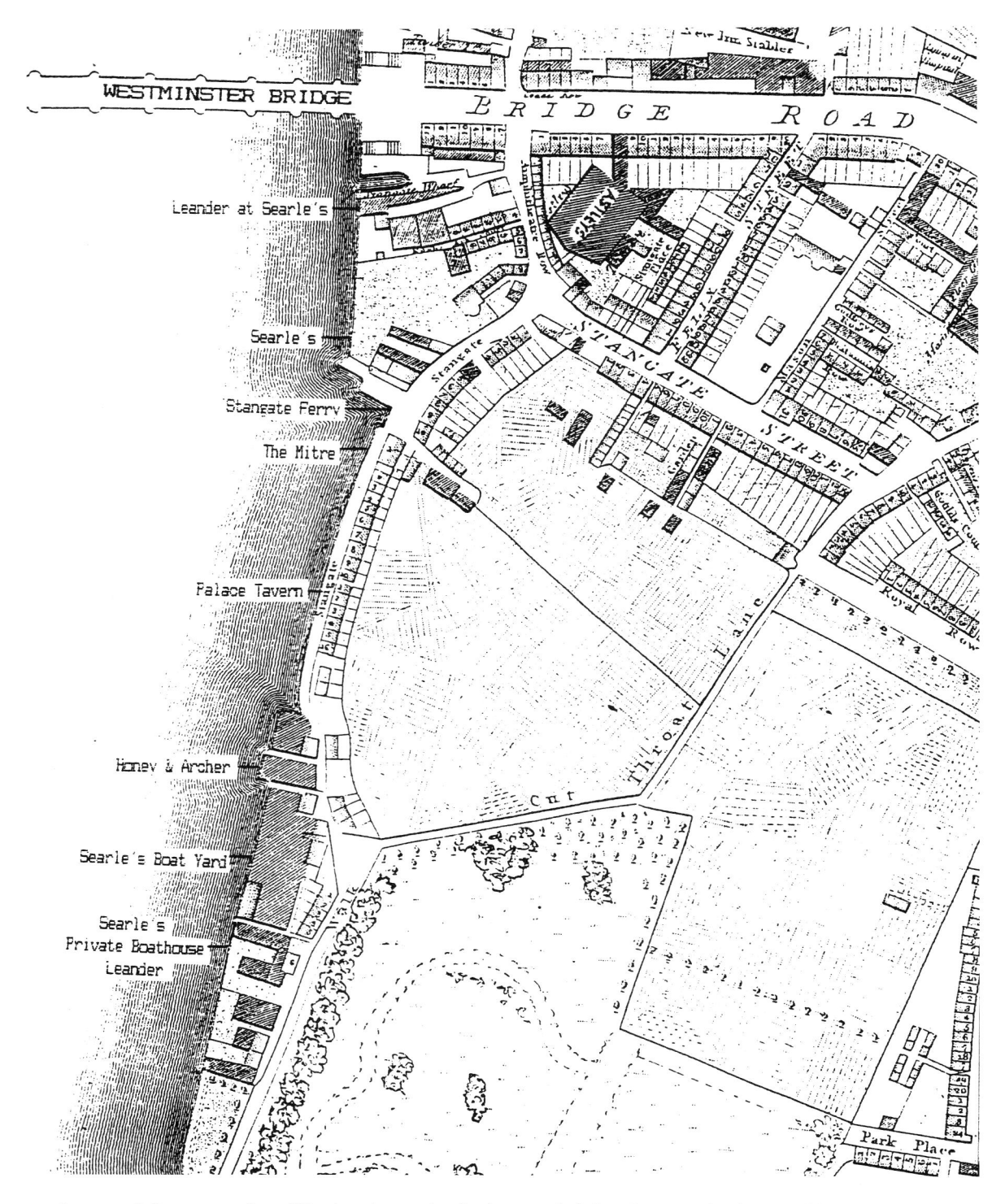

4 A map of Stangate, 1819. The boathouse in the bottom left-hand corner is the one illustrated in Plates 3 and 4.

I

Cock of the London Water
1818–1839

The Club's history is full, overfull some may say, of mysteries and assumptions. One of the assumptions has long been that the Club's first quarters were at Searle's Yard at Stangate, alias Lambeth, alias Bishop's Yard, that is to say, a site on the Surrey shore, upstream from Westminster Bridge, on land now buried beneath St Thomas's Hospital. This was a reasonable assumption since there is a picture hanging in the Clubhouse, which is captioned:

> Drawn by E.F. Lambert, Engraved by H. Pyall Westminster Bridge, Surrey Shore
> Searle and Sons respectfully beg to acquaint the Nobility, Gentry, and the public in general that they have constantly for sale and hire, Boats of every description adapted for parties of pleasure, viz. Shallops, Cutters & Wherries, Funnies, Skiffs, Sailing boats and Fishing Punts, any of which may be got up in the first manner at a few days notice and forwarded to any part of the Kingdom. Merchants and Captains' Commissions attended to with Punctuality and Dispatch.
> The above picture was presented to Leander by Miss Searle. The original quarters of the club can be seen on the right.

There is no date on the picture (Plate 3) but in living memory this has been supposed to be 1831. Nor is it known when it was presented to the Club but no one has seriously questioned the belief that Leander's original quarters were on the balcony in that picture. After all, what better provenance could there be than the evidence of a Miss Searle? But in recent years another picture has come to light (Plate 4) which appears at first sight to be identical, but on closer inspection, the one hanging in the Leander clubhouse shows the premises of Searle & Sons, while the other, which appears in a book entitled *Sporting Life – An Anthology of British Sporting Prints*, by Paul Goldman (British Museum, 1983), indicates that the premises belong to Lyon & Co. The second print is described as being an aquatint by Henry Pyall, after a painting by E.F. Lambert, published by W. Lyon (the boatbuilders) in 1831.

Another difference is that the Lyon balcony is open and larger than Searle's, which has a roof, and careful inspection reveals that it is the Searle version that has been altered. It was quite common, before the advent of photography, for commercial artists to 'adapt' original pictures to suit the requirement of customers and no doubt Searle and Lyon, or one of them at least, had this particular drawing altered for their own advertising purposes.

Research in Lambeth Palace Library by Richard and Ken Hylton-Smith has revealed that the Searles held leases at Stangate wharf, Lambeth, from 1729 until after 1857, and at Bishop's Walk, Lambeth, from 1773 until after

1853. They were one of the largest boat-building establishments on the London river, with branches at Eton and Cambridge, and held a Royal Warrant from Queen Victoria.

There is no record at Lambeth Palace of William Lyon ever holding a head lease and the likelihood is that the premises always belonged to Searle with Lyon being his sub-tenant. Probably there was originally a small covered balcony, with Leander renting 'quarters' above the 'west wing' of the boathouse. This would substantiate Miss Searle's claim, though it does not follow that these were necessarily the first quarters that Leander ever occupied. We know, from Colquhoun's correspondence, that the Club boats were housed and maintained by Searle, whilst the crews were changing at, and boating from, George Renshaw's Yard, which appears to have been situated a short distance upstream from Searle's. *Bell's Life* reported in 1831, the reputed year of both pictures, that Lyon had opened a new Subscription Room extension at the west (upstream) end of his Stangate Yard, *Bell* commenting that this would fill a long felt need. This would explain the difference in the prints, and in all probability Lyon opened his new Rooms as an independent venture, not in partnership with Searle.

All this is, of course, pure speculation, but it may well be that Leander, accustomed to the privacy of their own quarters, with a fine view over the river, did not relish the prospect of the hurly-burly of an extablishment offering a number of 'Rooms', not to mention 'bar facilities', to different customers, and moved to Renshaw whilst leaving their boats in the care of Searle.

The various clubs at that time were not large and the founding fathers of Leander Club limited their membership to fifteen, which seems small, but was no doubt dictated by the way they operated. The practice was to meet on specified days – by the mid-1850s we know that the rule was Tuesdays and Fridays at 5 o'clock in the afternoon – to make up a crew, or crews, which then proceeded to their chosen destination, down to Greenwich or up to Putney, perhaps, where they took dinner at some riverside hostelry before returning to Lambeth. In September 1824, *Bell's Life* wrote of 'the many Rowing Societies now making the water gay every afternoon, to the great pleasure of the public, and the great advantage of the Red House at Battersea, the Star and Garter at Putney, and the Castle and other inns at Richmond and Teddington'.

All Leander's members were required to attend on rowing days and were fined if they did not give good reason for their absence in advance, since an absentee meant that a waterman had to be employed to fill his seat. In coxed boats a waterman took the rudder lines and provided the coaching. Some members were scullers and some were pair-oar partners, so fifteen was a manageable number. The earliest accounts show that in 1847 the entrance fee was £5, which would be the equivalent of at least £150 in modern terms, with an annual subscription also of £5. There was also a 'one-off' retiring fee of £5 for those wishing to remain in the Club but not on the active list. If the Club's income did not cover the Treasurer's expenditure, mostly payments to watermen, boat hire and meals, there was a whip-round at the end of the season to balance the books.

5 The start of a race at Westminster Bridge, 1826

In the *Badmington Library* volume on *Rowing* (1898), R.P.P. Rowe and C.M. Pitman state that: 'The records of those (early) days speak of Leander matches against time and in long rows of many hours' duration; in no cases of races over measured and comparatively short distances; and it was doubtless in achievements of the former kind that the earliest Leander crews made their reputation. Of the advance to the next or actual racing stage Leander tradition tells us nothing, and it is not until we come to the club's matches with the Universities – with Oxford in 1832 and Cambridge in 1837 – that we have any record of the performance of Leander crews in races.

There were, nevertheless, races between other individuals and groups in the 1820s and 1830s. In 1826 *Bell's Life* reported a 'race for a Prize Wherry presented by the Gentlemen of the Funny Club, from Westminster Bridge round a boat moored off the second windmill (of which there were a number pumping water from the river to the city) beyond Vauxhall, down the Surrey shore, round a beacon below Westminster Bridge and back through the centre arch of Westminster Bridge'.

In the same year there was 'A Grand Amateur Rowing Match for 200 sovereigns, for gentlemen picked from the various crack clubs on the river'. Six pairs raced from the Red

House to the new bridge at Hammersmith. What seems to have been a repetition of this race took place in August 1827, when one of the rowers was a Mr Bishop, a Leander man later to become the first umpire at Henley Regatta, who, with his partner, Mr Cannon, was leading at Putney but unfortunately 'fouled one of the small arches of the bridge', which would have been the old wooden bridge. The report states that the winners, Attwood and Bayford, took thirty-seven minutes to cover the distance of 'about seven miles'. If that were true, it would have been a remarkable achievement, equivalent to covering the present-day Boat Race course in a little over twenty-two minutes, and one must remember that it was a very different river in those days, with no embankments and bordered by extensive mud flats and marsh land, so that the river was wider and the tide must have ebbed and flowed more slowly. The map, however, suggests that the distance would have been nearer to five than to seven miles, which makes the time more credible.

We are now on the threshold of great events, and at the beginning of eight-oared rowing. Eight-oared boats had begun to come into fashion in the second decade of the century, Eton having acquired their first eight-oar in 1810, Westminster following suit in 1818. We do not know when Leander acquired their first eight-oar, but they did not own one when Christ Church suddenly appeared on the Tideway in 1828 and had the temerity to challenge any gentlemen of the lower part of the river Thames, to row from Westminster Bridge to Putney. Leander, by then acknowledged to be 'Cock of the London water', responded to the challenge.

The *Sporting Magazine* reported that the Christ Church men 'took the precaution of enquiring into the "pulling qualities" of the men who were likely to be picked as their adversaries, and lost some of their enthusiasm on learning of the reputation of the Leander men. However, a few days later . . . when the coxswains of *The Arrow* and *Leander*, the former a four-oared wherry, the latter a six-oared cutter, and the coxswain of the *Christ Church*, were showing their respective boats, some chaffing took place between them.' This led to a meeting with Mr Slater, a leading Leander member, who was at pains to let them know that Leander owned no eight-oar of their own but that they had no objection to rowing the match in a boat which had just been built by Honey & Archer for Trinity College, Cambridge, notwithstanding that she had been sent back by them as 'not worth a damn'.

This was, however, a piece of astute gamesmanship for which the 'Brilliants' (another contemporary soubriquet for Leander men) were to become renowned. The trap having been set, Leander insisted on racing for a substantial purse of 200 sovereigns, over £6,600 by today's standards. In fairness to Leander one might add that Slater could have claimed not only that the Club owned no eight, but that they had no crew either. *Bell's Life* reported later that Leander had made up 'a mixed crew composed of members of Leander and the 'celebrated Arrow four, who had only entered their boat on the morning of the race, without training or a single practice'. In the event, the Leander eight defeated the Oxonians by no less than seventy yards.

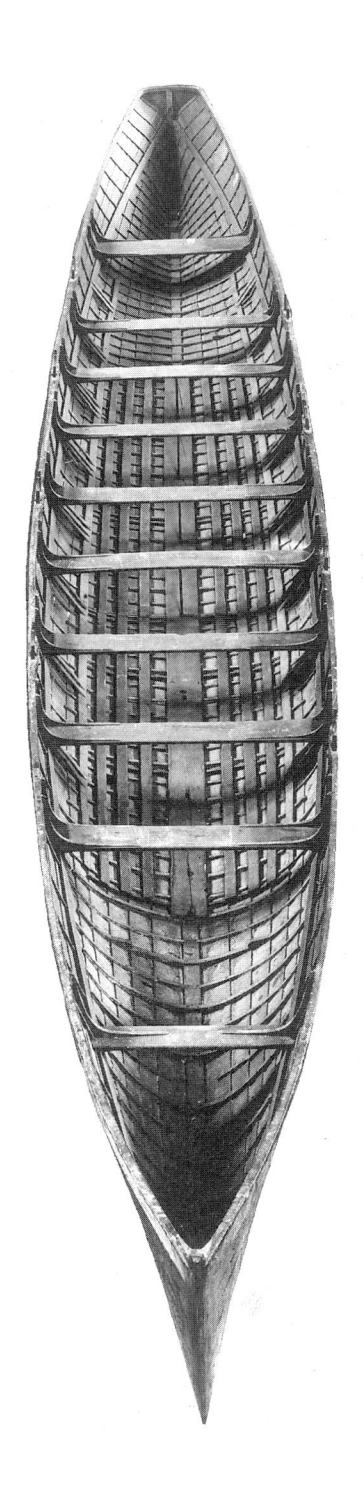

If we think that two hundred 1828 sovereigns was a high price to pay for losing to the wily 'Brilliants', consider the fate of the Guards amateurs, who the following year challenged the Arrow, all but one of whose crew were Leander members, to race from Vauxhall to Kew for a stake of £1,000 – something over £30,000 at today's values. 'The race created enormous excitement', *Bell's Life* reported on 4th July, 1829, '... amongst the numerous companies' boats we observed *Emerald*, *Leander*, *Corsair* (Slater's boat), *Trinity*, *William Frederick* and many others, several of which were manned by crack watermen.... A steel rudder, of very light construction, was made for *Arrow*'. *Arrow* led all the way and won by fifty seconds in one hour and three minutes. The crew then continued on up river to dine at Richmond, as they could well afford to do!

Mention of the special steel rudder casts an interesting light on the then current racing rules. There were, of course, no codified rules of boat racing, but simply agreements for particular matches. There was a draw for stations at the start but thereafter any crew which drew ahead was entitled to cross over into its opponents' water, which thereupon became their water. Furthermore, 'fouling' was permitted unless barred by the match agreement. Today we regard deliberate fouling as a form of cheating, but that was certainly not the case in the more robust Victorian era. It was quite common for the leading crew to ram the opposition's fore-quarter, to drive it ashore or into a bridge to prevent overtaking. The tactic for the

6 (*left*) The Oxford boat of 1829

7 New London Bridge under construction, 1825, with the Fishmongers' Hall and Old Swan stairs, the starting point of the Doggett's Coat and Badge race, in the background

trailing boat was to ram its opponents' stern in the hope of dislodging or damaging their rudder, so it made some sense to have it fashioned in steel.

In 1829 an event took place far from the tideway which was nevertheless to have a profound effect on amateur rowing everywhere. This was the first University Boat Race between Oxford and Cambridge at Henley-on-Thames. The enthusiasm which greeted this event, which was said to have attracted 20,000 spectators to the quiet market town in the Thames Valley, before the advent of trains, and when the principal means of access was on or behind a horse or on 'Shanks's nag', brought instant recognition of the possibilities of eight-oar racing and was a major factor in encouraging the local gentry, ten years later, to stage the world's first open regatta. The comment passed by the correspondent of *London Society* – 'Never shall I forget the shout which rose among the hills' – passed into rowing folklore.

The spotlight did not alight on Westminster that year, but *Bell's Life*, in their 'Retrospect of the late Aquatic Season' in December, reported that: 'On Wednesday, 8th July, the Gentlemen Amateurs at Messrs Rawlinson and Lyon's, Stangate, gave their second annual Purse of Sovereigns, to be rowed for from Westminster to Putney'. Already the amateurs boating from the many yards in the Westminster area had become patrons as well as customers of the watermen on whose services their recreation so much depended.

Bell's Life also gives us an interesting insight into wager racing in a description of a match, from Westminster to Putney on 26th May 1830, between F. Hornemann of Leander and a Mr Revell. There was a stiff breeze, it seems, so the *Leander*, 'beautifully steered by an "old un" (probably Jem Parish), served him (Hornemann) as breakwater, while the *Arrow*, paddling by his side, cheered and helped him at his work'.

History was made by a Leander member in August 1830, when Henry Wingfield presented the Silver Sculls which are still competed for annually under his name, 'on condition that the winner rows from Westminster to Putney, at half flood, whoever challenges him, on every 10th August'. Originally this race was a sweepstake in which the winner took the cash after deduction of the running expenses, as well as the title 'Champion of the Thames'. A Leander man, J.H. Bayford, won this first race from a field of eight, seven of whom were members of the Club.

On the same day, 15th August 1830, when *Bell's Life* reported the first contest for the Wingfield Sculls, they also recorded an event which revealed Leander in a less attractive light. A professional match for 'Searle's Sovereigns' was stopped for a foul on one of the competing watermen, Campbell, who declined to re-start on the grounds that he had been leading when the race was called off, declaring that if the race was re-started he would stop his principal rival, Williams. Sure enough, when the race reached Horseferry, about where Lambeth Bridge now stands, Campbell, 'accompanied by an amateur', rammed Williams and 'general conflict was the consequence, at the conclusion of which the men were ordered back to their stations'. Worse was to follow, for Campbell then laid in wait for Williams at Vauxhall, where 'a lad in a skiff took hold of the head of Campbell's boat, and the *Leander* galley coming up, all on board unanimously agreed to "row him over" and "cut him down"'. This was no sooner said than done, and the upper strake on Campbell's wherry stove in, his boat sunk, and both Campbell and the amateur who accompanied him were severely injured, the former by a heavy blow from an oar on the shoulder which was levelled at his head, and the latter on the right arm which became powerless. One might have hoped for a sequel from *Bell* in the following week, but none was forthcoming.

In the same 1831 issue in which *Bell's Life* announced that William Lyon (late of Rawlinson and Lyon) had established 'Lyon's Aquatic Subscription Room', it was recorded that '*Leander* and *Arrow* are about to form one club, which, with the *Emerald*, will shortly make their appearance on the river'.

There was no subsequent report of any sighting of the merged clubs, but it was a busy summer with two eight-oared matches for Leander. The first was against Eton College at Eton. We know that Leander won but no more beyond the names of the crews recorded in the *Eton Boating Book**. The second was a match against Oxford University. After the first Oxford and Cambridge Boat Race in 1829 there had been no return match in 1830. The

---

*This, the earliest named Leander eight-oar, comprised Bishop (bow), Evans, Wood, Howard, Hume, Weedon, T. Bayford, A. Bayford (stroke), and Cannon (cox)

official Boat Race *Centenary History* reports that Cambridge issued a challenge but that the race was stopped owing to the cholera epidemic then raging in London, no doubt spread by the increasingly foul state of the London river. To make up for the disappointment the captains of the Cambridge college eights challenged the university crew to a race on 29th November which was also cancelled at the request of the Vice-Chancellor 'on account of the cholera then prevalent in Sunderland'. The presumption was that 'Doctor Haviland, at whose instigation the Vice-Chancellor had put a stop to the race, confounded the term "rōwing" and "rŏwing", and whilst anxious to check any debauchery in the latter class of men, by a slight mistake was the means of preventing the healthy exercise of the former'.

Oxford, being that much closer to the metropolis, sought a match against Leander, to be contested at Henley, which was agreed for 18th June, Leander insisting on a stake of £200 a side. So far as is known, this was the only occasion on which either of the Universities raced for a wager. *Bell's Life* reported a week later: 'On Friday the London gentlemen left town for Henley and took up their quarters at the Red Lion. Noulton of Lambeth was selected to steer them. At about 6.30 the contending parties arrived in their cutters near Hambledon lock to row from there against the stream to Henley Bridge, which is reckoned two and a quarter miles.

'Mr Hume and Mr Bayford were appointed umpires on the part of the London gentlemen, and Mr Lloyd and another gentleman on the side of Oxford. The Oxford gentlemen won the toss and took the inside station. . . . In less than a dozen strokes the London gentlemen almost astounded their opponents by going about a boat's length in advance. The Oxonians. . . . made a desperate effort, coming within a painter's length. On nearing the goal the exertions of each party were increasing. One London gentleman (Mr Shaw) seemed so much exhausted that it was feared he would not hold out. . . . Noulton, seeing this and fearing the consequences, . . . said that "if the Londoners did not give it her it would be all up with them". The Londoners did give it her, and the consequence was that they became victorious by about two boats' lengths. The distance was rowed in eleven and a half minutes. The exertions at the conclusion of the contest became lamentably apparent. Captain Shaw nearly fainted and had to be carried ashore; Mr Bayford had to retire to bed immediately; so also did one of the Oxford gentlemen. The others were more or less exhausted'.

Notwithstanding their exhaustion on the Saturday, the Leander men rowed down to London on Tuesday – a distance of about forty-four miles, being greeted on their way by cheering and cannon, and, on arriving at Searle's, by a *feu-de-joie*. One might add that if they really covered the distance from Hambledon lock to Henley Bridge in eleven and a half minutes, that would have been the equivalent of covering the Henley regatta course in about 6 min. 45 sec. Supermen indeed – or could it be that *Bell's* man erred on the side of enthusiasm?

He was certainly showing enthusiasm, tempered with caution, in the following year when he wrote, on 10th June 1832, that, 'yesterday evening week the members of the Leander

Club rowed their annual oars match for a dinner and wine. The distance was from Westminster to Putney, and the match was well contested. . . . We are given to understand that the Leander crew are open to row any club composed of Oxford gentlemen from Westminster to Putney. Should a match take place we think the Leander men will suffer for their temerity, for the majority of members we know are not equal to many of the Oxford amateurs'.

There was no response from Oxford to Leander's overtures in 1832, and no evidence that any formal challenge was ever made. It was to be five years before Leander was involved in another major contest, by which time *Bell's* correspondent seems to have changed his opinion as to the strength of rowing amongst the university men, for in 1836, after they rowed their second University Boat Race, this time over the championship course in London, he wrote: 'We cannot say much for either party. Their style is bad for the Thames, whatever it may be for Oxford or Cambridge waters'.

However that may be, the challenge, when it came, was from the Cantabs, who had been unable to arrange another Boat Race in 1837 with Oxford, whom they had defeated in the previous year. *Bell's Life* of 9th June 1837, under the heading 'Grand Match between the Leander London Club and the Gentlemen of the Cambridge University', reported:

> This highly interesting eight-oared match came off on Friday evening, from Westminster Bridge to Putney, with the tide. The contest was one rather for glory than for gain, but excited a greater sensation throughout aquatic circles, not only in London and the Universities, but in various parts of the country, than has been witnessed for many years. . . . From the non-consent of the Oxonians to row the 'old-fashioned distance', from Westminster to Putney, it may be presumed, originated the challenge from the Cambridge gents to pull that distance with the long-existing and highly respectable Leander Club. That this club should have been selected by the gentlemen of Cambridge was certainly not anticipated, for it is well known that, during the eighteen or nineteen years which have elapsed since its formation, the members of it have never entered into any competition of the kind*. . . . With the exception of an occasional oars match between themselves. . . . and winning, it may be added, the scullers' match for the single sculls, they have never come out in a body to contend against any Club or any set of amateurs in a cutter contest.
>
> Notwithstanding such was the fact, and notwithstanding that several members of the Club, whose former extraordinary feats excited admiration, by the science and stamina displayed, had now become somewhat impaired by long service, still the Leander Club, for the honour of the London river, determined on accepting the challenge of the Collegians. Immediately the match was made more than ordinary interest was excited, and as the Club had only ten or eleven 'working' members to select a crew from, the Cantabs, who had the

---

*Bell's Life is wrong here, as readers will have realised already (see pages 14, 15).

picking of the entire University, became the the favourites at 5 to 4.

As the time for the match drew near, however, a sudden revolution in the betting took place, and 6 and 7 to 4 was offered on Leander, which odds, on the day of the race, went begging. It is impossible to account for this extreme change in the betting, but we presume it was in consequence of the speculative gentry looking more to the bygone achievement of several of the Leander crew than to the youth of their opponents, and forgetting that the Cambridge gentlemen at the present time row better and stronger than perhaps they ever did in any former season.

Cambridge had suggested that gentlemen steerers should be appointed but acceded to Leander's request that their own waterman, James Parish, should steer the Leander, William Noulton of Lambeth then being selected to steer Cambridge. On the afternoon of the match, although the rain occasionally came down in torrents, a strong muster of eights, sixes, and fours congregated between Westminster and Vauxhall bridges, together with a vast number of other boats, the Richmond steamer, which was to follow the race, being crowded with passengers, among whom were many fashionably attired members of the fair sex. The cutters afloat included several from Oxford and Cambridge, and from the Gloucester River Club, Worcester Boating Club, and an eight from Westminster School. Mr Bishop of Leander umpired from the bowseat of the old Leander eight, manned by watermen. Cambridge won the toss, taking Middlesex. *Bell's* report continued:

The following were the names of the gentlemen who formed the respective crews:

Cambridge		Leander
(Mr William Noulton)	Coxswain	(Mr James Parish)
Granville	Stroke	Hornby
Fletcher	No 7	Lewis
Penrose	No 6	Dalgleish
Brett	No 5	Sherrard
Keane	No 4	Lloyd
Budd	No 3	Wood
Green	No 2	Layton
Nicholson	Bow	Shepheard

A finer or more even crew than the Cambridge we have not seen for some time ... Youth and strength appeared combined and, on coming to the match, they were loudly cheered by their friends. The Leander gentlemen were also hailed with enthusiasm; and although there were two or three who had evidently seen many summers, yet their previous exertions ... and the confidence depicted in the countenances of the crew, still caused them to be favourites.

The Leander, the instant the word 'off' was given, jumped in advance, and slashed away in such excellent style that opposite Moberly's they were at least a boat's length ahead. As soon, however, as the Cantabs had overcome the first shock, they gallantly went to work, and overhauled their opponents hand over hand. Off the Horseferry, 'Little Noulton' gained a trifling advantage for the Cambridge by steering inside the ballast machine lying off there, the Leander going outside, which, perhaps, could not be avoided, but the latter still came out nearly half the length of their cutter in advance. Between this and

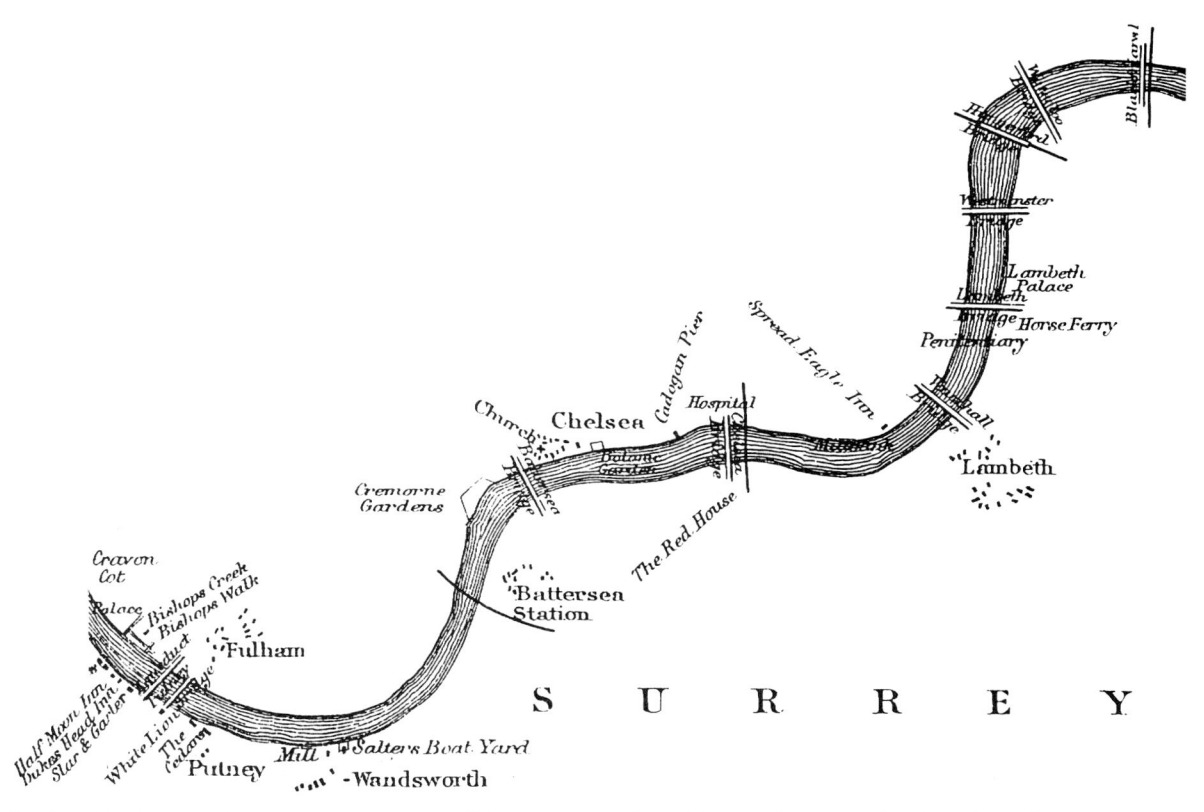

8 A mid-nineteenth-century map of the Thames from Blackfriars to Putney, showing the old Championship course

Vauxhall the Cambridge came alongside, and a desperate and manly struggle ensued for the superior station, which the Cantabs gained, and went under the bridge slightly ahead of the Leander. At the Red House the Leander was at least two boat's lengths in the rear, but they pulled steadily and apparently with a determination of giving the leading party plenty of work to maintain their advantage. Off Cheyne Walk there were some hopes that the Leander would eventually draw the draft by the Cantabs. Mr Layton, Mr Hornby, and one or two others, were particularly conspicuous for the strenuous and spirited manner in which they kept at their work...

The Cambridge crew, however, upon seeing their opponents gradually gaining on them, slashed away again with increased vigour, and after passing through Battersea Bridge, were well ahead. In the upper part of Wandsworth Reach the Leander made a desperate effort to overhaul the headmost men, and at every stroke drew nearer to them, but as the remaining distance was but short, the Cambridge men succeeded in passing under the middle arch of Putney Bridge in advance, winning, however, by only seven seconds. The match was rowed in 30 minutes and 12 seconds*, and a better or more spirited contest was perhaps never witnessed . . .

Several of both crews appeared rather baked at the conclusion.

The crews and their friends, totalling fifty, later dined at the Star and Garter. Proposing a toast to the winners, Hornby, Leander's captain, said that the manner in which Cambridge had dragged their boat by the Leander, (although several of his party were bald-headed and perhaps not so good as they were formerly**, had surprised him and must have excited the admiration of all. Replying, Granville, the Cambridge stroke, commented that if one or two of the Leander men were 'bald-headed', it must be remembered that his own crew were 'beardless'.

On the day following the race the *Morning Post* lamented: 'Yesterday the pride of the Thames, the beautiful, the brilliant Leander, which has stood above the foremost for years against every club on the river, yesterday sustained defeat; but their gallant conduct deserves the highest compliment. Never did men row with so much game'.

With so much goodwill in the air one might have hoped for a happier sequel when Leander asked for, and were granted, a return match,

*According to W.F. Macmichael (*The Oxford and Cambridge Boat Races*, 1870), the time for this race was variously reported as 30 min. 12 sec. and 30 min. 15 sec.

**Macmichael also reports that the Leander men 'averaged thirty-six summers'.

9 Lord Justice Brett (Viscount Esher)

which took place the following year on 10th June over the same course. Alas, it was not to be, for this time the Brilliants resorted to gamesmanship rather than 'gameness'. The Leander crew had only one change from that of the previous year, Bishop replacing the stroke, Hornby. Leading from the start, Leander never permitted Cambridge to get by them. At the finish Cambridge claimed a foul, the umpire, Mr Searle, then declaring 'No Race'.

Following this debacle, Brett, who had again been in the Cambridge crew, proposed through a letter in *Bell's Life* that there should be another race, James Layton, for Leander, countering that Leander did not accept the umpire's decision and considered that they had won the race and did not need to re-row it. In a further letter, Brett wrote*: 'We were at first, as in the former year, left behind; but on coming up to you at the Horseferry, we most unexpectedly found ourselves against a barge on the one side, and your boat on the other, fully proving that Parish had closed upon us and would not let us room to proceed on our proper course. Noulton upon this was anxious to proceed also to waterman's practice, and to endeavour to break the rudder of your boat. We, however, thinking that there might have been some accident in the case, insisted on backing water, and yielding the Middlesex side of the river to you.

'This we did, gave you a considerable start, and pulled up to you on the Surrey side, and were again crossed. We still insisted on Noulton yielding to you; but at the Red House, finding all hopes of being allowed to pass useless, and convinced that you were sanctioning your steerer's conduct, we told him to run into you, and there broke an oar, etc. We then asked the umpire whether the race was fair or foul and upon his answering that it was foul, we put up our oars to claim the match.

'Our own boat at that time was half full of water; but seeing that you had procured another oar, and had pulled away for about two hundred yards, we started after you and pulled up to you in less than half a mile. After Chelsea Bridge we again left you and actually crossed and recrossed the river, to discover whether or not you would allow us to pass. Being again crossed within ten yards of Wandsworth Meadows, the wrong side of the river, we gave you a last start, and ran into you as you passed through Putney Bridge'.

This race has sometimes been cited as an example of disgraceful behaviour on the part of Leander. Unsporting it certainly was, particularly since, in the previous year, they had allowed the Cantabs to row past them without interference. But the case is not quite so straightforward as that. Despite Brett's assertion that it was no more than an 'honourable competition', there undoubtedly was a wager at stake. We do not know whether specific terms had been agreed, but by current practice the leading crew would have been entitled to cross into whichever station it wished, and it was Cambridge, on Brett's own evidence, who twice ran into Leander. Nor can one help feeling that if their superiority in speed was as great as he inferred, then by spurting and veering widely from Leander's course they should have been able to get by before Leander had time to cut them off. The umpire, in *Bell's Life*, said: 'I considered the terms of the match to have been broken by each party. In fact there was scarcely anything but fouling from Vauxhall to Putney'.

One of the problems was that University men never accepted the principle of fouling as a legitimate means of winning, and never in their own races employed professional steersmen. To the Londoners, on the contrary, wager racing, professional coxswains, and fouling were all part of the game.

There is no record of any matches in 1839, although *Bell's Life* reported that the Dolphin Cutter Club had issued a challenge 'hoping for four members of the Leander gentlemen to come forth against them, and were disap-

---

* An early example of the writer's legal mind. He later became Lord Justice of Appeal and Master of the Rolls.

pointed at not having an opportunity of contesting the distance from Westminster to Putney against some of the crew of the "Brilliant Cutter"'. The Dolphin men subsequently backed themselves heavily against King's College Club, and lost.

The main event of 1839, of course, was the inauguration of Henley Regatta, which heralded the arrival of a new era in rowing history. Leander did not participate but rowed up to see what it was all about. According to the *Herald* of 15th June, they arrived from London, drenched with rain, about 11 o'clock, and 'rowed the distance, each heat, with the racing boats in good style'. They cannot, however, have rowed up from London during the night, so perhaps they slept at Eton or Maidenhead. The regatta programme included two heats and a final in the Grand Challenge Cup, and one race for the local Town Cup fours. According to the *Herald*, the second heat of the Grand was rowed immediately after the first and we must draw our own conclusions as to the literal accuracy of the report.

Bell's Life reported that at the time of the regatta 'an oars-match for a purse, subscribed by the Leander gentlemen for the London watermen present, took place and was won by H. Campbell and J. Phelps, starting from the bridge to row round the island and back'.

10 The race for Doggett's Coat and Badge, 1838, at Blackfriars Bridge

2

Lean Years
1840–1855

Although London's river, with its plentiful supply of boat-yards and professional watermen situated in the heartland of the city as it then was, proved a fertile seed bed for recreational amateur boating, changes in the environment were afoot in 1840 which were not favourable at all. The river itself was London's main sewer, and the rapid expansion of the metropolitan area during the opening decades of the nineteenth century brought serious problems of pollution, prompting a Leander member in 1857 to describe it as 'the largest navigable sewer in the world'.

Where the banks were not already built up the river was wider than it is today, and bordered with mudflats. The embankments were constructed mainly in the middle years of the century: the Victoria Embankment from Blackfriars Bridge to Westminster, for example, took six years to build between 1864 and 1870, and the Chelsea Embankment between Chelsea and Battersea Bridges was completed in 1874. The rebuilding of the Houses of Parliament began in 1837 and was a huge engineering project, while new bridges also began to appear. All the materials for these works had to be brought in by water, generating a hostile environment and unwelcome traffic for the small boats used by the rowing fraternity, who also had to contend with the passenger steamboats which, by the 1840s, were providing regular services between London Bridge and Chelsea.

London Old and New (W. Thornbury and E. Walford, 1873) described the area adjacent to Searle's Yard:

> That part of the Thames known as Stangate Bank, where the hospital (St Thomas's) now stands, had long been of ill repute – ill-looking, ill-smelling, and of evil associations. Even the construction of the Houses of Parliament on the opposite shore – even the building of the handsomest bridge in Europe, that of Westminster – failed to redeem its hideous aspect, overladen as it was with dank tenements, rotten wharves, and dirty boathouses. But the time came when it was decided to construct the southern Thames Embankment, and the necessities of its construction compelled a large reclamation from the slimy foreshore.

Though the author may have been unsympathetic to things aquatic, his message comes through loud and clear: Stangate was not a salubrious area.

While the steamships continued to appear in ever increasing numbers, the building of the railways improved communications between central London and the towns and villages upstream, so that by the 1850s a resident in town could conveniently travel to Putney to take his exercise, instead of rowing up there from Lambeth.

The second phase of Leander's history witnessed the withering away of the multitude of small private subscription clubs, until Leander was the sole survivor, while rowing moved upstream from Lambeth to Putney. In 1845, the Oxford and Cambridge Boat Race moved to a course from Putney to Mortlake, and the following year, a race for the World Professional Sculling Championship moved to the same course for the first time. The Wingfield Sculls continued on the old course until 1848 when they switched to a course from Putney to Kew Bridge, a distance of six miles, before changing in 1861 to what became known as the championship course from Putney Aquaduct to the Ship at Mortlake.

The new decade started auspiciously for Leander. Having decided by one vote not to compete at Henley in 1839, they were clearly encouraged by what they had observed then and made their first entry for the second Henley Regatta the following year, winning the Grand Challenge Cup. The Oxford colleges had been forbidden by the University authorities from entering under their college names and so Wadham appeared as *The Admiral*, University College as *The John Cross*, and Brasenose as *Childe of Hale*, names which may still be seen today on the bows of boats belonging to those colleges. Westminster School raced as *The Queen Bess*, so may have been under a similar restriction. Leander themselves raised an objection of a different sort, querying the eligibility of the Cambridge Subscription Rooms (London) to compete in the Grand, but a meeting of the Stewards at the London home of their President, Lord Camoys, ruled that the Cambridge men 'were fully qualified to contend for the Cup'. However, the Rooms did eventually withdraw, leaving a total of eight entries, of which Brasenose also withdrew.*

The *Badmington Library* saw the event as more then just a sporting occasion, quoting an unnamed newspaper report:

> As the boats on the first day passed the different stands erected for the occasion, which were crowded with beauty, wealth and fashion, great was the anxiety to ascertain the condition of the contending crews, their style of rowing, and to which boat the superiority of their *toute ensemble* should be awarded. The King's College adopted a modification of the London (Leander) colour, which was selected some years since, we understand, when the London gentlemen rowed against the Oxonians. The King's College crew mounting light crimson, the very colour Leander wore, in mistake; their proper colour, in fact, being scarlet though entered as red, a dull colour which no tasteful crew would think of wearing who wished to show off in the midst of a bright green scenery. The Etonians came forth looking like a clear sky, their colours being azure with a silver tassle ... The Leander went down first ... their appearance being very tasteful 'gay without being gaudy', and

---

*The current rule admitted 'any crew composed of members of any of the Universities of Oxford, Cambridge, or London, the Schools of Eton and Westminster, or the Officers of His Majesty's Army or Navy, also members of any Club established at least one year previous to the time of entering'.

the crew seemed to be in lively spirits without showing the least levity.

The same report referred to Leander as 'London's Pride, the Brilliant Leander'. We cannot be sure whether the soubriquet 'Brilliants', used quite frequently at that time, referred to the Club's performance on the water or to its distinctive colours, but the description 'light crimson' here seems to be the first reference to Leander's racing colours. In the first *Rowing Almanack* of 1860, Leander's colours were officially described as red. Today the official description is 'cerise', which, if one looks at the modern blades, is fanciful, to say the least. Ancient Leander blades are of a much darker hue, which, allowing for the darkening of old paint, might well have been the 'light crimson' mentioned above. Perhaps, when it became customary to declare club colours in regatta programmes, somebody decided that 'cherry red' was a more accurate description – hence 'cerise'.

In their first ever race at Henley Regatta in 1840, Leander had no difficulty in disposing of University College and the Etonian Club, Oxford. In the final they met Trinity College, Cambridge, who, as holders, having won in 1839, were not required to race in the heats. Trinity led off the start but then, according to *Bell*, one of the Leander men 'gave a cheer and in an instant they made a burst, gradually drew ahead and, although their opponents worked most manfully at their oars, maintained the lead during the remaining distance, rowing it in 9 min 15 sec'.

The umpire, Mr Bishop, was carried in an eight-oar cutter manned by London watermen and once once again there was a purse subscribed by 'Lord Kilmorey, the members of Leander Club, and many others', for a sculling match for the watermen, 'which gave great delight to hundreds who had never seen a contest in such light boats; the men racing in the wager wherries mostly belonging to the gentlemen of the London Scullers Club.'*

After Henley, Leander made their first foray into the provinces, winning the Liverpool Cup in July. They returned in 1841 to win the Victoria Cup and Salver. At a period when they had difficulty in mustering an eight in their home waters, Leander seem to have made a habit of supporting new regattas. In the following year, they raced in Norwich, and then for three years made successful forays to Erith.

In an age when the London clubs, if not the University clubs, regarded fouling as part of the game, it was perhaps too much to hope that the harmonious racing of 1840 would be repeated at Henley in 1841. The Henley course at that time was manifestly unfair, since it started at the top of Temple Island and finished just below the bridge, with the Poplar Point bend, where the present day finish is situated, offering a huge advantage to the Berkshire station. For the Bucks crew to win it was more or less essential for them to gain a sufficient lead at Fawley to be able to cross over to the Berkshire shore before reaching Poplar Point.

In the only heat in 1841, University College, Oxford, clashed with the Cambridge Subscription Rooms in trying to get in front of them at the Point, but sportingly stopped rowing and allowed them to get away. Leander, rowing in the final as holders, on the other

---

*Records of Henley Royal Regatta, by H.T. Steward.

11 Leander trophies from the 1840s
Top left: Erith Regatta
Top right: Victoria Cup, Liverpool
Bottom left: Liverpool Regatta
Bottom right: Erith Regatta

hand, were less altruistic. Like University, they had the bad luck to start on the Bucks side and ran into the Cambridge Rooms while attempting to cross over. Cambridge stopped and tossed their oars to claim a foul. Leander rowed on to the finish, where Mr Bishop disqualified them. Though the decision was clearly right, R.C. Lehmann records that 'the result on the tempers of the Leander men was disastrous. They retired to their tent to nurse their wrath'. This could well have been no exaggeration, for Leander did not return to Henley for another seventeen years.

However, after the 1840 Regatta, Leander's captain, Dalgleish, was so sure that Leander could win that he issued a challenge for 1,000 guineas a side. Not surprisingly, the Cambridge men were not attracted by the idea of risking something in excess of £30,000 modern money to gratify the Londoners' ambitions. Nor indeed did they immediately respond when Leander offered to row 'for love', 'since', as *Bell's Life* put it, 'this was the second time their contests (with Leander) had ended in a similar manner'. Later they relented and a return match did take place in London, but in conditions which proved too rough for the Cantabs, unaccustomed to Tideway waters, so that they lost by more than a minute. Happily, a convivial dinner in the evening helped to restore harmony between the two clubs.

As a postscript to this race, it might be added that when the Henley clubhouse was opened in 1897, and the first Honours Boards set up to commemorate Leander's entries in the Grand Challenge Cup, the 1841 crew were omitted. This could have been an oversight, for there were other omissions in later years, but perhaps those presiding at the time concluded that the 1841 episode was best forgotten.

A Short History of Leander Club (R.D. Burnell and H.R.N. Rickett, 1968) states that, in 1842, Leander's membership was so small that they could not raise an eight to accept a challenge from Oxford, although the Club was prepared to race in fours. 'This, though perhaps not realised at the time, was indicative of the coming plight of the private Subscription Clubs. In the next fifteen years the whole balance of power was to shift towards Oxford and Cambridge, with the University Boat Race becoming the great aquatic event of the year'.

In 1843, the Royal Thames Regatta was founded on the reach between Chiswick and Putney, Leander being among the founding patrons. According to *Bell's Life*:

> This Regatta was established ... at the instance of a few gentlemen jealous in the cause they had espoused, at a time when the great increase in steamboats on the river had almost deprived the watermen of their occupation, and by diminishing the number of both amateur clubs and rowers, had taken away the support of an industrious class of mechanics employed in boat building. As soon as the project was announced, many noblemen and gentlemen residing on the banks of the Thames, the Universities of Oxford and Cambridge, and principal London boat clubs, cordially responded to the appeal, and HRH Prince Albert kindly consented to become the Patron of the Regatta.

Royal Patronage was then a yardstick of success, so the new Tideway venture got off to a more auspicious start than its rivals at Henley, which had to wait until 1851 before becoming 'Royal'. The Royal Thames was a different sort of regatta, run by and for rowing men, with a wider range of events, including events for the watermen, whereas Henley was run by the local townspeople for the purpose of promoting interest and trade in the town. Although Henley was judged a success when it was founded, it faced serious difficulties in finding an adequate entry because of problems of transportation, and certainly regarded the Royal Thames as a dangerous rival. *Jackson's Oxford Chronicle* in 1847 even referred to 'the annual event at Henley' as ranking 'next to the Thames Regatta, as the most important and attractive in the kingdom'.

Leander entered for the premier event, the Gold Cup for eights, in 1843. Although involved in a false start and a foul in their first heat, they qualified for the final, but did not turn up, probably saving themselves for the Silver Cup for fours, which they won. They tried again for the Gold Cup in 1844 but, without the services of their usual professional coxswain, Jem Parish, found themselves crowded out by the two most redoubtable amateur coxswains of the day, Oxford's Arthur Shadwell and Cambridge's Tom Egan. Leander had one last unsuccessful try for the Gold Cup in 1848 but the days when such a small group could produce an effective eight were clearly numbered. The Brilliants were to wait almost thirty years for their next eight-oar success, and then with a very different sort of crew.

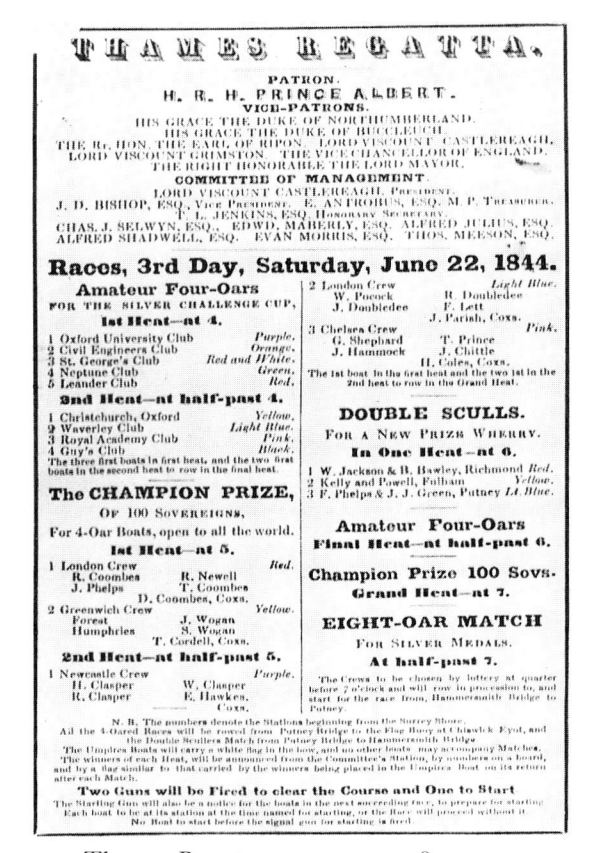

12 Thames Regatta programme, 1844

The days of the Royal Thames Regatta also came to an end in 1850. Some said this was due to an ill-advised rule whereby their principal trophies became the permanent property of any club winning three times in succession. They also faced an intractable problem in trying to run a major regatta on tidal waters, where the hours of racing were limited by the turning of the tide, and where the banks were open to the public without payment. Henley were the main beneficiaries of the decease of the Royal Thames Regatta. Not only were they left unchallenged as the premier regatta, but in the following year they inherited the patronage of Prince Albert.

The earliest surviving rules of the Club are those for the 1844 season and tell us what the Club was like at that time. It was composed of seventeen members (the original membership is believed to have been only twelve or fifteen), exclusive of retired members, and most of the other rules were as outlined earlier in these pages, the annual subscription remaining at £5. The 1844 rules also stipulated, 'That the uniform of the Club be a green waterman's coat, lined with red shalloon, a buff waistcoat, with gilt buttons marked LC, white elastic cotton shirts, with sleeves, white trousers, and a black hat; any member coming to row otherwise, to be fined half-a-crown'. Periodical meetings, to be considered Club days, for the purposes of business, were to be held out of the rowing season, commencing in November each year. Other rules dealt with the appointment of the Secretary, Treasurer and two Auditors, with their duties. The election of members was by ballot; three black balls to exclude. The Rules were followed by the earliest list of members that we have: Messrs F.W. Adey, T.B. Bumpstead, P. Colquhoun, T.H. Fellows, H.W. Fellows, G. Jeffreys, T.L. Jenkins, A.A. Julius, S. Newman, G. Peacock, C. Pollock, E.W. Shepheard, W.L. Smart, H. Thompson, S. Wallace, H. Webber and H. Wood. These were, of course, the seventeen active members and did not include any who might have been on the retired list at the time.

In 1845, Leander recorded their first win in the Diamond Sculls, which had been instituted at Henley in the preceding year. The main interest in the event was the appearance of J.W. Conant of St John's College, Oxford, in an outrigger, the first to be seen at Henley. In his opening heat he met T.B. Bumpstead, a Leander member although he was representing the London Scullers Club, and left him standing. Strangely, Conant was last in the final, which was won by Leander's S. Wallace on a foul from H. Chapman of the Crescent Club. Leander had no four or eight this year, but the St George's four in the Stewards' Cup were said to have been the old Leander under another name. No evidence has been found to support this, although the St George's crew might have consisted of old Leander members before the 1844 list. At any rate, Leander can rest content not to claim them, for, after being robbed of victory by the umpire's decision after an initial verdict of 'dead heat', they are said to have 'reviled the Henley Stewards in language more pagan than parliamentary'. But then again, perhaps there was some provocation. Herbert Steward, in his *Records of Henley Royal Regatta*, thought that there 'seemed to have been some informality' about the appointment of the judge who declared the dead heat, which was overruled by Bishop as umpire.

All we know of Leander's activities in 1846 is that they were present at the race for the Professional Sculling Championship of the Thames between Coombes of Vauxhall and Campbell of Putney. The print of this race in the Henley clubhouse shows the accompanying Leander crew wearing black hats, but not the green coats and buff waistcoats prescribed in the first rule, which were presumably discarded when rowing. Also displayed in the clubhouse is the Leander flag which is believed to be the one depicted by the artist flying on the Leander boat on that occasion.

The oldest surviving documentary record in the possession of the Club is an account book for the years 1847–1859, on the flyleaf of which appears the following memoranda on payments to club watermen:

> *Parish if he attends as early as two o'clock*
> *has per diem*   *10/-*
> *If after that hour*   *8/-*
> *Watermen on the usual club days*
> *and hours are paid*   *1/-*
> *Apprentices on the same occasions*   *5/-*
> *Watermen hired but displaced by*
> *the arrival of a member*   *2/6*
> *The 'Jack in the water' each time*   *6d*
> *The Coxswain and Watermen are allowed 'Tea' in addition to the above pay. At Putney this is fixed at 1/6 per head by agreement, but at Richmond and Greenwich the charge is 2/6 each*

On that basis, Parish's remuneration, at present-day values, would have been something in excess of £15, but we do not know whether he worked for the Club other than on the two weekly 'club days' nor whether he received a retainer out of the rowing season. The Jack's sixpence was one twentieth of Parish's daily fee, so seventy-five pence in modern money, but did 'each time' mean each day he attended the crew, or each time he went into the water to push out, or bring ashore, a club crew? The 'tea' allowance of two shillings would be about £3 today.

The early Leander is always thought of as being a very small club, but the club, as opposed to the active oarsmen's list, must have been larger. The first documentary proof of this comes in the earliest surviving Minute Book, for 1854, which actually names twenty-two active members and twenty-one on the 'retired' list. It is also apparent that there was a significant turnover in 'actives', as one might expect, since these were, in effect, signing up for active rowing during the current season. As we know from the 1844 rules, retired members could use the Club's boating facilities but not take their places in the formal twice-weekly club crews. One wonders how strictly this rule was enforced. If a waterman had to be hired at seven shillings, the equivalent of £10.50 in modern money, to take the place of an absent 'regular', it is a fair guess that if a retired member was available he might well have been pressed into service.

That retired members did sometimes row, even on 'club days', is born out by this report in *Bell's Life* on 1st June 1849:

> The members of Leander Club were on Friday last honoured with a visit from royalty. Prince Henry of the Netherlands having been long desirous of witnessing aquatics in England, availed himself of the opportunity which his presence in this country, as ambassador extraordinary to his royal relative, the Queen of Great Britain, of gratifying his desire. The members of the Leander mustered in great strength to honour and welcome His Royal Highness to the banks of the Thames, and soon after five o'clock they started from Westminster in two eight-oar cutters to row to Putney against a strong tide. Among the old members we noticed Messrs Layton, Julius, Wood, and Lewis (of whom only Wood appears in the contemporary list of subscribing members), and W.F. Hornemann, who

accompanied the Prince from London to show him over the various boat-yards, and explain the late improvements in boat building. After this part of the business had been gone through, His Royal Highness honoured the club with his company at dinner, which, considering the shortness of the notice, was served up in excellent style by the artists at the Star and Garter. The Prince is well known as the President of the Royal Netherlands Yacht Club, and in honouring the Leander Club with his company was treading in the footsteps of his father (the late King of Holland), who, while Prince of Orange, occasionally rowed with this club.* His Royal Highness was elected an Honorary Member, and is, we believe, the only one ever elected.

The year 1849 marked the end of an era, for Leander's entry in the Stewards' Cup was to be the last appearance of the 'Cocks of the London water' at Henley for many years, and the truth was that the whole 'London water' was in decline.

Henley Regatta was also struggling for survival. For the previous two years the Stewards' Cup had gone to Christ Church by default as the sole contenders. In eight events in 1849, only the Diamond Sculls, the Silver Wherries (the Goblets) and the local sculls event required heats.

Bell's account of the Stewards' is of some interest:

*This is the only record of the Club having had a royal guest crew member at some earlier date.

The Second Trinity Boat Club, Cambridge, was originally the only boat entered for this race; but the resolution of the Stewards to allow post entries until the 7th inst. was the means of rescuing this cup from the perils of a 'walk-over' and again introducing the Leander to the admiring denizens of Henley. It is now eight years since the club has made its appearance at any regatta in earnest, and with the intention to win, for its success at Erith in 1845 and its failure at Putney last year are well known to have arisen from anything but attention to those all important parts of rowing – paddling practice and condition . . . On Tuesday last they again made their appearance to measure their strength with the Second Trinity, and as they only had ten days practice they cannot be surprised at our saying that they had not that rowing – the pull together – and that regularity which winning Leander crews have always exhibited. The wonder is how, with so little training, they rowed as they did, for the time occupied in the race was only half a minute more than in the race for the Grand Challenge Cup.

The contest is soon described. The Leander dashed away all at once, took the lead directly, increased it at every stroke, took their adversaries' 'water', and won by several lengths with ease. They were, as a morning contemporary observes, 'evidently a crew of great capabilities' and their opponents were four of the crew in the Grand Challenge Cup.

A minor mystery is that Henley records show P. McC. Colquhoun as coxswain of this crew. Colquhoun was an oarsman, not a cox, and *Bell's Life* has C. House as the steersman, although the latter was not a member. However, Henley were not strict about coxswains in those days and there was actually one occasion when two clubs found themselves matched in a final with the same cox, a Leander man being called in to arbitrate. It was not until 1867 that a rule was passed requiring all competitors to be members of the clubs they represented for at least three months.

It seems that practice did not make this Leander crew perfect despite *Bell's Life's* opinion, for after Henley they went on to race at the newly founded Cliveden and Maidenhead Regatta, and lost.

In 1850 came news of the demise of the Royal Thames Regatta, perhaps well received in Henley-on-Thames but hardly welcome on tidal waters where one of its primary objectives had been to support the professional watermen, whose livelihood was increasingly threatened by new bridges and steamer traffic on the London water. To soften the blow, Leander instituted a new waterman's race in 1851: the Leander Apprentices Coat, Badge and Freedom.

This match, to be sculled annually in old fashioned wager boats, was open to all Thames apprentices whose masters hailed from stairs above London Bridge, and who had completed the fifth but not exceeded the seventh year of their apprenticeship. The prize consisted of a green coat trimmed with silver, a massive silver arm badge, and the amount of the winner's fee on taking up the Freedom. The race seems to have been financed by subscriptions, usually a

13   Leander Badge

guinea per head, from current and retired members, but lists do not appear in the accounts every year. One entry refers to 'Freedom £6.15s.0d'.

The Coat and Badge were offered at least up to 1860, but no examples were known to survive until 1987, when a Coat and Badge came up for auction in London and was purchased and renovated, with help from members in the United Kingdom and the United States. This treasure, for so it was to Leander, had been won by Samuel Beckett of Fulham in 1859 and passed down through his family. Beckett is named in the Minutes for 1858 as having finished fifth in that year, for which he won £1.0.0. The Minute noted that he would be eligible to compete again in the following year. Unfortunately, the secretary then got as far as to write: 'The race was as follows . . .' but did not add the account of the race.

The relationship between the professional watermen and the gentlemen amateurs during the first half of the nineteenth century, and indeed for some time after, was a special one, a mix of formal class segregation and mutual respect, which often amounted to affection. James Parish, 'Jem', Leander's waterman from 1831 to 1848, and known as 'The Man in Green', is a case in point. His picture hangs in the clubhouse today, showing him resplendent in his Club uniform, a loyal servant whose word carried authority somewhat in the manner of a Guards drill-sergeant. The *Short History of Leander* wrote of him:

> A past master in an era when deliberate fouling was an accepted part of boat racing, it is understandable that his prowess was less appreciated without than within the ranks of the Club, which presented him with a testimonial in 1848. The best-known story concerning Parish is in the *Bell's Life* account of the 1852 University Boat Race, when the Leander eight-oared cutter was swamped by the wash of steamers below Barnes Bridge. As she sank by the bows, and Parish saw disaster approaching, he called to Mr Harrison, the Leander stroke, 'Give me your oar, sir, to hang on by, for I cannot swim'. Mr Harrison, now *'nante in gurgite vasto'*, gallantly tossed him the oar, saying, 'Nor can I'.

An example of the relationship between Parish and the members of Leander emerges from the Club records of 1854. Howard Fellows, Club Secretary from 1847–1853, was about to emigrate to the Antipodes and the members were presenting him with a commemorative silver tankard. Parish submitted a humble request to be allowed to make a case to protect this on its journey to Australia. The Committee than passed a resolution, 'That James Parish, coxswain to the Leander Club, having expressed a desire to contribute towards the Fellows testimonial, by presenting a case for the purpose of holding the tankard, this meeting do signify their entire approbation of such participation on the part of that old and trustworthy servant of the Club in their expression of regard of that gentleman, and take this opportunity of thanking him as well as in their own names as that of his absent patron, for the zeal for the welfare of the Club, and the goodness of heart which evidently prompted him in making this request'.

The presentation was made at a dinner which, at Fellows's request, was held at The Lion, Newcastle Street, Strand, in which Fellows had been mainly instrumental in installing Parish. This must have been a riverside hostelry at that time, for until the building of the Embankment, the Strand, as its name implies, bordered the foreshore of the river. The 1854 Minute Book contains a set of the printed Rules showing that the subscription had been raised from five pounds to five guineas, and the limit on membership had increased to twenty-five, plus retired members, who included most of the familiar names from the preceding decade, as well as the Secretary, Patrick Colquhoun, who seems to have been the only survivor from the 1847 list.

The most important event in 1854 was the founding of the Thames National Regatta, the initial prospectus for which bemoaned the fact that the London River, with all its resources, presented no aquatic festival, whereas in the provincial towns, wherever the slightest facilities existed, local regattas abounded. It was proposed to hold the new regatta over the same course as the defunct Royal Thames Regatta from Putney Bridge to Chiswick Eyot, which was now easily accessible by railway, steam and road. Subscriptions raised £533.5s.0d (in excess of £16,000 at present-day rates). Leander donated ten guineas in addition to staging its Coat and Badge race as part of the festivities. There were events for Watermen, Landsmen, and Boatmen of the Coast, and an eight-oar race, North of England versus the South, with cash prizes totalling £360, excluding apprentices' coat-and-badge events. There were also events for Tradesmen and Gentlemen, for presentation cups. Unlike the earlier Royal Thames Regatta, the new regatta was scheduled for the second week in August so that it would not clash with the now 'Royal' Regatta at Henley. A glance at the clubs involved in the foundation of the new regatta is interesting. Forming the Committee were representatives of Triton, Meteor, Argonaut, Wandle, Leander, Thames (no connection with the later Thames Rowing Club), Ilex and Herne. In addition, we find on the Subscribers' List, Nemesis, Neptune, Northumberland Boat Club, Thames Unity Club of Lambeth, Volante – and the Arrow, which, according to *Bell's Life*, it may be remembered, had joined with Leander thirteen years earlier, further proof of the fluidity of the early London clubs.

The other event of importance to Leander in 1854 was the presentation by Charles Goolden of the Goolden Cup, to be contested annually by single scullers, members of the

14   The Goolden Cup

Club, over the traditional championship course from Westminster to Putney.

There were also problems with Searle's this year. Colquhoun had to write to Searle to protest that 'the Leander Club has learned with regret that you did on the 26 April last let out the Leander Club boat without having previously denuded it of the Club insignia, and to request you to erase the name and alter the paint of that boat and its oars forthwith, and to express the dissatisfaction of the Club, etc, etc'.

It was not long before Searle was in trouble again. In May we find him writing to Colquhoun to acknowledge a letter from the latter, but clearly defending himself from

15 Coat of Arms on the Goolden Cup

whatever was the basis of the complaint by stating that Edward Searle had seen 'both the eight and four afloat some time before the arrival of the Leander Club coxswain, so that he had only to step on board and put the boats ashore at Renshaw's. We have given orders that, for the future, they are to be ready at Renshaw's hard every Tuesday and Friday at five o'clock, according to your instructions'.

A more serious complaint followed in June, a special committee set up to examine a new eight-oar cutter supplied by Searle and Sons reporting that:

> The rowlocks do not flare out sufficiently from the shoulder of the boat, the result of which is that the oars being at an awkward and not a right angle with the rowlock as they should be ... are extremely difficult to feather properly ... This fault the committee considers to arise from the boat being built wall sided after the model of outrigged boats, and from the saxboard being put on almost or quite perpendicularly ... Secondly that the boat is too short from the bow rowlock to the nose by about 3 feet according to the lines upon which the rest of of the boat appears to have been built, and therefore between each stroke is utterly destitute of that power of 'shooting' evenly while the oars are on the feather ... Thirdly that the upperworks of the forward part of the boat are pinched like a packing case so that every swell makes a clear break over her instead of being shot off ...
> Fourthly the Committee draws attention to the fact of the boat being built of unseasoned stuff so that the skin has started clear away from the timbers in some places ... many strakes too are cockled twisted and warped.

Searle suggested that the old and new Leander cutters should be placed side by side for inspection. Alas, there is no record of the outcome, but since Leander continued to patronise Searle's Yard one must assume that harmony was restored. It is noteworthy, though, that Leander were acquiring a new in-rigged boat in 1854 although outriggers had been available since 1847.

The Minute Book of 1854 is unlike any modern Minute Book. Thanks to Colquhoun, who tended to use it partly as a personal diary, it tells us a great deal about what Leander was like at the time. The 1854 Minutes include a

On Saturday August 19th 1854 Colquhoun Rotton and T.L. Wood started from London by rail to Chertsey, whence shouldering their traps & boat tackle they walked to Shepperton Lock, intending there to take ship for Oxford, but finding that contrary to expectation the ship had been stowed on a barge which might be expected at Sonning the same evening, they determined to make for that village to wait for her arrival, being minded if it were possible to push on to Pangbourne, where beds had been ordered at the Elephant & Castle in pursuance of this they took fly to Staines Stats whence they travelled by train in great state, having, like the Grants of Tullochgorum, "their piper playing before them", almost incessantly to Windsor to the somewhat discomposure of their cotenants of the Railway carriage — waited at Windsor some 2 hours

16 MS of Patrick Colquhoun's account of the river trip to Oxford, 1854

light-hearted Appendix in which Colquhoun describes, in the third person, two remarkable long journeys in his randan skiff*, the first from Guildford to Littlehampton-on-Sea, and the second from London to Oxford and back. The following is from the Littlehampton Log:

> Colquhoun and Rotton having determined to explore the Wey and Arun, the former a judge being on Circuit at Guildford ... together with Ellis H, had on the third of August rowed Colquhoun's randan skiff up to Guildford from Weybridge, distance 18 miles, Locks 11, charge 5/-.
> On Saturday Wood, Harrison, Colquhoun, Rotton, start from Guildford at 4 pm and arrive at Loxwood ... at about 9, where they sleep at the Public House there called the Onslow Arms, having passed 18 locks ... and through Sidney Wood ... At 6 am on Sunday morning they start, taking a bargee to open the locks which all go with a winch, they arrive at the last lock at 9.30 and finding little tide against them do not arrive at Houghton Bridge till 11, where there is an excellent Public worthy of great commendation. They start again at 1 o'clock and arrive at Littlehampton at 3 where they bathe and wait the turn of the tide at 6. The tide takes between 2 and 3 hours to run up to the first lock which is nearly three hours row. Arrive at 9 and row throughout the night arriving at Loxwood at 5 am ... arrive at Guildford at 1.20 pm on Monday.

*A randan – there is one on the right of the 1831 print of the yard at Stangate mentioned on page 21 (Plate 3) – can be propelled by three scullers, or by an oarsman at bow and stroke with a sculler in between, or by two oarsmen alone.

The distance was estimated to be about fifty miles from Guildford to Littlehampton.

The second long distance trip that August was more eventful. The Log, which must be heavily abridged here, was written with considerable humour but a fine disregard of punctuation, by Colquhoun, and reminds one strongly of Jerome K. Jerome's classic *Three Men in a Boat*.

Setting off on Saturday, 19th August, Colquhoun, Rotton and T.L. Wood arrived at Shepperton Lock, only to find that their boat was on a barge on its way to Sonning, where they had to spend the night as the barge did not arrive until the next morning. They then set off on 'a most laborious day's work, it being necessary (owing to the bigotry of certain magisterial priests who refuse to let the locks be opened on Sunday) to tow the boat by locks on land ... At Caversham Lock the barbarous people showed us much kindness by helping us tow her here which wd. have been hard to do without them ...'

They found a winch at Whitchurch Lock, which they opened and went through and refused to pay. They also opened Goring Lock and pushed on to Cleeve Lock where, 'whilst pioneering through a willow plantation with the ship, (they) were overtaken by one demanding payment for Goring Lock, granted, as his aid was required to tow ...' They arrived at Wallingford Lock where the towing was tedious, about 250 yards and being unassisted although half the town were looking on. At Benson's Lock they 'had a row with the drunken host of a public who, failing to induce them to stop at his Potikin, demanded payment for trespass on his meadow towing past the lock, refused, as he had consented to it himself. He then held on by the painter, which, after a council of war carried on in *Lingua Franca*, Colquhoun cut, and the other two backing water, they glided gently beyond his reach and sped on amid mutual slang in which the *Santissima Trinidad* was not worsted'.

They arrived at Shillingford Bridge in the dark and the next morning reached Culham Lock, after which the river became so shallow and clogged with weeds that towing became necessary, which was difficult as the shrubs on the bank kept catching the towing line, but they eventually reached their next overnight stop, Abingdon. The following day they had a very wet row to Oxford with the river full of weeds and slept well at the Mitre.

'Tuesday being flush day* for the barges, the ship started about 10 with an excellent stream, bringing them down in great style to Abingdon, where there were many barges taking advantage of the same. Passing these, rowed merrily on unimpeded by weeds till, after passing Day's Lock, they came in sight of a pair-oar having for crew two men in brown rowing, cricket, and general field sport toggery, indifferent oarsmen, hen steering . . . to Wallingford, where both ships disembarked to victual crews . . . buckled to at work again and pass without adventure beyond a successful resistance to demand for Sunday toll at Whitchurch . . . and down to Sonning where, it now being too dark to proceed, put up for the night.

'Next day . . . down to Henley, that Paradise of oarsmen, where, however, except to rest for a stroke or two to fully admire the beauties of that magnificent reach, they halted not, barring locks, anywhere before Maidenhead . . . even the pastry of Marlow, so known to fame**, failed to stay their onward course. About that time the sun became exceedingly strong and burnt through jerseys like nothing at all, and the weather had brought out the anglers in heaps . . . At Maidenhead this vast number of Cockney anglers . . . became a bore, for so thick were they dotted about the river, that it was next to impossible to bathe without an indecent exposure to some half score of hens. C & R, not having the fear of the world before their eyes or elsewhere, had a dip . . . and necessarily married W. forbore . . . At Penton Hook, the *Trinidad* having got in before a family in a punt, the latter could not get in before a barge hove in sight inopportunely, notwithstanding paterfamilias threatening to pitch the boy of the Lock into the pound'.

They eventually reached Shepperton Lock in heavy rain at about 8 o'clock on Wednesday, 23rd August, the total distance covered being just over 127 miles.

At this period, the only officers named in the Club rules were a secretary and two auditors. The *Short History* shows also an honorary treasurer but there is no sign of any such office in

---

*'Flush Day' – at that time many of the locks on the Upper Thames were still 'Flash' or 'Flush' locks, with no gated lock basins. The water was held back by a barrage of paddles which could be removed to allow boats to pass. The consequent loss of water resulted in the upper reaches becoming too shallow for navigation. There were therefore twice weekly 'Flush Days', when barges carrying coal from Warwickshire to London passed downstream in convoy from Oxford on the flush of water.

**Marlow was then renowned for meat pies. Urchins, hurling abuse at passers-by, used to call out, 'Who ate puppy pie under Marlow Bridge?', the story being that a local landlord disposed of an unwanted litter of puppies in this manner.

17 An old flush lock

the contemporary Minutes, which, incidentally, were described as 'Logs' in nautical fashion.

Business was transacted at the dinners which invariably followed each outing and in principle members could propose motions, including the election of candidates, and these motions then came up for discussion on the second club day after proposal during the summer, or at the next 'periodic' meeting during the winter months. The 1854 Minute Book reveals a closely knit society of friends, who mostly lived or worked in the City, dedicated to recreational rowing, occasional wager matches, club competitions, long distance voyages, such as the two described above, and the patronage of professional watermen. The Brilliants were not equipped for competitive eight-oared rowing beyond their own home waters, nor, one would think, were they much interested in change, but change was about to overtake them.

No Minute Book survives for 1855, and there is no record elsewhere of significant activities around Lambeth, but in retrospect one can see that there were small developments at Henley which were to lead to more important developments in the following year. Henley Regatta had become, and indeed had hitherto largely been, the preserve of Oxford and Cambridge Universities and colleges. It was therefore only the 'norm' that in 1855 Oxford faced Cambridge in the Grand

Challenge Cup, whilst Balliol faced Trinity Hall in the Ladies' Plate, there being no other entries in either event. The only representatives of tidal waters were the likes of H.H. Playford and A.A. Casamajor in the Silver Goblets and Diamonds. However, for the first time there were invaders from the provinces. Royal Chester were entered in the Stewards' Cup, in which they easily beat Lady Margaret Boat Club, Cambridge, and in the Wyfold Cup, which had been designated in that year for coxed-four competition, they also won easily against Wargrave, who had entered only to make a race, knowing they had no chance.

In 1856 Royal Chester returned with higher aspirations, and the first keelless eight ever to be seen on the Thames, built by the Tyne boat builder, Mat Taylor*. In her, they won both Henley's coveted eight-oared trophies. They also entered, apparently with the same men, for the Stewards', Visitors' and Wyfold Cups but without further success. Although no contemporary reporter said so, this invasion was not popular with the Oxbridge men. An objection to Chester's entry in the Ladies' Plate was rejected, but in the following year the Committee was persuaded to change the rules, limiting the Ladies' to colleges from Oxford and Cambridge, and to Eton and Westminster. The Londoners, one may surmise, returned to tidal waters to brood.

Leander were present, not as competitors but as spectators. The Secretary provided a small sketch map to show where they were to put up their boat, and where to find beer and beds. He also recorded in his log that 'after attending races up till 4 o'clock . . . started for Windsor 24 miles. Beered at Cookham and arrived at Windsor where the crew re-embarked in the train for their homes'. On the next day they rowed on down to Hampton, and on the third day to Putney, from where the professional waterman, Campbell, ferried the boat back to Lambeth for five shillings. That seems to be a fair indication of Leander's *modus vivendi* at that time.

The event which took place during 1856, arising no doubt from the dissatisfaction of the Tideway oarsmen at their inability to produce eight-oar crews to compete at Henley, actually occurred on 9th April, before the opening of Leander's 1856 season. No mention was made in the Minutes, but in all probability its significance for Leander's future was not recognised.

A Mr Josias Nottidge, who had partnered Casamajor under the Wandle colours in winning the Silver Goblets in the previous summer, sent out a circular calling a meeting at the Craven Hotel in the Strand, and there proposed the formation of a new club 'whose members should meet periodically in town to discuss the interests of rowing', but those who had responded to Mr Nottidge's summons evidently had more radical ideas. They did not favour 'talking shop', but they did favour the forming of a new rowing club. Before the evening was out, the London Rowing Club had been well and truly founded. Rowing on the London waters would never be quite the same again. Indeed, that is an understatement, for the formation of London Rowing Club shifted the centre of gravity decisively from Lambeth

---

*C.M. Pitman states in his *Record of the University Boat Race* (1919) that the first keelless four was built by the Tyne boat builder, Harry Clasper, in 1847 and was used by Oxford at Henley to win the Stewards' Cup in 1852.

to what was then still the country village of Putney, and sounded the death knell of the score or so of small private clubs which had hitherto catered for amateur oarsmen in the metropolis – all, that is to say, except the Leander Club.

The principles on which the new club was to be run were soon clearly set out. The founders had had enough of the small associations which demanded high subscriptions and then had to levy fines to increase their income, and very often surcharges at the end of the season as well; and which had too few active members to support eight-oar rowing, and too few boats to allow recreational rowing to continue on days when club members were involved in any sort of racing. No doubt they were also disenchanted with the heavily polluted river downstream, and the increasing interference of steamer traffic. They wanted a large club with a fixed subscription, and a fleet of boats to cater for all who chose to turn up.

Within three weeks, they had recruited 106 members, boats had been purchased, rooms hired at the Star and Garter Hotel, Putney, and a tent erected nearby to house their boats. On 22nd May 1856, the first London Rowing Club crew 'made its debut on the bosom of old Father Thames.'

It is no exaggeration to state that the foundation of London Rowing Club revolutionised the rowing scene in London. The foundation was too late to permit London to enter at Henley Regatta in 1856, but four of its new members competed in the colours of the Argonaut Club and won both the Stewards' and Visitors' Cups from Royal Chester. The small clubs which had not been absorbed by the new giant soon faded away, with the exception of Leander, and a new and potent force had appeared at Henley.

The dramatic change in the situation might well have spelled the end of Leander, but ultimately the Brilliants rose to the new challenge.

18 The Thames at Lambeth Palace, 1850

3

Chrysalis Years
1856–1890

While the foundation of London Rowing Club undoubtedly set in motion a train of events which led to great changes in the second half of the nineteenth century, a perusal of the Leander books of that period gives no indication that the worthies of Stangate were aware that the wind of change was blowing. On the contrary, it was very much 'business as usual'.

At this point Leander were entering what could be described as a 'chrysalis' stage in their history. They may still have been referred to as the 'invincible Brilliants', and no doubt saw themselves as such, but the world in which they had earned that title was withering away; and the new rowing world in which reputations were to be made was at Henley and at that moment beyond their grasp.

In the meantime Leander's Charles Goolden was insisting 'that the (Goolden Cup) match be rowed in old-fashioned wager boats (at least he recognised that they were "old-fashioned") not outrigged and that the rowlocks be in a plane with the saxboard and that no evasion of the rule in its plain and obvious interpretation be allowed'. Wager matches were originally rowed in working wherries, but the problem was that when these were used for racing they could not be made narrower, and therefore faster, by reducing the beam, without sacrificing the leverage. This the professionals sought to overcome by building boats which were narrow on the waterline, but having widely flared gunwales and saxboards to increase the span between rowlocks. The boats so designed were highly unstable in windy conditions and it was this practice which Goolden was banning.

Leander's programme for July 1856 was typical and indicative of what the Club was then all about:

14 July. 12 members met and proceeded down to West India Docks where they dined as guests of ship-owner Walter Bovill. The Secretary noted that the feed by Bovill on board the *Sir Robert Sale* at 6 o'clock (was) soup, fish, cold viands, cheese with a flood of claret and champagne; after that, songs, the party leaving by the 10.30 train, 28 present in all ... The party went off very well, 'all more or less or rather more than less' (No need to enquire more or less what?)

18 July to Erith for excellent dinner at Crown, did not get back till 12.30 having been nearly run down off Greenwich by a steamer.

26 July boat sent up to Staines from Richmond and crew by 3.45 train. Rowed to Eton and then up to Surley to meet Westminster School, also 'had a slash down with Eton' in their outrigger.

5 August. Mr Smith expressed his desire 'that members be permitted to wear the straw hat with Red Ribbon'.

(There is no indication whether this proposal was accepted.)

The log for 16 June 1857 included a newspaper report stating that Leander had 'ordinarily exhibited during the season a scullers' contest, a pair-oar race, and an eight-oar race with Westminster, and on Tuesday they commenced the season with the addition of a randan race over the old-fashioned course from Westminster to Putney'. The crews (all Leander members) were made up with reference to the places they hailed from:

London – Messrs Prior, Bovill and Willoughby
Westminster – Messrs Colquhoun, Goolden and Wood
Eton – Messrs Davis, Smith and J. Davis

Westminster led first but were washed by a steamer off Pimlico and then forced off course by barge traffic, so that London passed them at Chelsea and finally reached Putney about six lengths ahead, with Eton a further eight lengths behind Westminster. Conditions were said to be very hard.

Apart from this new event, Leander's programme for 1857 followed the familiar pattern but the significant action was all taking place upriver. The Great Western Railway opened their branch line from Twyford to Henley, and London Rowing Club made their first entry for Henley Regatta under their own colours, winning the Grand Challenge Cup from Oxford University.

Both Oxford and Cambridge were anxious to meet the new challenge in 1858. The light blues were able to do so, but Oxford, who felt they had been robbed by a damaged oar in the preceding year, found they could not make up a crew. Four of them, together with a like number of Cantabs who were not rowing in their university crew, therefore approached Leander to enquire whether they could compete under Leander colours. This must have posed a considerable problem to a club which had hitherto kept its membership so exclusive, limited to twenty-five members, and, so far as can be judged, had never elected any candidate for the express purpose of racing for the Club. However, in May, after rejecting a proposal that the limit on their membership should be dropped altogether, they agreed to raise it to thirty-five. After discussing the merit of hiring an old boat which was said to be very 'tender' and unlikely to survive more than one regatta, they also agreed to purchase a new outrigger from Mat Taylor.

In the thirty years since the foundation of Henley regatta, this was only the third appearance by a Leander eight, and the first since the debacle of 1841. Drawn against Cambridge University, they were leading at half distance but Cambridge then moved ahead to win by three lengths, going on to defeat London Rowing Club in the final by half a length.

It has to be said that Patrick Colquhoun, though a tower of strength to Leander's administration for so many years, was not by nature one of the world's most generous characters. One can almost hear him remarking 'What did I tell you?', writing in the log:

Racing of the seediest description; in fact, there was but one race, Camb: LC who held them halfway, having the inside, but Cambridge then drew past and won by two lengths clear. No 7 LC had had a 3-inch cut in his stern in the morning for a deep-seated boil and of course was worse than useless in the Boat. In no case however would they have won having not trained long enough or enough together.

The old Secry thinks they must another year turn their attention to the following points. Longer and more severe training as to time. More severe training as to distance. More forbearance from the pleasures of society. To row the stroke out at the end swish, whatever blade they choose, to have too their oars covered. In a word more punishment.

It is moreover suggested that if the Club can sell this boat they should do so and try Jowitt whose form is far more perfect than that of Mat Taylor, and that some more definite instructions should be given him, for it is clear the LC, had it followed out the above programme, must have won.

The year ended with a grand banquet for Colquhoun in the Great Hall of the Freemansons' Tavern to celebrate his appointment to the Supreme Court of the Ionian Islands. His departure was a loss not only to his contemporaries at Leander, but to students of Leander history today. He was replaced by Thomas Wood, who retained the office for less than two years. The Club's 'Log' became no more than brief jottings and notes of expenses and elections.

It seems that the intention to continue competition up-river was there in 1859, for in April a new eight and four were ordered, but in the following month a note recorded that it had proved impossible to make up a crew for Henley. Eight years were to pass before Leander's next entry.

19   Sir Patrick Colquhoun

At the last meeting in 1859 Wood handed over to Arthur Lonsdale, a recent Oxford Blue who had stroked the unsuccessful 1858 Leander Henley crew and so was one of the Club's new generation. Clearly there was at last some willingness to see progress, for in January 1860, Bovill suggested that there should be a change in the club uniform and a committee was set up to report in July. Unfortunately, the Minute book for the years 1856–1860 ended at the beginning of 1860 and the succeeding volume is missing from the archives, so there is no record of what was decided about costume, nor of other important matters which must have been under discussion.

The last entry in the old book, recording a

meeting on 27th April, reads: 'A long discussion ensued as to the propriety of lowering the subscription of the Club, after when it was resolved that steps should be taken to see how far it could be done consistently with keeping the Club out of debt'. This in itself is a further indication that the wind of change was beginning to blow, for one of the common complaints against the old small clubs had been the high subscription rates which they necessarily had to charge. The recruitment of younger members from Oxford and Cambridge may well have aggravated this problem.

Although we lack the Minutes to give us details, we know that the limit on membership was removed altogether in 1860 or shortly after, and no doubt this was one of the steps taken to avoid running the Club into debt. The decision may also have been influenced by the failure to make up a Henley crew in 1859.

Frustratingly, the 1860 minutes end just when the most important decision was about to be made, for this was the year in which Leander finally deserted Stangate and moved to Putney. Rooms were hired at the Star and Garter Hotel, and a plot of land rented on which a tent was erected to house boats. Presumably finance prevented what was still a club of only a few dozen members from building immediately. Four years later the boat tent site was purchased by London Rowing Club to build their clubhouse and Leander then took a long lease on the adjoining plot of land, and set about raising money to build a home of their own.

Membership does not seem to have risen very quickly after the removal of the limit but we do know that the first Captain was formally appointed in 1863, indicating that Leander rowing was moving in a new direction; in earlier times crews had been made up by the Secretary and 'captained' in action by their strokes. Herbert Steward was the first to be elected for the express purpose of raising and leading a crew.

According to Pitman, a new Rule book was drawn up in February 1862, and probably the offices of President and Captain were added to those of Secretary and Treasurer. A committee was also first elected at that time. Previously the Club's business affairs had been decided by all members who were present on the routine Club days, and that meant, in theory at least, the whole membership of the Club, since attendance on Club days was obligatory. With members being elected from Oxford and Cambridge, that obligation ceased to be practical. An elected committee had become a necessity, and thenceforward meetings were held in the City, usually at the office of the President or Secretary. Later, as numbers increased, the practice arose of holding the Annual Meeting in conjunction with the annual dinner, at a London club or restaurant – the Pall Mall, the Criterion and the Café Royal all being favoured at different times. This practice continued until after the Second World War and had at least two merits: it ensured a quorum for the meeting and encouraged short speeches. The cynical sometimes also suggested that it priced the young, and therefore potentially subversive, out of an opportunity to criticise the establishment.

Herbert Steward took over as Secretary in 1866 and since that date Minutes of general meetings, but not committee meetings, have been preserved. There does survive in the archives, however, handwritten in copperplate on 21st March, a summons to a committee meeting at No 4 Upper Charles Street, Westminster. Nine candidates were elected, including two undergraduates, whilst one candidate was turned down, but Steward's Minutes were very different from Colquhoun's of old. They provided a detailed record of business transacted but without the chat and scrapbook element of their predecessor.

On 15th February, Steward presented plans for the proposed Putney clubhouse, stating that the money would be raised by £10 debentures (approximately £350 today), bearing interest at 6%. This produced a proposal that a general meeting of the Club should be called to consider the matter, but this was defeated by 15 votes to 12. It was then resolved, *nem. con.*, that the Committee should proceed as soon as possible with the building, subscribers to the debentures having already produced £535. On 16th March the Secretary wrote to the Conservators of the Thames:

> Dear Sirs,
> The Leander Club proposes erecting a large and expensive Boathouse and Clubrooms on the Banks of the Thames at Putney at the site shown by the accompanying plan. As the towing path there is very narrow and the Banks in a very dilapidated condition, I venture to ask on behalf of the Club if they will take into consideration the question of repairing the Banks and constructing a sloping causeway as they did last year on the adjoining site for the use of the London Rowing Club.
> I am, etc.

The reply came back with dispatch which would be remarkable today, that the Conservators agreed to the request.

The move to Putney evidently fired the Club's ambitions, for on 27th April they held Trial Eights, and crews were duly entered for the Grand and Stewards' Cups at Henley. The eight lost their heat to First Trinity, Cambridge, by under a length and must have been frustrated then to see Trinity withdraw from the final. In the Stewards', the Leander stroke broke his blade passing the White House, but at the time they were trailing University College, who went on to win the final from Kingston with some ease.

By the time of the following General Meeting in February 1867, the Secretary was able to announce the completion of the boathouse except for the fittings and water supply, but had also to report that the cost had greatly increased because of the treacherous nature of the soil, which had made it necessary to drive piles to a depth of 25 feet over nearly all the site. That was perhaps not altogether surprising considering the building stood on the foreshore of the river. It was agreed to ask members to contribute by donation towards the cost of fitting out the clubhouse, and to support a further issue of £5 debentures to cover the deficit in the building fund.

There was an entry at Henley again this year, in the Stewards' Cup, Leander losing their heat to the Oxford Radleian Club. They also received, and predictably rejected, their first invitation to sample international rowing from the International Regatta of the Universal Exhibition, Paris. The invitation was passed to the Captain who took no further action, no doubt mistrusting the intentions of the organ-

20 The 1866 Grand eight

l to r (back row) W.J.S. Cadman, F.H. Kelly, H. Watney, R.A. Kinglake
(centre) C.C. Scholefield, J.H. Etherington-Smith, J.G. Chambers
(front) J.H. Forster, F. Walton (cox)

21 The 1866 Stewards' four

l to r (back row) Etherington-Smith, Cadman
(centre), Kelly
(front) Forster, Walton (cox)

isers, if for no other reason than because they were foreigners. In passing, it is interesting to note that at a time when the British rowing establishment were making heavy weather of defining 'amateur status', those same foreigners had decided the problem admirably and succinctly – 'The Races are open to Amateurs only. Are not considered Amateurs: Waterman, Bargemen, Long-shoremen, Jacks-in-the-Water, all men who belong to a boat builder's yard, and men who have been paid for Rowing.' If Henley and the tideway hierarchy had accepted that definition, much subsequent heartache might have been avoided.

Funding the new boathouse was still causing problems in 1868, when the trustees were authorised to raise a mortgage of £500, but accounts in subsequent years indicate that the Club was running at a modest profit and paying off its debts, but enthusiasm for competitive rowing seems to have faltered. Steward resumed the role of Captain whilst remaining Secretary and appealed for a younger man to take on the responsibility for the rowing in the following year. There were then to be five different captains in the next six years, without any Leander crew appearing at Henley.

Without doubt, there was activity at the

Putney clubhouse, for in 1869 there was a complaint about the large quantity of rowing clothes left around which was becoming a great nuisance. This in turn prompted a request that more lockers should be provided, to which the Committee agreed, imposing a charge for these and those already in place.

While in the early years at Westminster Leander had ruled as 'Cock of the London Water', the 'Invincibles', the 'Brilliants', all titles bestowed by others and not self-sought, the world they had once dominated had since disintegrated around them and they were ill-equipped for the new rowing world that had replaced it. Although they had moved to Putney, they were reluctant to change the pattern of their activities, and they practically disappeared from the competitive rowing scene. When they finally re-emerged, their progress was at first unsure, but the days when metamorphosis was to take place were not too far distant.

The quick succession of captains ended with the election in 1875 of John Goldie, who was to give his name to the Goldie boathouse on the Cam. He raised a Leander crew containing six fellow Cantabs and one Oxonian, which rowed past First Trinity and Molesey between Fawley and the White House to record Leander's first win in the Grand since 1840. The four stern oarsmen also won the Stewards' Cup with some ease.

No doubt this experience convinced the Committee of the benefits to be derived from an intake of university men, to which they responded by reducing the subscription for undergraduates to half a guinea.

In 1876 Goldie's men lost in a heat of the Grand to a University College and Brasenose composite crew, and in the following year Goldie was unable to raise a crew at all. Indeed, there were no more Henley entries until 1880, when T.C. Edwards-Moss won the Grand with seven Oxford men, but he was unsuccessful in 1881 in both the Grand and the Stewards'.

One might say that at this point the formula had been found for producing Leander crews, but not for winning. In all but two of the next nine years Leander's flag was flying at Henley, but with no greater success than a place in the final of the Stewards' and the Grand in 1887.

In the meantime, in 1886, there occurred an event of great significance, though of no immediate effect. At a Special General Meeting, convened on 1st January, and attended by forty-three members, the Committee reported on 'A Scheme for Establishing an Upriver Boat and Club House'. One might imagine that this presaged a move to Henley, but this was not so: various options were to be considered. The Meeting agreed unanimously that an upriver boathouse should be established, and the various options mentioned were Henley, with 19 for and 19 against; perhaps Molesey, but not above Shepperton (6 for, 29 against); Cookham (20 for, 16 against). When the alternatives of Cookham or Henley were put to the vote, 21 were for Cookham, 20 for Henley, while 26 to 8 voted for the Putney boathouse to be retained.

It was eventually agreed that the Committee 'should take steps towards raising money and otherwise carrying out the scheme for an Upriver Boat House at Cookham, but that no contract be entered into without the consent of the Club in a General Meeting'.

Some may ask 'Why Cookham?' The short

22 *(above)* The Tottenham Charger, 1868

23 *(right)* Cup from the British Regatta, Paris, 1867

The charger, now in the Club's possession, contains a set of five winning Boat Race medals for 1864–1868, won by C.R.W. Tottenham, a unique record for a cox, and two Grand Challenge Cup medals for 1866 and 1867, also won by Tottenham as cox of the Oxford Etonians.

The cup is the individual prize won by Tottenham at the Paris Regatta of 1867

answer is probably 'Rudie Lehmann'. R.C. Lehmann was an activist in all matters acquatic and was already becoming influential with the young, whom he coached and entertained at his home – at Cookham, which was a fashionable riverside residential area. At the same time the choice does suggest that members were yearning not so much for a headquarters for competitive rowing as for a social country annexe to Putney.

The more discerning reader may also see the members' enthusiasm for expansion, alongside their evident reluctance to pay more money, as an indication that the membership was getting younger. In the following year, one member actually proposed, but was prevailed upon to withdraw, a motion 'for the remission of arrears (overdue subscriptions) to date'. There was a proposal in 1887 to suspend the concessionary rate to under-graduates of half a guinea, which, one assumes, was bringing in more young candidates than were welcome. The proposal was withdrawn but was symptomatic of what was to follow a few years later.

The introduction in 1886 of the New Course at Henley, when the finish was moved downstream to Poplar Point, had radically changed the spectator facilities, and in 1887 G.D. Rowe, who was now Leander's Secretary, announced that arrangements were being made for hiring rooms at the Royal Hotel for the use of Leander Club during the summer at a rate of £100 per annum. No doubt this was to disarm criticism from those who believed that they were to get new upriver premises at Cookham, whilst at the same time catering for the changed regatta requirement. The announcement prompted a request 'that steps be taken for securing an enclosure or barge for the Club, for the purposes

24   George Rowe (Spy cartoon)

of lunch and tea at the forthcoming regatta'.

George Rowe succeeded in providing an enclosure in 1887 on Temple Island, and during the closing years of the nineteenth century, and indeed until the outbreak of the war in 1914, private enclosures for clubs, including Leander, were a regular part of the Henley scene. Leander continued to rent rooms at the Royal Hotel, across the road from Henley Station, though not for the whole summer, Rowe arranging in 1889 for a club room, for the period 15th June to 13th July, for fifty

March 1889 by a sub-committee appointed to consider the possibility of a 'composition payment' in lieu of an annual subscription, and the creation of Honorary and Life memberships. The report tells us much about the Club. The sub-committee found that the number of members at the end of 1888 was approximately 440, of whom about forty were abroad, or without addresses, leaving some 400 paying members. The Treasurer, however, stated that only 339 had paid their subscriptions for the year 1888.

On this basis, the sub-committee calculated the Club's income as:

		Guineas
55	undergraduate members @ 10s 6d each	27½
4	honorary members @ 1.1s	4
339	members @ 2.2s	678
	Thus showing an annual income of	£709½

The sub-committee estimated the future annual expenditure for the boathouse (rent, rates, repairs, an attendant, sundries), printing, stationary, petty cash, repairs to boats etc, and subscription to Henley Regatta, plus 10% for contingencies – as about £300. In addition, expenses of the crew at Henley (£150) and a new racing boat and oars (£50) totalled £200, giving an annual expenditure of £500.

These figures did not make any provision for a club room at Henley, as the sub-committee had been led to believe that the experiment of the previous two years had not met with the success that had been expected. It was also thought by the sub-committee that it was not within their province to speculate on any probable increase in numbers, and they had also not taken into consideration the expense of the Island enclosure as it had been self-supporting,

25 'Rudie' R.C. Lehmann (Spy cartoon)

guineas. Charles Gurdon, later to become a County Court Judge, objected, in eloquent terms, to this step on the grounds of extravagance, 'but', Rowe minuted, 'after a brilliant debate of considerable duration, Mr Lehmann proposed and Mr Glynn seconded that the club rooms at Henley should be given up, but this motion was eventually rejected by an overwhelming majority'.

That the Club was certainly not short of funds at that time is evidenced in a report in

26 C.W. Kent

and had indeed yielded a small profit. Altogether, the above figures showed that the Club had a surplus income of £120 per annum.

The report went on to propose that any member paying the full subscription for ten years should become an Honorary member at one guinea p.a.; or after twenty years should become a Life member without further payment. Alternatively, Life membership should be available on payment of £20 on election, £15 after five years, or £7.10s after ten years' subscription.

The scheme, estimated to cost £111.6s p.a., was approved for introduction in January 1890. Those who wrestle with club budgets today must surely wonder at the confidence and financial stability which enabled their predecessors thus to cut their presumed profit margin to £8.14s on a turnover of a fraction under £745.

At the meeting at which the report was presented, the Treasurer commented in passing on the length of the wine bills at Henley which revealed the consumption of sixteen dozen hock. Presumably this item must have been included in the £150 expenses of the crew. Hock, sometimes diluted with water, was a favoured training beverage in that era and was even recommended as such in an article in the *Rowing Almanack*.

Wine bills may have been shorter in 1890 for only a Stewards' four went to Henley, to lose their heat, by two feet, to Brasenose, who went on to win in the final. The stroke of the Brasenose four was C.W. Kent, who was later to become one of Leander's most successful strokes. The account of this race, written by Herbert Steward for the Regatta history, was a masterpiece of understatement:

> Brasenose seemed ahead half way up the Island, but at the top of it Leander were ahead, and led by a quarter of a length at the quarter-mile mark. Brasenose, however, led at Remenham, but the crews were again level at Fawley. Brasenose led slightly at the three-

quarter mile post, but the boats were alongside at the mile post. Off Phyllis Court Leander seemed to be getting the best of it, but Brasenose passed the post first by two feet.

For the future there would be little risk of complaints about celebratory drinks, and perhaps a lesser consumption of hock by the Henley crews, for the breakthrough was about to occur. The *Short History* commented: 'It may seem remarkable that the "brilliant", the "invincible" Leander of the early years, thus stood, in 1890, with only five wins to its credit after fifty-two Henleys, but from now onwards the pick of the University oarsmen came in, and the story was different'.

27 The Leander Enclosure, Temple Island, 1891. This is one of a series of late Victorian Henley scenes by Dickenson & Foster

4

Metamorphosis
1891–1899

Chrysalis, the title of the previous chapter, naturally leads to the metamorphosis in Leander's history. It did not all happen at once, of course, but lifting the restriction on membership numbers, reducing the subscription for undergraduates, the consequent influx of younger members, and the opening of the clubhouse at Putney, all contributed towards making change possible, so that in 1891 an unprecedented run of success at Henley began. The 'Brilliants' and the 'Invincibles' were back in business.

The most potent single factor in the process was the special relationship which grew up between Leander and Oxford and Cambridge. It cannot be said that this relationship was sought or fostered by the Club during the early days; indeed, it was at first opposed by some of the elders. At a Special General Meeting on 20th March 1893 a new rule was proposed by Herbert Steward, seconded by John Goldie, which read:

> That a Resident Undergraduate of Oxford or Cambridge is not eligible for Election unless he has rowed in the University Eight, University Trial Eights, or in one of the first three boats on the river in the Eights at Oxford or May Races at Cambridge, or has won the University Fours, Pairs or Sculls, or has rowed for the Grand Challenge Cup at Henley, or has won any other race at Henley except the Thames Cup.

A number of amendments were put forward and rejected but a proposal by Duncan McLean and Rudie Lehmann, to add the words 'or may seem specially desirable to the Committee' was accepted.

The result, with this amendment, came to be known as the University Qualification Rule, and became a corner-stone of Leander election policy. There is no doubt that the intention was to limit the intake of undergraduate candidates, but the result was the opposite, for the new rule transformed Leander from a numerically small metropolitan club into the largest rowing club in the land, strongly orientated towards the two senior Universities.

The reason is not far to seek. Publishing a list of qualifications, to which only the most successful oarsmen of the day could aspire, made Leander membership something special in itself. Simply being a 'Leander man' became a cachet of rowing prowess, and although the rule applied only to undergraduate candidates, it inevitably set the standard for all other elections.

The University Qualification Rule, with minor adjustments, remained in force for almost a hundred years, until it was swept away by a new Constitution in 1985, which states:

> The qualification for Ordinary membership shall be good fellowship and proficiency in oarsmanship. In the election of Members special consideration

shall be given to candidates who have rowed with distinction at their Universities or in international competition or at major regattas or races. A candidate who has not achieved such proficiency, but who, because of his services to the sport of rowing may seem desirable to the Committee, shall also be eligible for election as an Ordinary Member.

Today's eligibility rule is expressed differently but the principle remains unchanged. Only those who have already demonstrated their skill on the water, or their willingness to devote time and effort to serving the sport, can hope to be elected. This is a fundamental difference between Leander and all other rowing clubs.

It has sometimes been said that Leander is not a 'rowing club' but a 'social club for distinguished oarsmen'. This claim is like a red rag to a bull to those who insist that Leander is first and foremost the world's premier rowing club. The subject may be emotive but there is really no conflict between the two points of view. On the one hand Leander has always been dedicated to the support and practice of rowing at the highest level. Before the Amateur Rowing Association, as the sport's governing body in the United Kingdom, assumed responsibility for producing international crews, Leander was by far the major provider of such crews, and today still provides more oarsmen for Britain's Olympic and World Championship crews than any other club, often more than all the others together. By those criteria Leander is certainly the country's premier rowing club, but that does not make it purely a rowing club in the usual sense.

The Club's membership was nudging the 1,000 mark a hundred years ago, and today stands at around 2,800 exclusive of Associate members; yet the number who race under Leander colours in any particular year seldom exceeds twenty and is often less, so ambition to row for the Club has never been a significant factor in applications for membership. Ninety-nine percent of Leander men join for 'good fellowship' (the first condition in the rules), for the social facilities, because they wish to support the rowing, and for the prestige of belonging to the only club which requires a rowing qualification.

Although a special relationship with Oxford and Cambridge developed, there were always some non-university members, but the fact that there was a guaranteed intake each year from these two universities, particularly in December after the Trial Eights, and in June after the summer bumping races, meant that by 1900 the Club had acquired a strong Oxbridge bias which was effectively self-generating. The special relationship grew to be so strong that the Presidents and Secretaries of the two University Boat Clubs were given ex-officio seats on the Leander Committee.

Leander's reliance on the 'Oxbridge Connection' stood them in good stead for some sixty years, and is still in operation today. However, the annual intake of Oxbridge men began to fall off after the Second World War, due to changing academic, financial and social circumstances at the two Universities, and Leander responded by looking for potential recruits from other sources, but this is jumping ahead of our story.

If Leander's relationship with Oxford and

Cambridge was fruitful in terms of recruitment, it was positively bountiful in terms of rowing success at Henley. Having won the Grand Challenge Cup only three times by 1890, Leander won it twelve times in the next fifteen years, the other winners being Trinity Hall and Third Trinity from Cambridge, and New College, Oxford. Memories fade and today some may find it hard to appreciate the dominance of university rowing until the end of the first half of the twentieth century. In the first 104 regattas at Henley, until and including 1953, the Grand Challenge Cup was won eighteen times by crews from one or other of the senior universities, twenty-two times by college crews and twenty-six times by Leander, manned almost exclusively by Oxbridge oarsmen. Foreign crews won nine times, and there were twenty-nine wins by other British clubs, many of whose crews also included Oxbridge oarsmen, so at least seventy percent of all British Grand winners were at or from Oxford and Cambridge.

One may wonder why so many of the top university oarsmen chose Leander rather than, for example, London or Thames, who offered more extensive rowing facilities. Paradoxically, the probable answer is that Leander's limited rowing programme was the very thing that attracted them. They could not row for a club until after the conclusion of Eights Week at Oxford or the May Races at Cambridge, by which time most other clubs' Henley crews were settled. So Leander, needing only a handful of oarsmen and a coxswain each year, had found a useful and profitable niche in the rowing world.

How Leander managed to succeed with such a limited programme is an interesting question. Outside the two leading universities, there was no competitive winter rowing until the institution of the Head of the River Race on the Tideway in 1926, but at Oxford and Cambridge there was a full programme – the Fours in October, followed by the Trial Eights and then the Boat Race, and while the final Leander crew often had only two weeks together before racing at Henley, most of the oarsmen had been racing together in various crews for a long time.

The system adopted by Leander was to appoint as Captain a recent, or sometimes a current, Blue of proven talent, who knew, and was known to and respected by his peers. During the winter the Captain would cast his net amongst those he considered to be sufficiently talented. All would be asked to get themselves fit and would be invited to row at weekends at Putney or Henley, and to be available for a fortnight of full-time rowing before the regatta. If there were not enough men to make up an eight during the winter, it was not hard to find substitutes. At the same time, the Captain would enquire at Oxford and Cambridge to find out whether there were current Blues who did not expect to have a viable college crew to row for at Henley. This latter point was considered important because it was an unwritten understanding that Leander would not poach oarsmen from college crews.

The Captain's brief was to produce a crew for the Grand and Stewards' Cups. Both events were usually covered by the same men and a common pattern was for the old Blues to double up in the Stewards', or sometimes the Goblets, so that they would have extra work during the last fortnight of practice to help them get racing fit. Any undergraduates were

28 Looking across the river to the site of the Henley clubhouse

expected to be fit already after rowing in the Boat Race and bumping races and they filled the remaining places in the eight. If the Captain was unable to muster sufficient talent, he would enter only a four, or no crew at all, which occurred not infrequently. It was a disappointment if there was no Leander crew in some years but the reason was well understood, and to have no crew from time to time was deemed to be less damaging to prestige than putting on a poor crew. Entering the lesser events was not considered.

In 1892 there was a proposal to rent a boathouse from Hobbs at Henley. Perhaps those who had raced in 1891 had not appreciated the spartan changing quarters and plunge bath fed directly from the river, which the Regatta then provided above Henley Bridge. Surprisingly, no enthusiasm was shown for this proposition. Then, in 1896, came news of an event which was to change every aspect of Leander life: at a Special General Meeting following the Annual General Meeting at the Café Royal that year, the Secretary, George Rowe, reported that the Committee had been engaged for some months in preparing a scheme for building a clubhouse and boathouse at Henley.

Unfortunately no Committee Minutes survive from that era, so we do not know precisely when or how Henley came to be substituted for the proposal to build at Cookham, which had been provisionally approved in 1886. Perhaps this occurred in 1892, when the Club first rented rooms at the Royal Hotel, and the logic of having quarters where the action took place, rather than at Cookham, must have become apparent.

One may surmise that Rowe had been at work for some time, for the scheme was already well advanced and the finances had been worked out. The Club would need to have an annual revenue of at least £65 more to run the new premises, which was to be achieved by imposing an entrance fee of one guinea for undergraduates, and two guineas for ordinary members.

Future members, Rowe said, would have to pay for the support of an institution which added such large attractions to membership of the Club, and current members were invited to give or lend voluntarily the sum necessary to inaugurate the new scheme. This was estimated to be £2,500 and already £1,800 had been promised in amounts ranging from £1 to £200 – partly in donations and partly in debentures redeemable by drawings at par but not bearing interest.

The Henley Corporation offered a lease of the Nook Enclosure, land that had been a Regatta Enclosure when the Henley finish was at the Red Lion steps, for seventy-five years at £25 a year rent, that being the longest lease which the Corporation had the power to grant. Plans were in the course of preparation for the building which, besides ordinary club accommodation, would contain a Ladies' dining-room and a Ladies' water closet, as well as sleeping accommodation for twenty-one members.

The proposal to introduce an entrance fee was carried by 57 votes to 6, which, in the circumstances, was just as well, and the proposal to proceed with the Clubhouse was carried *nem. con.*

No time was wasted, for at the following General Meeting on 1st April 1897, Rowe

29   George Rowe

declared that he particularly wished to retain the office of Honorary Secretary that year in order to see the new boathouse at Henley successfully put into operation. He reported that £2,673 had been promised by members towards the boathouse fund and bore witness to the great debt which the Club owed to Herbert Steward. 'The thoroughness and completeness of the work', he said, 'were sufficiently proved by the number and profusion of certain sanitary details'. He referred, no doubt, to the monumental brass and copper work which is still a feature of the ground floor plumbing, though no longer in the pristine brightness of a hundred years ago.

So the 'Pink Palace', as it came to be known, was indeed put into operation in 1897, and

George Rowe duly resigned as Secretary after eleven years in office. In recent years, the interior of the clubhouse has been extensively altered and modernised, but Steward's design served the Club for some sixty years.

Leander still regarded itself as primarily a Metropolitan club and the Henley clubhouse as a country retreat for use mainly in the summer months. The large number of bedrooms contributed to this role, though they were spartan by modern standards, with minimal furniture and, of course, no heating or running water.

It was not until after the Second World War that some refurbishment was carried put to enable members to stay at the Club with their wives, but members working in the City used to take a room at Leander for a week in the summer, commuting by train from Paddington. In this they were encouraged by the boating facilities, for, apart from the racing boats, there were always a club eight and four, as well as pairs and sculling boats, available for members' use. Old men's scratch crews boated in the evenings with some regularity, and there was space for members' own boats, while the Club provided a fleet of punts, skiffs and dinghies, maintained by a full-time boatman.

The Ladies' dining-room occupied what is now the members' bar, with the Ladies' 'water closet' mentioned by Rowe behind it, overlooking the garden entrance. Except for occasional private parties, I cannot recall that it was ever used as a dining-room, but teas and drinks were served on request. The heart of the clubhouse was the members' room, which then extended through from the landing to the balcony overlooking the boathouse forecourt. There was no bar, but a waiter service of drinks in the members' room. Teas and drinks were also served on the lawn.

The Henley clubhouse of that era was not the administrative headquarters it has become today, except in so far as the resident Steward had an office from which to run the clubhouse itself. Club business in the wider sense was conducted by the officers from their homes or places of work, which may explain why so many of the early record books are missing from the Club archives. Committee meetings were held in London, in later years often at the Great Western Hotel at Paddington.

Leander's metamorphosis from a relatively inactive club to a triumphantly successful one began in the closing decade of the nineteenth century, when the Club won the Grand Challenge Cup at Henley eight times, and should have won it nine times, as will be explained below. With oarsmen of the calibre of Guy and Vivian Nickalls, Reggie Rowe and Cherry Pitman on board this success was perhaps assured, but it was C.W. Kent, stroking at 10 st. 10 lb., who led the first charge.

Bill Kent had already stroked Brasenose College to the final of the Grand in 1888 and 1890, and won the Stewards' once and the Visitors' Cup twice. Then, in 1891, he stroked an all-Oxford Leander eight to their first Henley victory in ten years, but only after a dead-heat in the opening round of the Grand with Thames Rowing Club, who had four Cambridge Blues, P. Landale, A.M. Hutchinson, S.D. Muttlebury and J.C. Gardner, on board. At the first attempt, Leander led by a length at Remenham Farm, but Thames, sheltered from a gale force wind by the infamous Bucks 'bushes', drew level at the Mile. At the lower end of Phyllis Court,

30 The Henley clubhouse soon after completion

Thames led by a few feet, which they held almost to the winning post, but Leander pulled back to force the dead-heat. In the re-row the following day, in calm conditions, Leander won quite easily, and went on to beat London Rowing Club in the final, establishing a new record time for the course – 6 min. 51 sec.

For the next three years, Leander won the Grand more easily, though Thames pushed them to half a length in the final in 1894. Thus in 1895 Leander, and Kent, stood on the threshold of a unique fifth successive win, and when they went for the start of their first heat against Cornell University, they were confidently expected to win without difficulty.

Describing the race, H.T. Steward wrote in the *Henley Records*:

> On the Umpire giving the caution 'Are you ready?' several of the Leander crew called 'No', which, owing to a strong wind blowing off the Bucks shore, the Umpire did not hear, but gave the signal to start. The Cornell crew went off, one or two of the Leander crew rowed a stroke, but the others did not, expecting the Umpire to call them back. He, however, thinking Leander had only made a bad start, did not do so. Cornell consequently rowed over the course alone, Leander not racing.

Inevitably, there was much criticism of the umpire, who, it was said, should have called Cornell back; and of Cornell, who could, and perhaps should, have stopped of their own accord. Today, when the Corinthian view of sportsmanship is unfashionable, some might not echo that sentiment. Yet, in that same regatta in 1895, St John's College, Oxford, did indeed stop when Eton caught a crab at the start of the final of the Ladies' Plate – and went on to lose, but with honour, which was appropriately rewarded by victory for the same crew in the Thames Cup. With hindsight, one might say that it was also foolish of Leander not to chase after Cornell, for they might have won despite being left on their stakeboat. In the semi-final, Trinity Hall were half a length behind Cornell at Fawley but caught them at the Mile, when the Americans stopped rowing.

An unhappy side effect of the Cornell episode was the ill-feeling it engendered on both sides. Undoubtedly there was prejudice among the ranks of the British rowing establishment, and the public, against foreign entries in general and American entries in particular, and the flame was fanned by indignant articles in the American press, and, it may be added, by one anonymous letter which Rowe preserved in the Leander archives:

> New York, July 11th, 1895
> To whom it may concern:
> If you think because you are on the other side of the water that you are going to damn the Americans and my native country called 'America' you are very much mistakened. You tried to do it early in the 1756 period but you know the consequences. We are not what you take us to be, but I can tell you what you are, 'a lot of old Johnny Bulls, who think there are no one like themselves'. When the *Vigilante** lost last spring what did you English do but hiss at her crew and jeer them; are you treated like that when you come here? *NO*. When Cornell lost all you did when the Cornell boys cheered you was hiss them in self defence. They will get there yet. Do you think you would come here and damn the Americans right in their own country? You know you wouldn't, but why behind her back? If I was in the crowd when some of you Englishmen damned America I would have punched his or her head off. How dare you say anything against the United States of America. xxxxxxxxxx I have crossed this out because I do not wish you to read it as it may drop you dead. I hope in the future that you will keep your words to yourself and not express yourself like that again in public.
> One of the Americans you have injured.

In 1896, Leander were led back to victory again by another of the Club's great strokes, and in later years coach and administrator, in the person of Harcourt Gold, who had previously stroked Eton to victory in the Ladies' Plate in the three preceding years. Leander won their heat easily against Yale University, the semi-final by half a length from New College, and the final easily against Thames.

This was an era when Oxford were dominant in the Boat Race, fed by a seemingly inexhaustible supply of Etonians, most of whom

---
*After a dispute during races for the America's Cup

31 Vivian and Guy Nickalls, in whose honour the Nickalls Challenge Cup was presented to Henley by their father, Tom

were going to Magdalen and New College, and it never suited Leander when colleges were particularly strong, since this meant that they were likely to enter their own crews in the Grand. New College were a case in point in 1897. With W.E. Crum at seven and Arthur Whitworth at stroke, they robbed Leander of another Grand win by two feet and equalled the record set by Leander in 1891. However, the Club found some consolation in turning the table on New College in the Stewards' Cup, while E.R. Balfour and Guy Nickalls also won the Silver Goblets.

Whitworth was to become a staunch supporter of Leander. He was a frequent resident during the summer months and a not infrequent scourge of the Committee at Annual General Meetings. I have two fond memories of 'Witter' as he was generally known. After his retirement to live in Hove, he became a compulsive writer of letters to *The Times*, and whenever I wrote a report* describing some crew as lacking, or displaying 'a good stride', I could rely on Witter to protest to my editor that 'striding was something one did on dry land, not on the water'. I also recall that during the 1948 Olympic Regatta, when he found me in a somewhat nervous state in the Leander garden, after the Italians had beaten me in a heat of the Double Sculls, he insisted on administering a large glass of club port, which sent me to bed relaxed and happy.

*The author then being the Rowing Correspondent of *The Times*

By the close of 1897, Leander's metamorphosis was complete. The club of a couple of dozen members, based on a commercial yard at Lambeth and exercising twice weekly in wager boats and cutters, had moved into a purpose built boathouse at Putney, and then made the quantum leap to a second upriver clubhouse at Henley. The all important link with Oxford and Cambridge had been well and truly forged, and a membership of thirty-three in 1870 had risen to 233 in 1880 and 531 in 1890. In 1897 it stood around 800 and was still growing by about forty members a year. On the river, Leander crews had emerged from the chrysalis and were up and flying.

At the Annual General Meeting in 1898, the Treasurer remarked on the success of the 1897 crews in spending money, a cash balance of £1,260, not to mention £2,800 subscribed to the boathouse fund, having been transformed into a deficit of £646.1s.0d. On the other hand, he admitted, there was now a magnificent clubhouse at Henley. Nobody appeared to be concerned about the expenditure and the accounts were received with acclamation, but at a Special Meeting strategically held late in the evening, just in time to prevent half those present from leaving the room, the Treasurer explained 'as briefly and delicately as possible, that the Club might someday be in want of revenue' and proposed that those claiming Life membership after ten years should in future pay one guinea. This was passed unanimously.

An unexpected threat appeared in 1898, primarily to the Royal Regatta, but also to Leander's cosy new quarters at 'The Nook'. This came in the form of a Bill presented to Parliament by the Great Western Railway for the building of a loop line between Marlow and

32 Don Burnell

33 'Tarka' (Harcourt Gold) by Spy

34 Gold as a Leander oarsman

Henley. The line would have spanned the river on three iron girder bridges, running up the valley behind the regatta enclosures on a high embankment, crossing the main road near Remenham Lane. It later transpired that the object was not so much to improve the Great Western service to Henley as to prevent any other company providing a rival service. After fierce lobbying, the Bill was withdrawn.

On the river, this was a vintage year for Leander, the Club taking both the Grand and the Stewards' Cups in the same year for the first time, the Grand with perhaps more in hand than the verdicts of a length, half a length, and three-quarters of a length over Balliol, London RC, and First Trinity suggested, since, after being on level terms near the bottom of the enclosures in all the races, Gold seemed to have no difficulty in opening up a safe lead approaching the finish.

The Grand-Stewards' double would surely have been achieved again in 1899 but Gold,

Burnell and Carr all rowed for their college, Magdalen, in the Stewards', which they won easily. In the semi-final, they stopped when their opponents, Trinity, Cambridge, hit the booms near the start, offering a re-row, but as there had already been one re-start after the crews collided, this was not allowed. With Carr, Burnell and Gold at five, six and stroke in the eight, Leander won the Grand without difficulty. This was the first appearance, too, of one of the Club's great coxswains, G.S. Maclagan, who went on to steer six winning Leander Grand crews as well as recording other victories.

Recent events on the river and the successful launch of the new clubhouse ensured that Leander entered the new century with optimism, and the Secretary's reports confirm this. The balance sheet was back in the black and finances were buoyant, the clubhouse was increasingly used, and the Club enclosure, sited in the meadow below the White House, thanks to the generosity of George Rowe, was proving most popular. That Leander was being criticised in some quarters for enjoying a monopoly of British rowing was regarded as something of a compliment. Herbert Steward took the opportunity at the annual dinner to comment that London Rowing Club had been in a similar position in earlier years, and that 'just as in the Eighties Leander had had the bad luck to meet crews just a little better than their own, so they were now fortunate enough to send crews a little better than those opposed to them'. There was no reason to suppose, in the closing years of the Victorian era, that this happy situation would not continue in the opening years of the new century.

35 The Leander Enclosure, White House Meadow, in the late nineteenth century by Dickenson & Foster

36 *(top)* A late-nineteenth-century photograph showing the Putney boathouse, built in 1866, to the right of London Rowing Club, the building in the foreground

37 *(bottom)* The boathouse, since demolished, is now the site of the King's College School boathouse

PART TWO
1900–1996
by
Geoffrey Page

38 H.T. Steward.
Captain 1863–1865 and 1868; Honorary Secretary 1866–1879; President 1892–1915

5

The End of An Era
1900–1914

Although nobody could have realised it at the time, 1900 marked a milestone in British rowing, in the form of the first Belgian entry at the Royal Regatta. The Belgians' appearance that year arose from a decision by the Henley Stewards to place the Belgian Rowing Federation on the same footing as France, Holland and Germany, who were allowed to enter for Henley later than other foreign crews which were required to be 'vetted'.

In addition to American universities, French and Dutch crews had appeared in the Grand and Stewards' in the 1890s but none had had the effrontery to win a heat. In 1899, Hammonia, Hamburg, reached the final of the Stewards' but otherwise the overseas contenders in these events had been defeated, although the Amsterdam students, Nereus, had become the first overseas winners of the Thames Cup in 1895. In 1892 the Dutch sculler, J.J.K. Ooms, also from Amsterdam, had taken the Diamond Sculls abroad for the first time, although strong doubts had been expressed as to whether he was an amateur within the Amateur Rowing Association's definition.

However, the appearance of the Belgians in 1900 was greeted with some consternation by the English rowing establishment. Who were these extraordinary new arrivals, wearing sock suspenders whilst rowing, and, some said, stubbing out evil smelling cigars as they climbed into their boat? They rowed with swivels and broad blades in a most unorthodox manner, a long-sliding, short-swinging, high-rating heresy that offended the purists and was described in the *Rowing Almanack* as 'their peculiar style of rowing', although the writer was forced to admit that their boat ran remarkably well.

Nevertheless, they soon enjoyed cordial relationships with their British opponents and the public. Even Don Burnell, who was not renowned as an internationalist, was never heard to say an ill word about two of the best known Belgians, Oscar de Somville and Victor de Bisschop from Ghent, with whom he eventually became on very good terms.

British rowing at that time had paid little attention to what had been happening on the Continent but rowing had been developing there for many years – Searle's Yard, for example, had frequently shipped boats as far afield as St Petersburg – while European Championships had been introduced in 1893. These, however, went unremarked by a British rowing community still focused on the Boat Race and Henley. The British had never even heard of the two small clubs, Club Nautique and Sport Nautique from Ghent, which were to create such a furore at Henley in the first decade of the twentieth century, though Belgian rowing had been a powerful force on the Continent for several years. The thirty-five Belgians who rowed in the Grand at Henley up to 1910 had amassed a total of 108 individual European

Championship gold medals between 1898 and 1910, albeit from only a small number of competing nations.

Not that the Belgians were instantly successful at Henley. In 1900, Harcourt Gold, 'Tarka' to the rowing fraternity, had been forced to stand down from the Leander crew through illness, taking over the coaching so successfully that Burnell, when replying to the toast to 'The Crews' at the next Annual Dinner, remarked that Gold was a good man to have out of the boat. F.O.J. Huntley, inevitably known as 'Foj' in a community espoused to nicknames, took over the stroke seat, while John Payne, a rare newcomer from London Rowing Club, came in at six. The Belgians, in the colours of the Club Nautique, caused some dismay by leading to the bottom of the enclosures but Leander then went past to win by three quarters of a length, to the considerable relief of home spectators.

Leander went on to beat First Trinity by half a length in the final and four of the eight also took the Stewards', to give the Club an encouraging start to the new century.

The Belgians returned in 1901 and this time Leander defeated them rather more easily in the first round of the Grand, but that year the University of Pennsylvania became the first overseas crew to reach the final, beating London and Thames on the way. Burnell was now Captain of Leander, with Payne rowing again, as well as three Cambridge recruits in W. Dudley Ward, C.J.D. Goldie, and R.B. Etherington-Smith. All three had helped to turn the tide for Cambridge after Oxford's longest sequence of Boat Race wins, in which Gold, Burnell and Carr had featured, an example of how Leander has always succeeded in

39 'Ethel' R.B. Etherington-Smith by Spy

bringing together old rivals. Dudley Ward, the father of the actress Penelope Dudley Ward, who was popularly supposed to have inspired Noel Coward's song *Don't put your daughter on the stage, Mrs Worthington*, had a liking for the fleshpots and was known, on occasions, to turn up for training still dressed in white tie and tails. Perhaps another example of Corinthian ethos, but nobody questioned his ability in a boat.

Once again, it was left to Leander to uphold the traditions of British rowing and the final attracted a huge crowd with many American supporters. At a time when Leander, the uni-

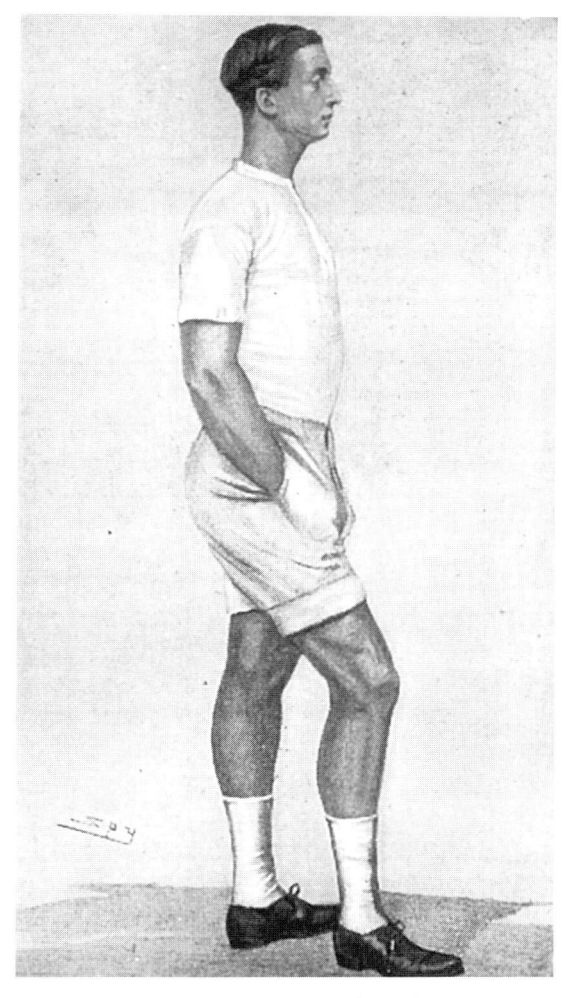

40 W. Dudley Ward by Spy

versities, and most clubs were using fixed rowlocks and short slides, Penn, like the Belgians, used swivels and long slides, so the final of the Grand in 1901 became as much a battle of styles as an international match. Penn led initially but Leander had their bows in front at Fawley and gradually drew away, amid tremendous enthusiasm from the crowd, to retain the trophy by a length. However, the four from the eight failed to keep the Stewards', Third Trinity winning easily in the final.

The parochial outlook of British rowing at that time was made clear a few days after the 1901 Regatta when correspondence in the Press questioned whether Henley should remain open to the world. The controversy went on for some months and in the autumn the Leander Committee, together with those of other leading clubs, were asked by the ARA for their views on a proposal by W.H. Grenfell, MP, an Oxford Blue from the 1870s, later to become Lord Desborough, that Henley should exclude 'foreigners and colonials'. The Committee, by a narrow majority of 9 to 7, rejected Grenfell's proposal and then approved, by the same majority, a proposal that 'while the Committee consider that Henley Regatta is not a suitable occasion for Foreign Competitions, they are of the opinion that Foreign Entries should not be refused until a satisfactory scheme has been devised and is in working order for contests with Foreigners elsewhere in the United Kingdom.'

A special meeting of the Henley Stewards in November decided by a large majority that 'it is inexpedient that any alteration in the Rules of the Regatta be at present made.' The Stewards also passed, by 13 votes to 2, a proposal that 'no professional coaching should be allowed in the preparation for Henley Regatta, except in the case of scullers.'

The Belgians had intended to compete again at Henley in 1902 but to their disappointment had had to withdraw when their boat was damaged in transit. It was also a disappointing year for Leander, whose eight, consisting entirely of Oxford Blues, failed to retain the Grand. They proved to be no match in the final for Third

Trinity, stroked by 'Boon' Gibbon, twice the winning Boat Race stroke for Cambridge and on leave from the Gunners, with six other Cambridge Blues behind him. Trinity had disposed of the only overseas entry, Argonaut Rowing Club, Toronto, in their semi-final, and they also retained the Stewards'.

Leander had accepted an invitation to compete at Cork Regatta for the International Cup, a 3-ft. 6-in. trophy then valued at £250, which had been paid for by public subscription and presented by Lord O'Brien, the Lord Chief Justice of Ireland, in celebration of the Coronation of King Edward VII, and also of Cork Exhibition. With an entry of thirteen eights, including Emmanuel College, Cambridge, and two Oxford Colleges, University and Magdalen, as well as the Berliner Ruder Club, this was considered by the *Rowing Almanack* to have been the most important event (in rowing, presumably) ever to have been held in Ireland. Leander came through the heats to defeat the Germans in the final by two lengths.

This was the first time since the Henley clubhouse had been built that Leander had ventured so far afield. Thus Cork marks the beginning of an interest by the Club well beyond the narrow boundaries of Henley. The pressure to strike out was increasing, for in 1902 the Committee had declined an invitation from Steve Fairbairn to compete in Australia, while invitations to compete in Hamburg in 1904 and in the first Canadian Henley, in August 1905, were also declined. Nevertheless, the Club was beginning to spread its wings and it was symptomatic that in 1902 'Flea' Fletcher suggested to the Committee that 'junior' Leander crews might be sent to minor Thames regattas, although no resolutions were forthcoming following the ensuing discussion. However, it was an interesting foretaste of things to come, foreshadowing the Leander Cadet scheme of the 1960s by over half a century.

In 1903, Leander regained the Grand when defeating Third Trinity by six feet in a memorable final, although the Club failed to prevent Trinity from taking the Stewards' for the third year in succession. Six of the Leander eight then rowed in the crew that competed for the Champion Cup at the Metropolitan Regatta, the principal regatta after Henley, for the first time since 1888, when the Club had lost to Thames. This time Leander had no trouble in taking the trophy, winning easily from London. This crew then returned to Cork, where they were opposed by only two Irish crews and won very easily. The losing finalists, Dublin University, had earlier won the Thames Cup at Henley and as a result of that victory had been invited to join Leander, if they cared to. 'If we cared!' wrote one of the crew. 'There was no greater honour we could have desired.'

Leander retained the Grand in 1904 and 1905. In the latter year, the Belgians, in the colours of SN de Gand and back after an absence of four years, and the Vesper Boat Club of Philadelphia provided the first foreign opposition since 1902, Leander defeating the Americans in the semi-final and the Belgians in the final. It was a very good Henley for the Club, the Stewards' four, stroked by the veteran Guy Nickalls, finally ending Third Trinity's four-year hold on the trophy. In the same year Frederick Septimus Kelly, the Australian-born but Eton-educated Oxford

41 Cork International Cup, 1902

42 *(top)* Leander Trophy, presented to Cork City Regatta

43 *(bottom)* Cork International Cup, 1903

44 F.S. Kelly sculling

Blue, who had won both the Grand and the Diamonds in 1903, repeated the double, setting a new record time for the Diamonds of 8 min. 10 sec., which was to stand until 1938.

As had become the custom by this time, foreign entrants for the Grand were elected honorary members of the Club during the Henley period, which, in Vesper's case, was subsequently to prove something of an embarrassment since they were later found, contrary to Henley's regulations, to have been financed by public subscription, with the result that the Stewards later decided that no future entry from Vesper would be accepted. A proposal by Fletcher that no entries should in future be allowed from the United States was defeated.

Leander's win in the Grand in 1905 was the Club's twelfth victory in fifteen years, an indication of Leander's dominant position in English rowing during this period, though the supply of top men was beginning to dry up. Indeed, in 1906 the Captain, Etherington-Smith, informed the Committee that he had decided with much regret not to enter an eight for the Grand as he had been unable to form a crew 'capable of worthily representing the rowing of the Leander Club.' After a long discussion, Rudie Lehmann proposed that 'the Captain of the Club be instructed to enter a crew for the Grand Challenge Cup' but to this was added a rider proposed by Cherry Pitman: 'In the event of his being able to raise a crew which in his opinion fairly represents the rowing of the Leander Club but not otherwise.' The proposal and the amendment were carried by five votes to two but in the end the Club did not put on an eight for the first time since 1890, with what many considered to be disastrous results for English rowing. The Belgians, this time the CN de Gand, at last carried off the Grand, becoming the first overseas crew to do so. However, Leander did at least retain the Stewards', thanks mainly to repeated spurts by Nickalls to hold off Third Trinity's last efforts by two feet.

If Leander's failure to put on a crew to defend the Grand did indeed lead to the Belgians' success, no such case can be made for 1907, when SN de Gand defeated Leander in the second heat of the Grand, though the purists claimed that it was the so-called 'sculling style' that had been developed by the stroke, Duggie Stuart, that let the side down. Stuart had been the stroke of that year's victorious Cambridge crew and at Henley was backed in the Leander eight by four others from that crew, but his style was much criticised by those versed in traditional Orthodox methods, of which Leander had been the prime exponents for many years. Leander led to the bottom of Phyllis Court wall but the Belgians then passed them to win a good race by a length, going on to beat Christ Church, who were experimenting with the Belgian style, by a length in the final.

In 1908, the Olympic Regatta was held at Henley and as early as the spring of 1907 the Henley Stewards had decided that no foreign entries would be accepted for the 1908 Royal Regatta since the Olympic regatta was to be held only three weeks later. This decision went unremarked at the time but after the Belgians' win in 1907 the Stewards were accused of unsporting behaviour by those who were under the mistaken impression that they were trying to prevent the Belgians from defending the Grand in 1908. However, the Belgians let it be known that they would not have considered competing at the Royal Regatta when it was so close to the Olympic event and neither of the two eights that were ultimately to represent the United Kingdom in the Olympics competed at Henley in 1908.

With British rowing still smarting from the

45   D.C.R. Stuart by Spy

humiliation of two successive Henley defeats by the Belgians, the ARA selectors decided to turn to some of the old hands to restore the nation's pride and letters were sent to ten veterans in January 1908 to ask them to make themselves available. 'We fully appreciate this will entail on you considerable expenditure of time and energy but on the other hand we would point out the importance that well tried oarsmen should be available at the present time, to regain such rowing prestige of the country as has been lately lost, and to defend that which remains.'

Among those answering the call were Guy Nickalls, then in his forty-second year, and Don Burnell, then thirty-six. These two eventually rowed in the Leander eight, which became known variously as the 'Old Crocks' and the 'Ancient Mariners'. Despite the presence of the two most senior members mentioned above, the average age of the crew was twenty-nine years and six months – mere youngsters by comparison with the Leander crew that raced Cambridge in 1838, reported earlier in these pages, who, according to H.T. Steward, averaged thirty-seven years, which might account in part for the considerable gamesmanship to which that crew resorted!

The Olympic rules in 1908 allowed for each nation to enter two crews for each of the four events. The winning 1908 Boat Race crew, Cambridge, stroked again by Stuart, had been selected first to represent the United Kingdom. Leander were later chosen as the second string, although there had been a ticklish moment when Nickalls had threatened to withdraw a few days after the final list of those selected had been announced. Since March he had been rowing in a four with Burnell, Escombe and Etherington-Smith but when he was nominated only as a spare man for a different Leander four, who had recently been formed and selected, together with the Stewards' winners, Magdalen, he wrote to the selectors in a huff, resigning from the eight. 'If

46 Guy Nickalls by Spy

I am not good enough to row in the four', he wrote, 'I am not good enough to row in the eight.' An emergency meeting of the selectors on 4th July deputed Fletcher to talk to him and he was eventually sufficiently mollified to stay with the eight.

The Belgian Grand crews each year,

47 Leander beating the Belgians in the Olympic Regatta, 1908

although rowing in the colours of either the CN or SN de Gand, were in fact composite crews drawn from both clubs, but in 1908 there was some dispute between the two clubs and the Belgian Olympic eight, rowing as the Royal Club Nautique de Gand (the Royal prefix had been accorded to them as a result of their triumph in the Grand) contained only four of the 1907 Grand crew, although all eight were European champions. They were expected to offer a stern challenge once again to the cream of Britain's oarsmen and while the Leander eight dealt with Hungary and Canada on their way to the final, Cambridge fell to the Belgians by one and a third lengths, so once again Leander found themselves as defenders of British prestige in the final.

The weather was perfect and it was in every sense a golden day. Leander took an early lead and by the Mile had clear water over their opponents, eventually coming home a good two lengths ahead for a memorable victory. The course had been lengthened for the Olympics to 1 mile 880 yards but Sir Theodore Cook, in his report in *Henley Races*, calculated that Leander had probably been moving as fast as any eight that had ever rowed at Henley up to that time.

48 Winning Leander crews and coaches framed in the 1908 Olympic Regatta winning-post.

49 The Leander Olympic eight in training at Henley, 1908

50 Duke Street, Henley, decorated for the Olympic Regatta, 1908

51 John Fenning and Gordon Thomson, winners of the Olympic coxless pairs, 1908

Magdalen beat Leander in the final of the coxless fours and two Leander pairs fought out the final of the coxless pairs, J.R.K. Fenning and G.L. Thomson defeating G.E. Fairbairn and P. Verdon, Fenning and Verdon having been specially elected members of the Club less than a month previously.

Some years later, in 1914, the Olympic eight's boat was smashed in a road accident while being transported from Putney to Henley and a section was converted into the C.D. Burnell medal cupboard which is to be found today in the Club drawing-room.

The 'Brilliants' may have given the British public the result they so desperately needed to restore national pride but by using several experienced veterans, Leander had not solved its problems for the next few years. In 1909 Leander were unable to produce an eight of the standard of their crews in the first few years of the decade and the Belgians, their private dispute happily resolved, and with seven previous winners of the Grand aboard, carried off the Grand for the third, and as it proved, last time. Wins in the Silver Goblets were Leander's only successes at Henley in 1909 and 1910, while in 1911 the Club could not raise any crews for Henley and no Captain was elected.

Henley in 1912 was memorable for the visit of King George V and Queen Mary and a huge crowd attended. Although the regatta was held only two weeks before the Olympic Regatta at Stockholm, this did not deter the designated Olympic eights from Australia and Canada from competing, while Leander put on the eight, based on the Magdalen winning Grand crews of 1910 and 1911, which had already been selected to represent the United Kingdom. New College had been chosen as the second British eight but they were defeated in their heat of the Grand by the Australians from Sydney Rowing Club.

Leander defeated London and Thames for the right to meet Sydney in the final, which was followed by the Royal visitors. The crews were overlapping the whole way, with the Australians leading by a third of a length at Fawley and half a length at the Mile. Both crews were exhausted in the final stages, the Australians holding out to win by three quarters of a length.

At Stockholm, Leander, who had replaced C.E. Tinné with E.R. Burgess, met the Australians in the second round. The latter, who had also made one change since Henley, led by three-quarters of a length at the 1000-metre mark, striking the higher rate. However, a determined spurt by their Magdalen stroke, Philip Fleming, took Leander past to reverse the Henley result and win a fine race in a fast time. Leander went on to beat the Germans from Berlin with rather less difficulty and then met New College, who had disposed of Sweden on their way, in an all-British final.

Fleming, taking no chances against a crew stroked by R.C. Bourne, who had that year established a Boat Race record by stroking Oxford to victory for a fourth successive time, led by nearly a length at 500 metres, Leander eventually winning the gold medal by a length. Angus Gillan, rowing five in the eight, had also rowed in the winning Olympic four in 1908 and so at Stockholm became the first Briton to win two Olympic rowing titles.

Leander, with four of the 1912 Olympic eight and coached by Guy Nickalls, at last won

52 The winning Leander Olympic eight at Stockholm, 1912

the Grand again in 1913. In their heat against the Canadians from the Argonaut Rowing Club, they equalled the course record of 6 min. 51 sec., set in 1891 by Leander. In the final against Jesus College, Cambridge, G.E. Tower, that year's Cambridge stroke, took Leander off at 48 and Jesus never saw them again.

In the fateful summer of 1914, few of those who attended Henley had any apprehension that it would be five years before there would be another Henley regatta, and had they known, the superstitious might have regarded the defeat of all four home crews in the first round of the Grand as ominous.

Leander went out by a length to the Harvard Junior Varsity eight, and, for the first time, all four semi-finalists were overseas crews, the final being an all-American affair, Harvard defeating the Union Boat Club of Boston. All the Harvard crew survived to return fifty years later, when they presented Henley with a replica of the Grand Challenge Cup to replace the original which was nearing the end of its days.

The Grand had now been won by overseas crews five times in nine years and the eclipse of British rowing in 1914, more devastating than the earlier defeats by the Belgians, inspired an *In Memoriam* notice in *The Times*: 'In loving memory of British rowing, which passed away at Henley on Saturday, July 4th. Deeply lamented by many sorrowing followers, who hereby place their regret on record.'

All was not lost, however. In the Stewards' final, Leander raced a much heavier German four, Mainzer Ruder-Verein, three of whom had been in a four that had defeated Leander by two feet in a heat of the Stewards' the previous year. (The Germans were later disqualified in the final that year against New College, who were stroked by Bourne.) In 1914, despite some erratic steering, the Germans were clear at Fawley, but Bourne, now stroking Leander, began a sustained spurt at the Mile and gained rapidly. The Germans suddenly cracked at the bottom of Phyllis Court wall and stopped, leaving Leander to paddle in alone. Another omen, perhaps, for the more serious struggle to come.

During the years that preceded the Great War of 1914-18, the Club had experienced a number of domestic developments. In 1900, George Rowe, whose close involvement in providing the Temple Island enclosure in 1887 and in the creation of the Henley clubhouse have been recorded earlier in these pages, made the White House Meadow, between the present sites of the Remenham Club and the Regatta enclosure, available for an enclosure for Club members. This enclosure was in use until 1914, but although it was initially a success, the numbers using it declined steadily in the last few years before the outbreak of the First World War.

The Committee were much concerned with taking steps to avoid gate-crashing at the White House Meadow and to avoid tickets getting into the wrong hands. The Minutes note that in 1905 the Committee had had to warn a member to be more careful after complaints had been received about 'certain undesirable females' to whom he had given enclosure tickets. His assurance that this would not happen again and his apologies were accepted.

The same year, the strong feelings against professionals, which had developed during the last part of the ninteenth century, were illustrated by a letter from the Secretary to a member expressing the views of the Committee (and his own) of the member's conduct in entertaining a professional at the Henley clubhouse. Tantalisingly, no further details were minuted.

In view of the Club's view on professionals, the Committee's attitude to Guy Nickalls' coaching of Yale University for remuneration shortly before the war seems somewhat ambivalent. A letter from Nickalls setting out the circumstances was discussed by the Committee in 1914 but it was decided to take no action at that time and it was ordered that the letter should 'lie on the table', the intervention of the War presumably allowing the matter to be dropped altogether.

The terms of membership continued to exercise the Committee, who had several times considered the possible election of overseas members, but had elected only a few as Complimentary or Honorary members. As long ago as 1889 Prince Eric of Turn and Taxis had been elected a Complimentary member 'in consideration of his purpose to introduce and encourage amateur rowing in Austria', although amateur rowing in that country had certainly been established by the 1860s, if not earlier.

In 1899, a Harvard cox then resident in England was also elected as a Complimentary member, and in 1907 two other Harvard men were proposed as members, but their election was postponed while a sub-committee considered altering the rules to provide for the election of a class of Honorary membership with certain restrictions so that foreign oarsmen could not be elected to the full privileges of membership. The sub-committee proposed that 'no candidate shall be eligible unless born in the UK or resident therein' and 'to elect as temporary Honorary members representatives of foreign or Colonial Boat Clubs when visiting this country.' The first resolution was passed at a Special General Meeting in 1907 but the second was adjourned *sine die* on the grounds that this might curtail rather than increase the powers of the Committee. It is not clear from the Minutes, however, on what grounds the two Harvard men had already been elected as full members before the 1907 SGM, though it has to be presumed that they were resident in the UK.

Following the Royal visit to Henley in 1912, the Prince of Wales was elected an Honorary Life member of the Club in 1913.

Suddenly and with little warning to many in England who had scant knowledge of the tensions that had been building up in the Balkans, the Great War erupted in the late summer of 1914 and what can still be considered, despite the death of King Edward VII in 1910, as the Edwardian era in England came to a sudden end. Life was never to be quite the same again and many of those who had recently competed at Henley were never to return from the resulting carnage of the war. Prominent among these were many distinguished Leander oarsmen, including Olympic gold medallists F.S. Kelly, A.G. Kirby (Captain of Leander in 1910 and 1912), G.S. Maclagan (the Secretary of the ARA) and R.H. Sanderson.

Spy cartoons of three distinguished Leander oarsmen

53 'Bush' Johnstone   54 'Flea' Fletcher   55 'Cherry' Pitman

6

Regeneration
1915–1939

The First World War brought an almost complete cessation of rowing from 1915 to 1918, although there were some charity regattas and schools were able to organise private fixtures.

Apart from the heavy casualties resulting from the war, some of the pillars of Leander also succumbed through age or illness during this period, notably, in 1916, Herbert Steward, aged 76, the Club's President from 1892, and also Chairman of Henley from 1894 and of the ARA from 1897 until his death. The author of the first records of Henley races, he was described in the *Rowing Almanack* as the 'father' of the amateur rowing world. Leander held no AGMs until after the war, Steward eventually being succeeded in 1919 by George Rowe.

Another faithful servant of Leander, Reginald Gridley, also died in 1916. Known to his many friends as 'Boss', he had been Captain of the Club from 1885 to 1887, and had also served as Secretary to the Club and to the ARA.

In 1917, the Club's oldest member, T.B. Bumpsted, died at the age of 94. He had made his first Henley appearance seventy-four years previously, winning the Diamonds and the Wingfield Sculls in 1844. A member of the Club in 1843, he had been re-instated as an Honorary Life member in 1909.

In 1915, the Club Committee offered the Red Cross board and lodging for six convalescent officers at the clubhouse for one guinea a week but no further details are forthcoming from the Minutes, which were inevitably rather brief during this period. They dealt mainly with a few domestic affairs, a major one of which concerned the misappropriation of Club money, as well as wines and spirits, by the Steward and his wife, who were dismissed. However, in view of their many years of good service, no criminal proceedings were taken. The Club's bank was blamed for cashing cheques drawn in the Club's favour for the Steward, which was against the Club's specific instructions, and the upshot was that the clerk who had made the transactions was required to discharge part of the debt by doing clerical work for the Club.

By 1919, the clubhouse was in urgent need of decoration and repairs and these, together with repairs to the boat yard and raft were immediately carried out, so everything was was quickly ready for the Club's post-war regeneration.

The war had resulted in major transformations to society and the 1920s were very different from the pre-war years, though, so far as Leander was concerned, much continued as before. The war had resulted in the loss of many fine men who might otherwise have become the nation's leaders in the post-war era, but women began to take a more active part in society, their role having been changed by their considerable contribution to the war effort, in nursing the wounded and in factories and on the land, with the resulting emancipation which the Suffragettes had fought so hard but vainly to achieve before the war. Society

1 London: Westminster Bridge from the north on Lord Mayor's Day, 1746, by Canaletto

2 The Thames on Lord Mayor's Day by Canaletto, probably also 1746

3 *Above*: Searle's Yard at Stangate

4 *Right*: Lyon's Subscription Room showing the alterations to the right-hand side (see page 21)

5 Lambeth, 1851. An oil painting of Stangate, now the site of St Thomas's Hospital, by R. Pembery

6 Print of the Great Race between the scullers R. Coombes and C. Campbell, accompanied by Leander (in the foreground) and other crews, approaching Hammersmith, 1846

7 Henley Regatta from Phyllis Court, c 1853

8 A Leander oarsman in Club uniform with the Great Race as background (detail from a watercolour by Paddy Page)

9 The Leander Coat won by Samuel Beckett in 1859

10 Henley Regatta, c. 1877, by James Tissot

11 Henley Regatta, 1880, by Walter Field. The standing figure, lighting his pipe in the boat on the right, is Herbert Steward. Among those seated are Walter Bovill and Sir Patrick Colquhoun

12 James Parish, waterman to the club in its early days

13 Two views of the clubhouse, c. 1990

14 Geoffrey Page and Peter Coni in conversation, Henley, 1988 (watercolour by Paddy Page)

15 Blades from 1898 and 1992 – note the deep red of the 1898 blade

16 Richard Burnell in his capacity as a rowing correspondent, Lucerne

17 The Under-23 gold medal eight, 1987:
S. Bell, J. Richards, T. Collerton, J. Blunt, K. Almand, P. Rudaz, H. Trotter, P. Hubbard, S. Gruselle (cox)

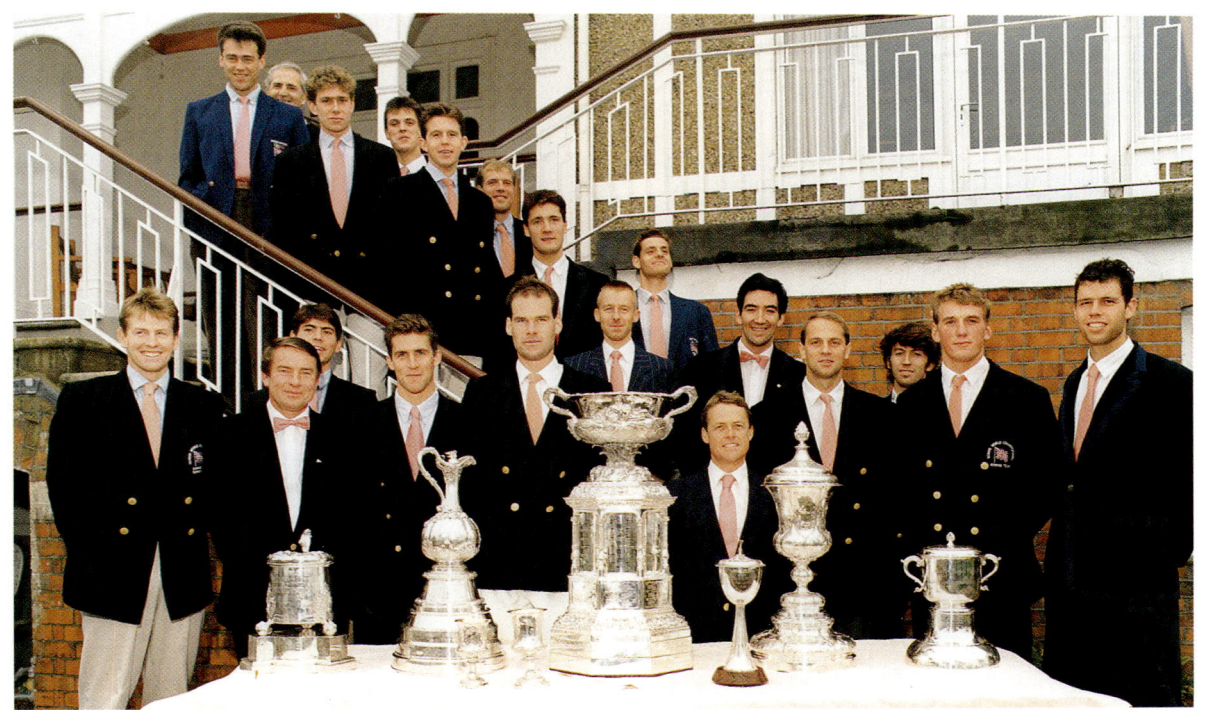

18 Leander Henley winners, 1991

On steps, l to r: Richard Stanhope, Terry Dillon, Snr, Rob Bartlett, Justin Waller, Dave Luke, Pete Bridge, Terry Dillon.
Ground, l to r: Henry Trotter, Jürgen Gröbler, Richard Phelps, Nick Burfitt, Simon Berrisford, Adrian Ellison, Pat Sweeney, Gavin Stewart, Steve Redgrave, Jim Walker, Matthew Pinsent, Cal Maclennan.
Absent: Garry Herbert

19 Redgrave and Pinsent on the way to their gold medals in the 1992 Olympic Regatta, Banyoles, 1992

20 Redgrave and Pinsent with their gold medals, Banyoles, 1992

21 Steve Redgrave with Henley trophies and medals

22 Redgrave and Pinsent winning the Olympic coxless pairs, Lake Lanier, 1996

23 Job completed: a victory handshake at Lake Lanier

24 Bill Windham, President of Leander from 1993 (watercolour by Paddy Page)

became freer and the end of fighting, while it led to hardship and unemployment for many, brought a natural release of tension for others. The post-war generation, the Bright Young Things of the 1920s, were intent on enjoying a new-found freedom, and the rapid advance of the motor-car led to greater mobility, with more people exploring the contryside, the increasing use of the rivers being one of the results.

Rowing at Leander in the twenty years between the wars followed its traditional pre-war pattern, the crews getting together a few weeks before Henley, sometimes for longer periods as the Club began to become more involved with the Olympic Games every four years, and with other occasional ventures abroad; at the same time the Club's social activities began to increase. Excursions in skiffs and punts, with which the Club was well stocked, became increasingly popular, while there were also frequent outings for scratch crews, for which members would often travel down to Henley and stay at the Club at weekends.

As far as more serious rowing was concerned, it was still almost exclusively based on the close relationship with Oxford and Cambridge. Indeed, relations between the Tideway clubs and Leander became strained in the early 1920s and deteriorated as the decade progressed, partly because of the rapid improvement of Tideway rowing which created a fierce rivalry, and partly because of what was generally regarded as Leander's Oxbridge 'bias'. Another factor could well have been the resentment by Leander's old guard of Steve Fairbairn's controversial methods which were bringing many successes to Thames, and later to London, Rowing Clubs, but which were regarded by traditionalists brought up in the Orthodox school as a threat to the true ideals of rowing.

Whatever the real cause, the Club Minutes of this period make frequent references to doubts concerning the election of members of the Metropolitan clubs; it was felt that such members should be elected only in special cases. In 1926, after several long discussions in Committee, which emphasised that the rowing qualifications of candidates should have been attained primarily at Oxford and Cambridge, the matter was postponed *sine die*.

The following year the Committee rejected the nominations of three members of London Rowing Club on the grounds that they were still active members of London, and in 1928 the election of Charles Rew, despite his having won the Grand with Thames in 1923, was also turned down on the same grounds. Finally, a resolution in 1929, stating that the 'membership of the Club being now in excess of 1,500, and consisting primarily of University oarsmen, the Committee consider that the election of members of other rowing clubs, who have attained their rowing qualifications as members of such clubs, should be strictly limited' was passed unanimously.

The Metropolitan clubs were not the only ones to come under the Club's scrutiny. Antipathy to the Fairbairn 'style' was behind the lengthy discussion that took place in 1928 over the election of candidates from Jesus College, Cambridge. Although they were third on the river at Cambridge, some of the Committee questioned whether their rowing justified their election, but eventually the Jesus men were accepted.

While the refurbishment of the Henley clubhouse had been carried out in the 1920s, another matter to occupy much of the Committee's attention during this period had been the future of the Putney boathouse for which the lease was renewed in 1920 on a yearly basis with a rent of £1 a week; and then in 1924, the Club took out a seven-year lease. Hubert Hartley, who was on the Leander Committee, became the owner of the boathouse in 1928 and with the lease due to expire in March 1932, Hartley offered to resign from the Committee in order to avoid prejudicing his position, but this was rejected.

In 1930, Imperial College, who were then boating from Thames Rowing Club, contemplated making an offer for the boathouse site, with accommodation for Leander included, but the college eventually decided to build a boathouse next to Thames. In 1931, the Club Committee decided that the time was ripe to send a circular to members asking for their views on the future of the Putney boathouse. Opinion was strongly in favour of the boathouse being retained and the Committee unanimously agreed to this and also to retain the boatman. In 1932 the Club arranged an annual lease with Hartley, with first refusal should Hartley decide to sell. A sub-committee set up to look into the question of developing the boathouse on the lines of the Metropolitan clubs advised that the cost was too great and further consideration of a scheme along these lines was shelved. However, a suggestion that a house at Putney might be taken during the winter months with a view to putting crews together to practise for Henley and upriver regattas in 1933 was considered possible, although the Captain at the time, Harold Rickett, considered that it was unlikely that there would be enough men available to justify this. Nevertheless, authority was given for the Captain to take a house should he be able to raise a crew, though this was never taken up.

In 1933, the University of London Boat Club also considered making an offer for the Putney boathouse, again with facilities for Leander, but after protracted negotiations, they, too, abandoned the idea and soon after built their own premises at Chiswick.

Eventually, in the autumn of 1937, Barclay's Bank came up with an offer which suited the Club well, and in May 1938, Hartley agreed to sell the boathouse to the Bank, with one bay for Leander boats, common use of the first floor and the flagstaff, and the services of the boatman employed by the Bank, while Cambridge were to be allowed to continue to use the boathouse as they had done for many years. The Club was to pay the bank £60 per annum, the latter paying all the outgoings such as gas, water, boatman's wages, and so on. The agreement was to be in force for ten years and to continue thereafter, subject to twelve months notice on either side. The sale was duly completed, which relieved the Club of the considerable expense of maintaining its own premises at Putney.

So life at Henley continued much as before. In 1932, the Club began its link with HMS *Leander*, a new cruiser which was commissioned that year and became the fifth ship in the Royal Navy to carry this name since 1780. The Club presented a piece of silver plate to the wardroom and the ship's officers were made Honorary members, the Captain and officers being guests at the 1933 annual dinner.

56   A Charles II porringer and cover, presented by the Club to *HMS Leander*, and returned to the Club when the ship was de-commissioned

Two of the *Leander's* officers continued to be guests at the Club's annual dinner until 1938, when the *Leander* left for New Zealand.

Fred Pitman, who had been the Club's Treasurer for thirty-eight years, had, in 1934, succeeded George Rowe as President on the latter's death after a long period of failing health. Rowe, as these pages have already shown, had rendered eminent service to the Club over many years. A further link with HMS *Leander* was forged when, soon after his election, Pitman was entertained by the ship's officers at Gibralter.

In 1919, Prince Henry of Gloucester, who had rowed in a lower boat at Eton during the war, was elected an Honorary Life member of the Club, the Duke of Kent later joining him in this capacity in 1937. In March 1936, The Club had received another Royal seal of approved when King Edward VIII honoured the club by agreeing to become Patron. However, after his abdication in December that year, he resigned from his honorary positions and was followed as the Club's Patron by his successor, King George VI.

The re-establishment of rowing in the country after the war had begun a month after the signing of the Armistice in November 1918, when W.A.L. Fletcher proposed at a meeting of the Club Committee that the ARA's affiliated clubs and the Secretaries of regattas should be invited to a meeting to consider what steps should be taken to revive amateur rowing.

The meeting was duly convened by Leander and held in January 1919 at the Temple, with George Rowe presiding. There was a large attendance. Fletcher proposed that, while it would not be desirable to revive Henley Royal Regatta that year, an interim regatta, run by the Henley Stewards, should be held as well as some other regattas (those on the Thames under the auspices of the Thames Amateur Rowing Council). Both proposals were passed unanimously.

In February 1919, Fletcher was elected Chairman of the Henley Committee of Management but, sadly, he died only a few days later. He had been gassed in the war, which had weakened his resistance to the lethal influenza epidemic that was sweeping Europe.

Seven events were put on for the Henley Peace Regatta in 1919, Leander presenting a cup for Allied Fours. This was won by the Leander Service Crew, who beat the American No 1 Service Crew in the final. The same Leander crew also won the Wargrave Manor Cup for senior fours.

By the end of the year, rowing throughout the country had made a remarkable recovery. The University Boat Race was revived in 1920, in which year the Olympic Games were held in Antwerp, but the latter event was not without its opponents and at a June meeting of the Leander Committee to discuss a possible Olympic entry from the Club, George Rowe expressed his strong disapproval of international rowing contests in general and of the Olympic Regatta in particular, although, unhappily for us, no outline of his arguments appears in the Minutes.

Despite the President's views, the Captain, R.S. Shove, was authorised to ask the ARA to

57 The Leander Cup, Henley Peace Regatta, 1919

enter a Leander crew for the Olympic Regatta. However, at Henley, now back to its full Royal Regatta status, Leander lost the Grand to Magdalen, with the result that the Leander eight that subsequently represented the United Kingdom at Antwerp were based on five of the Magdalen eight, one of whom was G.O. Nickalls, son of the great Victorian and Edwardian oarsman, Guy Nickalls, a member of the victorious 1908 Olympic eight. Two Cambridge Blues, including Sidney Swann from pre-war days, and Shove filled the remaining seats, with Cherry Pitman coaching.

58 The 1920 Leander eight at Henley

The Olympic Regatta brought British rowing face to face with the professional approach of the Americans and gave a foretaste of the direction in which the Olympic Games were to move. The Americans had selected twenty-five men in January and, according to Pitman, had rowed more than thirty races by the time they arrived in Antwerp, three weeks before the Regatta. They were accompanied by a second crew to act as pacemakers, and by a doctor and masseurs, together with their own cooks to prepare special food. By comparison, the Leander crew's preparation was amateurish in the extreme. They had trained together for only five weeks and were severely handicapped through poor organisation by the British Olympic officials, with the crew having to endure long drives over rough roads, while there was also inadequate provision for suitable meals. Nevertheless, despite this, they beat Switzerland, the reigning European champions, and then Norway, to reach the final, where they were narrowly defeated by the Americans.

In the circumstances, their narrow defeat was a praiseworthy performance. The *Almanack* reported that in paddling to the start 'the contrast between the two styles was remarkable. The Americans, with their exaggerated swing back, looked as if they had taken more out of themselves in paddling to produce the same pace as was produced by Leander. The latter, with their long, steady swing, sharp beginning and well held out finish, were perfectly together and looked the picture of what an English crew should be.' This report was, of course, written by Pitman himself.

Leander led from the first stroke and were a third of a length ahead at the 500-metre mark. With both crews flat out, Leander had increased their advantage to two-thirds by 1000 metres and held this to 1700 metres, when the Americans began to close up. They caught Leander with 100 metres to go and sheer physical strength gave them the verdict by one second in a time of 6 min. 5 sec. after a magnificent race. It was the beginning of the American stranglehold on the Olympic eights which was to last for forty years.

The *Almanack* commented that the 'truly wonderful time', accomplished on the dead water of a canal, was five seconds faster than the world record for 2000 metres set on much livelier water at Stockholm and, corrected for the Henley distance, would probably have beaten the Henley record of 6 min. 51 sec. by some seven or so seconds.

The following year Leander won the Grand with only two of the Olympic eight, 'Gully' Nickalls and 'Dink' Horsfall, the stroke, in the crew. This was the period when Tideway rowing was undergoing a revival initiated by Steve Fairbairn, and while Leander won the Grand again in 1922, beating Thames in the final, Thames, coached by Fairbairn, were successful in 1923, when a slightly shorter experimental straight course was introduced.

Early in the summer of 1923, Leander received an invitation from the organisers of the Canadian National Exhibition at Toronto and the Canadian Association of Amateur Oarsmen to send an eight to a regatta to be held in August in conjunction with the exhibition, the CAAO believing that Leander's presence would be an enormous stimulus to Canadian rowing. The Club Committee originally declined the invitation on the grounds that the races were primarily an advertisement for the Trade Exhibition, and also that the expense was too great, the Club not being prepared to accept an offer of £1,000 towards their expenses from the CAAO. There was also the difficulty of assembling a thoroughly representative crew who could find the time to visit Canada. However, the younger active members were keen to go and the Captain, Humphrey Playford, persuaded the Committee to change its mind, the visit being authorised providing that £800 could be raised by subscription from Club members, the Club agreeing to underwrite a further £200.

The crew, stroked by Oxford's winning American stroke, 'Pussy' Mellen, with Gully Nickalls at seven, were all Blues, five of whom had rowed in a slow and ponderous Leander eight that had failed to survive their heat of the Grand, but despite appalling conditions on Lake Ontario, with only two calm days during the fortnight's training, Cherry Pitman, coaching once again, brought the crew to peak form on the day.

By a stroke of good fortune for the worried organisers, the weather relented for the two days of the regatta and the water was calm. Leander overwhelmed Toronto University in their heat over the course of a mile and a quarter, while the American champions, the Undine Barge Club of Philadelphia, defeated the Argonaut Rowing Club by half a length in a high-rating race. In the final the next day, in front of a huge crowd, Leander had established a lead of one and a half lengths after two and a half minutes and eventually won comfortably by that margin. Pitman reported in the *Almanack* that the crew 'had proved once more

59 The Leander eight training at Toronto, September 1923

60 The Leander eight for Toronto, July 1923

that a really good crew rowing in the orthodox English style can beat a good crew rowing in the no-swing-and-all-leg-drive style and by their example and encouragement they were able to confer a benefit on our Canadian brothers of the oar.' While Pitman's enthusiasm is understandable, the truth was that the opposition was not of Grand standard. However, the visit was an enormous social success.

In 1924, with the crews starting on the Berkshire side of Temple Island, the present Henley course was used for the first time. Only Mellen and Nickalls from the Leander Toronto crew rowed in what the *Almanack* regarded as a rather moderate Leander crew that regained the Grand, beating Thames in the semi-final by half a length after the crews had been level at the Mile. In the final they had a desperate race with Jesus College, Cambridge, before winning by six feet.

Two of the Leander eight. Nickalls and R.S.C. Lucas, had won the Silver Goblets in 1920 and 1922 in Magdalen colours, and, rowing for Leander in 1924, they were expected to win again but their heat against Hampshire and Phillips of Magdalen resulted in one of the most extraordinary races in Henley's long history. The official account of the race reads:

> It was not generally known, however, that as well as being famous oarsmen they were no mean amateur carpenters and always carried a set of tools. While waiting at the start, stroke, thinking that the boat was unnecessarily heavy, cut away some of the bigger timbers and on the first stroke bow pushed his stretcher through the skin and she started to leak.

61 The Toronto Trophy won by the Club, 1923

Gully's version was rather different. He said the boatman had not replaced the bulkhead which he had removed in order to move his seat nearer the bows. Whatever the cause, the result was disastrous, but they might have survived their heat had they not stopped when ahead and waited for their opponents after the latter had hit the booms. The official account continues:

> On re-starting Nickalls and Lucas again took the lead and were a long way ahead at Fawley ... Here it became obvious that something was wrong for the boat was floating lower and lower in the water. In spite of the handicap they kept

well ahead and it became more of a race against the leak than against their opponents. At the Mile Post it was clear that the leak was gaining on them fast and at the bottom of the Enclosure the cut-water disappeared and then the boat sank amidst execrations that were visible but inaudible at the winning-post.

Hampshire and Phillips, unaware of the situation, were not a little surprised to find their opponents swimming and stopped rowing. Eventually, they paddled in to complete the course and immediately offered to re-row the race but the Committee ruled that, as they had passed the finish, the race was over and that a boat must abide by its accidents. The Magdalen pair did not survive the next round but were more successful in later life, Hampshire becoming a Director of ICI and the father of the actress, Susan Hampshire, while Wogan Phillips eventually became Lord Milford, the Communist peer.

The Henley of 1924, again an Olympic year, was not a vintage regatta. There was no outstanding English eight in the Grand; in the winning Leander eight, Mellen, being American, was ineligible for Olympic selection but the Club was not prepared to change the crew. Thames had already announced their intention of seeking selection and Cambridge, the Boat Race winners, declined to row a trial against them, so Thames were eventually chosen for the eights, in which they could finish only a disappointing fourth in Paris.

Mellen, Nickalls and Lucas again filled the three stern seats in the 1925 Grand eight which defeated Thames in the final, equalling the 1891 Fawley record in the process, but Nickalls and Lucas, without resorting to carpentry, failed in their heat of the Goblets and were also in the losing Stewards' four.

The Grand was retained in 1926 but the Club lost the final of the Stewards' to Thames. The following year, meeting Thames in the Grand for the fourth year in succession, they were beaten by two lengths, Thames going on to win the final from London, who were now also reviving under Fairbairn's tutelage. Leander also lost the final of the Stewards' to Thames, who were then at the highest point in their history, and the Club had no Henley success that year.

The unhappy situation between Leander and the Tideway clubs was exacerbated in 1928 when Gully Nickalls, who had been Captain of the Club from 1924 to 1926 and was still a member of the Committee, opted to row for Thames in the Grand, an unprecedented move. Nickalls had tried to persuade the stroke of the 1927 Thames-winning Grand eight, Jamie Hamilton (Hamish Hamilton, the publisher), to stroke Leander in 1928, but Hamilton remained faithful to Thames and turned the tables on Leander by making it a condition of his rowing with Thames that Thames persuaded Nickalls to row seven for them. Hamilton told me years later that this created a furore at Leander and that Nickalls was practically expelled from the Club. However, he was quickly forgiven and was back on the Committee by 1930 and ultimately, in 1962, became the Club's President.

Nickalls had his eye on the 1928 Olympics and believed that the Thames eight, with six of their 1927 Grand crew rowing again, were

62   Guy & Gully Nickalls with George Rowe at Henley in the 1920s

his best bet for selection. In this he was correct as Leander produced a very poor crew that went out in their heat of the Grand to First Trinity, who in turn lost in the final to Thames, Nickalls thereby recording his seventh win in the Grand, a tally that has yet to be beaten. Thames ultimately went on to represent Britain at the Amsterdam Olympics, where they lost narrowly in the final to the University of California, Gully earning a second silver medal to add to his 1920 silver.

Nickalls retired from active rowing in 1929, by which time London were replacing Thames as the main Tideway threat to Leander's supremacy. However, Leander produced a strong crew to beat London in the semi-final of the Grand, and Thames in the final. This was Leander's fifth Grand win since the war but London finally triumphed in 1930, beating Leander in the final to record their first win in the Grand since 1890. In August London went on to win the eights and coxless fours at the first British Empire Games at Hamilton, Ontario.

In 1931, the Club Committee had difficulty in finding anyone to take on the Captaincy and Alexander McCulloch, the 1908 Diamonds winner and Olympic sculler, was a late appointment. The recent successes by London and Thames meant that these clubs were once again attracting university oarsmen, which was weakening Leander's hold on what had been traditionally the Club's main source of talent, with the result that, despite McCulloch's efforts, the Club was unable to raise any crews for Henley that year.

It was a different matter in 1932, another Olympic year. The Olympics were by now beginning to assume a greater importance, especially as, with Cherry Pitman as its Chairman, the ARA's attitude had become more positive. For the first time for many years, the Club elected a resident undergraduate, the Cambridge President, Harold Rickett, as Captain, and Rickett and Gully Nickalls were nominated by the Club to serve on the ARA's selection committee.

The fast 1932 Cambridge crew won the Boat Race comfortably and the full crew represented Leander in the Grand, beating London, with five of their 1931 winning Grand eight, in their heat. The final, against Thames, was, in effect, an Olympic trial and a fine race developed, the crews overlapping throughout. Leander led by half a length at Fawley but continuous spurts by Thames kept reducing the lead, only for Leander to regain their half length as each effort faded, and they eventually won by this distance.

Leander were then selected as the British eight for the Olympic Regatta at Long Beach, California, Thames, the Stewards' winners, going as the coxless four, and the Goblets

63 Leander beating Thames in the Grand, 1932, to win Olympic selection

winners, the Oxford Blues Hugh Edwards and Lewis Clive, as the coxless pair.

Racing was on sea water and the heat was extreme. The eight reached the final but were caught napping at the start and produced a rushed row. Even so, although they finished fourth, they were only three-quarters of a length behind the American gold medallists, California. Italy were a foot behind the winners and Canada a further half length back, a canvas ahead of Great Britain.

Earlier, the pair had won with some ease and 'Jumbo' Edwards, rowing as a substitute for a sick man in the Thames four, took a second gold medal in the coxless fours.

Rickett declined the Captaincy in 1933 and once again it proved difficult to find a successor, a current Oxford Blue, W.D.C. Erskine-Crum, finally being persuaded to take the office as late as May, and it was hardly surprising that he could produce only a Stewards' four that lost in the semi-final. An exceptional Pembroke four won the final from London, who had earlier won the Grand once again by a quarter of a length from the Berliner Ruder Club.

Kenneth Payne, who had rowed in the 1932 eight, was the current Cambridge President and took on the Club Captaincy in 1934. Cambridge, beginning to move away from their long Orthdox tradition towards the Fairbairnism then prevailing on the Cam, and with four Fairbairn-trained men in the boat, but still using fixed pins, had won the Boat

64 The record-breaking Leander eight paddling down for the final of the Grand, 1934

65 Leander beating Princeton University, USA, in the final of the Grand, 1934

Race in very good conditions, breaking all the course records. Payne raised an outstanding Leander Grand eight, consisting of seven current Blues, four from Oxford and three from Cambridge, the eighth man gaining his Blue with Cambridge the following year.

A prolonged drought, coupled with fine weather, resulted in very fast conditions at Henley. In the Grand, Leander, also on fixed pins despite a general move towards swivels in other quarters, and stroked by Ran Laurie, with Payne at six, first met London, who included seven of their 1933 winning Grand eight. London were clear after the Barrier but Leander drew level at the bottom of the enclosure and drew away to win by a length, the record falling at every point. The following day, in another close race with Thames, in which Leander led by a third of a length at the Mile and finally won by half a length, they clipped another second off the course record, bringing it down to 6 min. 44 sec. In the final, Leander had a marginally easier race against Princeton and beat the American students by three-quarters of a length in 6 min. 45 sec, for the Club's seventh Grand win in the fifteen regattas since the war, and its twenty-third overall, a record no other club has approached before or since.

That year the Club made an exception to its much quoted resolution of February 1929, which barred active members from another club from membership of Leander, by electing Jack Beresford, who had competed throughout his active career with Thames. Beresford, in addition to his many Henley successes, had already won two Olympic gold medals and two silvers as a sculler and oarsman and was to win another gold medal in 1936. However, Rowland George, a member of the 1932 Thames winning Olympic four, in which Beresford has rowed, and W.W.H. Cane, who had won the Grand with London in 1933, were rejected at the same meeting.

Another mixture of dark and light blue oarsmen represented the Club in the Grand in 1935, reaching the final, only for their stroke, David Winser, to come off his seat at the start, a fine Pembroke eight rowing away to win comfortably.

The middle 1930s saw a notable increase in overseas crews competing at Henley and 1935 marked the appearance of the first of some outstanding crews from Zurich, who were to create controversy in British rowing circles, supporters of both the Orthodox and Fairbairn camps each claiming that the Swiss were rowing on their principles, although their coach, Arthur Dreyfus, maintained that he had been influenced by the excellent Pembroke Fairbairn four that had beaten the best Continental fours at Mainz Regatta in 1933. This had been his first experience of Fairbairn rowing and he began to coach his crews through Fairbairn's books and through correspondence with him. In 1934 Zurich won five Swiss championship titles and the 1935 Zurich four won the Stewards' with consummate ease before going on to take the European title that summer. Their sculler, Rufli, won the Diamonds.

In 1936, another Olympic year, competition for the Grand was exceptionally strong, with Zurich entering for the first time, together with the Union Boat Club, Boston, and Tokyo Imperial University, who had set tongues wag-

66 Leander losing to Ruder Club, Zurich, one of the outstanding Swiss crews of the 1930s, in the final of the Grand, 1936.

ging by striking phenomenally high rates when winning at Marlow. Pembroke defended the trophy with five of their winning 1935 eight included, while Leander put on a potential Olympic eight stroked by Ran Laurie, the current Cambridge stroke, and with Tom Askwith from the 1932 Olympic eight, and winner of the Diamond Sculls in 1933, at four, and the outstanding Oxford oarsman of the period, Conrad Cherry, at five.

The selectors had decided to pick the Olympic crews on Henley form and the draw for the Grand worked out well in this respect. In their heats, Pembroke and Leander beat Thames and London respectively, both by less than a length, but Pembroke then went out to the Americans. Tokyo, with spurts at 50 and 56, beat Quintin, who were making their first venture into the Grand, only to be overwhelmed by the Swiss, who paddled home in their semi-final.

Leander beat the Americans by a length in the other semi-final but in the final they could not match the pace of the Swiss, who went away fast to lead by three-quarters of a length at the first signal. Laurie spurted at the Barrier but the Swiss then went away again. They had half a length of clear water at the Mile and won, easing up, by a length and a quarter. The Swiss went on to retain the Stewards', clearing Leander in the final by the top of the Island, while Rufli retained the Diamonds.

All this did not augur well for Britain's Olympic hopes. Hitler was using the Berlin Games as a powerful propaganda exercise and it was no surprise that the Germans took five of the seven events at Grünau, missing out only in the eights and double sculls, Jack Beresford taking his third Olympic gold medal in the latter event.

The Leander eight had been selected but rearranged after Henley, with Hugh Mason and

67 Leander beating Thames in the final of the Stewards', 1937

Desmond Kingsford coming into the crew, and Noel Duckworth, the Cambridge cox, taking over over the rudder lines. At Grünau they lost their heat to the Americans, represented by Washington University, by one third of a length after leading 200 metres from the finish, but won their *repechage* from Canada and France. However, once again Britain could finish only fourth behind the USA, Italy, and Germany. One second separated the first three, with Italy again only a foot behind the winners, but Britain were over a length further back. The Swiss, making the mistake of doubling up, were sixth and last, and their coxless four were only third. London, stroked by the Oxford Blue, Jan Sturrock, took the silver medal.

Considerable comment had been made in 1936 on the refusal of the entry for the Grand by the Australian Olympic eight on the grounds that it was a police crew, which fell foul of the ARA's and Henley's archaic rules of amateurism. The following year the ARA removed all references to 'manual labour' and 'mechanic, artisan or labourer' from its amateur definition, although this did not come into effect at Henley until 1938.

Sturrock was Captain in 1937 and proposed to enter an eight for Frankfurt and Hamburg Regattas but had to abandon the idea when he failed to raise a suitable crew. He did find a crew for the Grand, but, despite including himself and Cherry, they went down in their heat by half a length to London, the latter then losing to the ultimate winners, 'Wiking' from Berlin, the 1936 Olympic bronze medallists, who recorded Germany's first win in the Grand by beating Jesus by half a length.

Leander did have a success, however, winning the Stewards', surprisingly for only the first time since 1914. With Sturrock and Cherry in the crew, they beat Thames in the final.

69 Laurie and Wilson winning the Silver Goblets, 1938

In November 1937, Sturrock was reprimanded, but not too severely, by the Committee for signing, as Captain of Leander but without the Committee's approval, a joint letter with Peter Jackson the Captain of London, and Jack Beresford, for Thames, appealing for funds to take a crew to the Empire Games Regatta to be held in February 1938 on the Nepean River in Australia. Beresford eventually raised a composite eight drawn from Leander (Sturrock), London, Thames, and Kingston, to represent England, and they duly won by three-quarters of a length from Australia.

The Club did not raise a Grand eight that year but the Stewards' Cup was retained, with Con Cherry, now the Club Captain, at three and Ran Laurie stroking. At bow was Jack Wilson, who, with Laurie, scored a notable double for the Club by winning the Goblets. It was the beginning of a famous partnership.

This was the year of the Munich crisis, with the threat of another catastrophic war already looming, and the 1939 season took place against this ominous background. Cherry was again Captain of Leander and asked the Committee for their views on the possibility of the Club entering a Wyfold four composed primarily of young members likely to be available to the Club in future years, but although the Committee agreed to this, it did not materialise in 1939 and many more years were to pass before the Club entered for any but the top Henley events.

The 1939 Grand eight was strong on paper, with four of that year's winning Cambridge crew, three of the 1938 winning Oxford crew, including Cherry and the stroke, Brian Hodgson, plus the Cambridge Olympic oarsman, Desmond Kingsford. They ought to have been formidable but had too little time together and lost their heat by half a length to Jesus, whose only Blues were Alan Burrough, the Cambridge President, and Joe Savill.

Jesus were the only home crew to reach the semi-finals, where they went out to the ultimate winners, Harvard, who beat the Toronto Argonauts in the final. It was painfully reminiscent of the fiasco in 1914, when Harvard's victory presaged the First World War, their 1939 win, as it turned out, doing the same thing for the second war.

Leander did not defend the Stewards', which went again to Zurich, and so the Club's distinguished pre-war run ended on a disappointing note.

Conrad Cherry and Desmond Kingsford were among those to lay down their lives in the ensuing conflict, together with many others who had appeared at Henley in the 1930s, a sad closing of the pages of another chapter in the long history of the Club.

69   Con Cherry

7

Revival and Survival
1940–1953

When war broke out, Con Cherry was still Captain of the Club and remained in this office until he lost his life on active service in 1943, a great loss to the Club and British rowing. The majority of the Committee were not engaged on war service and continued to run the Club, the clubhouse remaining open to members on a restricted basis, with the Steward, Potter, also acting as assistant secretary. Members continued to be elected from time to time, the Club's strict rowing standards for membership remaining in force. In 1941, the American Ambassador, Averill Harriman, was elected an Honorary member during his stay in the country.

Rowing did not cease completely, with an Oxford and Cambridge Boat Race taking place at Henley in 1940, at Sandford in 1943, Ely in 1944, and Henley again in 1945, the crews being awarded wartime Blues and many of them being elected members of Leander. Torpids and Eights were held in modified form at Oxford, and similarly the Lents and Mays at Cambridge.

There were also inter-school races and in 1943 the Committee decided to elect, with the help of the school coaches, some school oarsmen who, but for the war, would have gone further with their rowing. Among a number of Etonians, Radleians and Salopians elected that year were Antony Rowe, a future Oxford President and winner of the Diamond Sculls, Archie Nicholson, a future Cambridge President, and Peter Sutherland, a future Captain of the Club.

During the war, the Club at various times became the quarters for the officers of six different regiments and for the American Army Medical Corps. The officers of the Border Regiment presented a silver salver to the Club in 1941 in recognition of the hospitality they had received during their stay at the clubhouse.

In January 1942, the Club's President, Fred Pitman, died, having been a member of the Club for nearly sixty years and a member of the Committee of Henley for forty-six. As in the First World War, no Annual General Meetings were held and since there had been a precedent in 1916, it was at first decided that the election of a new President should be deferred until the end of the war. Later in the year, however, H.A. ('Bertie') Steward, invoking Rule 3, proposed that Pitman's brother, His Honour Judge Pitman KC, 'Cherry' Pitman to the rowing world and President of the ARA, should be elected President by the Committee. This was seconded by Stanley Garton and passed unanimously.

Ill-health forced Pitman to stand down at the 1946 AGM, the first since 1939. The Committee nominated Steward in recognition of his long and loyal service to the Club, for which he had been Secretary from 1921 to 1942, and whose father had been President from 1892 to 1916. However, Brigadier J.H.

Gibbon was also proposed by R.M.A. Bourne but Steward was elected by 49 votes to 23. Unhappily, he died in February 1948 after a long illness and was succeeded by Lord Bruce of Melbourne, an old Cambridge Blue and former Prime Minister of Australia. It had been decided that in future the President's period of office should be limited to five years and Lord Bruce was elected under this rule.

With victory in Europe in May 1945, regattas quickly revived and rowing made a quick recovery. A one-day regatta was held at Henley over a shortened course on the 7th July, for the Hedsor Cup for Schools, presented by Harcourt Gold, the Danesfield Cup for Open Eights, presented by Stanley Garton, and a sculling race for the Barrier Cup, presented by Bertie Steward. Leander did not compete.

During the war, British oarsmen had somehow contrived to find places to row all over the world and many began to return home in 1945 ready and anxious to continue from where they had left off in 1939. It seemed as though the clock had been turned back when Oxford, reverting to fixed pins under the tutelage of the pre-war Orthodox coach, Peter Haig-Thomas, won the first post-war Boat Race. In 1947, with both crews using fixed pins, Haig-Thomas coached the winning Cambridge crew.

In a material sense, the Club survived the war well, with the Henley clubhouse and the Putney boathouse, still shared with Barclay's Bank, both still intact. The Committee were empowered to appoint trustees of the Club in 1947 and the following year the Club bought the freehold of the Henley clubhouse for £3000. Subscriptions were raised to four guineas in 1948, with Life memberships being introduced for members over the age of 65 on payment of £100. The total membership in 1946 was over 1600 and the income from subscriptions in 1948 was approximately £5000. However, with repairs and redecoration needing urgent attention, the financial situation was precarious in the immediate post-war period, the Club making a loss of over £1000 in 1947, mainly through extensive repairs. For a few years, as part of an economy drive, the clubhouse was closed from September to April, except for rowing, but in 1952 it was opened to members in a limited fashion during the autumn and winter months.

On the river, the need in the immediate post-war years was to restore the Club's rowing to its traditional high level. In the event, the revival was quick and successful. The first full post-war Henley in 1946, which was honoured by the attendance of Princess Elizabeth on the introduction of the new schools' event for the trophy named after her, was a mixture of pre-war veterans and a young post-war generation. Among the former were Richard Burnell, a 1939 Oxford Blue and son of the great oarsman of the Victorian and Edwardian era, 'Don' Burnell, Hugh Mason, from the 1936 Olympic eight, Jack Bradley, stroke of the 1934 record-breaking Cambridge crew and of the fine 1933 and 1934 Pembroke winning Steward's fours, and his brother Pat, who had rowed for Shrewsbury in 1937 and 1938. These four combined with four of the 1946 Oxford winning eight to form the Club's Grand eight, coached by Haig-Thomas and the Club's non-rowing Captain, Gully Nickalls. The former also coached the Stewards' four and the Goblets pair.

Among the six Grand entries were the Ruder Club, Zurich. None of their pre-war oarsmen was in the crew but they disposed of Thames in the semi-final to meet Leander, who had beaten Kingston and Trinity Hall, in the final. The Swiss led by a canvas at the Barrier but Leander were ahead at the Mile and drew away to win by three-quarters of a length. Jack Bradley also stroked the Club's winning Stewards' four, one of whom, J.F. Burgess, also took the Goblets with his twin brother, C.G. Burgess, having disposed of a Uruguayan pair in the semi-final and a Danish pair in the final. The Burgess twins were still only eighteen-years-old and remain to this day the youngest winners of this event. It was an auspicious start to the Club's post-war era, and a month later Burnell won the Wingfield Sculls.

The following March, Jack Beresford took the Burgess pair and the Maidenhead sculler Bert Bushnell to Argentina. Bushnell won all three of his races but the pair succeeded only in the last of theirs. Unhappily, the twins were seriously injured in a car crash soon after and were unable to defend the Goblets in 1947. Neither competed at Henley again.

Zurich re-appeared in the Grand in 1947 and this time included three of their 1939 winning Stewards' four, one of them their winning Diamonds sculler, Rufli. The Leander eight included four of the previous year's winning eight, including Jack Bradley at stroke, and three winning Cambridge Blues, but this was, at last, Jesus's year, the Cambridge College producing an outstanding crew which beat Leander by half a length before overcoming the Swiss and, in the final, a Dutch crew from Delft. This was Jesus's third Grand win and their first since 1885. The Club's Stewards' four failed to retain the trophy, losing their heat to the ultimate winners, Thames.

In 1948, the Olympic Regatta was to be held at Henley once again and various attempts were made by the ARA to form a composite eight but after early trials the plans came to nothing and the selectors, with the Olympics to be held a month after the Royal Regatta, fell back on the old policy of choosing Britain's representatives on Henley form.

In what he regarded as being in the best interests of British rowing, in view of the forthcoming Olympics, Haig-Thomas took the unique position of helping with the coaching of both crews for the Boat Race, which Cambridge, despite catching a crab early in the race, won in record time, while Thames won the Head of the River Race.

There were no foreign entries for the Grand, in which six of the Cambridge crew, plus the spare man, Paul Massey, and Ian Lang, a 1947 Blue, rowed in Leander colours. The Cambridge and Jesus stroke, Chris Barton, unhappy with the Orthodox style and fixed pins favoured by Cambridge, opted for his College eight, with one Pembroke man included, the Henley Stewards having admitted composite crews for this Olympic year only, while Bert Barry had put together a crew drawn from the NARA clubs on the Lea and Thames, rowing as Leetham, but they failed to survive their heat against Kingston.

Leander drew Thames and led by a third of a length until shortly before the Mile, where Thames drew level and then went away to win by half a length. Thames went on to overwhelm Jesus/Pembroke in the final, the stern four of the Thames eight also retaining the

70

71

72

Leander's post-war revival, 1946

70 Beating Ruder Club, Zurich, in the final of the Grand
71 Beating Oriel College, Oxford in the final of the Stewards'
72 The Burgess twins beating Secher and Paerregaard in the final of the Silver Goblets

Stewards', which provided the selectors with a dilemma, since Urs Burkhard in the Thames eight was Swiss and therefore ineligible to represent Britain in the Olympics. In the end, the selectors plumped for a re-vamped Leander eight, with Barton, who was adapt at switching between the Jesus and Orthodox styles, coming in to stroke, and Brian Lloyd, a Cambridge freshman who had learnt his rowing in Australia but had yet to win his Blue, at three. Thames were selected for the coxless fours.

The Henley of that year saw the re-appearance after ten years of the 1938 Goblets winners, Ran Laurie and Jack Wilson, who had been in the Sudan on colonial service in the intervening years, Wilson almost losing his life after being speared by a deranged woman under the spell of a witch doctor. The pair, on leave from the Sudan, resurrected their partnership and, representing Leander once again, scored a remarkable victory ten years after their first success, beating the Australian Olympic pair-designate in the final, to be selected for the Olympic coxless pairs.

Another unexpected selection was that of Richard Burnell and Bert Bushnell for the double sculls. Burnell had competed unsuccessfully at Henley with Dick Winstone of Kingston, going out in a semi-final to the Belgians, the ultimate winners. The selectors suggested that Burnell should try to combine with Bushnell, the losing Diamonds finalist who had the previous year won the Wingfields, which Burnell had not defended. Despite a considerable difference in physique, Burnell being three stone heavier than Bushnell, this new double worked almost immediately and they won an Olympic trial. Tony Rowe, in Leander colours, had lost in the second round of the Diamonds to the Australian Olympic sculler, Mervyn Wood, but was selected for the Olympic single sculls.

The start for the Olympic Regatta was at the top of Temple Island which allowed three crews to race abreast over the 1880-metre course. The British eight reached the final with the United States (the University of California) and Norway. Britain led by half a length after 500 metres but the Americans drew level at 1000 metres and then went away to win comfortably, with Norway third, the United States having now won the Olympic eights every time since 1920.

The Thames four rowed below form and failed to reach the final, while Rowe went out in the semi-final of the single soulls after a dramatic race which ended in a torrential downpour. Rowe had a close race to 1000 metres with the American sculler, Jack Kelly, the 1947 Diamonds winner and son of the triple gold medallist from the 1920s, John B. Kelly, before Kelly junior drew away and looked to have won the race. But Kelly was caught just before the finish by the Uruguayan Edouardo Risso and lost by a few feet, Risso going on to take the silver medal behind Merv Wood.

It was not all failure for Britain, however. Indeed, there were two notable triumphs: Laurie and Wilson put on an immaculate exhibition of pair-oared rowing to take the gold medal, and Bushnell and Burnell followed this by leading all the way in the final of the Double Sculls to win comfortably from Denmark and Uruguay. Burnell's win completed a unique family double, his father having won the Olympic Eights, also at Henley, forty years earlier.

73 An outstanding pair. Laurie and Wilson winning a gold medal in the Olympic Regatta, 1948

74 Laurie and Wilson receive their gold medals, 1948

75 Bushnell (bow) and Burnell (stroke) competing in the 1948 Olympic Regatta

76 Bushnell and Burnell after winning the Olympic double sculls

Burnell took over the Club Captaincy in 1949 and put together a strong Grand eight, stroked by Pat Bradley. The other seven were all Oxford or Cambridge Blues, with Burnell at six and Bill Windham at five. They beat London and Trinity College, Oxford, and, with virtually no stream, equalled the 1934 course record against the latter. In the final, against Thames, who included four of their 1948 winning eight, Leander led from the start and were two lengths ahead at Remenham Club, eventually winning by one length. This was the last occasion on which the Grand was won by a crew using fixed pins.

The Stewards' four, drawn from the eight, failed against the ultimate winners, Trinity, Oxford, who were stroked by the Oxford Blue, Christopher Davidge, with Tony Rowe at three. Bushnell and Burnell also failed in their heat of the Double Sculls, losing to the Olympic silver medallists, Ebbe Parsner and Aage Larsen of Denmark.

The ARA, with the 1948 Olympics in mind, had finally become affiliated to the international federation, FISA, in 1947, Thames representing Britain in the European Championships that year in the coxless pairs and fours, both reaching their finals. This new departure was, in the long run, to have a significant effect on British rowing, with the ARA beginning to focus on the annual European Championships in addition to the Olympics.

In 1949, Bushnell and Burnell competed in the double sculls in the European Championships on the Bosbaan, Amsterdam, reaching the final via the *repechages*, but they could finish only fifth, the Danes taking the gold medal.

In the autumn of 1949, Burnell was invited by the ARA to select an eight to represent England in the Empire Games to be held in New Zealand the following February. With Pat Bradley stroking, the eight consisted of five Leander and three Thames men. The venture was an unmitigated disaster, the eight suffering a series of unforeseen setbacks, which included the withdrawal through ill-health and ultimately the death of their original coach,

77 Leander equalling the course record when beating Trinity College, Oxford, in the semi-final of the Grand, 1949

'Two-Legs' Hellyer, and equipment going astray in New Zealand, so that they were forced to train with antiquated borrowed equipment. They were well beaten by Australia and New Zealand, but Tony Rowe salvaged some English pride by taking the single sculls silver medal behind the Australian 1948 Olympic Champion, Mervyn Wood.

By 1950, domestic rowing had settled back into the familiar pre-war tradition, and Oxbridge college rowing was still at the top of the Henley tree. Some outstanding Lady Margaret crews had begun to have several successes and many crews began to adopt in varying degrees the Cambridge college's long lie-back and low rates of striking. In 1949, in winning the Ladies' Plate, LMBC had lowered the Henley course record by one second, beating Leander's best time in the Grand that year by the same margin. In 1950, entering for the Grand with seven of the 1949 crew rowing again, they were fancied by the pundits to win, but, after being clear of Harvard at the three-quarter mile in their heat, they were rowed down by the American students and lost by half a length.

Leander, stroked by Davidge with Burnell and Bradley also in the crew, were once again short of practice compared with their opponents but they comfortably beat Dartmouth Rowing Club, USA, in their heat before losing a close race to the Dutch student crew, Njord, Leiden, who were in turn beaten by Harvard in the final.

Leander also lost the final of the Stewards' to Hellerup, Copenhagen, after hitting the booms and bending a rigger, but the Club had one notable success when Tony Rowe became the first home winner of the Diamond Sculls

78 A.D. Rowe, winner of the Diamond Sculls, 1950

since Tom Askwith's 1933 victory. In September, Rowe competed at Philadelphia for the Philadelphia Gold Cup but was beaten by Wood by seven seconds and Kelly by two.

A Goldie eight based on the Lady Margaret eight won the bronze medal in the 1950 European Championships and at the end of the year Richard Burnell, the anonymous Rowing Correspondent of *The Times*, commented that British rowing was becoming increasingly international in character. 'There are many', he wrote, echoing similar opinions expressed in the Press fifty years earlier, 'who would like to see English rowing remain a domestic affair, who disagree on principle with the Olympic Games, Empire Games and European Championships, and would even like to see a limit to foreign participation at Henley. There is something to be said for their feelings but it has been proved in so many spheres that the clock cannot be put back . . . Foreign crews will

79 Tony Rowe leading Rob van Mesdag past Temple Island in the final of the 1950 Diamond Sculls

continue to come to Henley in increasing strength and it is a compliment to us that this should be so. Equally, the growing demand to send British crews abroad will not be denied.'

Among correspondence that followed Burnell's article was a letter from the well-known Tideway oarsman and Leander member, Charles Rew, advocating 'a competent selection committee empowered to select oarsmen from any club or college they choose, and to have those men at their entire disposal (as far as rowing is concerned) for twelve months for coaching and welding into a crew. This, of course, would mean taking twenty-four of the best oarsmen ... in the country away from their own clubs ... for the twelve months preceding the Olympic Games.' Burnell answered that, while clubs might be prepared to accept this, the universities could not, because of, among other things, academic requirements. In another letter, Jack Beresford thought that, in any case, the solution lay with the Tideway clubs. 'If they could pool their resources, which would include former university oars, still in their prime and perhaps more cunning at twenty-five than twenty-one, a first-class crew could row together for at least a year before the next Olympics.'

All this was an early indication of the thinking that was to have a profound effect on British rowing, and not least on Leander's, with the eventual introduction of a national squad. However, it was to be some years before this would be realised or the domestic scene changed significantly, but it was probably the germ that led Ronnie Symonds, one of the architects of the successes of Cambridge, Lady Margaret and Thames in the early post-war years, to assemble a composite Grand eight in Leander colours, in April 1951, as a potential Olympic crew for 1952.

However, 1951 was to prove Cambridge's

year, beginning with the light blues easily winning the Boat Race at the second attempt, Oxford having sunk soon after the start on the first. Cambridge then went on a triumphant tour of the United States, during which they beat Harvard and Yale and other American universities.

At Henley, Leander's Grand eight contained one member of this Cambridge crew, Bill Windham, and four former Cambridge Blues, one Oxford Blue, and two Thames men, who had decided that it was in the national interest for them to co-operate. Stroked by the 1950 Cambridge and Lady Margaret stroke, John Crick, under Symonds they adopted the Lady Margaret 'style' but unfortunately they also acquired some of the worst faults arising from the long lie-back. Having subbed in this crew while Windham was in America, I can say that this was the most uncomfortable and artificial rowing I had ever experienced.

Four of the nine entries for the Grand were from overseas, headed by the Italians from Varese, who were the full 1950 European Champion eight, six of whom had also won the eights in 1947 and 1949. The others were two Dutch student crews and a Spanish eight from Barcelona. Leander won a close race by half a length from Njord but then went out to Lady Margaret, who were stroked by the Olympic silver medallist, Brian Lloyd, one of five of the 1951 Cambridge eight in the crew. Lady Margaret, striking only 32, led Leander by half a length at the half mile and by one and a quarter lengths at the three-quarter mile, maintaining this lead to the finish. Lady Margaret won the final by a length from Laga, Delft, who had beaten the Italians with surprising

80 Ronnie Symonds (oil painting by Geoffrey Page)

ease in their heat and Barcelona in their semi-final, also by a large margin.

The Club was represented in the Stewards' by the Clare four, stroked by the Cambridge stroke, David Jennens, but they lost in the final to Thames, while Rowe lost in the first round of the Diamonds. However, Richard Burnell and Pat Bradley won the Double Sculls without being unduly pressed. This was the last Henley appearance for these distinguished Leander stalwarts.

Cambridge crews won the Grand, Ladies', Visitors', Wyfold, Goblets, and, but for an untimely crab, would also have won the Thames Cup, while the Pembroke sculler, Tony Fox, took the Diamond Sculls. It was a light blue triumph exceeded only by the *annus mirabilis* of Cambridge rowing, 1887, when Cambridge colleges carried off eight trophies.

Cambridge then crowned their 1951 season when the Goldie eight, stroked by Jennens, won the European title, the first for Britain, by six feet from Denmark at Macon.

At the end of this season, Symonds decided that a Tideway-based eight might provide the best chance of producing an Olympic eight for Helsinki in 1952 and he took on the Captaincy of Thames, with the Cambridge Blue, Alastair Macleod, as his Deputy Captain. Captain of Leander in 1951, Macleod had rowed in the Leander eight that year and three others from that crew joined him at Thames.

The ARA selectors decided to wait until after the Boat Race and the Head of the River Race before making any announcement about Olympic representation. When Cambridge unexpectedly lost the Boat Race by a canvas in a blizzard and Thames could finish only third behind moderate crews in the Head, the selectors invited Brian Lloyd, then Captain of Leander, to form an eight, reserving the right to hold a trial in June should the crew not look like coming up to scratch. Trials for fours, coxless pairs, and double and single sculls were also to be held in June. This was definitely a step towards moving with the times.

Lloyd had, in fact, had an eight based on the Cambridge 1951 crew in training for some time, a departure from the Club's traditional practice of putting crews together a few weeks before Henley. After the Head, Macleod resigned his office at Thames and rejoined the Leander squad, and the crew that ultimately represented Leander in the Grand contained six of the 1951 Cambridge crew plus the cox, John Hinde, together with one of the 1952 crew and Macleod. Harold Rickett, the Cambridge finishing coach, took charge and the crew were not in the end required to row a trial.

In the small boat trials, the coxless four, all Cambridge Blues and stroked by Adrian Cadbury, were the only Leander crew to win and they were selected for Helsinki.

Because of the Olympics, the Australian Olympic eight, Sydney Rowing Club, were the only overseas entry for the Grand and met Leander in the final. Leander had clear water at the first signal but the Australians had reduced this to one third of a length by the mile and this was still the difference at the last signal, though Jennens's final spurt gave Leander the verdict by half a length. Helped by a strong following wind, the winning time shattered the record by five seconds.

The selected coxless four did not compete in the Stewards', which went to the Thames four that included three former Leander oarsmen, the Blues Peter de Giles, Graham Fisk and Paul Massey, and which competed as the coxed four in Helsinki.

The Olympic Regatta was a major disappointment. For the first time, Britain won no medals, the eight, both fours, the coxless pair and single sculler, Tony Fox, all finishing fourth. The eight's failure was a particular blow, with the Australians taking the bronze medal, but the appearance for the first time of the State-backed Soviet crews, who took the silver in the eights and won the single sculls, and of the Germans, also for the first time since the war, gave notice of the rising standards that were to come.

In *The Times*, Burnell commented later that it was arguable that the Olympic Games were

81 Leander beating Sydney Rowing Club, Australia in record time in the final of the Grand, 1952

so disruptive of our domestic rowing that they were not worth the trouble involved, and it was time to understand that, if we did compete, we could not muddle through. However, for the next few years British rowing continued along its traditional path.

In 1952, the Club sustained a great loss with the death of Sir Harcourt Gold. A fine oarsman and coach in his time, 'Tarka', the Chairman of the ARA from 1948 and of Henley from 1945 to 1951, had been, in 1949, the first man to be knighted for services to rowing. His contribution to British rowing, and in particular to Leander and to Henley, over a period of more than half a century, had been outstanding.

The previous year, the Balliol-educated Crown Prince Olaf of Norway had been elected an Honorary Life member of the Club. Then, following the death of King George VI in 1952, the Club was honoured when the new Queen, Elizabeth II, consented to become Patron of the Club, the Duke of Edinburgh accepting Honorary Life membership.

The Club won the Grand again in 1953 with a crew containing five of the Helsinki eight. Stroked by Cadbury, they beat the only overseas entry, 'Metro' (Union-Sportive Metropolitaine des Transports, Paris) in the final. Four of the Club eight also won the Stewards'. Leander had now won the Grand twenty-six times and it was their fourth win in the eight regattas since the Second World War. However, in 1953 the wind of change began to be felt on the Henley reach and British rowing was soon to face a formidable challenge from overseas.

The 1953 Leander eight did not continue

after Henley and no British eight went to the European Championships that year, the 'Metro' eight taking the bronze medal behind the Soviet Union and Denmark, the Soviets also winning the coxless pairs and taking silver medals in the coxed fours and double sculls. The world rowing scene was beginning to take on an ominous new look.

Three Presidents:
82 Lord Cottesloe (1952–1961)
83 Viscount Bruce of Melbourne (1948–1951)
84 G.O. Nickalls (1962–1966)

8

New Challenges and A Changing Scene
The 1950s and 1960s

While the rowing world was undergoing significant changes, the Club Committee continued to occupy themselves mainly with domestic problems, some of the Minutes sounding strangely anachronistic. In 1953, for instance, they record some unacceptable behaviour by a member, who, having booked a room for the night and saying he would arrive by 10pm, had eventually done so at 2.30am 'in an excited condition; had woken a member sleeping in the Club; and had brought in his chauffeur and valet to sleep in the Club bedrooms.' The Secretary was instructed to write to him in inform him that such conduct could not be tolerated. The Minutes of the next meeting report that the Secretary had received a reply from the member's mother, but unfortunately for us, did not elaborate.

In the same year the question of members' dress when using the Club was raised and it was decided that flagrant cases of *déshabillé* should be brought to the attention of the President, 'who would instruct the Hon. Sec. to communicate with the offender in appropriate terms.'

A later Minute records that 'an attractive lady with two dogs, introduced by Mr Geoffrey Milling, had been seen in the Club on the Friday of the Regatta, contrary to regulation 10.' The problem, however, was not the lady's presence but that of the dogs and it was agreed that dogs could be taken into the garden but not into the Club itself.

A more serious matter was the disappearance of the Club clerk with £150, the insurance stamp money. He was never traced but the Committee informed the police that even if he were to be apprehended, they would not prosecute.

Redecoration of the dining-room and the establishment of a small bar in the Ladies' drawing-room, from plans drawn up by Ronnie Symonds, were also undertaken during this period.

On the river, in 1954, the Club, encouraged by the ARA selectors, assembled a crew for the Grand made up of men who would all be available for the Empire Games to be held in Vancouver in August. Six were from the winning 1953 Grand eight, with stroke to four unchanged. The bowman, Ted Pain, had been a gold medallist in the 1950 Empire Games with the Australian eight and the Leander eight were potentially another fast combination, but once again they had too little time together to cope with the strong challenge that was to come.

In 1954 came the largest overseas entry that Henley had ever received up to at that time. It was marked by the first appearance of crews from the Soviet Union, who entered an eight for the Grand, two Stewards' fours, who were not doubling up in the eight, a Goblets pair (the reigning European champions), a double scull and the Olympic champion, Yuri Tukalov, in the Diamonds. The pattern of

Henley was being changed by the appearance for the first time of a full national team, complete with team manager, coaches, doctors and physiotherapists. Although only two of the foreign entries were in the Grand, both were formidable, being the 1953 European gold and silver medallists. The Soviet eight, Krylia Sovetov, had been unbeaten since finishing second to the US Navy crew at Helsinki in 1952, and both they and Kvik, Copenhagen, had their complete 1953 crews.

The Soviets' unusual and distinctive style had an effect on observers somewhat similar to that of the Belgians at the beginning of the century. The eight, in particular, were beautifully together and their boat ran with no noticeable check. Their rhythm was very exaggerated, with a marked slowing of the hands, almost a pause, as they passed the thighs on the recovery, followed by an acceleration up the slide and a lightning catch. They did not row a long stroke and sat upright at the finish. Those accustomed to the traditional variations in British rowing found their pace hard to assess.

They did not have to wait long for this to become clear. The first Soviet crew to race, the Krylia Sovetov Stewards' four, won their heat against Thames despite hitting the booms below Fawley. The following day the Soviet eight demolished Kvik by three lengths, and then had an unexpectedly hard race against Thames, winning by half a length after having been led to Fawley, while Leander, who had a bye, beat Lady Margaret by three-quarters of a length.

Much had been expected of the Leander eight in the final but in the end they proved to be no match for Krylia Sovetov, who led by a length at Fawley and then rowed right away to win by two and a half lengths. They later retained the European title.

In the Stewards', the Leander four, drawn from the eight, went out in their heat to a Copenhagen four that failed to make the final. This was won, inevitably, by Krylia Sovetov, who, with Tukalov coming in at bow, later became the European coxed four champions.

British rowing took a heavy drubbing at Henley, six of the seven open events going abroad. Worse was to follow at the Empire Games, for which, as a result of Henley form, the Thames eight replaced Leander, but, using the Leander boat, which did not suit them, they never hit their true form and were beaten by the Canadians, none of the other English entries recording a win.

In the European Championships, two of the Leander Grand eight, David Macklin and Christopher Davidge, were chosen for the coxless pairs. They rowed without a rudder, which led to some comment at the time, and in view of this and their short time together, they did well to battle along in a blustery following cross-wind in the final to take the bronze medal, the Soviet Goblets winners finishing second behind Denmark.

A depressing season for British rowing ended with Cambridge, who had lost the 100th Boat Race, losing all three of their races on a visit to Japan.

The following year, six Henley trophies went abroad again. Davidge was unable to raise an eight for the Grand, in which a new Soviet eight were beaten in the semi-final by the Empire Games champions, rowing as Vancouver RC, the Canadians going down narrowly in the final to Pennsylvania.

Leander were well beaten in the final of the Stewards' by the 1954 winners, Krylia Sovetov, and the Russians also retained the Goblets. Later, a sub-standard British team failed to reach any finals in the European Championships, an inauspicious build-up for the 1956 Olympics.

Just before Henley in 1956, the Club suffered a sad loss when Ronnie Symonds died while swimming off the Channel Islands. A brilliant coach and a charming man, he had recently done much to restore the fabric of the Club.

The Soviets did not appear at Henley that year, the main overseas challenge coming from the Swedish 1955 European bronze medallists and an exceptionally powerful French Army eight. The Club put on an eight that included Davidge and Tony Leadley, who had rowed in the 1953 and 1954 Leander eights, but in their heat they were unable to deal with a moderate Jesus crew, losing by half a length. Jesus lost their semi-final to the French Army, despite having been given a bonus lead of two and a half lengths when the French stroke came off his seat on the second stroke. The French then beat the Swedes by a length in the final.

The Leander Stewards' four, once again drawn from the eight, lost their heat to the ultimate winners, Thames, and it was another bleak Henley for the Club.

The 1956 Olympic Games were held in Melbourne in November and so European Championships were also held earlier that year at Bled. The ARA invited twenty-nine oarsmen and three coxswains to trial on the Tideway for an eight for both. Of the six Leander candidates, only Simon Tozer, plus John Hinde, the cox, made the eight which went to Bled, Christopher Davidge and Tony Leadley going as the coxless pair. The eight were never right and failed to reach the final, in which the French Army took the silver medal behind Czechoslovakia. The pair also failed narrowly to reach their final and the whole lot went back into the melting pot for Melbourne, Davidge eventually coming in to stroke a re-organised eight, in which Tozer held his place. However, they never found a uniform technique and were well below the Olympic standard, failing, with the rest of the British entries, to reach even the semi-finals. It was Britain's worst Olympic performance ever and showed how far the country had slipped down the international ladder. At the inquest after the Olympics, many critics called for an improvement in technique and fitness in British crews.

The Russians contested five events at Henley in 1957. The Club did not raise an eight for the Grand, two overseas crews once again contesting the final. Krasone Znamia went out to Cornell in their semi-final, in which the course record, in calm conditions, was lowered by a remarkable eight seconds. All three home eights lost their heats by large margins and Cornell beat their compatriots from Yale by half a length in the final.

Leander lost their heat of the Stewards' to a new Krylia Sovetov four but it was a happier story in the Goblets, in which Leadley and Davidge beat in turn American and Soviet pairs to reach the final, where they had a fierce battle along the enclosures with the Austrian 1956 European silver and Olympic bronze

85 Leadley and Davidge waiting to receive their gold medals as European coxless pairs champions, Duisburg 1957

medallists before winning by one-third of a length. The Leander pair then went on to take the gold medal in the European Championships at Duisburg, with the Austrians second, and, despite erratic steering, they broke the coxless pairs record. This was only the second European title won by Britain and went some way towards restoring Britain's badly damaged prestige.

The Club was once again without a Grand entry in 1958 and for the fourth year running no home crew reached the final. The only Leander entry were the Goblets pair, Leadley and Davidge, who eliminated Buldakov and Ivanov of the USSR, three times the European champions, in their semi-final. They then went on to beat Streuli and Kottman of Switzerland, the European coxed pair champions in 1954 and 1955, in the final. Sadly, the Leander pair were unable to retain their title in the European Championships at Poznan, finishing only fourth. The whole British team suffered from severe food poisoning and the pair were among those weakened by this.

Before Henley, Leadley and Davidge had been surprisingly beaten in the trials for what were now designated the British Empire and Commonwealth Games by an Isis pair, Stuart Douglas-Mann and Jonathan Hall, who later lost at Henley to the Swiss pair in the semi-final. The Club lost a coxed four trial and so were not represented at Padarn, in Wales, where England won three gold medals, the first in these Games since 1938.

In 1959 there was a notorious mutiny at Oxford, led by an American, Reed Rubin. The President, Ronnie Howard, successfully quashed this and Rubin and a fellow American, the Olympic gold medallist Charlie Grimes, were among those who did not row in the winning Oxford crew. At Henley, however, they rowed in the Leander Grand eight, in which Tony Leadley rowed at six. They took the unusual step of entering for the Marlow Grand, only to lose by two lengths to Thames in the final. As luck would have it, they drew Thames again at Henley, losing by one and a quarter lengths, but Harvard beat Thames comfortably in the final, the trophy going abroad for the sixth successive year.

Leander were represented in the Double Sculls by Davidge and the Australian 1956 Olympic single-sculls silver-medallist and reigning European champion, Stuart Mackenzie. There were only two other entries, both British, and the Leander double won without difficulty. Mackenzie also recorded his third successive victory in the Diamonds, but in Sydney RC colours. Sidney Rand, representing the Club for the first time, reached the semi-finals and was selected to represent Britain in the European Championships at Macon but failed to reach the final.

These championships were notable for Karl Adam's remarkable winning German eight from Ratzeburg. Using a short boat, an eccentric rig which put four and five in tandem and stroke and bow on the same side, and long oars with short wide blades, they started at 50 and were never below 40. They were three lengths ahead at 1000 metres and, finishing at 48, they eventually won by ten seconds. Germany took four and the USSR two of the seven gold medals. Of the six British entries, only Richard Norton and Hugh Scurfield in the coxless pairs reached the finals, finishing fourth. Once again the international standard seemed to be slipping out of Britain's reach, let alone Leander's.

Early in 1960, Thames introduced Macon-type oars on the Tideway and these were quickly adopted by many clubs, while Jumbo Edwards, Oxford's chief coach, designed his own version with special lightweight looms, with which Oxford won the Boat Race, while Cambridge continued to use conventional blades. Oxford decided to stay together with the Olympics in mind, rowing in the Grand as Isis. In earlier years they would have rowed in Leander colours and the result was that, for the fourth time in six years, the Club had no entry in the Grand or the Stewards'.

In 1958 a new club, Barn Cottage Boat Club, had won the Stewards' with experienced oarsmen. The intention was that Barn Cottage would provide composite crews with international representation the goal. In 1960, they combined with Molesey and rowed as the latter in the Grand, the eight splitting into Barn Cottage and Molesey fours for the Stewards'. With Davidge stroking the eight, they beat Oxford in the final of the Grand and the Barn Cottage four won the Stewards', the Molesey four losing their semi-final after breaking a blade on the booms. Eventually Oxford went to the Rome Olympics as the eight and the Molesey/Barn Cottage fours as the coxed and coxless fours.

Leander's only interest at that Henley was in the Diamonds, in which the Club was represented by Rand and Mackenzie, the latter

86 Stuart Mackenzie (*left*) beating Teodor Kocerka in the final of the Diamond Sculls at Henley, 1960

beating the former in the third round and going on to record his fourth successive win, beating the 1955 European champion and winner of the Diamonds in 1955 and 1956, Teodor Kocerka of Poland, by half a length. A week later, Mackenzie again beat Kocerka at Lucerne but ill-health prevented him from representing Australia in the Olympics.

Rand won the ARA single sculls trials and went to Rome, where Britain contested all seven events on Lake Albano but only the coxless four, stroked by Davidge, reached the finals, finishing fifth. The Germans, who took three gold and two silver medals, finally broke the United States' grip on the eights, the Americans finishing only fifth. The USSR took two golds and a silver.

The emergence of university crews rowing in the summer, including strong crews from the University of London, and of new composite crews from recently formed clubs, such as Barn Cottage and Lou Barry's Tideway Scullers, was beginning to provide a serious challenge to the traditional clubs, such as London and Thames, and also to Leander. Indeed, Leander's pre-eminent position in British rowing was being steadily eroded, not least because many of those who, in the past, might have rowed for the Club, were being attracted elsewhere. In addition to this, the number and quality of top overseas crews continued to increase and while, in 1961, there was only one overseas entry for the Grand, this was the formidable USSR Navy Sports Club eight. Leander was represented, after a gap of four years, by an Oxford eight containing four of their Olympic eight and three other Blues, while the Molesey eight contained six of their 1960 winning Grand crew. These two drew each other, Leander leading all the way to win by one length. In the semi-final, Leander led Thames by only a quarter of a length at the Mile but then drew away to win by one length. However, they were no match for the Soviet crew's greatly superior weight and strength, losing by two and a quarter lengths. Leander withdrew from the Stewards' and the Soviet Trud Club won a straight final from Thames.

The Soviet sculler, Oleg Tjurin, beat Rand in the Diamonds but lost to Mackenzie, who was representing the Sydney club, Mosman, and recorded his fifth consecutive win, equalling J. Lowndes's record set from 1879 to 1883.

It was indicative of the way things were going that Leander broke with tradition by entering a four for the Wyfold Cup. An entry for the Wyfold had been approved in 1958 but did not materialise, and when the Captain, Peter Sutherland, announced to the Committee in May 1961 that a Wyfold four were among the five Henley entries he was proposing to make, the Committee did not demur at this major break with the Club's traditional policy of entering for only the major Henley events. At a subsequent Committee meeting it was unanimously decided that 'the Captain should aim to enter his crews for the senior events in the country, such as the Grand and the Stewards', and any international event, but should be permitted to enter his crews for any lesser event if he felt that by doing so he would give them experience which would be advantageous in obtaining his ultimate object . . .' but it was stated that such crews should row in plain zephyrs. This paved the way for the introduction of the Club's cadet scheme a few years later.

The four that competed in the Wyfold hardly fitted these conditions. Containing a former Cambridge Blue and a recent Oxford President, in former days this four would have competed in the Stewards', but it was a further indication of the rising standard of the minor Henley events that the four lost easily in the third round.

The Grand eight were unable to continue after Henley and Molesey went as the eight to the European Championships, finishing fifth, but Britain won a medal in the Double Sculls when George Justicz and Nick Birkmyre, the Henley winners, took the silver medal.

In 1961, although Club crews were often training on the Tideway, the Club parted with the remainder of its interest in the Putney boathouse but was allowed the use of its facilities and half a bay for rack space.

For the Grand in 1962, Leander put on a crew which included one Cambridge and five Oxford Blues, stroked by Oxford's Olympic stroke, Mike Davis. Molesey had their 1961 eight with one change, the Cambridge Blue, John Beveridge, coming in at four. The holders, the USSR Navy Club crew, also had only one change from their 1961 eight. With Pennsylvania, Yale, and Moto Guzzi from Italy, four of whose crew had been in the winning eight at the previous European Championships, and the 1961 Thames Cup winners, the University of London, also competing, this was arguably the strongest ever entry in depth for the Grand.

Leander again drew Molesey and equalled the Barrier record when leading by half a length, but Molesey, never striking less than 40, went through before the Mile, to win by three-quarters of a length. The ultimate winners, however, were the Russians, who beat Moto Guzzi by a third of a length.

The Club had more luck in the sculling events that Henley, with the 1961 European silver medallists, Justicz and Birkmyre, now representing Leander, retaining the Double Sculls, and Mackenzie, back in Leander colours, registering a record sixth and final win in the Diamonds. In his semi-final, Mackenzie had been involved in an unfortunate incident when he had been warned on several occasions for washing his Polish opponent, Kubiak, when only a bare length ahead. Despite this, Kubiak gradually overhauled Mackenzie until the latter's lead at the Mile was only three feet. Mackenzie then appeared to falter but as soon as the Pole had drawn ahead, he spurted. Kubiak was then warned but before he could move over, Mackenzie appeared to hit his puddle and caught a crab. Kubiak crossed the line several lengths ahead but was disqualified after Mackenzie appealed. So incensed was the Polish team manager, Teodor Kocerka, that he immediately withdrew the other Polish entry, a Goblets pair. It left an unpleasant taste in many British mouths since the general feeling was that Mackenzie should have been disqualified for his frequent infringements earlier in the race. It was an unfortunate end to Mackenzie's distinguished Henley record.

Mackenzie went on to represent Great Britain at the first World Championships which were inaugurated at Lucerne that year, but he finished second to his old adversary Vyacheslav Ivanov, the 1956 and 1960 Olympic gold medallist and reigning European champion. Justicz and Birkmyre could finish only fifth but went on to take the gold medal in the Commonwealth Games at Perth, Australia.

Henley 1963 was the wettest for many years but at least the Russians did not compete. The Club Minutes reveal that, despite increasing standards at Henley, the Leander Grand eight did not start training together until April and it was not surprising that they were well beaten by the University of London, who confirmed their rise to the top in British rowing by taking the Grand for the first time, defeating Cornell in the final by three-quarters of a length, though they could manage only fifth place in the European Championships at Copenhagen, where Germany again won the eights.

That Henley saw the re-introduction of a coxed-four event, equivalent to the Stewards' class, for the Prince Philip Cup. Leander did not put on a four for this nor for the Stewards', Auckland RC, New Zealand, emerging as the first winners of the new event. Mackenzie joined Davidge, who had returned to the Leander fold, for both the Goblets and Double Sculls. They won the former, beating the 1958 European Champions, Veli Lehtelä and Toimi Pitkänen of Finland, in the first round and the Amlong brothers of Vesper BC, Philadephia, in the final, but they lost in their heat of the Double Sculls to the ultimate winners, Alwin and van der Togt from Holland. Justicz and Birkmyre did not compete.

That Henley was Davidge's last. He had competed every year since 1947, taking the Silver Goblets three times, the Grand twice, and the Stewards', Double Sculls, Ladies' and Visitors' once each, six of these wins in Leander colours. This was the best individual post-war Henley record at that time, and in addition to these successes, he won one gold and one bronze medal in both the European Championships and the Commonwealth Games.

His active career was, however, not quite finished. His pair with Mackenzie, together with a new Leander double, Peter Webb and Arnold Cooke, competed in the European Championships, the pair finishing fifth and the double qualifying only for the newly introduced small finals, for seventh to twelfth places, in which they finished eighth but ahead of the Dutch Henley winners.

On the social side, HMS *Leander* had expressed an interest earlier that year in renewing contacts with the Club, which resulted in a party of the ship's officers lunching at the Club after the Regatta.

A rather more unusual social activity by the Club was the adoption of a baby hippo at Whipsnade Zoo, members of the Club being entertained by the Director of the Zoo at a naming party, during which the hippo was duly named Leander and presented with a Club cap, which was hung in the compound. There were reports in the national dailies and baby Leander made several TV appearances, all of which amounted to good publicity for the Club.

In 1963, the wind of change finally reached the ARA. As the result of memoranda from two pressure groups, the ARA's administrative organisation and international rowing policy underwent major changes. Two of the most significant of the latter were the appointment at the end of the year of Jim Railton, a Loughborough-trained former athlete and 100-metre runner, as Director of Training, and

87 Christopher Davidge

the decision to set up a national squad for the first time. The ARA also continued to search for a suitable site for an international-standard 2000-metre multi-lane rowing course.

In December, the ARA appointed Jumbo Edwards as chief coach to the national squad which was to be formed in the autumn of 1984 after the Tokyo Olympics. Under the title of the Nautilus Club, the scheme eventually failed as the country's top oarsmen preferred to sit on the fence to await developments, and in its first year Nautilus entered only moderate crews for the Grand, Stewards' and Prince Philip.

Meanwhile, domestic rowing carried on normally but a special feature of Henley's 125th Anniversary Regatta in 1964 was the return of the complete Harvard eight that had won the Grand in 1914. They went for a ceremonial outing and presented the Henley Stewards with a replica of the Grand Challenge Cup to replace the existing one which was suffering from wear and tear. In return, the Stewards gave them a commemorative dinner at Leander.

Conditions at Henley were fast and there was an outstanding crew for the Grand from Viljnus, Lithuania. The Leander eight included seven Oxford Blues and had won the Marlow Grand but they lost their heat at Henley to Thames after having had clear water at Remenham Club. They were still leading by a quarter of a length at the last signal but fell to pieces as Thames launched their final attack at 42 and went past them to win.

However, no British crew could get near Viljnus, who won all their races with verdicts of 'easily'. They equalled Cornell's 1957 record when beating Harvard and then lowered the Fawley and course records against Thames, taking seven seconds off Cornell's time. In the final, against the University of London, Viljnus broke the Barrier record and lowered their own Fawley record by two seconds, though, in winning by 18.2 seconds, they were actually two seconds outside their record at the finish. It was a rout for British rowing.

In the Stewards', a Leander four drawn from the eight reached the final but lost easily to the Tideway Scullers, who had now taken over from where the Barn Cottage/Molesey composites had left off. This was the Scullers' first Henley win.

Once again, it was in the small boats that Leander found success, the Club having no fewer than four entries in the Goblets, which resulted in an all-Leander final, the Cambridge Blues Kiely and Lecky, American and Canadian respectively, beating Hall and Napier by two lengths.

Justicz and Birkmyre returned in the Double Sculls and met the Club's other entry, the 1963 representative double, Webb and Cooke, in their heat, in which the boats overlapped all the way. Justicz and Birkmyre put in a tremendous final spurt to win by a quarter of a length and went on to beat a Danish double that had finished seventh in Copenhagen in the final.

Justicz and Birkmyre did not continue after Henley and Webb and Cooke were selected for the European Championships in Amsterdam,

88 Webb and Cooke leading Justicz and Birkmyre along the Enclosures in a heat of the Double Sculls at Henley, but the latter went on to win

where they were the only British crew to reach a main final, taking the silver medal. In the eights, Viljnus, outstanding at Henley, were beaten into second place by the Ratzeburg eight by two-hundredths of a second, which put the current state of British rowing in perspective.

The double were unable to repeat their Amsterdam form at Tokyo, finishing seventh. However, the Tideway Scullers four, to which the selectors had made two changes, making them in effect the first ARA composite crew, won the silver medal in the coxless fours.

Leander was now no longer able to raise crews for the Grand capable of reaching winning standard, and none of the home Clubs could either, which resulted in two overseas crews, Vesper, the American Olympic winners, and Ratzeburg, the silver medallists and European champions, producing one of the most memorable Grand finals in Henley's long history. The Germans, never below 39, were always slightly ahead and gained their revenge for their Tokyo defeat by half a length, demolishing all the records set by Viljnus the preceding year, the full course time by an astonishing seven seconds. In two years, the Grand record had been lowered by fourteen seconds.

The Club won the Prince Philip that year but it was with an 'adopted' crew consisting of four Americans from Yale who had filled the stern seats of that year's winning Oxford Boat Race crew. They broke the record at every point, but, representing the United States in the European Championships at Duisburg, they were outclassed and finished eleventh. Leander had other representatives at these Championships in the shape of an unlikely double, Nick Cooper and Stuart Mackenzie. Put together for the Championships, they had little chance and finished eighth.

In 1966, the international scene took on yet another new dimension when the German Democratic Republic were allowed by FISA to compete separately from the German Federal Republic. In 1965 there had been three East German entries for Henley, Gorny and Bergau winning the Goblets, and in 1966 they descended on Henley with a vengeance, winning five of the six major events. Of Leander's entries in the Goblets, Double Sculls and Diamonds, only Nick Cooper and Arnold Cooke in the Double Sculls reached their final, losing to an East German double.

In the remaining years of the decade, the Club suffered one of its leanest spells, with no wins in any of the top Henley events, but the Club Committee, having taken stock of the situation and anxious about the Club's dwindling status as the result of rapidly rising standards, had already taken a bold decision. Convinced that one answer lay in recruiting young oarsmen from rowing schools to build up a nucleus for the future, and after the rowing masters of the leading rowing schools had been consulted, the Leander Cadet scheme was set up, with the active support of Peter Sutherland and John Hall-Craggs. The Cadets were recent school leavers nominated by their school coaches and made their first Henley appearance in 1965 in the Thames Cup with a crew who had all rowed in the Princess Elizabeth Cup the previous year. Although they lost by half a length to Pembroke College, Cambridge, they were the acorn from which an oak was soon to grow.

The Cadets' Thames Cup eight lost again the following year, while a Cadet Wyfold four reached the semi-final, losing to the ultimate winners, Norwich Union.

Success finally came to the Cadets in 1968. Training through the winter and coached by Derek Drury, who had produced the outstanding Emanuel School crews of the previous few years and was now teaching at Shiplake College, they won the Thames Cup event at Reading and the Marlow Eights. With three former Emanuel oarsmen and the ex-Radley oarsman, Tim Crooks, at six, they had clear water at Henley by the Barrier in their first three heats of the Thames Cup, but on the unfavoured Bucks station, which had been affected by a severe rainstorm, they were pushed much harder by Bedford, winning by a length. Back on the Berks station in the final, they romped away from Cornell, the holders, to win by four lengths, but so great was their superiority that the result was clearly not affected by the inequality of the stations.

The Cadets also entered for a new coxed-four event that year, the Henley Prize, the coxed equivalent of the Wyfold Cup, and renamed the Britannia Cup the following year. The Cadets reached the semi-final before losing to the eventual winners, Crowland, but a Wyfold four lost in the second round. One of the latter four, Vic Pardhy, a former Captain of Boats at Emanuel, was still a junior and later won the single sculls at the third National Youth Championships. He went on to take the single sculls bronze medal in the second FISA Junior Championships, which later became the World Championships for Juniors.

The Cadets had quickly made their mark and they retained the Thames Cup for the next two years. In 1969 the Henley Stewards decided to introduce a system of selecting certain crews in the draw, mainly to prevent early clashes between overseas crews or obviously outstanding crews, and that year Leander were one of five selected crews in the Thames Cup. The official *Henley Records* stated:

> Leander were much faster than any other crew in the event. They disposed of Garda Siochana, Isis, and Harvard, all well thought of and the latter two selected crews, by an aggregate of more than eight lengths, on their way to the final. Only Harvard, in the semi-final, led them briefly off the start.

In the final, against the previously unbeaten Pennsylvania freshmen, Leander led by two lengths at Fawley and crossed the finish line three lengths ahead.

In 1970, the Cadets took the Thames Cup event at Reading for the third year running but unexpectedly failed to retain the Marlow Eights. However, they again dominated the Thames Cup at Henley. They were clear at the Barrier in every race and in the final beat London, stroked by the Oxford Blue, Fred Carr, who had beaten the Marlow winners, Quintin, in their semi-final. Leander's winning time was only one second slower than that of the winning Ladies' Plate crew, the Dutch students from Aegir, Groningen.

The validity of the Cadet scheme had been proved and its main aim, to provide the Club with top-class oarsmen for the future, was eventually realised in the following decade, when eight members of the three winning Thames Cup crews became full internationals.

Meanwhile, in 1967 the Club had tried once again to find a Grand crew of the right class and was represented by the full Cambridge crew. Although the order had been shuffled, this was a losing Boat Race crew and inevitably succumbed easily in their heat to an East German crew who were not their best eight. On their way to an easy win in the final, the Germans also beat Oxford, with six of their winning Boat Race crew. All six of the major trophies went overseas again and the Thames Cup, for which Leander had not entered that year, also went overseas. It was another black Henley for home crews.

The Leander cadets come good with clear wins in the Thames Cup
89 *(Top)* Beating Cornell University, USA, by 4 lengths, 1968
90 *(Bottom)* Beating the University of Pennsylvania, USA, by 3 lengths, 1969

9

Moving With the Times
The 1970s

The Club's 150th anniversary occurred in 1968, in which year the Club President was Harold Rickett, who was also that year elected as the first President of the ARA. The anniversary was celebrated with a ball on July 6th and a dinner two days later, the Monday before Henley. The Duke of Edinburgh had been unable to attend the dinner but made a short visit to the Club on July 11th.

At the dinner, an Appeal had been launched with a target of £25,000 to settle some outstanding liabilities and to complete the modernisation of the clubhouse, as well as to improve the boating facilities. Work carried out in 1963 and 1964 had cost £17,771 but much remained to be done. The intention was for a better social club to increase the profitability of the Club's facilities, as well as to promote a more active rowing scene. The Appeal ran for eighteen months but fell short of its target, standing at just over £21,000 when it was closed. At the same time, expenses in running both the clubhouse and expanding rowing commitments, which now included the Cadet scheme, were escalating and the Club's finances were in a serious state.

To accompany the launch of the Appeal, Harold Rickett and Richard Burnell produced *A Short History of Leander Club*, in which the closing paragraphs read:

> In the past ten years the Club may seem to have suffered a recession, compared with the dominant position it enjoyed in the past. Yet in these same ten years, besides earning two gold and two silver medals abroad, Leander has won nine Henley trophies. No other club, and indeed no single country, has won as many in the same period. Nor, of course, has Leander passively accepted the position as regards eight-oared and four-oared rowing. The Club may enjoy a reputation for conservatism but the gentleman who made the gibe about the hippopotamus* really missed the point. For, wherever it may direct its nose, the hippopotamus is also a remarkable example of adaptability. And the fact is that no other club, in the past hundred years, has changed so much, in its membership, in the premises and facilities it offers, or in its approach to rowing. It is this ability to trim its sails to the winds of change which has made Leander the Club it now is, and enables its members confidently to look to the future, and to believe that the historian of the 200th anniversary will have equally good cause to call the toast:
> 'CORPUS LEANDRI SPES MEA'.

Brave words, but these pages have already shown that the Club was facing some real problems if it was to regain its traditional place

---

*A newspaper report had suggested that the hippopotamus was the only aquatic creature, apart from the members of Leander, which kept its nose permanently in the air.

in English rowing. The hard truth was that the Club had not won the Grand or Stewards' for fifteen years, while wins in the Goblets in 1964 and the Prince Philip in 1965 were by transatlantic oarsmen in Leander colours, and the two Diamonds' wins in this period were by an Australian. In fact, only four 'home-grown' oarsmen – Davidge, Leadley, Justicz and Birkmyre – had featured in the Club's nine wins between 1957 and 1967, a situation that was not encouraging if genuine Club crews were to succeed again. The Club had been upstaged, first, by Barn Cottage and Molesey, and later by the Tideway Scullers. Both London and Thames, realising that only the small-boat events were within the range of club crews, had stopped competing in the Grand by 1967. It was against this background that the Leander Cadet scheme had been created.

A handicap had been that the country's top oarsmen had been shuffling between clubs while seeking their best chances of Henley wins and international selection. Several of them had won at Henley with three different clubs. This scattering of the country's most talented oarsmen, while it brought relative success to various private armies, was counter-productive when it came to finding top-class international representative crews. Recognising that many of the crews competing in the top Henley events were, in effect, composite, the Stewards in 1970 allowed composite crews to compete as such in the major events.

In January 1969, Harold Rickett had resigned as President of the ARA on doctor's orders. Sadly, it was too late and he died within a fortnight. He had retired as Chairman of Henley in 1965 after fourteen years in that

91 Harold Rickett with the Queen Mother, Henley 1964

office. An immensely influential figure in the rowing world, his death was a great loss to British rowing in general and to Leander in particular. His successor as Club President was Derek Mays-Smith, but he, too, was already mortally ill and died the following year, to be succeeded in turn by Rickett's brother, Graham.

Another of the Club's stalwarts, one of the last of the Victorian and Edwardian giants and the oldest surviving Blue, Don Burnell, died at the end of the year at the age of 93. In addition to his 1908 Olympic gold medal, he had won the Grand four times and the Stewards' three times. A Henley Steward for fifty years, he was President of the Club from 1952 to 1957.

An addition to the Club membership that year was Thomi Keller, the President of FISA, who was elected an Honorary member. Six years later, he was elected a Henley Steward.

Leander was represented in the 1969 European Championships at Klagenfurt by the former Oxford Blues, Jock Mullard and Peter Saltmarsh, in the coxless pairs. They had won the ARA trials but failed to reach the last twelve at the Championships and a full British team again won no medals.

The most fruitful outcome from Klagenfurt, however, occurred on land. The ARA, realising that urgent remedies were required, held discussions with a Czech national coach and Olympic bronze medallist, Bohumil Janousek, and later than year he was appointed as the ARA's first full-time national coach. This was the catalyst for significant changes in the organisation and direction of Britain's international aspirants. It was to have a major effect on club rowing, especially Leander's, in the 1970s, although domestic rowing was not immediately affected by the arrival of 'Bob' Janousek, who was busy learning English and assessing the standard of British rowing.

In 1970, the potential Leander Grand eight won the Marlow Grand for the first time since 1964 but against crews of only Thames Cup class. The Grand eight included seven men from the recent winning Thames Cup eights, plus Mullard, and at Henley beat Dartmouth College, USA, in their heat before succumbing to the Groningen students, Aegir, by three-quarters of a length after a close race. At least the Club had produced a competitive Grand eight again. Aegir eventually lost the final to Vorvaerts, Rostock, by only half a length. The opponents of the winning Cadet Thames Cup eight in the final, mentioned earlier in these pages, were the Aegir second eight.

Overseas crews again carried off all the major trophies, as well as the Ladies', Wyfold and Princess Elizabeth. It was the worst ever Henley for home crews, a clean sweep that offered Janousek only the prospect of a new broom for British rowing.

The Leander Grand eight competed at Amsterdam after Henley but finished only fifth behind the Tideway Scullers. Two of the eight, Tim Crooks and Glyn Locke, then formed a pair for the ARA trials but, with only three days' practice, they lost in the final and the Club was not represented in the World Championships at St Catharine's, Ontario, where none of the British entries reached a main final.

A major development in 1971 was the new 2000-metre multi-lane course at Holme Pierrepont, near Nottingham, which was now nearing completion and meant that good training facilities were at last becoming available. In February, Janousek began to move tentatively towards a national squad and invited leading coaches to form a steering committee to programme the activities of Britain's top oarsmen and scullers. There were compulsory training weekends on the new course in May, followed by early trials in sculls, pairs and fours in June, the best eights having trials to sort out the fastest and so release members of the other crews to make up small boats, with the Rotsee Regatta at Lucerne to be used as the final trial for the team for the European Championships.

In the first assessments in May, the Scullers' eight twice beat Leander over 2000 metres, which left the Club with no option but to try again in the smaller boats. In June, Locke and Crooks won the coxless pairs trial and they were selected for Lucerne.

This new policy had not yet meant a clear division between the Club's domestic oarsmen and its international aspirants, and Locke and Crooks, who easily won the pairs at Marlow, also rowed in the Club eight that retained the Marlow Grand. This crew, composed of former Cadets, might have been considered rather a forlorn hope for Henley, but they very nearly upset the selectors' applecart. With only three entries for the Grand, one of which was the Cairo Police, who were not in the Grand class, Leander's heat against the Tideway Scullers was virtually the final. Leander led by three-quarters of a length at the Barrier and held this to Fawley. The Scullers then challenged hard and Leander led by little more than a canvas at the Mile the Scullers moving ahead at the bottom of the enclosures to win a fine race by half a length. They were unpressed by the Egyptians in the final.

The two clubs' second eights met in the semi-final of the Thames Cup, where it was the turn of the Scullers, with three internationals in their crew, to be rowed down. There was little between the crews until the last signal, where the Scullers led by a few feet, but the pressure was too great for one of their crew, who stopped rowing, Leander coming home alone. This race took a lot out of the Leander eight as well and they lost the semi-final by one length to Kingston, who in turn lost in the final by a third of a length to the Harvard lightweights.

However, Locke and Crooks at last brought Leander a win in a premier event, taking the Goblets when beating two Cambridge Blues, Chris Dalley and Robin Winckless, rowing for Quintin, in the final. The modest overseas entry that year meant that of the top Henley events, only the Diamonds went abroad.

At Lucerne the following weekend, Britain reached five finals but won none, Locke and Crooks finishing fifth in the Coxless pairs. In the European Championships at Copenhagen, the pair were eighth, but no other British entry finished higher.

At these Championships, Janousek, who was officially still only a consultant to the British team, told them that they were still 'playing at rowing' and asked for more dedication, warning them at the same time that they could not expect results overnight.

The outcome was that for the 1972 Munich Olympics the selectors decided to form a squad of oarsmen to be totally detached from domestic competition and based initially in London, Cambridge and Henley, with Janousek in overall charge. A key decision was that only members of the squad would be considered for the Olympics. It had been lack of this backing that had doomed the Nautilus scheme to failure and it effectively ended the private armies of recent years. This revolutionary policy, for such it was, received the endorsement of the ARA Council and had the full support of oarsmen and coaches. The pattern of domestic rowing was being changed irrevocably and Leander was going to have to come to terms with it. From this point, the story of the Club's top oarsmen becomes closely interwoven with that of the national squad and in the next few years, Leander men played a vital part in the development of Janousek's squad, many of them holding key positions in the top crews.

Until 1974, squad men were available to row for their clubs in the Head of the River Race and in 1973 the Club won the Head for the first time with an eight who were all squad members, stroked by Dick Lester. In 1975, Janousek's ARA eight, entered as such and stroked by Tim Crooks with three other Leander men behind him, annihilated the opposition in the Head, winning from the Tideway Scullers by a massive thirty-five seconds and taking six seconds off the Scullers' 1964 record time. The Leander Club eight, with no squad members, finished fourth.

Janousek's squad for the Munich Olympics in 1972 brought home no medals, but the best performance came from the Leander squad double, Pat Delafield and Tim Crooks, who had done well at continental regattas and had won the Double Sculls at Henley, following this with a second place at Lucerne. At Munich the double qualified for the final, in which they set off at a cracking pace, to lead at 500 metres, but this was a suicidal effort and by 1000 metres they had been caught by the Soviet double. The writing was now on the wall and at 1500 metres they had been overhauled also by Norway and East Germany. With nothing left to give, they eventually finished fifth, the USSR taking the gold medal. This was Britain's best result and although the rest of the team all reached the semi-finals, none qualified for the main finals.

Janousek's first medal success came the following year through the Cambridge Blues, Mike Hart and Chris Baillieu. Competing at Henley as Leander/Cambridge University, they had won the Double Sculls, after having been involved in an epic semi-final against a Soviet double, Gennadi Korschikov, the 1972 Olympic champion, with a new partner, Juri Malischev. The Soviet double, leading by half a length at Fawley, where they broke the record, came almost to a standstill along the enclosures when they were caught by the British double, who went on to break the course record and beat a Swiss double, Isler and Ruckstuhl, in the final.

For the 1973 European Championships at Moscow, the last to take place before annual World Championships were introduced the following year, the Soviets had reverted to their winning Olympic double, Korschikov and Alexander Timoshinin, but they finished second to the East Germans, the British double taking the bronze, to win Britain's first medal since 1964.

Hart and Baillieu went on to have a distinguished career. In Leander colours, they won the Henley Double Sculls in 1975, 1977 and 1978, not having competed in 1976, an Olympic year. They took the World Championship bronze in 1974 and 1975, and the silver at the Montreal Olympics in 1976. In the *Rowing Almanack*, Desmond Hill wrote of this performance:

> They started really well but after 45 seconds they were last, having been hit by what Chris described as 'an enormous bloody gust'. On the far side West Germany had shot off like scalded cats but though they led at 500 metres they had been swallowed up at 1000, where the Russians were a length ahead, striking an effortless 30 and, on my notes, 'looking too good'. Even with the memory of their storming finishes in

92 Mike Hart and Chris Baillieu, winning the World Championship in Amsterdam, 1977

the past, I don't think anyone at this stage gave the Britons more than a very outside chance of a bronze, for they were four seconds from the lead...

The Hansens made their move at 1450 metres with the East Germans on their tail, and it was suddenly apparent that the Russians were totally one-paced.

The Britons were still fourth but within half a length of the DDR and by now Baillieu was in full cry. He went past Russia as though they were at anchor, cut down the East Germans 200 metres out and, for the first time ever, was overlapping the Norwegians on the line.

The Norwegians, Frank and Alf Hansen, who were also the reigning world champions, retired, temporarily, as it turned out, after the Olympics and in 1977 Hart and Baillieu won at Lucerne and then took the gold medal at the World Championships, Britain's first open-weight world gold, the lightweight eight having won their event earlier.

The Norwegians, whom Hart and Baillieu never beat, returned for the 1978 World Championships on Lake Karapiro, New Zealand, relegating the Leander double to the silver medal position, after which Hart retired. Both had earlier been awarded MBEs.

Baillieu was then joined by Jim Clark of Thames Tradesmen's, better known as an oarsman who had won three silver medals, but although the new combination won at Henley in 1978, they could finish only fourth in the World Championships that year and in the 1980 Olympics, after which Clark reverted to rowing.

Baillieu also had considerable success as a single sculler, winning the Wingfield Sculls four times and the Scullers Head a record nine times between 1974 and 1984, always in Leander colours. After his double with Clark broke up, he concentrated on single sculling,

93 Chris Baillieu, winner of the Diamond Sculls, 1981, 1982 and 1984

winning the Diamond Sculls in 1981, 1982 and 1984. He was Britain's single sculler for the World Championships in 1981 and 1982, finishing fourth and sixth respectively, and then tried once more in 1983 in a double with a young former Junior international, Joff Spencer-Jones of Bewdley. There were no overseas entries for the Double Sculls at Henley, Baillieu and Spencer-Jones winning their three races easily, to give Baillieu a record sixth win in this event. However, in the World Championships the double failed to survive the *repechages* and although Baillieu tried unsuccessfully to win selection as the single sculler for the 1984 Olympics, his long and distinguished international career had finally come to an end. Still smarting from his non-selection for the Olympics, Baillieu recorded his third Diamonds' and ninth and last Henley win, defeating Hugh Matheson, the 1979 winner, on his way to winning the final from the Danish world lightweight champion, Bjarne Eltang, by four lengths. Baillieu's voice has since become familiar as a BBC TV commentator for the Boat Race and international championships.

Having concentrated on small boats in 1972 and 1973, Janousek formed an eight for the 1974 World Championships. At Henley, rowing as Leander/Thames Tradesmen's, the ARA eight, stroked by Crooks, with three other Leander men, John Yallop, David Maxwell and Hugh Matheson, filling the other stern seats, easily beat the Tideway Scullers in their heat of the Grand, to meet the Trud eight in the final. The ARA eight took an early lead of three-quarters of a length but the Soviet crew went ahead along the enclosures, to win a fine race by half a length.

In the World Championships at Lucerne, using a unique set of carbon fibre reinforced oars with narrow looms, the eight hit their best form, taking the silver medal, one second behind the USA, with New Zealand, East Germany, the Soviet Union and West Germany behind them in that order. After years in the wilderness, it was something of a breakthrough.

The following year, the squad eight, again rowing as Leander/Thames Tradesmen's with six of the 1974 silver-medal eight included, were the only home crew in an entry of five for the Grand, the other entries being three from America and one from Canada. With Dick Lester stroking and with John Yallop, Richard Ayling, Tim Crooks and Hugh Matheson behind him, Leander men filled the five stern seats. In very fast conditions, Harvard broke Ratzeburg's 1965 course record by three seconds when beating the Union Boat Club,

Boston, who had four world champions in their crew, but later, with the wind registering 'nil', the Leander/Tradesmen's composite beat Vesper and equalled the new record.

All was set for a classic final but Harvard, with the stroke and six of the 1974 world champion eight, were completely outpaced by the ARA composite, who increased a lead of a length at the Barrier to three at the Mile and finally cruised home two lengths to the good, three seconds outside the new record. Although the honours were shared with three Tradesmen and their cox, Pat Sweeney, the Club, after a gap of twenty-two years, had at last put its name back on the trophy.

For the World Championships, which in 1975 were held for the first time at Holme Pierrepont, Janousek, to the immense disappointment of British supporters, split the eight into two fours, believing their chances of medals would be better in the smaller boats. This controversial decision did not quite pay off, both fours finishing fourth. In all, nine Leander men were in the British team that year; and also in the team the following year for the Montreal Olympics. At Montreal, when seven of the 1974 silver-medal eight, plus Dick Lester at stroke, competed in the eights, five of the crew again were from Leander. As in 1974, they hit top form at the right time and reached the final, of which Desmond Hill wrote in the *Rowing Almanack*:

> After New Zealand's searing start had given them a canvas in one minute and one and a half seconds at 500, Lester chose the East Germans' own spurt-point and bolted for home at 750 metres. He caught the Kiwis so defenceless that they rowed the third quarter four seconds slower than Britain and the DDR and were immediately out of the reckoning. I never clocked the British eight below 39, though they must have been fractionally lower at times. They led at 800 metres and, 300 metres on, had a third of a length as East Germany drew level with New Zealand. East Germany pulled back 0.3 of a second in the third quarter but the impossible still looked a real possibility. It was like watching your own club leading Manchester United five minutes from the end of a cup-tie – we were praying for the final whistle. It was, I believe, at this point that the BBC saw fit to cut off their sound radio commentary to make way for Max Bygraves, to such a furious reaction that their switchboard was jammed for an hour.
>
> Manchester United won in the end, of course, inching ahead 150 metres out, but it had been so desperately close that for both crews and supporters the reaction was more frustration at having come so close than delight at so splendid a silver. The delight still lingers . . . but what if there had been a following wind?

With the double also taking a silver, this was Britain's best Olympic result since the two gold medals in 1948.

Janousek resigned after the Olympics to become a leading boat builder but he had put British rowing firmly back on the international map. Leander had seven silver medallists at Montreal and the part played by the Club in Janousek's squads had re-affirmed Leander's position as the country's premier rowing centre.

While the Club's top oarsmen were playing their part in international rowing, the Club's non-squad oarsmen were also giving a good account of themselves. In 1972 they had a notable success, winning the Wyfold Cup for the first time. The Club four, though not a selected crew, were much the fastest crew in the event. In the final they led the South African squad four, Trident, by two lengths at the Barrier and eventually won by two and one-third lengths.

The Club had an excellent Henley in 1975. In addition to the successes of the double and the squad eight, the non-squad Club crews reached the finals of the Britannia and Wyfold. In the former, Leander were the pacemakers throughout, equalling the Barrier record in their opening heat and clipping a further three seconds off this and three off the Fawley record the following day without being pressed. The semi-final against University College, Dublin, proved to be their closest race, Leander drawing clear only after Remenham. In the final, Leander beat the Tideway Scullers by two lengths.

The Wyfold four, who earlier had also beaten the course record, had a tremendous tussle in their final with a high-rating Thames Tradesmen's four, the Tradesmen leading from the quarter mile. The crews overlapped until the last few strokes, when the Tradesmen drew clear, breaking the course record by a further three seconds to become the first Wyfold four to better seven minutes. The time was only seven seconds slower than the new Stewards' record set by Potomac, who bettered Quintin's 1965 record by five seconds.

In 1976, in the absence of ARA crews at Henley because of the early Olympic date, the Club entered a non-squad eight for the Grand, which, owing to the imminence of the Olympics, attracted only one overseas crew, the University of British Columbia, Leander drawing them in the preliminary heat. The Canadians led by half a length from the Barrier to the Mile, after which Leander began to reduce the deficit. Taking the lead just after the last signal, Leander then drew away fast to win by three-quarters of a length. In the semi-final against the University of London, Leander led by a length at the Remenham Club, holding off UL's final challenge to win by half a length. Against the Thames Tradesmen in the final, Leander were a few feet ahead approaching the end of the Island when a submerged log jammed their rudder, bringing the crew to a halt. The umpire, Kenneth Payne, ordered a re-row later in the day, when the crews raced level along the Island before the Tradesmen drew away to pass Fawley three-quarters of a length ahead. Leander had reduced this to half a length at Remenham but they could gain no more, the Tradesmen drawing away again along the enclosures to win by two-thirds of a length. Considering that the Club was without ten of its best men who were in the Olympic squad, this was a praiseworthy effort.

The Club lost in the final of the Thames Cup in 1977 to the fast squad lightweight eight, rowing in London colours, who later that year won the gold medal in the World Championships. The winning Thames Cup time was seventeen seconds faster than that of Trinity College, Dublin, in winning the Ladies' Plate.

The following year, Leander again lost to the London lightweights in a final that was not without drama. Leander were leading by three-quarters of a length at the Barrier when they struck a dinghy which had wandered onto the course, breaking two's blade. This led to a re-row later but Leander had gone off the boil and could not recapture their earlier form, losing by two lengths, a real tragedy for this excellent young crew.

However, Leander had their revenge in 1979. Stroked again by Chris Jones, backed by three others of the unfortunate 1978 crew, Duncan McDougall, John Pritchard and Gavin Sayers, they were unpressed on their way to the final, where they met the London lightweights for the third year running. Leander, determined not to be robbed again, stormed away from the start to reach the Barrier one length ahead. They had increased this advantage to nearly two lengths at Fawley, the lightweights making little impression thereafter. Leander won by one and a quarter lengths and, once again, the winning time was faster than that of the Ladies' Plate.

The eight had competed in several Continental regattas before Henley, taking a good third place at Salzgitter, near Hanover, close behind the British and West German squad eights. They were also third at Ratzeburg, less than three lengths behind the ARA eight, the winners, and then won the Marlow Grand, beating the University of California by two lengths.

In 1972, with the Holme Pierrepont course fully operative, the ARA had staged the National Championships of Great Britain for the first time, with squad crews winning all the major events except the eights, for which they did not enter. The Tideway Scullers' eight

94 Tim Crooks, winner of the Diamond Sculls, 1977 and 1978

95 Charles Wiggin and Andrew Carmichael, winners of the Silver Goblets, 1979

were the winners, a non-squad Leander eight taking the bronze medal. In the following years, Leander squad men took many gold medals but the highlight for the Club came in 1974, when Janousek's squad again carried off the five events for which they entered, Leander men figuring in all of them. The Club Cadet eight took the silver medal in the eights behind the Leander/Tradesmen's eight, while the coxless fours went to a Leander/Tradesmen's four drawn from the eight, with a Leander squad four second and a Leander/Scullers squad four third. The other half of the ARA eight took the coxed fours, a Leander squad member, Mark Hayter, was in the winning quadruple scull, and Hart and Baillieu won the double sculls. This multiple involvement gave Leander the men's *Victor Ludorum* by a massive points margin.

Other successes at Henley in the 1970s included wins by Tim Crooks in the Diamond Sculls in 1978 and 1979. In the latter year, Hugh Matheseon, then representing Thames Tradesmen's, beat the reigning world champion, the West German Peter-Michael Kolbe, who had twice defeated Crooks on the Continent that year. In the other semi-final, Crooks survived a desperate race with the selected Bulgarian sculler, Mincho Nikolov, coming from behind to win by half a length. Matheson had twice beaten the Bulgarian at the Nottingham International Regatta on the Holme Pierrepont course, and the scene was set for a classic Diamonds final. The scullers raced alongside each other to Fawley, where they were level, and Crooks then made his challenge to go clear by the three-quarter mile, where Matheson had nothing left to offer. The verdict at the finish was 'easily', which hardly did justice to a fierce struggle. Crooks later competed in the World Championships at Karapiro in New Zealand but he was unwell and could finish only eleventh.

A Leander squad pair, Charlie Wiggin and Andrew Carmichael, gave the Club a second win at Henley in 1979, taking the Goblets before going on to finish fourth in the World Championships.

Earlier that year a young Marlow sculler, Steve Redgrave, had risen to sixth place behind Baillieu in the Scullers Head, taking the junior pennant.

Three Presidents (watercolours by Paddy Page)

96 Derek Mays-Smith (1969–1970)

97 Graham Rickett (1970–1975)

98 Ran Laurie (1975–1980)

10

Renovation and Revolution
The 1980s

From Janousek's first tentative national squad in 1971 to the 1980 Olympics, twenty-four Leander oarsmen and a cox made between them sixty-seven appearances in the national teams, winning thirty individual medals: eleven Olympic silvers and two bronzes, and in the European or World Championships, two gold, eight silver and six bronze medals, a record unequalled by any other British club. Despite having to provide so many good men to the national cause, the Club, in addition to sharing Henley wins in composite crews, had, in its own name, won thirteen Henley trophies: the Double Sculls five times, the Diamonds, Silver Goblets and Britannia twice each, and the Thames and Wyfold Cups once each. This tally beat the next best total, by the University of London, by five. The 'Brilliants' had reclaimed their traditional reputation, but at a cost.

While the Club's rowing commitments had been increasing steadily, its overheads had continued to escalate alarmingly. A Club lottery, the Pink Hippo Club, launched in 1970, had not been as successful as had been hoped and got off to a slow start, bringing only small sums into the coffers. The introduction of Associate membership, with limited privileges, in 1975, which was intended to help with the social side, had helped to swell the income, as did some new Life memberships, but the expense of maintaining an ageing building and of staffing it, as well as an expanding rowing side, was increasing faster than income.

In the mid-1970s, Henley had moved its regatta office into the clubhouse, which meant converting the garage and punt shed area. An appeal to Life members helped to defray some of the cost of this, which was shared with the Regatta, who also, of course, paid rent to the Club, but this did not help with deeper-lying problems. In the event, the Regatta's tenure was short-lived, rapidly improving finances eventually enabling the Stewards to build their present impressive headquarters by the Bridge. These were opened by the Queen in 1986.

The expenses incurred in the necessary renovation of the clubhouse, as well as urgent repairs, continued to climb steadily and the Club's bank overdraft rose alarmingly. The setting up of a Boat Fund shop by Ken Hylton-Smith, and sponsorship by Pimm's and BP, among others, helped to finance the rowing programme and some work on the building, but it was becoming clear that a major appeal for funds was the only hope of the club being able to pay for important structural work on the clubhouse.

This was a period of re-examination of all aspects of the Club's affairs, which led to a proposal in 1981 to admit women members. For the first time, a woman had that year coxed a Boat Race crew, this distinction going to Sue Brown, the victorious Oxford cox, while the Henley Stewards, now under the chairmanship of the dynamic Peter Coni, proposed the introduction of two invitation events for women at that year's Royal Regatta. With a woman, Penny Chuter, a single-sculls silver medallist in the 1960 European Championships, now in charge of the national squad and coaching top men's crews, and women playing an increasingly large part generally in the sport, a Special General Meeting of the Club was called in April to consider a proposal by Richard Burnell, seconded by Coni, that Rule 1 should be amended to read: 'Men and women shall be eligible to be admitted to membership of the Club in any category'.

Burnell argued that women were achieving rowing standards and giving administrative services to rowing which would qualify them for election if they were men, but after a two-hour debate, the motion was defeated by 41 votes for to 86 against. An amendment to give limited admission to women who had ceased to participate in first-class competition and who had given outstanding service to the sport was more heavily defeated, by 105 votes to 25. Several speakers thought that it was likely, if not inevitable, that women would one day be accepted to membership but that the time was not yet right, the prevailing view of the meeting being that, in any case, sex equality was not progress. The chauvinists were able to breathe freely again.

At the Annual General Meeting that year, the President, John Garton, announced the launch of the Appeal and the setting up of a Leander Trust with charitable status in order to benefit from tax relief from covenanted subscriptions. Legally, this could benefit only the rowing facilities and expenses, not the social side.

By the time of the AGM in 1982 the Appeal

99 John Garton, President 1980–1983 (watercolour by Paddy Page)

had reached a total of £55,000, though much of this was convenanted and so was not instantly available cash. The Club also received a substantial sum from the Trust for the use of the rowing part of the Club premises, but the original plan of the Trust taking a full repairing lease on all or part of the clubhouse was not

Renovation and Revolution: the 1980s

major source of income but this would, of course, involve yet more capital expenditure.

Meanwhile, soon after he had been elected Club Chairman in 1981, Dorrien Belson had arranged with the Committee to undertake a complete review of the state of the Club buildings:

> This we felt obliged to face up to in spite of inheriting a dismal financial situation. Within a few weeks a whole host of problems came to light . . . Major work needed to be done on the roof; the Club's fire precautions were wholly inadequate; the kitchen equipment was way out of date, and the electrical wiring was for the most part not only out of date but actually dangerous. Both the Fire and Health authorities could have closed the Club, certainly for any functions, and indeed threatened to do so, but each relented after accepting our promise to put matters right as a matter of urgency.
>
> Almost the whole interior of the Club – the entrance, the public rooms, the changing-rooms and the bedrooms were in an utterly shabby and run-down state. The only redeeming features were the gentlemen's lavatories and urinals which stood out then, as indeed they do today, as an impressive example of Victorian architecture.
>
> The Tissot painting, which was then hanging in the dining-room, and which was later sold for £200,000, was insured for £2,000, but there were virtually no security arrangements and anyone could come and go as they pleased.
>
> Why, we asked ourselves, had such a prestigious Club ever have been allowed

100 Kenneth Payne, President 1983–1988 (watercolour by Paddy Page)

possible since the Trust had insufficient funds to undertake the obligations the lease would involve.

By the end of 1982 the Club's overdraft had reached £131,000 and drastic steps needed to be taken. The Committee realised that some commercialisation of the clubhouse could be a to fall into such a sorry state?

Realising the urgent need for action, the Committee grasped the nettle and set about tackling the numerous problems. It was a mammoth task, leading to endless meetings with accountants, lawyers, architects, builders, security experts and others ... We were fortunate to have a very able Committee dedicated to the job, plus the invaluable help of the then President – John Garton – who, with myself, must have averaged over two days a week at the Club ...

By early 1983 it had become apparent that as well as raising the money by the Appeal (the Leander Trust), it would also be necessary to raise the rate of the annual subscription. At the Annual General Meeting in June, the Committee proposed increasing this from £38 to £69 (ie £60 plus VAT). The Committee reckoned this would enable the Club to return to a firm financial footing within a year or so and also enable the Club to be restored to its former position of repute. The Committee were so convinced of the strength and justification of their proposal that they agreed unanimously to stand by it at all costs and not to offer themselves for re-election if it were to be rejected by the membership.

However, the AGM was clearly unsympathetic to the efforts made by the Committee. The Minutes of the meeting record:

> Mr Coni (speaking as Cassandra) said there was complete mismanagement and that the present Committee was just as bad as the previous ones. He had no confidence in it ... and made an adverse comparison of the present management of the Club with that of Henley Royal Regatta ... Mr Coni then said that the Committee was out of touch, in particular with how to generate income; he said that female membership was essential and that during the Regatta, Associate membership was of no use.

Coni then put forward an amendment to the Committee's proposal, calling for the annual subscription, with effect from 1st January 1984, to be £45, including VAT. The amendment was seconded and passed by 31 votes to 19.

Garton then adjourned the meeting temporarily so that the Committee could consider their position and when the meeting reassembled, Garton announced that the Committee regretted that they would not be able to continue to conduct the financial affairs of the Club on a subscription rate as low as £45. The meeting then adjourned for a month, but the resumed meeting did not refer to the subscription, a Special General Meeting having already been called for 25th September. Coni's remarks had been the trigger that set in motion what has become known as the 'Pink Palace Revolution', though this is perhaps unnecessarily sensational. Nevertheless, it was to have far-reaching effects. Between the meetings of 26th June and 25th September, the opposing factions stated their cases, both sending circulars to members, the latter over the names of Tom Boswell and Jeremy Randall, while 'out of court' manoeuvres were rife and discussions tended to become animated.

The large turn-out at the SGM, 240 Full and eight Associate members, meant that the meeting had to transfer to the garden, it being, fortunately, a fine day. The meeting was told that a breakdown of the 226 letters received in response to the Committee's memo revealed that 137 favoured the proposal to reconsider the subscription, 77 opposed it, and 12 were undecided. Randall stated that he and Boswell had also received letters but did not elaborate. When the matter was put to the vote, 127 were for the subscription to be reconsidered and 107 against, but as this was less than the two-thirds majority required, the motion was lost and the subscription for 1984 remained at £45. Belson records:

> It seems curious to me now, but such were the rules governing the conduct of the SGM in September 1983 that I had no opportunity to speak. Perhaps it was just as well because, apart from a number of local members, few others had any real concept of the appalling state the Club was in at the time our Committee began its work, and consequently were not fully aware of the pressing need for the urgent action we thought best to recommend. It would indeed have been very difficult anyway to have attempted to bring home to members the reality of the Club's extensive decay in 1981 without implying very serious criticism of previous committees. This is why it was not done then or at any other time. ... However much this situation has been glossed over, I feel bound to emphasise it now if only because it remains the key factor behind the events that followed.

The Committee had earlier confirmed that if their proposals were defeated, they would not stand for re-election and a new Committee was then elected, with Kenneth Payne as President, Tom Boswell Chairman, Jeremy Randall honorary Secretary and Maurice Buxton honorary Treasurer. Peter Coni, Richard Burnell, Chris Etherington and Chris Baillieu were also elected to the Committee.

> 'This result', writes Belson, 'was obviously a disappointment to our Committee, probably the first one to have undertaken such an immense amount of work and to have achieved so much in such a short space of time. We should certainly have liked to finish the work which we had started. We recognised, however, that judgements of this sort are rightfully made by the Club members, amongst whom there will always be differences of opinion.'

The Club's financial affairs improved after the September meeting but, whatever Coni may have thought about the Committee at the AGM, the groundwork for this had been laid as the result of their strenuous efforts. For two years they had tried to lay a solid foundation for the future welfare of the Club, and the position had already begun to improve at the time of the change of Committee.

The essence of the difference of opinion in the rival views was whether the members themselves should be responsible for helping to set their Club on a firm footing or whether the Club should seek outside help from commercial interests, and the latter view seems to have won the day.

By the end of 1983, the introduction of a contract caterer, the conversion of heating to gas, donations in response to an appeal to Life members, the sale of unused boats and improvement in financial management had reduced the overdraft to £79,000. A Building sub-committee, with Coni as Chairman, was formed and by 1985 work on the clubhouse had been carried out with an interest-free loan of £230,000 from the Trust, which also donated £25,000 towards boats and building work associated with rowing. The ship was back on an even keel.

An arrangement with Pimms, who in 1983 had become the Club's main rowing sponsor, to make their contribution through the Trust meant that the benefit over four years would be £34,000. A £20,000 sponsorship by Jaguar in 1985 also alleviated the position further. Another source of income was the Club shop which contributed £9,950 in 1986.

In 1984 there had been a small increase of £7 in the subscription and in 1986 this was again increased, without opposition, to £60.

Before the new regime, the Committee had for some time been considering selling some of the Club's assets, notably the painting by James Tissot mentioned above of Henley Regatta, 1877, as well as certain items of silver, though the latter decision was later rescinded. In 1986 the Club donated the Tissot to the Trust and, although doubts had been expressed by some experts about the painting's authenticity, the sale realised, after expenses, £188,000 for the Trust.

Amid all the upheavals, rowing continued as normal, the Club having an unusual win in 1980 when one of its internationals, Bill Woodward-Fisher, won Doggett's Coat and Badge. His grandfather, a professional waterman, had won the coveted Coat in 1911 but by 1980 the event had long since ceased to be a professional one. Woodward-Fisher outclassed his opponents and won by twenty-eight seconds.

Under Chuter's direction as Senior National Coach, the national squad continued much as before. The Moscow Olympics in 1980 were marred by a boycott, led by the United States, because of the Soviet Union's involvement with Afghanistan, but this was not supported by the ARA. The British Olympic eight contained four Leander men: John Pritchard, Malcolm McGowan, Allan Whitwell and Duncan McDougall. Wiggin and Carmichael were the coxless pair, Gordon Rankine was in the coxed four and Bailleu in the double with Clark.

Although the Olympics were inevitably somewhat devalued by the boycott, medals were still hard to come by, but the British team hit good form, and the eight reached what turned out to be a classic final. Britain led at 500 metres, but with less than a second covering the first five crews. By 1000 metres the East Germans had broken away to lead the field by nearly a length, the next four crews still being within a second of each other, with Britain fourth.

At 1500 metres Britain surged past Australia and the USSR, to move into second place. With the Russians trying to get back on terms, they and Britain were closing on the East Germans when Britain's rudder strings broke. With singular presence of mind, the cox, Colin Moynihan, later to become Minister for Sport, grabbed the rudder bar and steered the rest of the race with his hands behind his back. Britain were overlapping the East Germans at the finish, to take a well-deserved silver medal. With the coxless pair and four taking bronze medals, this was an encouraging beginning to the new decade.

The Olympic team did not compete at Henley, which had its biggest entry ever, boosted by national teams from countries boycotting the Olympics. These included the United States, West Germany, New Zealand, Canada and Norway, resulting in another clean sweep of the top events by overseas crews. At a less exalted level, Leander's non-squad fours did well to reach two finals, the Wyfold four losing but the other four in Britannia, which contained three of the 1979 winning Thames Cup eight, were too experienced and two strong for the Wallingford schoolboys, whom they outweighed by 28 lb. a man, and won by two and a quarter lengths.

Pritchard and McGowan were again in the squad eight in 1981, with Richard Stanhope stroking. At Henley, rowing as Leander/Tyrian, they disposed of Boston and Washington Universities on their way to the final, where they met an Oxford University/Thames Tradesmen's composite containing five of that year's winning Boat Race crew, plus Justice and Whitwell from the Olympic eight and the Olympic coxless pairs bronze medallist, Charlie Wiggin, at bow.

In a fierce headwind in the final, the ARA eight gained three-quarters of a length before being pulled back by the Oxford composite, the latter taking a lead of three feet at the Mile. Spurt and counter-spurt along the enclosures finally went in Oxford/Tradesmen's favour and they won an outstanding race by half a length. Oxford's stroke, John Bland, was so exhausted after the race that he was taken to hospital as a precaution.

These crews had another desperately close race in the National Championships, Leander/Tyrian, who had finished second at Lucerne, reversing the Henley result to win by half a length. The outcome was that, for the World Championships in Munich, the crews were merged, with Pritchard, McGowan and Stanhope combining with three of the Oxford eight and two Tradesmen. The new eight took another silver medal, this time behind the Soviet Union.

In 1982, the squad eight rowed in the Grand as Leander/London. With Leander providing the stern four, Andy Holmes, John Pritchard, Malcolm McGowan and Richard Stanhope at stroke, they beat the University of California, Berkeley, in a paddle in their heat. In the final, they met the University of London, who had accounted for the previously unbeaten Yale eight. The Leander/London composite went off too fast and did not settle but they still led by two lengths at Fawley before UL began to whittle away at the lead. UL were overlapping at the bottom of the enclosures and were still closing at the distance board, when Stanhope settled the issue with a final spurt, to take the squad eight home with half a length to spare, giving the Club its second shared win in the event.

The eight went on to win at the National Championships, but the British team had become increasingly unhappy during the year and performed poorly at the World Championships at Lucerne, the eight finishing ninth and last. After the heart searching that followed, Bob Janousek was brought back to co-ordinate and organise the men's squads, but results in the 1983 World Championships were again disappointing and Janousek resigned, asserting that a full-time professional was needed to run the ARA's international rowing. Penny Chuter was then put in overall charge of the 1984 Olympic squad, with the unenviable task of eliminating the rivalry among the squad coaches which had played havoc with selection for the previous two years.

A Leander-based potential Olympic squad coxed four were assembled and coached by Mike Spracklen. Spracklen had been responsible for the rapid progress of the young Marlow sculler, Steve Redgrave, who, after narrowly missing the double sculls gold medal in the Junior World Championships in 1980, had won the Double Sculls at Henley in 1981 and 1982, and had also taken the recently established Queen Mother Cup for quadruple sculls in the latter year. His ambition was to become a top-class sculler and in 1983 he had won the Diamond Sculls, beating Tim Crooks in the final, for his fourth Henley win in three years. However, he was persuaded by Spracklen to stroke the 1984 coxed four, to which he agreed with considerable reluctance.

With Andy Holmes of Leander at three, the former London University 1981 World coxed pairs bronze medallist, Richard Budgett, at two, Martin Cross of Thames Tradesmen's, a triple bronze medallist in coxless fours, at bow, and coxed by Adrian Ellison, this four were outstanding at Lucerne, which, it being an Olympic year, was held before Henley. The four knocked five seconds off the Rotsee coxed fours record in beating the East Germans into second place. Then, rowing as Marlow/Tyrian, they won the Prince Philip easily but, with Holmes at three, Leander at least had a share in the victory.

In the Grand, the Leander/London squad eight, who included McDougall, Pritchard (who had won a Blue at Cambridge that year), Adam Clift, and McGowan, with Allan Whitwell stroking, became the first crew to reach Fawley in under three minutes. They then lowered the full course record by three seconds, despite winning easily from the University of Pennsylvania, before going on to beat the University of Washington comfortably in the final.

The Los Angeles Olympics were also devalued through a rather pointless boycott by Eastern bloc countries, who gave a security risk as the reason, but it smacked of a *quid pro quo* for the US-led 1980 boycott. In the case of the British coxed four, however, it had little effect on the result since they had comfortably beaten the Soviet and East German fours at Lucerne. The British four came through the rising early-morning mist on Lake Casitas to win Britain's first Olympic gold medal in this class of boat, beating the United States by half a length. This was also the first British Olympic gold since 1948 and a first Olympic triumph for the four's coach, Mike Spracklen. It was, however, the only British success at Casitas, the eight finishing fifth.

Since 1980, the Club, despite putting on some excellent non-squad crews at Henley, had had no success with them. The standard of the lesser events had been rising rapidly because of the invasion of crews that were really rowing below their class. In 1981, Leander lost in the semi-final of the Thames Cup to the United States development squad, rowing as the Charles River Rowing Association, to whom the Club eight were conceding 32 lb. a man. The same year, the Wyfold four lost in the final to the Canadian squad crew, Hanlan. In 1982, the Club eight in the Thames

Cup were a selected crew and reached the semi-final again, where they met Goldie, who included six of the Cambridge Boat Race crew. Goldie had clear water at Fawley but Leander crept back, to overlap at the bottom of the enclosures, though losing in the end by half a length. Another massive Charles River crew beat Goldie by two lengths in the final, but questions were asked as to whether these crews should not have competed more appropriately in the Grand.

In 1984, with a new input of recent school oarsmen, several of them junior internationals, the Club was able to enter two eights for the Thames Cup, the B crew losing in the second round, but the A crew, stroked by Mark Buckingham, with Simon Berrisford at six and the Cambridge Blue, Roger Stephens, at five, reached the final, having lowered the event record against Harvard. However, they then came up against another crew competing below their true class, the South African squad crew, who were rowing as Cantabrigian, and lost by two lengths. The South Africans had previously lowered the record at all points, their overall time of 6 min.16 sec. beating by two seconds Leander's time, set two hours earlier. The Thames Cup record was now seven seconds faster than the Ladies' Plate best time and was only six seconds slower than the new Grand record set by the ARA squad eight. This again made a mockery of the Henley status rules.

The Leander A eight went on to win the eights at the National Championships and then represented England in the Home Countries International at Blessington, near Dublin, holding off a late charge by the Irish eight to win by six feet. This was the Club's first appearance in Ireland since the Cork International Regatta in 1903.

The conflict between the demands of the national squads and the clubs, which had been becoming tense in recent years, continued in the early months of 1985 and there was a growing suspicion that Chuter's squad was deliberately being kept large to restrict any challenge to the squad crews that might come from the clubs.

Be that as it may, the Club was able to run two eights again that summer, the second eight being lightweights who won the lightweight event at the Belgian International Championships at Ghent, and later took the lightweight title at the British National Championships.

That year the Henley Stewards introduced long overdue changes to the regatta qualification rules, the Ladies' Plate being opened to club crews, while entries for the Thames Cup, with the exception of schools, was limited to British and Irish crews. The Club therefore entered for the revamped Ladies' Plate, which predictably drew a large and strong entry, twenty-one of the permitted thirty-six crews coming from overseas. The Club had two entries since the lightweights, who had originally been entered for the Thames Cup, were moved up by the committee of management to the Ladies', together with London and Molesey, although these crews were all eligible for the Thames Cup. This controversial decision was clearly a mistake since the presence of these crews in the Thames Cup would at least have made the British entry more competitive.

The lightweights beat Eliot House, USA, in their heat, but then found that giving away 21 lb. a man to Harvard was too much of a handicap, and they lost by one and three-quarter lengths. The A crew, however, with five of the 1984 Thames Cup finalists in the boat, and who had won at Ratzeburg, were one of eight selected crews, defeating Georgetown University, USA, Molesey, Vesta and Princeton on their way to the final, where they met the Irish police, Garda Siochana.

In their semi-final, Garda had narrowly defeated a powerful but not fully fit Norwegian eight, Ormsund, who included the Hansen brothers and two former coxless-pair world champions, and the final was another classic, with the lead changing twice. My report of this race in the *Sunday Telegraph* read:

> Leander attacked the Irish from the start and by the Barrier had drawn out to a length ahead. Garda gradually pulled them back and by the Mile had taken a lead of a few feet.
>
> It looked all over but Leander were not yet done. At the bottom of the enclosures they raised their rate to 40 and the Garda could not hold them. In a magnificent race in, Leander squeezed home by a canvas to become the first winners of the open event.

More significant was the time of 6 min. 26 sec., which was one second faster than the winning Grand time, the first occasion since 1949 that this has happened, and which in theory made Leander the fastest crew in the Regatta.

Whether they could have beaten Harvard* in a straight race is doubtful, but Leander's performance must raise questions about the effect of the new status rules, while Ridley's Thames Cup performances make a farce of the new rules for that event.

Neil Campbell's Ridley schoolboys, who had won the Princess Elizabeth five times between 1970 and 1979, were not the sort of crew that Peter Coni had envisaged for his new Thames Cup, and with the lowered standard of the home crews, who, under the new rules, were subject to restrictions on status, Ridley led from start to finish in all their races.

For the World Championships at Hazewinkel, in Belgium, Simon Berrisford, who had rowed six in the winning Ladies' Plate eight, was brought into the British eight, a development crew who finished seventh.

In 1985 Redgrave reverted to sculling, winning the Diamonds again, but he failed as a single sculler in the World Championships. The following year, training at Leander but still representing his local club, Marlow, he was joined in a pair by Andy Holmes, who had rowed behind him in the Olympic four. With Spracklen again coaching, Redgrave competed at Henley in both the Goblets and the Diamonds, but in the latter he suffered a humiliating defeat in the final. Having gone off far too fast, he was sculled to a standstill by the Danish world lightweight champion, Bjarne Eltang. However, the pair, in Leander and Marlow colours, were far too good for the opposition, winning easily. Holmes had an unexpected second win as a last-minute substitute for the injured Joff Spencer-Jones, in the ARA eight, Nautilus, who beat Pennsylvania in the final of the Grand.

Holmes and Redgrave competed as a coxed pair at Lucerne, where, with Pat Sweeney steering, they beat the reigning Olympic and

---

*Harvard had beaten Princeton in an all-American final of the Grand, in which the ARA eight did not compete.

101 Ladies' Plate: Leander beating Garda Siochana, Ireland, by a canvas in the final, 1985 (note the cox in the bows)

102 Leander's winning crew racing in the Ladies' Plate, 1985

World champions, the Italian Abbagnale brothers, the winning time setting a new world record.

This was a complicated year for British rowing, with the Edinburgh Commonwealth Games, for which rowing had been resurrected at Strathclyde Park, and the World Championships, for the second time, at Holme Pierrepont. In the former, Holmes and Redgrave represented England in the coxed fours and coxless pairs, while Redgrave was also chosen for the single sculls, a demanding programme. However, the four and pair both won, and Redgrave took the single sculls, becoming the first English sculler to do so. His three gold medals were also a record.

Holmes and Redgrave then crowned their outstanding season by winning the coxed pairs at the World Championships, the Abbagnales just snatching the silver medal from the East Germans. The Nottingham lightweight double, Allan Whitwell and Carl Smith, won a second gold for Britain and the women won two lightweight silver medals.

In the 1987 New Year's Honours, Redgrave was awarded an MBE, but Holmes was left out, which, with Olympic, World and Commonwealth gold medals to his name, was regarded by the British rowing world as an unwarranted snub. However, the situation was put right in the 1988 New Year's Honours.

In 1987, Mike Spracklen, based at Leander, was chief coach to the ARA men and, after trials at the Royal Albert Dock, he took another crop of Leander's best men into his group. The ARA crews, with one notable exception, did not enter for Henley, preferring to compete at Amsterdam the weekend before. This led the

103 Mike Spracklen

Club's Secretary, Jeremy Randall, to write to the ARA on behalf of the Committee, accusing them, by not competing at Henley, of damaging the relationship between the national squad and those clubs which had released their oarsmen to the squad; and, in particular, of embarrassing Leander with its sponsors through the absence of almost all the Club's best oarsmen. The Committee's view was that, should the situation recur, the Club would feel obliged to seek a return to a selection system based on squads under club control rather than on the centrally organised system then being operated.

The exception mentioned above was the coxless pair, Holmes and Redgrave, who went for the Goblets again and immediately set about demolishing records, breaking the Barrier record in their opening heat, and the Fawley and full course records in the second

104 Andy Holmes and Steve Redgrave at Henley

round. The final, against the Soviet Pimenov twins, three times world champions, was full of drama, the race being stopped when two women in a canoe strayed into the path of the British pair and capsized. There was no damage to the pair but Holmes, in anger, punched a hole in the canoe but fortunately without damaging his hand. The pairs returned to the start and the Pimenovs then shot off at a phenomenal rate to lead by a length at the Barrier. They held this until Holmes and Redgrave began to overhaul them and then suddenly threw in the towel at the Mile and stopped, the British pair paddling home alone.

At Lucerne, Holmes and Redgrave went for both the coxed and coxless events, a formidable task at what is Europe's premier regatta. They won the coxless pairs but failed by a length to the Abbagnales in the coxed event.

The World Championships at Bagsvaerd near Copenhagen became a lottery when the wind caused a big difference between lanes, but Holmes and Redgrave, doubling up again as the finals of the two events were, for the first time, held on different days, won the coxless pairs, the Pimenovs taking the bronze medal behind the Romanians. However, in the coxed event, the British pair had to settle for the silver, again behind the Abbagnales, but it was still a remarkable performance.

To underline the Club Committee's earlier grumble to the ARA, the Club, in addition to Holmes, was strongly represented at these Championships. John Maxey, John Garrett and the cox, Vaughan Thomas, were in the coxed four, who, after having broken the world record earlier, were particularly affected by a poor lane in their final, finishing fifth. Berrisford was in the coxless four that finished fourth and Terry Dillon and Steve Turner rowed in the eight, finishing ninth.

In February 1988, a Leander eight, all squad members and based on the previous year's representative eight, defeated Oxford in training races at Henley. Still rowing as Leander for sponsorship reasons, this crew rowed right away from the field in the Reading Head, beating Oxford by twenty-four seconds, with a Leander Under-23 eight fourth. It was the beginning of a good season for the Club.

The winning Reading crew represented the ARA squad in the Tideway Head. Starting second, they finished a split second ahead of the squad first eight, who were the previous year's coxed and coxless fours. The Leander Under-23s also did well, winning the Page Trophy as the fastest upriver Thames crew.

Redgrave, still representing Marlow, had a fourth win in the Wingfield Sculls, breaking the sculling record from Putney to Mortlake, which had stood since 1933, by ten seconds. However, in the summer he rowed in the pair in Leander colours.

At Henley, the ARA squad reverted to rowing in their club names, no doubt partly because of Leander's pressure the previous year. The Olympic eight designate competed in the Grand as Leander/University of London, the seven Leander members being Richard Stanhope, Pete Beaumont, Terry Dillon, Steve Turner, Nick Burfitt, and Simon Jefferies, the cox. Among the entries were the Australian 1986 world champions, who were their country's potential Olympic eight. They met Leander/UL in the final, watched by the Princess Royal from the umpire's launch in relentless rain. This was a magnificent race, which I reported for the *Daily Telegraph*:

It is unlikely that there will ever be a better race at Henley Royal Regatta than yesterday's final of the Grand Challenge Cup in which the potential British Olympic eight snatched victory on the last stroke to beat the Australian Olympic eight by one foot...

The Australians, striking 40 to the British eight's 39, led by a quarter of a length at the first signal. By the Barrier the Australians had increased their advantage to two-thirds of a length and were rowing with machine-like uniformity,

In contrast, the British oars looked less well controlled. However, approaching Fawley, with the British at 35 to their opponents' 39, the lead began to diminish.

A push at 40 by the Australians took it back to two-thirds of a length but this effort was expensive and could well have cost them the race. By the Mile, with Burfitt taking the British eight to 38, the difference was only half a length.

However, at the last signal, with the Australians at 40 and maintaining their half length, it looked as though they would hold out. By now the crowd in the enclosures were on their feet and the noise was deafening.

Spurred on by this support, Burfitt made his last big effort. Suddenly the Australians were struggling. From the launch it was impossible to see who had won, but the British crew's reaction and the roar of the crowd made it clear what they thought. It took a photograph to

105 Grand, 1988: Leander/University of London defeat the Australian Institute for Sport by one foot

separate the crews and Britain had won...

Naturally the Grand tended to overshadow everything else but half an hour later there was another excellent home victory when the Leander four, another crew seeking selection for Seoul, beat the already selected American four in the Stewards' Cup.

The Leander four finished fourth in last year's World Championships and yesterday they were soon in charge. Steering impeccably, they were one and a half lengths ahead at the Barrier and emphasised their class by equalling the Barrier record.

On a day when records did not seem to be in jeopardy, this was a sign of real pace. Leander were two and a half lengths ahead at Fawley and eventually won easily after Penn hit the booms opposite the Stewards' Enclosure.

This was the Club's first win in the Stewards' since 1953, but what should have been another sure win for the Club in the Goblets unexpectedly did not materialise, the pair having had to withdraw after winning their heat, with Holmes suffering from an earlier rib injury that had plagued their training and which also forced them to miss Lucerne the following week.

However, the Club, enjoying its best Henley for years, again reached the final of the Ladies' Plate, where their opponents were Mercantile, Melbourne, the Australian Under-23 eight. Leander led by a length at Fawley, where their time was only four seconds slower than that of the Grand, but the Australians eventually came storming through along the enclosures to win

106 Leander/University of London beating Syracuse University, USA in the semi-final of the Grand, 1988:

107 The Leander four after winning the final of the Stewards', 1988

108 (*above*) Winners of the Champion Cup at the Metropolitan Regatta, 1988: P. Hamer, R. Phelps, H. Trotter, D. Badcock, C. Greenaway, P. Rudaz, R. Stephens, A. Almand, G. Herbert (cox)

109 (*right*) Ghent, 1988 – Guy Blanchard and Rupert Fane, winners of the Under-23 coxless pairs

by a length, equalling the record and only six seconds slower than the winning Grand time.

In the Club's largest ever Henley entry, the Wyfold four went out in the semi-final and the Britannia four in the quarter-final. There were also entries in both these events from the recently formed Leander non-representative club, Star and Arrow, the Wyfold four reaching the quarter-finals.

At the National Championships, the Club's Wyfold four won the coxless fours and then missed the gold medal by centimetres in the *Match des Seniors*, the Under-23 championships, the Italians getting their bows in front almost on the last stroke to win by 0.28 of a second, although Richard Burnell, standing immediately behind the judges, was convinced that Britain had won. Leander, with four men and the cox, Garry Herbert, from the Ladies' Plate eight, took the bronze medal in the eights.

The winning Stewards' four finished second to the East Germans at Lucerne, where the eight were third to the West Germans. But in the Olympics at Seoul both just missed medals, each finishing fourth, as did the coxed four, but once again the pair came to Britain's rescue.

With Holmes recovered from the various ailments that had beset him earlier, he and Redgrave again went for both the coxed and coxless events, taking the coxless pairs for their second individual Olympic gold medals, but they were bitterly disappointed the next day when they could manage only third place in the coxed pairs behind the Abbagnales and the East Germans, who were not doubling up. The Leander pair had raced over 2000 metres six times in a week and, because of unprogrammed delays, they had had to race two semi-finals within an hour, which proved too much for even this exceptional pair. To everyone but the pair themselves, this was once again a truly outstanding performance.

The Club's contribution to the Olympic team had been thirteen oarsmen and three coxes, plus a spare man, out of a total of twenty competitors. Penny Chuter had her contract renewed by the ARA, and Mike Spracklen, Leander's coach and chief coach to the Olympic team, received an OBE in the 1989 New Year's Honours.

Holmes and Redgrave ended their partnership after Seoul but both continued to train in 1989, Redgrave smashing his own record in the Wingfield Sculls by an astonishing forty-five seconds, taking the title for the fourth time.

Early in the year, Spracklen had proposed to Chuter that Leander should become a training base for the men's heavyweight squad for the current Olympiad, and the Club came to an arrangement with the ARA for the squad's use of Leander's facilities, with squad members from other clubs not being required to join Leander. Spracklen had also proposed that a development squad should be formed but when this did not materialise, mainly for financial reasons, he resigned in April as the men's chief coach, although he continued as Leander's chief coach and offered to coach any squad crews who wanted to train with him at Leander. Not surprisingly, this brought him into direct conflict with Chuter, who had taken over as chief coach.

In June, Penny Chuter's contribution to rowing was recognised by the award of an OBE

110 Simon Berrisford and Steve Redgrave, winners of the Silver Goblets, and silver medallists, in the World Championships at Bled, 1989

in the Queen's Birthday Honours, but this came at an unfortunate time. The Leander squad, who were fed up with constant disruptions and inadequate warning for trials, had decided to boycott national squad trials, to be informed as a result that they would be ineligible for selection. The disgruntled squad members met the ARA Executive on 20th June, pointing out that the structure of the squad scheme was unworkable, with Chuter having been given too much to do. However, the ARA Executive backed Chuter and warned the Leander defectors that, even if they were to beat squad crews at Lucerne, they would still not be considered for selection.

Meanwhile, having been unable to reach a compromise with Chuter, Spracklen had formed a Leander eight from the rebels. The eight, who included four of the Olympic eight and a 1988 junior coxless pairs gold medallist, Matthew Pinsent, were entered for the Grand and for the ailing Nottingham International Regatta, now international almost only in name, where the 'rebel' Leander eight won. However, after discussions behind the scenes there were hints that the defectors would be reinstated for Lucerne.

The Club's non-squad crews had no such

problems, and at early regattas in 1989, their Under-23s had a series of successes, winning seven events at Ghent, while at Duisburg, where at this stage there was no squad heavyweight eight, they carried the flag with some distinction, finishing third behind the East and West German eights. At Ratzeburg they won the Senior B (Under-23) eights on the Saturday after two fours from the eight had each taken a second place, and the next day the coxless four won the Senior B event, the coxed four coming second in Senior A class.

Simon Berrisford had joined Redgrave in a new pair but at Duisburg, notoriously unfair in certain wind conditions, the pair were beaten on a bad lane on the Saturday. In fairer conditions the next day they recorded an easy win.

In its 150th year in 1989, Henley drew another record entry. Conditions were again exceptionally fast and records fell like ninepins. Leander, the only British entry in the Grand, overwhelmed a Hungarian composite and then met a new West German squad eight, Hansa Dortmund. in a semi-final. Both crews went off at 46, the Germans gaining a lead of three-quarters of a length by the first signal. The Germans were never below 39 and Leander simply could not match this. Only when Leander mounted a challenge at 39 in the final stages did they reduce the deficit but to no avail, and the Germans won by half a length. In the final, Hansa Dortmund beat Dinamo, USSR, the 1988 Olympic silver medallists, by three lengths, becoming the first crew to break six minutes for the course, recording a time of 5 min. 58 sec.

Berrisford and Redgrave beat another Leander squad pair, John Garrett and Salih

111 The Leander four, winners of the Wyfold, 1989

Hassan, in the second round of the Goblets and then met the Pimenovs in a semi-final. Once again, the Soviet pair took an early lead but at the three-quarter mile the crews were level. The Pimenovs held on for a time but their steering became erratic, the Leander pair gaining rapidly along the enclosures to win by two and a quarter lengths. In the final, the Leander pair overwhelmed the West German Grabow brothers, who were twice world champions in coxless fours. Leaving the Germans trailing in their wake, Berrisford and Redgrave broke the course record by nine seconds.

Among other Club entries that year were a four for the Britannia and two for the Wyfold. In the latter, both crews reached the semi-finals, where the Under-23s lost to Nottinghamshire County, but the A crew, with Pinsent's junior gold medal partner, Tim Foster, at bow, beat an Italian four, with three world lightweight gold medallists aboard, by four lengths, and then went on to beat the Nottingham four in the final, lowering the Fawley record by seven seconds and the full course record by a remarkable seventeen seconds.

112 The Leander four, winners of the Britannia, 1989

The Britannia was now open to foreign crews but the Leander Under-23s were also in record-breaking form. Having disposed of Penn in the second round and Harvard in their semi-final, they lowered the intermediate and full course records in the final, beating Lea by two lengths. They were the first Britannia four to break seven minutes, their winning time of 6 min. 53 sec. being only two seconds slower than the Prince Philip best time, equalled that year in the final by the University of London.

An unhappy casualty of the squad unrest, however, was Andy Holmes, who had been in a squad four earlier but failed to find a place in a Henley crew. He finally retired from active rowing and in the autumn became a consultant to the French Rowing Federation. A double Olympic, World and Commonwealth champion, he had also won World silver and Olympic bronze medals, while among his Henley wins were one in the Grand and two each in the Prince Philip and the Silver Goblets.

At Lucerne, the Leander Grand eight came third behind the East and West Germans but over a length ahead of a UL/Oxford eight made up from the winning Stewards' and Prince Philip fours. The Club's winning Wyfold four finished a commendable fifth but the race of the regatta was the final of the coxed pairs, in which Berrisford and Redgrave, with Pat Sweeney again coxing, looked out of it when lying fifth after 500 metres, some two and a half lengths behind the leaders, the evergreen Abbagnales. However, all the chasing crews closed up on the Italians and in a remarkable finish, five of the six crews finished abreast.

The photo placed Jugoslavia first, one-hundredth of a second ahead of the East Germans. The Abbagnales were third, a further three-hundredths of a second behind, followed by Berrisford and Redgrave, another four-hundredths of a second down, with Poland fifth, three-fifths of a second behind Leander. As the Leander pair had been in the coxed boat for only a few outings since Henley, this was an encouraging result for them. Garrett and Hassan were second to the East Germans in the coxless pairs and a Leander double, Chris Skuse and Rob Luke, took the bronze medal in the lightweight doubles, one second behind the winners.

To help settle the rift between Leander and Chuter, the ARA ordered Chuter to appoint a chief coach for the men's squad, and David Tanner accepted the challenge. Common sense then prevailed and the Leander rebels were invited back into the fold for final trials at Nottingham. The Nottingham lightweights, who had also been at loggerheads with Chuter, continued to defy her, refusing to consider changes to their winning Ladies' Plate eight.

They put their case to the ARA appeals panel but they were not selected for the World Championships at Bled, in what is now Slovenia.

Despite a summer of considerable discontent, fourteen Leander men made the British team. Richard Phelps, Jonathan Singfield and Tim Foster were in a new young eight put together for Bled; Steve Turner, Gavin Stewart, Terry Dillon and Matthew Pinsent from the Leander Grand eight were the coxed four, with Vaughan Thomas coxing; and Pete Mulkerrins, Nick Burfitt, John Garrett and Salih Hassan were the coxless four. Berrisford and Redgrave went for both pairs, with Sweeney steering the coxed boat, Richard Stanhope was in the quad sculler and Skuse and Luke were the lightweight double.

At Bled, the team did not seem to suffer unduly from the earlier troubles. Berrisford and Redgrave had to settle for the silver in the coxless pairs behind the outstanding East Germans, Thomas Jung and Uwe Kellner, but they finished a disappointing fifth in the coxed pairs. However, the eight, despite their short time together, excelled in taking the bronze medal behind the West German Grand winners and the East Germans but narrowly ahead of the United States. The coxed four also took a bronze and after such a traumatic season, these results represented an almost miraculous recovery.

Leander had another ten men in the British team for the *Match des Seniors* in Amsterdam, the winning Britannia four being the coxed four, while three of the Leander Under-23 Wyfold four were in a composite eight, but the results were disappointing, only the eight from the heavyweight team winning a medal, a bronze, although the lightweights won a silver and a bronze.

It had been a difficult year but for Leander it had brought considerable success. Indeed, the decade ended with Leander still firmly established as by far the most important source of material for Britain's international teams.

11

Jürgen Gröbler and The New Order
1990–1992

In the autumn of 1989, British rowing, as well as the Club, lost the services of one of the world's outstanding coaches when Mike Spracklen left to become chief coach to the Canadian men. A sponsor had been found to enable Spracklen to continue as coach to Leander but Spracklen's offer to take control of the ARA men's heavyweight team, for expenses only, was ignored by the ARA, who failed to answer his letters before he left, reluctantly, for an interview in Canada. This was an unforgivable discourtesy to someone who had done so much for British international rowing, but Spracklen regarded it as a fair indication of the ARA's attitude to him. It was also an unforgivable error by the ARA, the Canadians giving Spracklen a contract until the 1992 Olympics. Spracklen continued as Oxford's finishing coach for the Boat Race, but his loss to the national squad was considerable.

Also in the autumn, the ARA abolished Chuter's post of Director of International Rowing and a new post of International Performance Director was created. There was too much opposition to Chuter's autocratic methods for her to be acceptable in this new post, which went to the highly successful chief coach to the juniors, Bruce Grainger. Brian Armstrong became the International Rowing Manager, David Tanner was re-appointed as the men's chief coach and Chuter reverted to a domestic role as the ARA's Principal National Coach.

However, all was not well with British rowing. Discontent among the clubs went beyond the problems with the national squads, a meeting of nineteen club Captains, held at Leander in February 1990, expressing dissatisfaction with the ARA generally and with the management of its financial affairs in particular.

Tension between Leander and the national squad continued in the new year but the Club provided six of the ARA eight which gave the squad their seventh successive win in the Head of the River Race. While the University of London had been allowed to keep their best men for the Head, Leander had lost so many to the squad that the Club withdrew its first eight as a protest, the second eight finishing ninth, one place behind the Cambridge Boat Race crew. However, the Club continued to provide men for the squad after the Head.

Berrisford had been involved in a collision while sculling at Henley before Christmas and this led to recurring back trouble which plagued training in his pair with Redgrave in 1990. The pair reached the semi-finals of the Goblets at Henley but Berrisford's back problems then forced them to retire. However, there were other strong British pairs competing that year, including a Leander/Star composite, Pinsent and Mulkerrins, and another squad composite, Martin Cross and Tim Foster. Pinsent and Mulkerrins lost in their semi-final to the Austrian world bronze medallists, Sinzinger and Bauer, hitting the booms near the finish in a close race. The Austrians then won the final by one foot from Cross and Foster.

In the Grand, after the ARA Leander/UL eight had beaten the Lithuanians, Zalgiris from Viljnus, they had to replace their sick stroke, Johnny Hulls, of London University, and lost their semi-final to the eventual winners, Hansa Dortmund, with four of their World Champion eight rowing, by two lengths.

Leander had no successes that Henley, the Prince Philip four being a less than serious entry, consisting of the four mature American Oxford Blues who had won the event in 1965. They paddled over in a gentlemanly fashion behind a fast Hansa Dortmund four, the Germans allowing them to lose by half a length before going on to beat a Bulgarian four in the final.

With Berrisford still injured, Redgrave was drafted into the ARA eight for Lucerne. Pinsent was also in the crew, who won in a blanket finish, with Spracklen's Canadian eight second and the East Germans third, three-tenths of a second dividing the three crews.

For the World Championships in Tasmania at the end of October, the nineteen-year-old Pinsent replaced Berrisford in the coxless pair, coached since Spracklen's departure by Pat Sweeney, but the new combination had been unable to compete at the pre-Olympic Regatta in Amsterdam, Redgrave having gone down with what was diagnosed as food poisoning, so they had to go to Tasmania without a race in open competition and did not attempt both pair events. They reached the final of the coxless pairs but, after a poor start, they never

113 Jürgen Gröbler

quite got on terms with the reigning East German world champions and were pipped for the silver medal by the veteran Pimenov twins.

Only eight Leander men were in the British team in Tasmania and results were generally disappointing, the two fours and the eight finishing fourth, while the Canadian eight narrowly missed the gold medal behind the West Germans in the latter event.

It was now that a highly important event took place in the story of British international rowing. During the previous year, following the loss of Spracklen, the Club had been negotiating with a former East German coach, Jürgen Gröbler, with a view to him becoming the Club's coach. Gröbler had been chief coach to the East German men's teams from 1978 to 1985 and was the women's chief coach from 1986 until the championships in Tasmania, after which the unification of the two Germanies was to lead to one German team, with the result that many East German coaches were seeking new posts abroad. Gröbler had been responsible for more than forty medal-winning crews at world and Olympic level.

The Club's decision to break with tradition by appointing a full-time professional coach arose from recognising the direction in which the sport was moving, and the realisation that this was inevitable if the Club was to retain its leading position in British rowing. Gröbler had visited the Club during the year and signed a contract as the Club's Director of Rowing in December 1990, taking up his post in January 1991. Needless to say, this added considerably to the Club's financial burden.

Gröbler's arrival was timely. The ARA, who had been advertising, without success, for a full-time professional chief coach to the heavyweight squad, immediately began negotiations with Leander to see if Gröbler could combine his work with Leander with helping the national squad, and it was agreed that he would be used as 'technical adviser' to the squad, with John Pilgrim-Morris acting as the squad co-ordinator, the latter resigning from the Club committee to prevent possible accusations of bias.

Not long after this, Grainger resigned as the ARA's International Performance Director, partly because of disagreement with Armstrong over the exact nature of his role, but also because he disapproved of Gröbler's appointment, not for personal reasons but because he believed that Gröbler had been placed in an invidious position. Mark Lees, the former lightweight chief coach, succeeded him.

Gröbler's efforts with Leander quickly began to bear fruit. With Redgrave and a recovered Berrisford back in the boat, the Club squad eight, all recent internationals stroked by Richard Phelps, won the Head, taking the Page Trophy as well as the Fairbairn Bust. The following day, rowing as Rentacrew, another alternative Leander *nom de guerre*, they registered a unique double by winning the Veteran's Head by well over a minute.

After the Boat Race, in which he rowed in the winning Oxford crew for the second time, Pinsent resumed his partnership with Redgrave, who had spent much of his time sculling while Pinsent was in the Oxford boat, regaining the Scullers Head title which he had last held in 1986.

Gröbler disconcerted Redgrave by making the pair change places, Pinsent taking over as stroke. Redgrave was unhappy about this at first but it was an inspired move. In this order they won at Cologne, setting an unofficial world best time. At Grünau Regatta in Berlin the pair beat the world coxless pair champions for the previous two years, Jung and Kellner, and at Duisburg they won on both days, tearing the field apart each time in the last 250 metres. Berrisford was now stroking the squad coxed four, who also won on both days against strong opponents.

At Henley in 1991, the surprise in the Grand was the defeat by a composite Soviet eight of the Canadians, who had beaten the German world champions at Duisburg. Hansa

Dortmund did not defend the Grand, in which the ARA eight, Leander/Star, had a bye to the final. Coached by London University's Australian coach, Marty Aitken, with Anton Obholzer, Richard Phelps, Richard Stanhope, and cox Garry Herbert in the crew, they produced an inspired row, to lead the 15 1/2 stone Soviet eight by a length at the Barrier. The Soviets had reduced the deficit to half a length at Fawley but their rowing then began to lose its edge. Leander/Star drew away again and as they streaked away for a memorable victory by two and a half lengths, several of the crew were punching the air along the enclosures, to be reprimanded later by Henley's Chairman, Peter Coni, for such un-British behaviour.

Steve Redgrave duly took his eleventh Henley medal, recording his fourth Goblets' victory, the pair having broken the Barrier record in their heat before dropping to a paddle. The following day, they lowered the Fawley record, again easing off afterwards, and in the final, against two Spanish internationals, they were paddling much of the way before Pinsent leapt to life at 41 along the enclosures, the pair drawing away at an astonishing speed to win easily.

The ARA squad had a memorable regatta, winning everything for which they entered, seven Leander men fighting out the final of the Stewards'. The Club was also represented in the winning Queen Mother quad and in the winning Prince Philip four, which Berrisford stroked. In the Ladies', a Leander/Molesey composite, with six Leander men aboard, won the final against a UL/Oxford composite by a length in a time only four seconds slower than that of the Grand final.

Gröbler had certainly got off on the right foot and it was an excellent Henley for Leander, the Club's competitors winning twenty individual medals, to justify their traditional soubriquet, the 'Brilliants'.

The Leander pair continued their winning run at Lucerne, where the Pimenovs were second. The coxed four also won but the eight were fourth, though less than a length behind the winners, Germany. Leander had eighteen men in the team for the World Championships in Vienna, the coxless four and double scullers, Rorie Henderson and Guy Pooley, drawn entirely from the Club. Three of the coxed four and the cox, and the coxed pair, except for the cox, were also from Gröbler's Leander squad.

Once again, Redgrave and Pinsent were outstanding. Unbeaten throughout the season, they won their heat and semi-final without being pressed, but in the final, with a tail wind that favoured their generally lighter opponents, they had to go considerably harder. Only fourth at 1500 metres, Redgrave began to encourage his younger partner. 'Come on, you're a world champion', he said, and Pinsent's now familiar finishing burn was again too much for their opponents. They cut through the opposition like a hot knife through butter, coming home with clear water ahead of Iztok Cop and Denis Zvegelj of Slovenia, with the Austrians third, lowering their own world record by a further five seconds.

The coxed four had arrived at these championships with hopes of a gold medal but they rowed well below their best in the final, missing the bronze medal by 0.2 of a second. The coxless four also failed, cracking near the finish of their vital *repechage*. They finished seventh overall, but the young and relatively light eight produced a storming finish in their final, snatching the bronze medal from Romania and overlapping the winners, Germany, and the Canadians, who were a close second for the second year running. With the lightweight four winning a gold, the lightweight women's four a silver, and the women's pair, Fiona Freckleton and Miriam Batten, winning bronze, the first ever openweight women's medal, the team at Vienna equalled the previous best British medal result.

Earlier, at the *Match des Seniors* at Naro in Sicily, a composite Under-23 eight, the national champions, with Pete Bridge and the cox, Neil Chugani, from Leander, had taken the gold medal, and a Leander coxless four a silver medal. In the single sculls, Leander's Charlie Holmes had missed the bronze by less than a length. Bridge later rowed in the coxed pair at Vienna. All this was encouraging for the forthcoming 1992 Olympics.

Early in 1992, the Club accepted an invitation to compete in South Africa's first international regatta for nearly thirty years, Gröbler taking a squad of fourteen, among them Redgrave and Pinsent. They trained on a dammed lake near Pretoria for three weeks before taking part in the Vaal Regatta, in which the squad set new records in all the events for which they entered, winning the coxless pairs, the coxed and coxless fours, and the eights. It was a welcome break from the drudgery of English winter training.

The bulk of the candidates for the men's Olympic team split into two groups, one based at Molesey and the other at Leander, and there was a strong rivalry between them. In the Head, the Molesey eight, all internationals, were the surprise winners, pushing Leander's internationals, with Redgrave and Pinsent included, into second place.

Pinsent had taken a year's leave of absence from his studies at Oxford to concentrate on the pair for the Olympics. Redgrave did not compete in the Scullers Head, which was won by Guy Pooley of Leander, the lightweight Peter Haining, also in Leander colours, taking third place. Pooley then retained the Wingfield Sculls, in which Haining was the runner-up.

Trials for the potential Olympic team at Holme Pierrepont in April produced a shock defeat for Redgrave and Pinsent, the Molesey pair, Jonny and Greg Searle, from the 1991 World bronze-medal eight, beating the Leander pair at their own game, rowing right away in the last 500 metres to win by two and a half lengths. It was an impressive indication of things to come.

However, the Leander pair soon quelled possible doubts about their future by winning on both days at Cologne, although on the Saturday, the Searles were not ready when the start was given and did not leave the starting pontoon. On the second day the Molesey pair went for the coxed pairs, in which they finished third, but less than a second behind the Polish winners.

That all was not well with the Leander pair was indicated when they were twice beaten at Essen, losing in the final on the first day to Cop and Zvegelj, the Vienna silver medallists, and on the second day they failed for the first time to qualify for the final, the Slovenian pair again beating them. However, since they were the reigning world champions, and despite their disappointing form, Redgrave and Pinsent became the first British crew to be selected for the Barcelona Olympics, leaving the Searles, with Garry Herbert coxing, to try for the coxed pairs.

Shortly afterwards, the pair's poor form was explained when Redgrave was diagnosed as suffering from ulcerative colitis, a chronic bowel infection, and he was ordered to take a rest, which meant missing Lucerne, where the Searles did well enough in the coxed pairs to earn their Olympic selection, as did the coxed four, the same crew as in the previous years, with Dillon, Burfitt and Berrisford from Leander. Two other Leander men, Garrett and Stanhope, were in the coxless four, together with Gavin Stewart, formerly of Leander but now with the Molesey squad, while Pooley was in the quad. The eight included Rupert Obholzer, Steve Turner, Richard Phelps and Ben Hunt-Davis of Leander and there were altogether thirteen of the Club squad in the Olympic team, who did not compete at Henley.

Leander had intended to enter for the Grand but a disagreement among the eight meant that they eventually entered as two fours, the Stewards' four containing three current Oxford Blues, while the Prince Philip four were squad members who had failed to win Olympic selection. The Steward's four lost in their heat to the Nottingham County lightweights, the 1991 world lightweight champions, who went on to beat a Spanish four, to whom they were conceding 30 lb. a man, in the final.

The Nottingham four almost achieved a unique double, competing also as a quad in the Queen Mother Cup, but they lost a hard-fought final by a length to the Swedish Lucerne winners.

The Prince Philip drew five entries, including a Molesey/Reading University composite, who were also squad members who had failed to make the Olympic team. They drew Leander in the first round and it was something of a grudge match. Leander had the upper hand throughout and Molesey, the more disgruntled of the two crews, realising that they could not win, stopped rowing before the finish line, which drew some unfavourable comments.

In the final, against the Tideway Scullers, who were stroked by the 1984 Olympic gold medallist, Richard Budgett, Leander won by three lengths, breaking the Fawley record by one second and the full course record by two.

Rorie Henderson and the Oxford Blue, Cal Maclennan, represented the Club in the Diamonds, Maclennan going out in the first round but Henderson progressed steadily and had the race of his life in the semi-final, where he met the American, Fran Reininger, a former winning Oxford stroke and a selected sculler. Reininger took the lead at the three-quarter mile and was then allowed by the umpire to wash his opponent. Henderson had a couple of minor shipwrecks along the enclosures but made a powerful sprint for the line, breaking the American in the last few strokes, to win by a third of a length.

In the final, Henderson met an Australian Olympic double-sculls silver medallist, Paul Reedy, who was warned for his steering early in the race and hit the booms when he over-

114 Rorie Henderson beating Fran Reininger by ⅓ length in the semi-final of the Diamond Sculls, 1992

115 Rorie Henderson with the Diamond Sculls, 1992

corrected. Henderson led by a length at the Barrier but Reedy had reduced this to two feet at Fawley and then pulled ahead to lead by a length at the Mile. The Australian was striking a higher rate than Henderson, and when the Leander sculler began his charge, Reedy had nothing left. Henderson was through in a flash and the race was over. This was the first home win in the Diamonds since Redgrave's in 1985.

Rowing was honoured at the Olympic opening ceremony at Barcelona when Redgrave, a double gold medallist at his third Olympics, and now fully recovered from his earlier illness, was chosen to carry the British flag, the first British oarsman to so so since Jack Beresford at the 1936 Berlin Olympics.

Before coming to Spain, the British oarsmen and scullers had undergone altitude training and heat acclimatisation, which was just as well as the heat and humidity were excessive at Banyoles, where the rowing took place. Otherwise conditions on the attractive lake were excellent, except when a morning fog on the third day caused racing to be postponed, as a result of which the last race of the day took place in a temperature of 100°F.

The racing was of the highest order and without doubt the outstanding crew of the regatta were Redgrave and Pinsent. Their main opposition came from the Slovenians, Cop and Zeveglj, and the Germans, Peter Hoeltzenbein and Colin von Ettingshausen, who had won at Essen and Lucerne. The British pair's tactics were simple: they set out to dominate the event and did so in their heat and semi-final. In the final, they were clear at the half-way mark, with less than three lengths separating the other five pairs. When Pinsent raised the rate at 1500 metres and again at 1750 metres, the British pair left their opponents trailing, crossing the line striking 42, two and a half lengths ahead of the Germans, who just beat the Slovenians for the silver medal. It was an awesome performance which earned Redgrave the distinction of being the first British oarsman to win a gold medal at three consecutive Olympics.

If not strictly part of Leander's history, although the Leander cox, Garry Herbert, was involved, no account of the 1992 Olympics would be complete without reference to the remarkable performance by the Searle brothers in the coxed pairs and in my Olympic report for *Rowing* magazine I wrote of both pairs:

> Somebody who might have suffered at Banyoles, in view of his earlier colitis, was Steve Redgrave, but in fact he appeared to be unaffected and with Matthew Pinsent in the coxless pair he was on tremendous form for the whole week. The pair looked likely winners from the start of their opening heat and there can have been few crews in any Olympics to have displayed such dominance. They won the final by the biggest margin of the regatta and were arguably the best crew competing in any event. The combination of Pinsent's rhythm and power and Redgrave's experience proved too much for any of their opponents, most of whom abandoned any hope of the gold medal early on and concentrated on the minor medals.
>
> If the coxless pair's great superiority

gave them comfortable wins, the coxed pair's races were all desperately close and won in the last few strokes. Jonny and Greg Searle, coxed by Garry Herbert, astonished the crowd with their almost unbelievable pace for the last 500 metres. In their opening heat, with only the winners moving directly into the semi-final, they finished at 44 and went through the Romanians in the last few strokes, to win by 0.56 of a second. In their semi-final they were in third place at the 1000-metre mark, which would have been sufficient to qualify, but again they went through in the closing stages to beat the Germans by about half a length, which gave them a centre station for the final.

Their victory in the final over the legendary Abbagnale brothers, the Olympic champions in 1984 and 1988, and seven times world champions, was sensational and it is not an exaggeration to say that it was one of the greatest in Olympic history. The Italians have always been a one-pace crew, unable to change gear in the later stages, but their speed over the middle part of the course has usually won them their races well before the last 250 metres. In the final it looked as though they were going to succeed in this once again and, like Redgrave, take their third successive gold medal. After 1500 metres they were two lengths ahead of the Romanians, who were fractionally ahead of the Searles. The young Molesey pair, urged on by Garry Herbert and tumultuous cheers from the strong British contingent of spectators, then went into overdrive. Greg Searle wound the rate up from 36 to 40, then 42, then 44, and suddenly it was clear that the Italians were in danger. Amid mounting excitement in the stands, the Italians cracked less than 100 metres from the finish and the Searles shot past to win by half a length. The Italians were almost caught on the line by the Romanians but just held on to take the silver medal. The British pair's last 500-metre time of 1:39.58 was their fastest in the race and they covered the second half of the course nearly three seconds faster than the first. A truly amazing performance.

Garry Herbert had played his part and, with his pink socks tumbling round his ankles, was caught weeping with emotion on the victory rostrum by TV cameras and this was widely relayed. His photograph was reproduced everywhere and caught the world's imagination. It was a memorable image of the release of all the pent-up emotions that accompany great sporting events.

Britain had not won two rowing gold medals in one Olympic regatta since 1948 but unfortunately the rest of the British team at Banyoles could not match these two superlative performances. Like most of the British crews, the eight had not been together long enough to get among the medals but they made the final by scraping in third in their semi-final. In the final, Mike Spracklen's Canadian eight took the gold medal from the USA and Germany, with Britain predictably finishing sixth. The coxed four rowed without fire and they and the coxless four failed to qualify for the A finals, although the coxless four did at least have the satisfaction of winning the B final. The quad looked ordinary and their spare man, Wade Hall-Craggs, a last-minute choice for the single sculls, was not surprisingly outclassed.

Many of the Olympics crews had not rowed together until after Lucerne; consequently they had not raced in their final orders before competing at Banyoles. However, in the autumn, the gold medals that had been won there did not prevent heavy criticism being directed at the way Mark Lees had run the national squad. After the promising performances in Vienna in 1991, the results at Banyoles, with the obvious exception of those of the pairs, led to further discontent among the squad oarsmen. The ARA responded by abolishing the role of performance director; and they then decided to invest full powers in the chief coaches of the various squads.

The obvious choice for the men's squads, heavyweight and lightweight, was Jürgen Gröbler, but he was still under contract to Leander. While Ivor Lloyd, the Club's long-serving Captain, realised that Gröbler was the sort of man the ARA should have employed years before, the details of his relationship with the Club had to be sorted out if the Club was not to be left exposed. Eventually it was arranged that Gröbler would be released from his Club contract, which was to have run until 1996, but that he would continue to oversee the programming, testing, and coaching of the Club's development squad — candidates for future national teams — until the following Henley or until someone else had been appointed.

Gröbler remained at Henley, however, and continued to coach Redgrave and Pinsent.

116 The Leander quad, winners of the Fours Head, 1992: N. Burfitt (bow), C. Maclennan, S. Redgrave, G. Pooley (stroke)

117 Leander veterans celebrate Henley's 150th anniversary, 1989

118 The 'Wednesday Club' on Len Habbitts's 80th birthday, 1988: *(l to r)* Douglas Wilson, Dick Hylton-Smith, James Macnabb, Bob Wilson, John Pinches, Sam Hall, Len Habbits, John Allen, Peter Allnutt, Ken Hylton-Smith

12

The Greatest of the Brilliants
1993–1996

By 1993, Steve Redgrave, at thirty, had become the best known oarsman in the world, and his pair with Pinsent was also famous. Both men were tall and immensely powerful, averaging 16½ stone and with high physiological profiles. Immediately after the 1992 Olympics, the pair had decided to dedicate themselves to winning again at Atlanta in 1996, with Redgrave determined to establish yet another record by taking an unprecedented fourth successive rowing gold medal.

In January 1993, in the New Year Honours, the Searles and Garry Herbert joined the growing list of rowing MBEs, a tribute to their Olympic success, but the same month the FISA Congress in Budapest made the controversial decision to recommend to the International Olympic Committee that they should admit lightweight events. These were subsequently admitted into the Olympic programme, but at the expense of the coxed fours and pairs and the women's coxless pairs, the lightweight events being men's coxless fours and men's and women's double sculls. This meant, of course, that future men's heavyweight teams would be reduced by six men and two coxes. The coxed fours and pairs, however, were to be retained in World Championships and the Searles, although they would have to look for an alternative event for Atlanta, decided to continue in their coxed pair for another year.

Meanwhile, Pinsent had returned to Oxford and was President of the OUBC, so the pair were not able to get together again until after the Boat Race. In the Head, Molesey, with six Olympic oarsmen, again defeated Leander, with five, but both finished behind the German squad eight, who included their Olympic silver medal pair and three of their Olympic eight. This was the first time the event had been won by an overseas crew. In the Boat Race, Cambridge, with Richard Phelps at four, beat Oxford, for whom Pinsent rowed at six, for only the second time in eighteen years.

Bearing in mind recent criticism about the short time the Olympic crews had had together, Gröbler started to assemble his crews in April and most competed at Henley. Redgrave and Pinsent were not affected by all this, of course, and carried on as before.

At Henley, in their heat of the Goblets, they became the first pair to break two minutes to the Barrier, lowering their own record by three seconds before easing off. In the final against the New Zealanders, Campbell Clayton-Green and Bill Coventry, they led immediately and were content to maintain half a length of clear water between the pairs as Redgrave was also competing in the Stewards', in which he was substituting for the injured Tim Foster. As Leander/UL, stroked by Ben Hunt-Davis, the four met serious opponents in the final in the form of a Hansa Dortmund four containing two world gold medallists. The crews overlapped all the way, both racing in at over 40, the home crew holding on to win a fine race by two-thirds of a length. Redgrave, for once, was exhausted at the finish but this win gave him his twelfth Henley medal.

The Molesey/Leander squad coxed four, stroked by Terry Dillon, won the Prince Philip from another squad four, Molesey/UL, but the Club was not represented in the Grand, which was retained by Hansa Dortmund, who were far too good for the CUBC/UL squad eight.

The Club's entries in the Wyfold and Britannia both lost. The Wyfold crew were the Under-23s who later finished fourth in the *Match des Seniors* at Joannina in Greece. At Henley, they lost in the final to the London lightweights, and the Britannia four were beaten in a semi-final by Goldie, who included three of their winning reserve eight which had won the Little Boat Race, and were stroked by that year's winning Cambridge stroke, Will Mason. Goldie lost the final to a Harvard heavyweight four, drawn from their Varsity eight, who were yet another crew rowing in an event well below their class. They broke every record in a heat, their overall time being three seconds inside the Prince Philip record. In the final, Harvard were five seconds faster than the winning Molesey/Leander Prince Philip four and their performance led to further changes to the qualification rules the following year.

Redgrave and Pinsent recorded another win at Lucerne, where Cop and Zeveglj were second and the New Zealand Goblets pair third. Britain also won three lightweight gold medals.

Two days after Lucerne, Peter Coni died. He had been seriously ill for some time and had handed over as Henley Chairman to Mike Sweeney but with a remarkable effort of will he had been able to present the prizes at Henley, delivering a speech with a firmness that belied his condition. In what turned out to be a farewell gesture, the Leander pair and the lightweight four both called him to the medal podium at Lucerne. Coni, FISA's treasurer at the time of his death, had played an influential role in British rowing for thirty years, and in Henley's recent increasing success and prosperity.

The Club was strongly represented once again in the World Championships at Roudnice in the new Czech Republic, and a number of erstwhile Leander oarsmen also competed while representing other clubs. Altogether, eleven British crews reached finals and the two pairs were again outstanding, both repeating their Olympic victories, but otherwise the heavyweights came home empty handed, although both Peter Haining, the lightweight sculler, and the women's lightweight four won, to give Britain an encouraging total of four gold medals.

Redgrave and Pinsent created some excitement when they were almost too casual in their heat and were nearly caught by a Croatian pair, and had to put in three or four 'thick 'uns' just before the line to qualify on a photo finish. Then they had to change boats shortly before the semi-final when Gröbler discovered a serious crack in Pinsent's stretcher support. They rapidly re-rigged their reserve boat and started cautiously in the semi-final and were behind the Germans at 1500 metres. Deciding that they were not going to let the Germans win, if only for psychological reasons, they threw caution to the wind, putting in one of their blistering final spurts, to win by two-thirds of a length. Back in their repaired boat for the final, they paced themselves well and did not take the lead until the last 250 metres, where they caught the Slovenians, after which the result was no longer in doubt. They eased off just before the line, beating Germany by three-quarters of a length, to retain the title they had won in 1991, with Cop and Zeveglj just missing the silver medal.

The Searles, still coxed by Garry Herbert, changed their tactics in the coxed pairs, shattering the opposition, and almost themselves, with a devastating burn at 1250 metres, moving from last to first in twenty strokes. They were clear at 1800 metres, where they began to run out of steam, but the damage had been done and they crossed the line still clear of the veteran Abbagnales.

In 1994, the German squad again won the Head, but this time Leander's internationals, with Redgrave at seven and Pinsent at four, moved into second place, just over two seconds behind, Molesey dropping to fourth. Two Germans also figured in the Boat Race, with gold medallists Thorsten Strepplehoff and Peter Hoeltzenbein rowing stroke and seven in the winning Cambridge crew.

With sculling by far the weakest link in the heavyweight squad, the Club had recruited a group from the junior ranks with a view to developing scullers for Atlanta, and some of these young scullers began to emerge in time for the early regattas in 1994. A promising Under-23 double, Robert Thatcher and Richard Rogers, took the bronze medal in the open event on the first day of the Paolo d'Aloja Memorial Regatta at Piediluco, where Redgrave and Pinsent won on both days, as did the squad eight and a young coxless four, with Leander members in both crews. The Club entered an Under-23 quad for the Queen Mother Cup at Henley and they survived two rounds before losing in the semi-final.

At Henley, Redgrave and Pinsent retained the Goblets but their victory was not the foregone conclusion that many had expected, with the German 1993 world silver medallists, Detlef Kirchoff and Hans Sennewald, and the Belgian Olympic and world finalists, Jaak Van Driessche and Luc Goiris, lurking in the field. However, the Leander pair streaked away from the Germans in their semi-final, to lead by two and a half lengths at the Barrier before dropping to a paddle for a surprisingly easy win. Against the Belgians in the final, the Leander pair were always in charge, although they were pushed sufficiently hard to equal, despite a cross headwind, their own record time to Fawley, where they led by two lengths. They eventually won comfortably to give Redgrave his thirteenth Henley win and his sixth in the Goblets. This equalled the record set in the 1890s by Guy Nickalls, in whose honour, and his brother Vivian's, their father Tom presented the Nickalls Challenge Cup that goes with the Silver Goblets.

Four national eights rowed in the Grand. The ARA eight, rowing as Leander/Cambridge University, six of whom and Garry Herbert, the cox, were from Leander, lost by half a length to the French eight in a semi-final. The American eight, with Spracklen now their chief coach, beat the Dutch eight and in the final rowed right away from the French, who had picked up a branch with their rudder but made no protest, saying that they had had a bad row anyway.

The Prince Philip was an all-British affair, the Club four meeting the Nottingham County four who were generally regarded as the fastest British four, in the final. Nottingham won by half a length, but they were at loggerheads with Gröbler because they had not met all the selection criteria and, having failed to resolve the issue with Gröbler, they were not in the end considered for selection.

At Lucerne, Redgrave and Pinsent faced a challenge from the the German Cambridge Blues, Hoeltzenbein and Streppelhoff, who had been waiting to race the Leander pair all season. With 500 metres to go, Leander were lying third, a length and a half behind the Germans and three-quarters of a length behind the early leaders, the Canadians Phil Graham and Darren Barber, the latter a gold medallist in the 1992 Olympic eight. It looked as though the Olympic champions were at last going to meet their match but again their immense power began to take effect. Striking an astonishing 45 in the closing stages, they broke the Canadians and caught the Germans a few strokes from the finish line. Their time of 6 min. 18.34 sec. shattered their own world record, set in the 1991 World Championships, by three seconds.

Redgrave and Pinsent again won the coxless pairs at the World Championships at Indianapolis for their fourth title in as many years, but this bald fact does scant justice to yet another heart-stopping battle in the final, in which the Germans produced another strong challenge. Once again, they were clear at 1000 metres, with Australia second and Britain third. By the 1500-metre mark, Britain had moved into second place but the Germans still led by a length. Here Pinsent raised the rate to 40 and, as before, the Germans began to wilt. With 250 metres to go, Redgrave and Pinsent had taken a narrow lead and finally crossed the line half a length ahead, Hoeltzenbein and Streppelhoff just holding off Richard Wearne and Robert Walker of Australia to take the silver medal.

Redgrave was also a surprise member of a new coxed pair. He was a last-minute replacement in the B final for Jonathan Singfield, who had fallen ill. With his 1984 coxed-four gold-medal partner, Martin Cross, who was making his eighteenth successive appearance in the British team, he won the B final.

The Searles were now in a new coxless four and took the bronze medal behind Italy and France, the 1993 world champions. The eights were won by the United States, who just held off a late challenge from the Dutch. The British eight, failing to make the A final, finished eighth. Spracklen's remarkable coaching record now included gold medal crews from three different countries.

The top international crews were presented with a new challenge in 1995 when a qualification system for the Atlanta Olympics came into operation at the World Championships at Tampere in Finland. Crews rather than individuals were to qualify but it meant that, even more than usual in a pre-Olympic year, crew selection in 1995 would have to be done with Olympic places in mind, especially as there would no longer be events for coxed fours and pairs at Atlanta.

Gröbler tried to smooth over the troubled areas that had affected his relationship with the Nottingham group and he attempted to combine Leander's candidates with Nottingham's. However, quite apart from psychological differences, the physical distance between Nottingham and Henley was always going to prove an obstacle, since none of the men concerned was prepared to move to the other's base, and nothing came of the plan.

Leander's internationals, who included Redgrave and Pinsent once again, made a rare entry in the Kingston Head, winning by thirty-seven seconds in a record time from the University of London. But a week later the Tideway title went abroad for the third successive year, this time to the fast Dutch national eight, who included five of the crew who had narrowly missed the world title the previous year. Leander, in second place, were three seconds slower.

Redgrave and Pinsent had trained briefly in Australia in the winter and at the squad trials, held in Hazewinkel in April, they again emerged as the fastest pair. Later, on the same course, at a regatta billed, somewhat meaninglessly, as the European Union Championships, they had their first real test of the season. Among the pair's opponents were the Australian 1994 bronze medallists, Wearne and Walker, with whom the Leander pair had trained Down Under. The Australians had been amazed by the weights shifted by Redgrave in the gym and at Hazewinkel Redgrave and Pinsent were out to capitalise on the psychological advantage that this had given them. Also competing were three French pairs, two of them drawn from the 1993 World champion coxless four.

Redgrave and Pinsent did not race as a pair on the first day at Hazewinkel, combining instead in a Club coxed four with two American Oxford Blues, Jo Michels and Laird Reed. The crew were destined for the Prince Philip at Henley and won on the Saturday at Hazewinkel, the Australians taking the coxless pairs in the absence of the Leander pair. The following day, Redgrave and Pinsent took on the Australian and French pairs and wasted no time in establishing their superiority. Going into the lead at once, they led by a length at 1000 metres, after which they delivered the *coup de grace*, taking another full length in twenty strokes. The Australians finished second with the best of the French pairs, Michel Andrieux and Jean-Christophe Rolland, third. For good measure, the coxed four raced an hour later and again won easily.

Redgrave had announced that Henley 1995 would probably be his last since the Olympic team would not be able to compete the following year because of the closeness of the dates of the two events, and if this was indeed to be his last Henley appearance, he went out in style, the pair winning the Goblets comfortably. The opposition was only moderate but in their semi-final the pair went for the record, lowering the Fawley time by three seconds and then taking a remarkable thirteen seconds off the course record, which Redgrave had set with Berrisford in 1989. In the final, the last race of the regatta, the Leander pair were content to paddle over in front of two lightweights until Pinsent suddenly unleashed the pair's full power, coming in at 43 to win by five lengths. Afterwards, ignoring Henley tradition, but with some justification, the pair paddled back down to the bottom of the enclosures before turning and coming back up the course, Redgrave waving to the crowd amid tumultuous applause. Although the Stewards frowned upon such exhibitionism, there can be no one who begrudged his intended farewell to the scene of so many of his triumphs by Britain's most successful oarsman of all time.

It was a fitting end to an excellent regatta, at which the pair, together with their American Blues, had won the Prince Philip for Leander, beating the Leander-based squad four by four lengths and demolishing the record at all points; the overall time was beaten by five seconds.

Redgrave now had fifteen Henley medals to his credit, by far the greatest number of individual wins in the 20th century and beaten in the previous century by only three men, one of whom was Guy Nickalls. Redgrave's seventh Goblets win broke Nickalls's record in this event, which led Pinsent to observe, 'I suppose they'll have to add a Redgrave Ladle'. A comparison between the Henley performances of Nickalls and Redgrave shows that Nickalls competed in sixteen Henleys between 1885 and 1907, winning twenty-two medals from seventy races, of which he lost ten. Redgrave competed in thirteen Henleys between 1981 and 1995, winning fifteen medals from fifty-eight races, of which he lost only three. In the Goblets, Nickalls raced sixteen times for six wins, Redgrave twenty-eight times for seven wins, and, of course, many times against far tougher opponents than those faced by Nickalls.

Leander's other interests that Henley included the ARA squad eight, Leander/Molesey, with four of the crew and the cox, Hayden Bass, from the Club. Stroked by Richard Rogers of Imperial College, they had a hard-fought race with the only other entry, the American squad eight, San Diego, who included six of their world champion eight. San Diego led by half a length at the Barrier, where they equalled the record set the previous year, and then took a second off the record to Fawley, having stretched their advantage to one length. The ARA composite then began to reduce the gap and the difference was only half a length at the last signal. With both crews flat out along the enclosures, the Leander/Molesey composite continued to gain but the Americans held on to win by a third of a length, one second outside Hansa Dortmund's 1989 record, becoming only the second eight to break six minutes for the course.

Of Leander's other entries, the best performance came from a new double, James Cracknell and Bob Thatcher, who reached the semi-finals before going down to an American squad double.

Fourteen Leander men were in Gröbler's squad at Lucerne, where the standard was exceptionally high, with several World champions tumbling, together with records. Redgrave and Pinsent had to overcome another strong challenge from the Australians, who once again found the pace too hot. They were passed eventually by the Italian and Croatian pairs, the latter with one of that year's winning Cambridge crew, Marko Banovic, at bow, but the Leander pair finished with clear water over their opponents.

The American eight provided one of the

major shocks of the regatta by failing to qualify for the final, which was won by the Russians, the ARA eight finishing sixth. The Leander squad coxed four finished fourth, having just managed to squeeze pass Wallingford, the Britannia winners, in the last minute.

All the Leander men were selected for the World Championships at Tampere, where the coxless pair were again the strongest British representatives, comfortably winning their heat and semi-final, in which they led from the first stroke and left their opponents to sort themselves out behind them. The final followed a similar pattern, although the chasing pack closed up approaching the finish, a fierce battle having developed for the minor medals. To British supporters it looked a closer run thing than it apparently was. 'We trod on it at 1000 metres', said Pinsent afterwards, 'and we knew the race was in the bag by 1500 metres. It was game over. We knew no one would get past us.' They finished nearly a length ahead of the Australians, who just beat the French pair, Andrieux and Rolland, for the silver medal. The win gave the Leander pair their fifth gold medal in as many years and their fourth world title together.

The Molesey/UL coxless four, with the Searles aboard, having beaten the Italian world champions by a split second in their semi-final, were narrowly pipped by the Italians in the final, to take the silver medal. The eight qualified for their final but on lane 1, which was affected by an unfavourable cross headwind, they could finish only sixth, the Germans taking the gold, the Dutch the silver and the reigning champions, the United States, the bronze. Haining took the lightweight single sculls title for a record third time, for which he later received an MBE, and the lightweight eight and the women's lightweight four and pair all won silver medals, the final medal tally being Britain's best ever. More importantly, the men qualified for four of the six heavyweight Olympic events, while the men's lightweight four qualified for their new Olympic event, and the women's openweight sculler, Guin Batten, also qualified. The others would have to try again for the few remaining places at the qualifying regatta at Lucerne the following year.

Redgrave and Pinsent went to Australia again for three weeks in January 1996 and then rowed in the winning Leander squad eight that won the Head by ten seconds from the University of London, the Dutch holders having scratched. This gave Redgrave his tenth Head win.

At Piediluco, in Italy, the pair won on both days, and they also won at Mannheim and Cologne, but a virus which ran through the Leander squad hit the pair and once again they had to miss Lucerne, as did the eight for the same reason. However, having had a successful run on the Continent, the pair had already been selected for the Olympics, together with the Molesey/UL coxless four. After the Lucerne Olympic qualifying regatta, the rest of the Olympic team were selected, with six Leander men, including Garry Herbert, the cox, in the eight. Also in the team were the Leander double, James Cracknell and Bob Thatcher, who had qualified at Tampere the previous year.

At Henley, where none of the Olympic team

competed, the Club non-squad eight reached the final of the Ladies' Plate, but they were unexpectedly outpaced by a Goldie crew containing five winning Cambridge Blues, losing by three and a half lengths, and the Club had no Henley successes.

The Atlanta Olympics were marred by major transport problems for crews and officials, delays often adding hours to the travel times, which did not help with over 90% humidity and temperatures often over 80° or 90° F. Most of the British team stayed in the Olympic Village, fifty-five miles from Lake Lanier, where the rowing took place. 'It is a shambles', said Redgrave, 'We have tried not to let it affect our build-up but obviously that has not been easy.' Eventually, during the regatta the pair and coxless four moved to Gainesville, which was only a few miles from the lake. However, the rest of the team stayed in Atlanta, which may, at least, be part of the explanation of why they under-performed.

Redgrave had the unique honour of being asked to carry the British flag at the opening ceremony for the second time, and the pair, and Redgrave in particular, came in for considerable media attention. On the day of the pair's opening heat, the media, despite formidable problems with the official buses, turned up in force.

The pair, then still living in the Olympic village, were so uncertain that they would arrive in time for their 9am heat that they persuaded the British Olympic Association to drive them to the lake in one of their official cars reserved for VIPs 'It has taken us four years to get here' said Redgrave, 'We are not going to let somebody's bad organisation interfere with our prospects.'

With none of their main rivals in their heat, Redgrave and Pinsent won easily enough in a paddle but they were unhappy with their row, having had, by their standards, a poor start. However, this win put them into the semi-finals, where they were made to fight hard by the American pair, Michael Peterson and Jonathan Holland, who had finished fourth at Lucerne. The Americans settled for what were probably the only tactics that might have defeated the reigning champions, rowing flat out for the lead. They were leading Redgrave and Pinsent by a length at 1000 metres but, as others had dicovered in the past, they had no answer when Pinsent applied the pressure, quickly falling back to fourth and eventually failing to qualify for the final.

The other semi-final was won in a time four seconds faster than Britain's by a new Australian pair, David Weightman and Bob Scott, the Lucerne winners, the previous year's silver medallists, Wearne and Walker, having failed to earn selection. Andrieux and Rolland of France were second. Despite their ultimately comfortable semi-final win, Redgrave and Pinsent had not established their superiority as they had done in 1992 and it was clear that the final was likely to be a cliffhanger, and so it proved.

Redgrave had been showing signs of stress during the week, British team officials saying he had been taciturn and generally uncommunicative, and he had added pressure on himself by declaring earlier that the Olympic final would be his last race. Both he and Pinsent knew that any mistake in the final could cost them the gold medal. 'It's been one of the toughest weeks of my life', declared Pinsent. 'As the race gets near, we both get quiet. I lose my appetite. Steve gets grumpy'.

They were not helped when someone let off a bomb in the Centennial Olympic Park in the early hours of the morning of the final, killing two and injuring over one hundred. Despite the widespread shock and anger that this caused, the Olympic programme was not interrupted, but all flags were lowered to half-mast.

Redgrave was unusually nervous as the pair paddled down to the start. For once, they were facing, in the Australians, opponents they had never previously raced. They were determined therefore to get an early grip on the race and drew ahead immediately, to lead the French by a length and a quarter after 1000 metres, with the Australians in close pursuit, the early challengers, New Zealand, having begun to fall back. By 1500 metres, the Australians had moved into second place and were beginning to look dangerous. However, Pinsent had something in reserve as usual, and although the Australians closed right up near the finish, Great Britain crossed the line half a length ahead, breaking their own Olympic record set in 1992 by over seven seconds, a fitting climax to the pair's outstanding career. Redgrave had looked totally exhausted for the last dozen strokes or so but Pinsent, who appeared to be capable of rowing another 500 metres, raised his arm in triumph as the pair crossed the line. Redgrave, drained physically and emotionally, slumped over his oar as Pinsent reached back to shake his hand. 'We had it from the start', said Redgrave afterwards. 'They were never going to catch us'. Watching the Australians closing fast at the finish, the anxious British spectators would have been happier had they known this.

This was the only gold medal won by Britain in any sport at these Olympics. Later the same day the coxless four, in one of the most competitive of the rowing events, were bitterly disappointed by having to settle for only the bronze medal. They finished about a deck length behind the winners, Australia, and the width of the bow bobble behind France, who were second. The world champions, Italy, were last.

With the exception of Guin Batten, who produced her best performance to date when finishing fifth in the women's single sculls, the rest of the British team were below their best, the men's eight finishing only eighth, the gold medal being won by the Dutch for the first time. The Leander double had to race in their heat and *repechage* with Guy Pooley substituting for James Cracknell, who had gone down with a virus. To avoid catching this was another reason why the pair had moved out to Gainesville. Cracknell was able to race in the C final, but he was not fully fit and the double finished only seventeenth overall.

Redgrave's distinguished career now included four Olympic gold medals, a unique achievement in rowing. He had also won seven World and three Commonwealth titles, in addition to his fifteen Henley medals. He had also won the Wingfield Sculls five times from 1985 to 1989 and the Scullers Head twice. The greatest British oarsman of all time and arguably the outstanding international oarsman of the century, his record may never be surpassed.

While Redgrave attracted most of the attention from the media, Pinsent's part in the pair's successes tended to be underestimated. By the end of the 1996 Olympics, he had himself won two Olympic gold medals and four World titles, as well as two World bronze medals. By the time of the final at Lake Lanier, he had become at least Redgrave's equal in the partnership, if not the stronger man mentally and physically. Still aged only twenty-five, he announced after the Olympics that he intended to continue, though with whom and in what class of boat had yet to be determined.

The pair's wins were also great victories for their coach, Jürgen Gröbler, who had been made an Honorary Life member of the Club when his contract with the Club had ended. One of his former East German oarsmen, Harald Jahrling, was the coach of the Australian pair.

So Leander's many triumphs on the water, stretching back over nearly two centuries, had reached new heights in 1996, with the golden pair the greatest of all the 'Brilliants'.

119   Steve Redgrave with his four Olympic gold medals, 1996

120 LEANDER WALTZ
   (courtesy of KPM Music)

This waltz was composed by a Leander member, John Arkell, and is often played in the Stewards' Enclosure during Henley Regatta

13

The Way Ahead

Immediately after the Olympic final, Redgrave, reacting to the enormous stresses, partly self-induced, involved in winning his fourth gold medal, announced that he never wanted to go again through the hell that he had endured for the previous few weeks. 'If anybody sees me anywhere near a boat,' he announced, 'he has my permission to shoot me! I never want to get into another boat in my life.'

However, he soon regretted this impulsive and emotive remark and it was not long before he began to feel the urge to carry on. To his surprise, he found that, after twenty years of competitive rowing, he missed the routine of training, and after a period of uncertainty about his future, he announced at a well-attended press conference at the Club at the end of November 1996 that he was to continue rowing after all until the Sydney Olympics in 2000. However, he had agreed with Pinsent that they would not resurrect the pair and the two of them opted to try for a four, backed by substantial sponsorship from the finance house, Lombard.

Meanwhile, the Olympic Regatta had not been the end of the 1996 international season. World Championships for the non-Olympic heavyweight and lightweight events, together with the junior championships, were held ten days later at Strathclyde Country Park in Scotland, when Leander's only representative was Chris Long, who finished tenth in the lightweight single sculls.

The separation of the non-Olympic events from the Olympic ones was the latest development in the continually evolving rowing scene, with no certainty that all the non-Olympic events would survive a further culling by FISA.

Leander's future, however, seems more assured, with its proven ability to adapt to the changing circumstances in which it has found itself over the years.

By the time of the centenary of the Henley clubhouse in 1997, the Club's long, if meandering, journey from its source on the tidal Thames in 1818 was in full flood. What, if they could return today, would those early 'gentlemen amateurs' from Stangate, with their private wager matches against carefully selected opponents, convivial lunches and dinners at riverside hostelries, or their wandering trips up the backwaters of Victorian waterways, make of today's generation of internationally orientated superstars, backed by sponsors and grants, operating from, to use current sports' jargon, from today's 'centre of excellence' at Henley?

Although those early Brilliants raced for substantial money prizes, they never for a moment considered themselves to be professionals. Professionals were those watermen and boat-builders who earned their livelihood on the river and raced each other for wagers and coats and badges, usually through the patronage of the gentlemen amateurs and the livery companies.

These watermen knew their place in the social as well as the sporting scene: they supplied and tended the boats and equipment used by the gentlemen amateurs, as well as steering and coaching them for wages. The fact that the amateurs also raced for money was neither here nor there, since they were generally from the leisured or professional classes, which automatically labelled them as gentlemen and therefore amateurs.

It was only when the Amateur Rowing Association, with several members of Leander involved, introduced in 1878 what was to prove a socially devisive definition, adopted by Henley the following year, of what constituted a professional, adding mechanics, artisans and labourers to the already accepted professional ranks of those who 'worked in or about boats' for a living, that rowing in Britain was split into two camps for well over half a century and led to the establishing in 1890 of the National Amateur Rowing Association, whose rules did not bar manual labourers.

Leander became the temple of amateurism in the late nineteenth and early twentieth centuries. Today's top 'amateur' oarsmen and women, with substantial financial assistance and subsidies from such organisations of the Sports Aid Foundation, as well as commercial sponsors, may find it incomprehensible that Vesper should have been banned from Henley for several years after 1905 because their Grand eight's expenses had been met by public subscription.

To today's Leander oarsmen, the Club's refusal to accept £1,000 from the sponsors of the Canadian National Exhibition towards their expenses to compete in the regatta at Toronto in 1923 must seem equally incomprehensible. All top competitors in every major sport today are professionals to a greater or lesser degree and rowing is no exception: nevertheless among the Olympic sports generally it has remained relatively unsullied by the intrusion of the media, which has helped to corrupt so many other sports. Because it is not easily televisual, rowing has not suffered in the way that athletics, football and, more recently, rugby, for example, have done.

Today, Leander upholds the best traditions of amateurism while accepting the reality of modern 'professional' competition, of which the Olympic Games are the prime example. At the same time, Henley maintains its position as undeniably the best preserved survivor of traditional amateur competition.

What, then, will the future bring, and in what ways will Leander need to move with the times in the twenty-first century? In the past, as the preceding pages have shown, the Club gradually shifted its ground according to the needs of the time, becoming, for example, an Oxbridge-oriented club in the 1890s before opening its doors to a wider membership in more recent years, notably with the Cadet scheme in the 1960s, and later with the arrival of national squads.

Since the arrival of these squads, which has meant, of course, that many of the Club's top oarsmen have not been available for its own crews, the Club has continued to register successes at Henley while also sharing wins with composite crews. It is confirmation, if one were needed, that Leander still plays a major part in the development of British rowing.

That this has been possible is largely due to the assistance of a number of voluntary coaches, whose combined efforts deserve more recognition than it has be possible to give them in these pages. Not least of these is John Peters, who has made an especially important contribution in recent years as the coach of Leander's younger crews, notably the Under-23 squad. Much credit should also go to Ivor Lloyd, who, as the Club's longest serving captain, has managed to co-ordinate the Club's rowing with international requirements with much skill. He took on the captaincy in 1985 and was continuing in that capacity at the time of writing.

As Appendix B shows, the Club's Henley record since its first success in the Grand Challenge Cup in 1840 is exceptional and is unrivalled by any other club, with twenty-seven wins in its own right in the Grand, together with six others shared in composite crews. Altogether, the Club has won Henley trophies on ninety-six occasions and shared in an additional seventeen wins. From a total of 835 races, the Club, including composite entries, has won 572 and lost 263, a remarkable record.

Appendix C shows that, in international rowing, Leander's contribution to Great Britain's representative teams since 1908 has been enormous and far outshines any other source of internationals in the United Kingdom.

While representing Leander in British teams, Club oarsmen and scullers have won thirty individual Olympic gold medals, thirty-three silvers and two bronzes. In World Championships, the total is eighteen golds, twelve silvers and eighteen bronzes, and in the now defunct European Championships, the tally was two golds, three silvers and three bronzes. Representing England in the Commonwealth Games or the former British Empire Games, Club members have taken two gold, nine silver and five bronze medals, a total of fifty-two gold medals, fifty-six silver, and twenty-eight bronze. None of the above includes the earlier medals won by Steve Redgrave, who, while rowing from Leander, was representing Marlow prior to 1988.

In recent years, Leander oarsmen have provided the backbone for British teams and since 1975 alone, against increasingly formidable opposition, Leander men have won seven Olympic, eighteen World and two Commonwealth gold medals, let alone twenty-nine silver and four bronze medals.

In today's highly competitive sporting scene, the development of first-class crews demands up-to-date facilities and equipment with all the back-up that is considered necessary for success: physiologists, physiotherapists and psychologists, in addition to full-time professional coaches, all of which results in always escalating costs.

Also vital to a club like Leander is an active social side with income from house activities to help defray the expenses of running both the building and the active rowing side. To generate such income, the house facilities have to be first-class as well. In recent years, there has been a steady improvement in these: the bedrooms now match those of good modern hotels and there are also meeting rooms and dining facilities to provide for the business conferences which are now held regularly at the clubhouse.

However, much remains to be done to the fabric of the building, and also to provide the extra facilities needed to expand the rowing activities.

The Leander appeal for funds, launched to coincide with the centenary of the Henley clubhouse in 1997, aimed primarily to provide the means to maintain the Club's pre-eminent position in British rowing by, among other things, expanding the Club's activities at both senior and development level, as well as making it feasible, at last, to admit women as members. In recent years, top women rowers and scullers have used the clubhouse while training as part of the national squad and, although the 1981 Special General Meeting rejected women as members, several speakers at the time considered it inevitable that women would one day be accepted. It would seem that, with the recent marked advance in the standard of women's rowing, together with the increasing acceptance of the important part played by women in the mixed society in which we live today, that time is now considerably overdue. Should women be admitted to active rowing membership, they would require changing and other facilities, and these were included in the imaginative and important plans for the future proposed by the Club Committee to celebrate the centenary of the clubhouse.*

These involved the demolition of the existing inadequate and antiquated changing rooms and gymnasium, which were to be replaced with up-to-date facilities for both sexes, including provision for medical and physiotherapy support. The number of bedrooms was to be increased but with the clubhouse being used for social and business functions, careful consideration was being given to ensuring a balance so that social activities, vital to ensure that the clubhouse paid its way, would not overwhelm the rowing side.

The total cost of all works was estimated at £2,313,000. A considerable amount by any standards, it was a formidable challenge and to raise the funds to realise these improvements, the Club would need all the support it could muster from every quarter. A submission for a grant was made to the National Lottery and this was eventually approved in the first week of January 1997, when the Sports Council announced that £1,500,000 would be allocated from the Lottery Sports Fund towards the redevelopment.

This generous contribution still left the Club to find £798,000 from other sources but at the time of the Lottery award, the Club had already been promised 75% of this, including some from the Leander Trust, and the rebuilding seemed assured.

Previously, towards the end of 1996, the Club had received a grant from the Foundation for Sport and the Arts towards the cost of employing a top international coach or coaches, with the proviso that any such coach should be available to help with coaching members of other clubs. As a result, the Club approached Harald Jarhling, chief rowing coach to the Australian Institute of Sport for the past seven years, who, as has already been recorded in these pages, had coached the Australian pair that had given Redgrave and

---

* A Special General Meeting of Leander Club, held on Sunday April 27, voted by a clear majority to admit women as members

Pinsent such a hard race at Lake Lanier. Jahrling accepted the invitation to become the Club's chief coach from February 1997 but later turned it down and the Club then resumed its search for another top-class coach.

In December 1996, Steve Redgrave was given the rare honour of being elected a Henley Steward, and this was soon followed by his being awarded the CBE in the New Year's Honours, the highest honour ever given to an active oarsman.

So Leander began 1997 on a high note and could look forward to the new century with considerable optimism and satisfaction. A long future seemed assured.

The Club has come a long way since 1818 and these pages have attempted to record the Club's traditions and its changing and developing character. No doubt it will continue to change and adapt in the twenty-first century, but it will remain, one trusts, for many decades to come, 'the pride of the Thames, the beautiful, the brilliant Leander' and the home of future Leander giants who will maintain the right to be called the 'Brilliants', and who will continue to raise their glasses to the Club's traditional toast:

CORPUS LEANDRI SPES MEA

PART THREE
FACTS AND FIGURES
by
Geoffrey Page

I
OFFICERS OF THE CLUB

Presidents
1866–1881   W. Bovill
1882–1891   Sir Patrick Colquhoun
1892–1915   H.T. Steward
1919–1934   G.D. Rowe
1934–1942   F.I. Pitman
1942–1946   C.M. Pitman
1946–1948   H.A. Steward
1948–1951   Viscount Bruce of Melbourne
1952–1956   C.D. Burnell, DSO
1957–1961   Viscount Cottesloe
1962–1966   G.O. Nickalls
1967–1969   H.R.N. Rickett, CBE
1969–1970   D.H. Mays-Smith
1970–1975   C.G. Rickett
1975–1980   Dr W.G.R.M. Laurie
1980–1983   J.L. Garton, CBE
1983–1988   K.M. Payne, MC, TD
1988–1993   R.D. Burnell, TD
1993–   W.A.D. Windham

Chairmen
1966–1969   M. Buxton
1969–1977   C.G.V. Davidge
1978–1981   C.M. Davis
1981–1983   D.B.E. Belson
1983–1989   T.A.G. Boswell
1989–1993   M. Hoffman
1993–   C.J. Rodrigues

Hon Treasurers
1845   E.W. Shepheard
1846–1857   T.B. Bumpstead
1858–1865   W. Bovill
1866–1881   C. Wigram
1882–1895   J.H.D. Goldie
1896–1934   F.I. Pitman
1934–1948   A.S. Garton

1948–1951   A. McCulloch
1951–1957   J.A. Macnabb
1957–1973   M. Buxton
1973–1978   J.D. Cazes, DFC
1978–1981   H.R.P. Steward
1981–1982   C.M. Davis
1983–1986   M. Buxton
1986–1989   M. Hoffman
1989–1991   E.H. Bainbridge
1991–1993   C.J. Rodrigues
1993–   J.D. Randall

Hon Secretaries
1845   H. Wood
1846   P. Colquhoun
1847–1853   T.H. Fellows
1854–1857   P. Colquhoun
1858–1859   T.L. Wood
1860–1864   A.P. Lonsdale
1865   H.C. Smith
1866–1879   H.T. Steward
1880–1883   A.W. Nicholson
1884–1886   J.A. Watson-Taylor
1887–1897   G.D. Rowe
1898–1903   R.C.M.G. Gridley
1904   C.J.D. Goldie
1905–1920   C.M. Pitman
1921   H.A. Steward
                E.D. Horsfall
1922–1942   H.A. Steward
1942–1946   P.C. Underhill
1946   K.M. Payne
1946–1950   G.D. Clapperton
1950–1951   J.A. Macnabb
1951–1956   A.T.M. Durand
1956–1957   M. Buxton
1957–1966   D.H. Mays-Smith
1966–1967   R.D. Burnell, TD

1967–1973	J.D. Cazes, DFC	1909–1912	A.G. Kirby
1973–1974	S.G.B. Underwood	1913–1914	A.S. Garton
1974–1978	H.R.P. Steward	1914–1919	A.F.R. Wiggins
1978–1981	J.D. Cazes, DFC	1920	R.S. Shove
1981–1983	R.S. Langton	1921	P.H.G.H.S. Hartley
1983–1989	J.D. Randall	1922	E.D. Horsfall
1989–1993	K. Hylton-Smith	1923–1927	G.O. Nickalls
1993–	J. Beveridge	1928	K.N. Craig
		1929–1930	J.C. Holcroft

Captains

1863–1865	H.T. Steward	1931	A. McCulloch
1866–1867	J.H. Forster	1932	H.R.N. Rickett
1868	H.T. Steward	1933	W.D.C. Erskine-Crum
1869	W.P. Bowman	1934–1935	K.M. Payne
1870	M.M. Brown	1936	W.G.R.M. Laurie
1871–1872	W.W. Wood	1937	J.D. Sturrock
1873	J.C. Tinné	1938–1943	J.C. Cherry
1874	S.D. Darbishire	1946	G.O. Nickalls
1875–1877	J.H.D. Goldie	1947	H.W. Mason
1878	M. Farrer	1948	G.O. Nickalls
1879	E.A. Miller	1949–1950	R.D. Burnell, TD
1880–1881	T.C. Edwards-Moss	1951	A.L. Macleod
1882–1883	E.V.V. Wheeler	1952	C.B.M. Lloyd
1883	G.D. Rowe	1953	W.A.D. Windham
1884	A.R. Paterson	1954–1955	C.G.V. Davidge
1885–1887	R.C.M.G. Gridley	1956	D.D. Macklin
1888	D.H. McLean	1957–1958	A.T.M. Durand
1889	S.D. Muttlebury	1959–1960	D.A.T. Leadley
1890–1891	W.F.C. Holland	1960–1962	P.B.D. Sutherland
1892	G. Nickalls	1962	J.L. Fage
1893–1894	W.F.C. Holland	1963	C.M. Davis
1895	R.C. Lehmann	1964	D.F. Legget
1896	C.M. Pitman	1965	R.D. Burnell, TD
1896	W.F.C. Holland	1966–1968	G.H. Brown
1897	G. Nickalls	1968–1972	J.K. Mullard
1898–1900	H.G. Gold	1973–1976	H.J. Twiss
1901–1902	C.D. Burnell, DSO	1976–1979	C.P. Etherington
1903	R.B. Etherington-Smith	1979–1981	A.C. McLean
1904	F.J. Escombe	1983–1985	D. Crockford
1905	C.K. Philips	1985–	I.B. Lloyd
1905–1906	R.B. Etherington-Smith		
1907–1908	B.C. Johnstone		
1908	R.B. Etberington-Smith		

2

LEANDER CREWS AT HENLEY ROYAL REGATTA

GRAND CHALLENGE CUP

1840 E. Shepheard (bow); H. Wood; S. Wallace; J. Layton; T.L. Jenkins; O. Ommanney; C. Pollock; A. Dalgleish (stroke); H. Gibson (cox)

Ht: bt University College, Oxford, easily, 9m 5s
Ht: bt Etonian Club, Oxford, easily
Final: bt Trinity College, Cambridge, easily, 9m 15s

1841 E. Shepheard, 10.2 (bow); J. Layton, 10.11; A.A. Julius, 11.6; – Ronayne, 11.8; T.L. Jenkins, 12.3; S. Wallace, 11.7; H. Wood, 10.12; A. Dalgleish 11.2 (stroke); H. Gibson, 11.0 (cox)

Final: lost on a foul to Cambridge Subscription Rooms, London.

1858 J. Wright, 11.2 (bow); P.P. Pearson, 11.8; T.H. Craster, 12.8; E.H. Fairrie, 12.10; E. Courage, 12.10; A.B. Rocke, 13.0; A.P. Lonsdale, 12.7 (stroke); E. Prior, 8.5 (cox)

Ht: lost to Cambridge University BC, 3 lths, 7m 43s

1866 C.C. Scholefield, 9.6 (bow); W.J.S. Cadman, 10.8; J.H. Etherington-Smith, 10.9; H. Watney, 10.12; J.G. Chambers, 12.1; R.A. Kinglake, 12.11; F.H. Kelly, 11.11; J.H. Forster, 10.0 (stroke), F. Walton, 7.6 (cox)

Ht: lost to First Trinity, Cambridge, ¾ lth, 8m 43s

1875 P.J. Hibbert, 11.5 (bow); W. Davy, 11.5; E.A. Phillips, 13.00; A.W. Nicholson, 12.11; C.S. Read, 12.9; H.E. Rhodes, 11.9; C.W. Benson, 11.6; J.H.D. Goldie, 12.6 (stroke), E.O. Hopwood, 8.6 (cox)

Ht: 1, Leander; 2, Thames RC; 3, London RC, 1¼ lths, 7m 30s
Final: Leander, 1; Molesey BC, 2; First Trinity, Cambridge, 3.2 lths, 7m 19s

1876 P.J. Hibbert, 11.5 (bow); A.B. Woodd, 11.6; T.K. McClintock-Bunbury, 12.0; F. Peabody, 11.8; M.G. Farrer, 12.1; A.W. Nicholson, 12.13; H.W. Benson, 11.8; J.H.D. Goldie, 12.4 (stroke); E.O. Hopwood, 8.6 (cox)

Ht: 1, University and Brasenose Colleges (OUBC qualification); 2, Leander; 3, Kingston RC 2 lths, 7m 23s

1880 R.H.J. Poole, 10.4 (bow); L.R. West, 11.0; F.H. Capron, 11.13; H. Sandford, 11.6; J.H.T. Wharton, 11.9; H.B. Southwell, 12.10; T.C. Edwards-Moss, 12.4; W.A. Ellison, 10.12 (stroke); G.L. Davis, 8.0 (cox)

Ht: 1, Leander; 2, Thames RC; 3, Jesus College, Cambridge 2 lths, 7m 6s
Final: Leander, 1; London RC, 2.1½ lths, 7m 3s

1881 R.H.J. Poole, 10.7 (bow); H. Sandford, 11.13; C.W. Moore, 11.11; F.H. Capron, 11.12; R.S. Kindersley, 13.5; W.H. Grenfell, 12.11; T.C. Edwards-Moss, 12.3; L.R. West, 11.2 (stroke); G.L. Davis, 8.0 (cox)

Ht: bt Eton College, easily
Final: 1, London RC; 2, Leander;
  3, Hertford College, Oxford 1 lth, 7m 23s

1883 G.C. Bourne, 10.10 (bow); F.M. Lutyens, 10.11; W.E.P. Austin, 11.8; G.D. Rowe, 12.0; D.H. McLean, 12.12; A.R. Paterson, 13.2; E.L. Puxley, 12.8; A.H. Higgins, 9.3 (stroke), G.L. Davis, 8.3 (cox)

Ht: 1, Twickenham RC; 2, Leander;
  3, Royal Chester RC, 4 lths, 7m 35s

1884 H.S. Close, 10.7 (bow); F.C. Meyrick, 11.12; C.R. Carter, 12.9; E.L. Puxley, 12.11; D.H. McLean, 13.1; A.R. Paterson, 13.6; R.A. Pinckney, 11.6; W.D.B. Curry, 10.1 (stroke); F.J. Humphreys, 8.3 (cox)

Ht: 1, Twickenham RC; 2, Leander;
  3, Kingston RC, 3 lths, 7m 25s

1885 W.K. Hardacre, 10.7 (bow); R.G. Gridley, 10.8; R.H. Coke, 12.5; S. Swann, 12.10; F.E. Churchill, 13.6; E.W. Haig, 11.12; St C.G.A. Donaldson, 11.10, F.I. Pitman, 11.9 (stroke); G.L. Davis, 8.2 (cox)

Ht: lost to Twickenham RC, 1¾ lths, 7m 17s

1888 W.F.C. Holland, 10.9 (bow); A.C. Maclachlan, 11.6; W.F.D. Smith, 10.12; H.R. Parker, 13.7; G. Nickalls, 12.1; D.H. McLean, 13.1; S.D. Muttlebury, 13.7; L. Frere, 10.0 (stroke); P.L. Hawkins, 8.4 (cox)

Ht: bt London RC, 2¼ lths, 7m 36s
Ht: bt Trinity Hall, Cambridge, 1½ lths, 7m 37s
Final: lost to Thames RC, ¾ lth, 7m 1s

1889 W.F.C. Holland, 10.6 (bow); C.W. Kent, 10.12; R.P.P. Rowe, 11.7; C.F. Lloyd, 12.9; S.D. Muttlebury, 13.10; P. Landale, 12.13; F.H. Maugham, 11.5; J.C. Gardner, 11.12 (stroke); D. Powell, 8.0 (cox)

Ht: lost to Thames RC, 1¾ lths, 7m 1s

1891 W.F.C. Holland, 10.7 (bow); J.A. Ford, 11.8; V. Nickalls, 12.8; Lord Ampthill, 13.8; G. Nickalls, 12.5; W.A.L. Fletcher, 13.9; R.P.P. Rowe, 11.9; C.W. Kent, 10.12 (stroke); L.S. Williams, 8.4 (cox)

Ht: dead-heat with Thames RC, 7m 38s.
  re-row: bt Thames RC, 2 lths, 7m 7s
Final: bt London RC, 1 lth, 6m 51s (record)

1892 H.B. Cotton, 10.0 (bow); J.A. Ford, 11.10; W.A.S. Hewett, 12.0; C.M. Pitman, 11.11; G. Nickalls, 12.10; W.A.L. Fletcher, 13.8; R.P.P. Rowe, 12.0; C.W. Kent, 10.12 (stroke); J.P. Heywood-Lonsdale, 9.2 (cox)

Ht: bt First Trinity, Cambridge, 1 lth, 7m 26s
Final: bt Thames RC, 3 lths, 7m 48½s

1893 W.F.C. Holland, 10.10 (bow); T.G. Lewis, 11.12; C.T. Fogg-Elliot, 11.7; J.A. Ford, 11.9; W.B. Stewart, 13.2; W.A.L. Fletcher, 13.6; R.O. Kerrison, 11.8; C.W. Kent, 10.10 (stroke); L.S. Williams, 8.4 (cox)

Ht: bt Magdalen College, Oxford, 1¼ lths, 6m 56s
Ht: bt Trinity College, Dublin, 2¼ lths, 7m 5s
Final: bt London RC, 1¾ lths, 7m 12s

1894 H.B. Cotton, 10.0 (bow); J.A. Ford, 12.0; M.C. Pilkington, 12.3; C.M. Pitman, 11.12; W.B. Stewart, 13.8; J.A. Morrison, 12.9; W.E. Crum, 12.1; C.W. Kent, 10.13 (stroke); D. Powell, 8.3 (cox)

Ht: bt London RC, 1 lth, 7m 18s
Final: bt Thames RC, ½ lth, 7m 22s

1895 C.W.N. Graham, 10.1 (bow); J.A. Ford, 11.12; H. Graham, 12.1; T.J.G. Duncanson, 13.5; W.B. Stewart, 13.5; C.D. Burnell, 13.6; M.C. Pilkington, 12.4; C.W. Kent, 10.11 (stroke), F.C. Begg, 8.7 (cox)

Ht: won by Cornell University, USA, Leander left on start.

1896 C.W.N. Graham, 10.2 (bow); J.A. Ford, 12.3; H.W.M. Willis, 11.12; R. Carr, 12.11; T.H.E. Stratch, 13.5; G. Nickalls, 12.3; W.F.C. Holland, 10.8; H.G. Gold, 11.9 (stroke); H.R.K. Pechell, 8.2 (cox)

Ht: bt Yale University, USA, 1¾ lths, 7m 14s
Ht: bt New College, Oxford, ½ lth, 7m 6s
Final: bt Thames RC, 2¼ lths, 7m 43s

1897 C.W.N. Graham, 10.2 (bow); J.A. Ford, 12.1; H.W.M. Willis, 11.12; R. Carr, 12.9; E.R. Balfour, 13.4; G. Nickalls, 12.7; C.J.D. Goldie, 11.12; H.G. Gold, 11.8 (stroke); H.R.K. Pechell, 8.4 (cox)

Ht: bt Thames RC, 1¾ lths, 7m 21s
Ht: bt Utrecht University 'Triton', 1¼ lths, 7m 11s
Final: lost to New College, Oxford, 2 feet, 6m 51s

1898 H.A. Steward, 10.11 (bow); W.B. Rennie, 11.7; J.A. Tinné, 11.11; H.A. Game, 12.1; C.D. Burnell, 14.2; H.W.M. Willis, 12.2; C.J.D. Goldie, 12.2; H.G. Gold, 11.10 (stroke); H.R.K. Pechell, 8.10 (cox)

Ht: bt London RC, ½ lth, 7m 12s
Final: bt First Trinity, Cambridge, ¾ lth, 7m 13s

1899 R.O. Pitman, 10.11 (bow); E.A. De la P. Beresford-Peirse, 11.0; H.W.M. Willis, 12.2; H.A. Game, 11.13; C.D. Burnell, 13.11; R. Carr, 12.10; C.K. Philips, 11.7; H.G. Gold, 11.11 (stroke); G.S. Maclagan, 8.7 (cox)

Ht: bt Balliol College, Oxford, 1¼ lths, 7m 11s
Ht: bt Trinity College, Cambridge, 1¼ lths, 6m 57s
Final: bt London RC, 1¼ lths, 7m 12s

1900 R.O. Pitman, 10.8 (bow); H.U. Gould, 11.8; Lord Grimston, 13.6; F.W. Warre, 12.4; C.D. Burnell, 13.9; J.E. Payne, 12.9; M.C.McC. Thornhill, 11.0; F.O.J. Huntley, 11.2 (stroke); G.S. Maclagan, 8.12 (cox)

Ht: bt Club Nautique de Gand, Belgium, ¾ lth, 7m 17s
Final: bt Trinity College, Cambridge, ½ lth, 7m 6s

1901 C.A. Willis, 11.1 (bow); H.J. du Vallon, 12.3; W. Dudley Ward, 12.7; G.McD. Maitland, 12.1; C.D. Burnell, 13.4; J.E. Payne, 12.12; C.J.D. Goldie, 12.1; R.B. Etherington-Smith, 12.6 (stroke); G.S. Maclagan, 8.9 (cox)

Ht: bt New College, Oxford, 1¾ lths, 7m 9s
Ht: bt Club Nautique de Gand, Belgium, 1 lth, 7m 8s
Final: bt University of Pennsylvania, USA, 1 lth, 7m 4⅖s

1902 T.B. Etherington-Smith, 11.3 (bow); D. Milburn, 12.2; J. Younger, 12.10; A.de L. Long, 12.11; C.D. Burnell, 13.10; F.W. Warre, 12.5; C.K. Philips, 12.3; G.C. Drinkwater, 11.4 (stroke); G.S. Maclagan, 8.10 (cox)

Ht: bt Kingston RC, easily, 7m 34s
Ht: bt London RC, 1 lth and 2 feet, 7m 28s
Final: lost to Third Trinity, Cambridge, 1½ lths, 7m 17s

1903 H. Sanger, 10.9, (bow); T. Drysdale, 11.10; B.C. Cox, 11.13; F.S. Kelly, 12.0; R.B. Etherington-Smith, 12.6; F.W. Warre, 12.8; F.J. Escombe, 13.0; A.K. Graham, 10.10 (stroke); G.S. Maclagan, 8.10 (cox)

Ht: bt Thames RC, easily, 7m 40s
Final: bt Third Trinity, Cambridge, 6 feet, 7m 9s

1904 W.H. Chapman, 11.2 (bow); F.S. Kelly, 11.12; B.C. Johnstone, 12.5; C.W.H. Taylor, 12.12; F.J. Escombe, 13.3; P.H. Thomas, 12.6; A.K. Graham, 11.0; R.H. Nelson, 11.1 (stroke); G.S. Maclagan, 8.11 (cox)

Ht: bt London RC, 1 lth, 7m 43s
Final: bt New College, Oxford, 1 lth, 7m 20s

1905 A.K. Graham, 11.3 (bow); F.S. Kelly, 12.1; B.C. Johnstone, 12.8; G.Nickalls, 12.12; F.J. Escombe, 12.11; P.H. Thomas, 12.7; R.B. Etherington-Smith, 12.5; R.H. Nelson, 11.2 (stroke); G.S. Maclagan, 8.9 (cox)

Ht: bt Jesus College, Cambridge, 1¾ lths, 7m 26s
Ht: bt Vesper BC, Philadelphia, USA, 1 lth, 7m 1s
Final: bt Sport Nautique de Gand, Belgium, 2¼ lths, 6m 58s

1907 H.C. Bucknall, 11.6 (bow); J.F.H. Benham, 12.3; H.M. Goldsmith, 12.5; R.V. Powell, 12.6; B.C. Johnstone, 12.12; F.J. Escombe, 12.11; E.W. Powell, 11.6; D.C.R. Stuart, 11.2 (stroke); G.S. Maclagan, 8.10 (cox)

Ht: bt London RC, 1¼ lths, 7m 33s
Ht: lost to Sport Nautique de Gand, Belgium, ⅓ lth, 7m 50s

1909 C.A. Gladstone, 10.11 (bow); R.W.M. Arbuthnot, 10.4; A.C. Gladstone, 11.6; B.C. Johnstone, 12.11; E.G. Williams, 13.0; J.S. Burn, 12.8; H.R. Barker, 12.4; R.C. Bourne, 11.1 (stroke); B.G.A. Scott, 8.10 (cox)

Ht: lost to Jesus College, Cambridge, ⅓ lth, 7m 19s

1910 C.A. Gladstone, 10.13 (bow); R.H. Owen, 12.8; C.R. le B. Smith, 12.11; J.S. Burn, 12.9; N. Field, 14.2; J.B. Rosher, 14.7; A.G. Kirby, 13.8; R.C. Bourne, 11.0 (stroke); B.G.A. Scott, 8.10 (cox)

Ht: lost to Magdalen College, Oxford, ¾ lth, 7m 13s

1912 S.E. Swann, 11.6 (bow); C.E. Tinné, 11.13; L.G. Wormald, 12.7; E.D. Horsfall, 12.6; J.A. Gillan, 13.4; A.S. Garton, 13.6; A.G. Kirby, 13.8; P. Fleming, 11.11 (stroke); H.B. Wells, 8.12 (cox)

Ht: bt London RC, 2½ lths, 7m 23s
Ht: bt Thames RC, 1¼ lths, 7m 25s
Final: lost to Sydney RC, Australia, ¾ lth, 7m 6s

1913 A.C. Gladstone, 11.3 (bow); S.E. Swann, 11.3; L.G. Wormald, 12.5; E.D. Horsfall, 12.5; C.S. Clark, 12.9; A.S. Garton, 13.8; F.F.V. Scrutton, 12.0; G.E. Tower, 11.10 (stroke); H.B. Wells, 8.12 (cox)

Ht: bt Argonaut RC, Toronto, Canada, 1¼ lths, 6m 51s
Ht: bt Thames RC, 1¼ lths, 7m 4s
Final: bt Jesus College, Cambridge, 1 lth, 7m 11s

1914 A.A. Swann, 11.11 (bow); S.E. Swann, 11.9; F.F.V. Scrutton, 12.7; A.F.R. Wiggins, 12,10; K.G. Garnett, 13.9; E.D. Horsfall, 12.5; C.E.V. Buxton, 12.3; D.I. Day, 11.0 (stroke); J.D. Walker, 8.7 (cox)

Ht: lost to Harvard Athletic Association, USA, 1 lth, 7m 37s

1920 J.P.I. Corry, 11.5 (bow); A.C. Beasley-Robinson, 11.9; A.A. Swann, 11.13; A. McCulloch, 13.1; P.C. Livingston, 13.10; R.S. Shove, 12.5; Rev S.E. Swann, 11.7; G.L. Thomson, 11.9 (stroke); R.T. Johnstone, 9.2 (cox)

Ht: bt Thames RC, 1½ lths, 7m 58s
Final: lost to Magdalen College, Oxford, 2 lths, 7m 24s

1921 J.E. Lawson-Johnston, 11.2 (bow); P.C. Mallam, 11.6; H.O.C. Boret, 12.0; H. Peake, 12.5; R.I.L. MacEwen, 13.1; J.H. Simpson, 12.5; Hon. J.W.H. Fremantle, 12.2; P.H.G.H.S. Hartley, 11.5 (stroke); R.T. Johnstone, 9.5 (cox)

Ht: bt KRZ de Maas, Holland, easily, 7m 15s
Ht: lost to Jesus College, Cambridge, 1 lth, 7m 25s

1922 P.H.G.H.S. Hartley, 11.7 (bow); H.O.C. Boret, 12.0; G.O. Nickalls, 12.5; D.T. Raikes, 13.11; A.B. Ritchie, 13.3; R.S.C. Lucas, 13.11; Hon J.W. Fremantle, 12.4, E.D. Horsfall, 12.7 (stroke); W.H. Porritt, 9.9 (cox)

Ht: bt Pembroke College, Cambridge, easily, 7.25
Ht: bt First Trinity, Cambridge, 1 lth, 7m 49s
Ht: bt Jesus College, Cambridge, ½ lth, 7m 44s
Final: bt Thames RC, 1 lth, 7m 36s

1923 P.C. Mallam, 12.0 (bow); H.O.C. Boret, 12.3; A.B. Ritchie, 13.7; D.T. Raikes, 13.8; H.B. Playford, 13.7; R.K. Kane, 13.7; G.O. Nickalls, 12.12, P.H.G.H.S. Hartley, 11.0 (stroke); A.W.F. Donkin, 8.8 (cox)

Ht: lost to Eton Vikings Club, 1¼ lths, 7m 4s

1924 D.C. Bennett, 10.8 (bow); G. Milling, 12.0; H.O.C. Boret, 12.3; J.E. Pedder, 13.2; H.R. Carver, 12.4; R.S.C. Lucas, 13.6; G.O. Nickalls, 12.13; W.P. Mellen, 10.9 (stroke); R.T. Johnstone, 9.6 (cox)

Ht: bt Christ Church, Oxford, 1 lth, 8m 5s
Ht: bt Thames RC, ½ lth, 8m 1s
Final: bt Jesus College, Cambridge, 6 feet, 8m 3s

1925 G. Milling, 12.0 (bow); H.O.C. Boret, 12.8; K.N. Craig, 12.2; A.D.B. Pearson, 13.10; H.B. Playford, 13.10; R.S.C. Lucas, 13.8; G.O. Nickalls, 12.13; W.P. Mellen, 10.11, (stroke); G.D. Clapperton, 8.0 (cox)

Ht: bt Granta (CUBC qualification), 1 lth, 7m 9s
Ht: bt London RC, easily, 7m 18s
Final: bt Thames RC, ¾ lth, 6m 53s

1926 G.E.G. Gadsden, 11.2 (bow); C.R.M. Eley, 11.5; K.N. Craig, 12.6; H.O.C. Boret, 12.11; H.R. Carver, 12.6; A.D.B. Pearson, 13.11; G.O. Nickalls, 12.9; T.D.A. Collet, 12.5 (stroke); G.D. Clapperton, 8.0 (cox)

Ht: bt Thames RC, ½ lth, 6m 59s
Final: bt Lady Margaret BC, Cambridge, 2 lths, 6m 56s

1927 G.E.G. Gadsden, 11.2 (bow); A.G. Wansbrough, 11.9; S.K. Tubbs, 12.8; H.O.C. Boret, 12.11; K.N. Craig, 12.8; H.T. Kingsbury, 14.5; G.O. Nickalls, 12.12; E.C. Hamilton-Russell, 11.7 (stroke); G.D. Clapperton, 8.0 (cox)

Ht: lost to Thames RC, 2 lths, 7m 6s

1928 A. Graham, 11.3 (bow); A.A.F. Haigh, 11.10; L.V. Bevan, 13.3; A.G.H. Willis, 12.5; J.C. Holcroft, 12.13; R.R. Waterer, 13.1; K.N. Craig, 12.9; J.S. Herbert, 11.5 (stroke); G.D. Clapperton, 8.0 (cox)

Ht: lost to First Trinity, Cambridge, 2 lths, 7m 41s

1929 E. Norman-Butler, 11.9 (bow); R.J. Elles, 12.1; H.R. Carver, 12.9; T.R.B. Sanders, 12.0; J.C. Holcroft, 12.8; J.B. Collins, 14.3; C.E. Wool-Lewis, 12.3; T.A. Brocklebank, 11.12 (stroke); J.K. Brock, 8.10 (cox)

Ht: bt London RC, 1 lth, 7m 54s
Final: bt Thames RC, 2 lengths, 7m 0s

1930 W.A. Prideaux, 12.6 (bow); H.R.N. Rickett, 12.6; J.C. Holcroft, 12.8; T.E. Letchworth, 12.6; M.H. Warriner, 13.13; R. Beesly, 12.10; A. Graham, 11.7; T.A. Brocklebank, 11.6 (stroke); G.D. Clapperton, 8.0 (cox)

Ht: bt University College, Oxford, 1¼ lths, 7m 17s
Final: lost to London RC, 1½ lths, 6m 59s

1932 D. Haig-Thomas, 11.6 (bow); K.M. Payne, 12.7; T.G. Askwith, 12.6; W.A.T. Sambell, 12.4; C.J.S. Sergel, 12.3; H.R.N. Rickett, 12.13; D.H.E. McCowen, 12.8; L. Luxton, 12.11 (stroke); J.M. Ranking, 8.0 (cox)

Ht: bt London RC, 1¼ lths, 7m 38s
Final: bt Thames RC, ½ lth, 7m 19s

1934 J.H.C. Powell, 12.3 (bow); J.M. Couchman, 12.10; J.H. Lascelles, 11.8; A.V. Sutcliffe, 14.0; P. Hogg, 12.9; K.M. Payne, 12.3; D.J. Wilson, 13.11; W.G.R.M. Laurie, 13.4 (stroke); J.N. Duckworth, 8.7 (cox)

Ht: bt London RC, 1 lth, 6m 45s (record)
Ht: bt Thames RC, ½ lth, 6m 44s (record)
Final: bt Princeton University, USA, ¾ lth, 6m 45s

1935 M.P. Lonnon, 12.7 (bow); J.H.C. Powell, 12.8; C.M. Fletcher, 13.4; A.V. Sutcliffe, 14.5; C.A. Noble, 12.10; J.M. Couchman, 12.8; T.G. Askwith, 11.9; D.M. de R. Winser, 11.8 (stroke); D.R. Rose, 8.6 (cox)

Ht: bt Thames RC, ¾ lth, 7m 17s
Final: lost to Pembroke College, Cambridge, 1¾ lths, 6m 52s

1936 A.D. Kingsford, 11.13 (bow); F.M.G. Stammers, 11.8; M.P. Lonnon, 12.13; T.G. Askwith, 11.13; J.C. Cherry, 13.9; J.M. Couchman, 12.10; D.J. Wilson, 12.12; W.G.R.M. Laurie, 13.4 (stroke); D.R. Rose, 8.8 (cox)

Ht: bt London RC, ½ lth, 7m 33s
Ht: bt Union BC, Boston, USA, 1 lth, 7m 17s
Final: lost to Ruder Club, Zurich, Switzerland, 1¼ lths, 7m 25s

1937 F.M.G. Stammers, 11.9 (bow); D.M.W. Napier, 13.0; P.H. Gaskell, 12.0; R.G. Rowe, 12.8; J.P. Burrough, 13.6; J.D Sturrock, 14.6; J.C. Cherry, 13.10; D.M. de R. Winser, 12.0 (stroke); G.J.P. Merifield, 8.2 (cox)

Ht: lost to London RC, ½ lth, 7m 30s

1939 M. Buxton, 12.10 (bow); C.B. Sanford, 12.2; H. Parker, 13.2; H.A.W. Forbes, 13.2; D.G. Kingsford, 13.2; J. Turnbull, 13.13; J.C. Cherry, 14.4; A.B. Hodgson, 11.12 (stroke); G.J.P. Merifield, 8.9 (cox)

Ht: lost to Jesus College, Cambridge, ½ lth, 7m 32s

1946 R.M.T. Raikes, 10.12 (bow); A.J.R. Purssell, 11, 11.6; P. Bradley, 12.7; H.W. Mason, 11.5; R.D. Burnell, 14.0; R.M.A. Bourne, 11.6; P.N. Brodie, 11.2; N.J. Bradley, 14.10 (stroke); G.D. Clapperton, 9.2 (cox)

Ht: bt Kingston RC, 1½ lths, 7m 50s
Ht: bt Trinity Hall, Cambridge, 1¼ lths, 7m 23s
Final: bt Ruder Club, Zurich, Switzerland, ¾ lth, 7m 1s

1947 A.P. Mellows, 12.0 (bow); R.M.A. Bourne, 11.6; P. Bradley, 12.10; H.W. Mason, 11.8; W.A.D. Windham, 12.13; I.M. Lang, 13.7; A.S.F. Butcher, 12.4; N.J. Bradley, 14.13 (stroke); J.N. Duckworth, 8.7 (cox)

Ht: lost to Jesus College, Cambridge, ½ lth, 7m 20s

1948 A.P. Mellows, 12.4 (bow); G.C. Richardson, 12.10; P.A. de Giles, 12.5; P.M.O. Massey, 13.9; E.A.P. Bircher, 13.5; I.M. Lang, 13.3; M.C. Lapage, 13.3; D.J.C. Meyrick, 11.5 (stroke); H. Mayman, 8.10 (cox)

Ht: lost to Thames RC, ½ lth, 6m 59s

1949 J.G.C. Blacker, 11.13 (bow); R.M.T. Raikes, 11.4; J.R.L. Carstairs, 12.4; J.R.W. Gleave, 12.9; W.A.D. Windham, 13.3; R.D. Burnell, 14.12; P.A. de Giles, 12.4; P. Bradley, 12.12 (stroke); A. Palgrave-Brown, 8.3 (cox)

Ht: bt London RC, ½ lth, 7m 10s
Ht: bt Trinity College, Oxford, ¾ lth, 6m 44s (equals record)
Final: bt Thames RC, 1 lth, 6m 54s

1950 A.P. Mellows, 12.8 (bow); D.J.C. Meyrick, 11.0; J.R.L. Carstairs, 12.4; P. Bradley, 12.13; E.A.P. Bircher, 13.3; R.D. Burnell, 14.4; D.N. Callender, 12.2; C.G.V. Davidge, 13.4 (stroke); J.E.C. Hinchcliffe, 9.3 (cox)

Ht: bt Dartmouth RC, USA, 3 lths, 7m 32s
Ht: lost to SR 'Njord', Holland, ½ lth, 6m 57s

1951 G.C. Fisk, 11.12 (bow); J.R. Johnson, 12.1; A.L. Macleod, 12.12; T.H. Christie, 13.13; W.A.D. Windham, 12.12; P.M.O. Massey, 13.12; P.A.de Giles, 12.4; J.L.M. Crick, 12.2 (stroke); J.G. Dearlove, 8.7 (cox)

Ht: bt SR 'Njord', Holland, ½ lth, 7m 15s
Ht: lost to Lady Margaret BC, Cambridge, 1¼ lths, 7m 7s

1952 D.D. Macklin, 11.13 (bow); A.L. Macleod, 12.8; N.B.M. Clack, 12.11; R.F.A. Sharpley, 13.7; E.J. Worlidge, 12.13; C.B.M. Lloyd, 12.8; W.A.D. Windham, 12.10; D.M. Jennens, 12.8 (stroke); J.F.K. Hinde, 9.2 (cox)

Ht: bt London RC, easily, 6m 44s
Final: bt Sydney RC, Australia, ½ lth, 6m 38s (record)

1953 D.D. Macklin, 11.6 (bow); R.M.S. Gubbins, 11.0; P.A. de Giles, 12.8; D.A.T. Leadley, 13.1; E.A.P. Bircher, 12.10; C.G.V. Davidge, 12.2; W.A.D. Windham, 12.6; G.A.H. Cadbury, 12.0 (stroke); J.F.K. Hinde, 9.3 (cox)

Ht: bt Lady Margaret BC, Cambridge, 1 lth, 6m 41s
Ht: bt Thames RC, 2 lths, 6m 44s
Final: bt Union Sportive Metropolitaine des Transports, France, ¾ lth, 6m 49s

1954 E.O.G. Pain, 11.10 (bow); D.D. Macklin, 11.10; H.M.C. Quick, 13.8; D.A.T. Leadley, 13.1; E.A.P. Bircher, 13.1; C.G.V. Davidge, 12.1; W.A.D. Windham, 12.10; G.A.H. Cadbury, 12.0 (stroke); J.F.K. Hinde, 9.3 (cox)

Ht: bt Lady Margaret BC, Cambridge, ⅔ lth, 6m 56s
Final: lost to Krylia Sovetov, USSR, 2½ lths, 7m 16s

1956 D.D. Macklin, 11.6 (bow); R.M.S. Gubbins, 11.3; J.G.C. Blacker, 12.5; D.A.T. Leadley, 12.8; S.G.D. Tozer, 13.9; C.G.V. Davidge, 12.8; R.H. Carnegie, 13.9; J.J.H. Harrison, 12.0 (stroke); J.F.K. Hinde, 9.4 (cox)

Ht: lost to Jesus College, Cambridge, ½ lth, 7m 46s

1959 C.K. Smith, 12.4 (bow); B.S. Mawer, 12.3; H.E. Fitzgibbon, 13.3; R. Rubin, 14.2; C.L. Grimes, 15.2; D.A.T. Leadley, 12.6; R.A.J. Southgate, 12.1; J.F.C.S. Clayre, 12.1 (stroke); S.G.B. Underwood, 8.11 (cox)

Ht: lost to Thames RC, 1¼ lths, 7m 6s

1961 P.C.D. Burnell, 12.9 (bow); R.L.S. Fishlock, 11.9; J.O.B. Sewall, 13.13; C.P.M. Gomm, 12.6; I.L. Elliott, 14.0; D.C.R. Edwards, 13.3; J.R. Chester, 12.9; C.M. Davis, 12.2 (stroke); J.M. Howard-Johnston, 8.11 (cox)

Ht: bt Molesey BC, 1 lth, 6m 40s
Ht: bt Thames RC, 1 lth, 6m 52s
Final: lost to Central Sport Club of the USSR Navy, Moscow, 1 lth, 6m 43s

1962 J.H.M. Edwards, 12.5 (bow); R.L.S. Fishlock, 12.0; M.J. Muir-Smith, 13.1; I. Wilson, 13.1; F.D.M. Badcock, 12.12; D.C.R. Edwards, 13.1; J.R. Chester, 13.1; C.M. Davis, 12.8 (stroke); P.J. Reynolds, 8.6 (cox)

Ht: lost to Molesey BC, ¾ lth, 6m 34s

1963 Hon R.A. Napier, 12.6 (bow); C.W. Holden, 11.2; M.H.F. Morley, 12.12; G.A. Hayter, 14.5; J.L. Fage, 13.2, M.J.W. Hall, 12.7; R.C.I. Bate, 12.9; S.C. Rand, 12.4 (stroke); G.C.H. Shakerley, 9.0 (cox)

Ht: lost to University of London, 2¾ lths, 6m 46s

1964 W.P. Andreae-Jones, 11.7 (bow); R.L.S. Fishlock, 11.8; D.C. Spencer, 13.3; A.T. Lindsay, 13.0; J.C.D. Sherratt, 12.10; D.C.R. Edwards, 12.12; J.R. Chester, 12.12; C.M. Davis, 12.2 (stroke); P.J. Reynolds, 8.7 (cox)

Ht: lost to Thames RC, ⅔ lth, 7m 8s

1967 C.D.C. Challis, 13.8 (bow); L.M. Henderson, 13.7; G.C.M. Leggett, 12.10; D.F. Earl, 13.11; P.G.R. Delafield, 14.6; N.J. Hornsby, 14.10; R.D. Yarrow, 13.8; R.N. Winckless, 13.4 (stroke); W.R. Lawes, 9.3 (cox)

Ht: lost to SC Wissenschaft DHfK, Leipzig, E. Germany, easily, 7m 6s

1970 V.J. Pardhy, 12.5 (bow); P.D.P. Angier, 12.6; R.J.S. Clarke, 12.9; J.C. Yallop, 13.13; J.K. Mullard, 13.4; T.J. Crooks, 13.6; G.A.S. Locke, 13.13; J.C. Pemberton, 12.11 (stroke); J.A. Easton, 9.5 (cox)

Ht: bt Dartmouth College, USA, 1⅔ lths, 7m 5s

Ht: lost to GSR Aegir, Holland, ¾ lth, 6m 34s

1971 V.J. Pardhy, 12.5 (bow); P.D.P. Angier, 13.5; C.M.C. Preston, 13.2; R.C. Lester, 13.3; G.A.S. Locke, 13.6; T.J. Crooks, 13.9; N.D.C. Tee, 12.11; J.C. Yallop, 14.9 (stroke); J.A. Easton, 8.1 (cox)

Ht: lost to Tideway Scullers School, ½ lth, 6m 47s

1974 (Leander/Thames Tradesmen's): W.G. Mason (TT), 11.2 (bow); L.D. Robertson (TT), 13.5; F.J. Smallbone (TT), 13.5; H.P. Matheson, 14.0; D.L. Maxwell, 13.7; J.C. Yallop, 14.12; T.J. Crooks, 13.10 (stroke); P.J. Sweeney (TT), 8.0 (cox)

Ht: bt Tideway Scullers School, 3¼ lths, 6m 53s

Final: lost to Trud Club, USSR, ½ lth, 6m 34s

1975 (Leander/Thames Tradesmen's): L.D. Robertson (TT), 13.0 (bow); W.G. Mason (TT), 11.10; J. Clark (TT), 13.8; J.C. Yallop, 13.8; R.J. Ayling, 15.0; T.J. Crooks, 14.0; H.P. Matheson, 14.4; R.C. Lester, 13.10 (stroke); P.J. Sweeney (TT), 8.3 (cox)

Ht: bt Vesper BC, USA, 1 lth, 6.13 (equals record)

Final: bt Harvard University, USA, 2 lths, 6m 16s

1976 D.E. Innes, 11.12 (bow); G.S. Innes, 13.7; D.J.D. Tatton, 12.7; N.C. Hardingham, 13.4; D.B. King, 13.12; W.R. Woodward-Fisher, 13.7; P.S. Gregory, 14.1; G.A. Rankine, 14.1 (stroke); R.C. Lee, 8.0 (cox)

Ht: bt University of British Columbia, Canada, ¾ lth, 6m 22s

Ht: bt University of London, ½ lth, 6m 26s

Final: lost to Thames Tradesmen's RC, ⅔ lth, 6m 25s

1977 (Leander/Thames Tradesmen's/Thames RC): D.B. King, 13.9 (bow); A.G. Mallin (TT), 13.0; J.H. Clay (LRC), 13.2; J.M. Pritchard (TRC), 13.9; P.S. Gregory, 14.5; W.R. Woodward-Fisher, 13.2; R.D. Milligan (TT), 12.13; C.G. Seymour (TT), 14.3 (stroke), R.C. Lee, 8.8 (cox)

Ht: bt Oxford University, 1⅔ lths, 7m 2s

Ht: bt Cornell University, USA, ¼ lth, 6m 47s

Final: lost to University of Washington, USA, 1 lth, 6m 27s

1978 (Leander/Thames Tradesmen's/London RC/Tideway SC) R.D. Milligan (TT), 13.8 (bow); J.H. Clay (LRC), 13.10; C.G. Seymour (TT), 14.3; W.R. Woodward-Fisher, 13.10; P.S. Gregory, 14.6; G.A. Rankine, 14.8; L.D. Robertson (TT), 13.7; N.P. Dale (TSc), 13.8 (stroke); R.C. Lee, 8.7 (cox)

Ht: lost to Trakia Club, Bulgaria, 1¼ lths, 6m 31s

1981 (Leander/Tyrian/Thames Tradesmen's): L.D. Robertson (TT), 13.12 (bow); M.D. Field (T), 13.10; G. Hill (T), 13.8; G.A. Rankine, 14.3; C. Seymour (TT), 13.8; J.M. Pritchard, 14.2; M.R. McGowan, 13.10; R.C. Stanhope, 13.1 (stroke); N. Weare, 8.0 (cox)

Ht: bt Boston University, USA, 2⅔ lths, 6m 53s

Ht: bt University of Washington, USA, 2¾ lths, 6m 34s

Final: bt Oxford University and Thames Tradesmen's RC, ½ lth, 7m 15s

1982 (Leander/London RC/Kingston RC): D. McDougall (LRC), 12.13; J.G. Suenson-Taylor (KRC), 14.3; J. Clark (LRC), 14.0; J.M. Beattie (LRC), 14.0; A.J. Holmes, 14.3; J.M. Pritchard, 13.10; M.R. McGowan, 13.12; R.C. Stanhope, 13.1 (stroke); S.M. Jefferies (LRC), 7.12 (cox)

Ht: bt University of California, Berkeley, USA, 1½ lths, 6m 36s

Final: bt University of London and Tyrian BC, ½ lth, no time taken

1984 (Leander/London RC): D. McDougall (LRC), 12.13 (bow); C.J. Mahoney (LRC), 13.3; S.F. Hassan (LRC), 13.10; J.M. Pritchard, 14.2; D.A. Clift, 14.0; C.G. Roberts (LRC), 12.13; M.R. McGowan, 13.12; A. Whitwell, 13.1 (stroke); Hon. C.B. Moynihan (LRC), 7.12 (cox)

Ht: bt University of Pennsylvania, USA, easily, 6m 10s (record)

Final: bt University of Washington, USA, 3 lths, 6m 22s

1988 (Leander/Univ of London): R. Stanhope, 13.13 (bow); P.R.K. Beaumont, 14.6; S.F. Hassan (UL), 14.8; G.B. Stewart (OUBC), 16.6; T.G. Dillon, 14.10; A.M. Obholzer (UL), 13.8; S. Turner, 14.7; N.J. Burfitt, 14.4 (stroke); S.M. Jefferies, 8.3 (cox)

Ht: bt Syracuse University, USA, 3½ lths, 6m 46s

Final: bt Australian Institute for Sport, Australia, 1 foot, 6m 17s

1989 N.J. Burfitt, 14.4 (bow); P. Mulkerrins, 14.1; M.C. Pinsent, 14.12; S. Turner, 14.7; G.B. Stewart, 16.6; T.G. Dillon, 14.10; R.C. Phelps, 13.12; J.G. Singfield, 13.7 (stroke); P.J. Sweeney, 8.6 (cox)

Ht: bt Csepel & Magyar, Hungary, 4¼ lths, 6m 46s

Ht: lost to RC Hansa Dortmund, W. Germany, ½ lth, 6m 9s (record)

1990 (Leander/Univ of London/Lea/OUBC): M.W. Norton (UL) 13.10 (bow); R. Thain (Lea), 13.9; J.L. Garrett, 14.5; G.B. Stewart, 15.11; J.G. Singfield, 13.9; R.C. Phelps, 14.1; J.W.C. Searle (OUBC), 13.5; R.J. Obholzer (OUBC), 13.9 (stroke); P.J. Sweeney, 7.12 (cox)

Ht: bt Club Zalgiris, Lithuania, USSR, 3 lths, 6m 38s

Final: lost to RC Hansa Dortmund, W. Germany, 2 lths, 6m 36s

1991 (Leander/Star/Thames Tradesmen's): M.P. Cross (TT), 14.1 (bow); R.C. Stanhope, 13.9; J.E. Cracknell, 14.13; J.W.C. Searle (MBC), 13.1; R.C. Phelps, 14.1; J.G. Singfield (Star) 13.7; A.M. Obholzer, 14.7; T.J.C. Foster (Star) 13.4 (stroke); G.G.P. Herbert, 8.0 (cox)

Final: bt Dinamo Club, Moscow, & Soviet Army Club, Kolomna, USSR, 2½ lths, 6m 22s

1994 (Leander/Cambridge Univ): R.D. Taylor (CUBC), 14.7 (bow); R.C. Phelps (CUBC) 14.6; R.H. Manners, 15.4; M.H.W. Parish (CUBC), 14.6; J.D.C. Walker, 13.10; F.B. Hunt-Davies, 14.13; P.A.J. Bridge, 14.9; J.E. Cracknell, 14.11 (stroke); G.G.P. Herbert, 8.8 (cox)

Ht: lost to SN Compiegne and Société d'Encouragement du Sport, France, ½ lth, 6m 16s

1995 (Leander/Molesey/Univ. of London): P.A.J. Bridge, 14.6 (bow); F.B. Hunt-Davies, 14.11; R.W. Hamilton, 14.12; A.P. Story, 16.12; J.D.C. Walker (MBC), 13.5; M.H.W. Parish (CUBC), 14.6; G.D.C.R. Smith (UL), 13.8; R.M. Rogers (MBC), 13.5 (stroke); H.C. Bass, 8.5 (cox)

Final: lost to San Diego Training Centre, USA, ⅓ lth, 5m 59s

STEWARDS' CHALLENGE CUP

1849 W.Bovill (bow); M.Shearman; T.H.Fellows; E.P. Wolstenholme (stroke); P.McC. Colquhoun (cox)

Final: bt Second Trinity, Cambridge, not rowed out.

1866 J.H.Etherington-Smith, 10.9 (bow); W.J.S.Cadman, 10.8; F.H.Kelly, 11.11; J.H.Foster, 10.00 (stroke); F.Walton, 7.6 (cox)

Ht: lost to University College, Oxford, not rowed out, 9m 34s

1867 W.J.S. Cadman, 10.13 (bow); G.H. Swinny, 11.12; R.A. Kinglake, 12.7½; J.H.Foster, 10.7½ (stroke); F.Walton, 7.5 (cox)

Ht: lost to Oxford Radleian Club, 2 lths, 9m 38s

1875 C.W.Benson, 11.6 (bow); H.E. Rhodes, 11.9; C.S.Read, 12.9; J.H.D. Goldie, 12.6 (stroke)

Ht: 1, Leander; 2, Thames RC; Royal Chester RC, disq. 8m 6s
Final: lost to London RC, 2½ lths, 7m 56s

1881 R.H.J. Poole, 10.7 (bow); H. Sandford, 11.13; T.C. Edwards-Moss, 12.3; L.R. West, 11.2 (stroke)

Ht: lost to Hertford College, Oxford, 2 lths, no time taken

1887 R.G. Gridley, 10.7 (bow); S.D. Muttlebury, 13.7; C.W. Moore, 11.6; F.I. Pitman, 12.0 (stroke)

Ht: bt London RC, not rowed out, 8m 7s
Final: lost to Trinity Hall, Cambridge, not rowed out, 7m 53s

1889 W.F.C. Holland, 10.6 (bow); P. Landale, 12.13; R.P.P. Rowe, 11.7; J.C. Gardner, 11.12 (stroke)

Ht: lost to Thames RC, 4 lths, 7m 47s

1890 G. Francklyn, 11.12 (bow); R.E.R. Brocklebank, 13.3; S.D. Muttlebury, 13.9; G. Elin, 10.12 (stroke)

Ht: lost to Brasenose College, Oxford, 2 feet, 7m 52s

1894 H.B. Cotton, 10.0 (bow); J.A. Ford, 12.0; W.B. Stewart, 13.8; M.C. Pilkington, 12.3 (stroke)

Ht: lost to Thames RC, easily, 7m 55s

1895 C.W.N. Graham, 10.0 (bow); J.A. Ford, 11.12; W.B. Stewart, 13.5; C.W. Kent, 10.11 (stroke)

Ht: lost to Thames RC, easily, 7m 58s

1897 C.W.N. Graham, 10.2 (bow); J.A. Ford, 12.1; H.W.M. Willis, 11.12; G. Nickalls, 12.7 (stroke)

Ht: bt London RC, easily, 8m 6s
Final: bt New College, Oxford, 2 lths, 7m 30s

1898 C.J.D. Goldie, 12.2 (bow); H.W.M. Willis, 12.2; C.D. Burnell, 14.2; H.G. Gold, 11.10 (stroke)

Ht: bt University College, Oxford, 3 lths, 7m 46s

Ht: bt Thames RC, not rowed out, 8m 12s

Final: bt New College, Oxford, 1¼ lths, 7m 42s

1900 R.O. Pitman, 10.8 (bow); F.W. Warre, 12.4; C.D. Burnell, 13.9; J.E. Payne, 12.9 (stroke)

Ht: bt Thames RC, easily, 8m 19s

Ht: bt Trinity Hall, Cambridge, 2½ lths, 8m 6s

Final: bt Trinity College, Cambridge, 1¼ lths, 7m 55s

1901 C.J.D. Goldie, 12.1 (bow); R.B. Etherington-Smith, 12.6; C.D. Burnell, 13.4; J.E. Payne, 12.12 (stroke)

Ht: bt London RC, 1¼ lths, 8m 5s

Ht: lost to Third Trinity, Cambridge, easily, 7m 54s

1902 C.K. Philips, 12.3 (bow); A.de L. Long, 12.11; C.D. Burnell, 13.10; F.W. Warre, 12.5 (stroke)

Final: lost to Third Trinity, Cambridge, easily, 8m 45s

1903 B.C. Cox, 11.13 (bow, steers); F.W. Warre, 12.8; F.J. Escombe, 13.0; R.B. Etherington-Smith, 12.6 (stroke)

Ht: lost to Third Trinity, Cambridge, 1 lth, 7m 59s

1905 H.A. Steward, 10.8 (bow); R.B. Etherington-Smith, 12.5 (steers); F.J. Escombe, 12.11; G. Nickalls, 12.12 (stroke)

Final: row-over (Third Trinity, Cambridge, scratched) 8m 26s

1906 A.K. Graham, 10.11 (bow); F.S. Kelly, 12.0; R.B. Etherington-Smith, 12.3; G. Nickalls, 12.4 (stroke, steers)

Final: bt Third Trinity, Cambridge, 2 feet, 7m 36s

1907 E.W. Powell, 11.6 (bow); F.J. Escombe, 12.11; B.C. Johnstone, 12.12; R.V. Powell, 12.6 (stroke, steers)

Ht: bt Ludwigshafener RC, Germany, not rowed out, 8m 40s

Final: lost to Magdalen College, Oxford, 3 lths, 8m 42s

1910 C.A. Gladstone, 10.13 (bow, steers); R.H. Owen, 12.8; A.G. Kirby, 13.8; G.L. Thomson, 12.4 (stroke)

Ht: lost to Thames RC, 1¼ lths, 7m 57s

1913 R.W. Fletcher, 11.6 (bow, steers); L.G. Wormald, 12.5; A.S. Garton, 13.8; F.F.V. Scrutton, 12.0 (stroke)

Ht: lost to Mainzer Ruder-Verein, Germany, 2 feet, 7m 36s

1914 A.A. Swann, 11.11 (bow); G.L. Thomson, 12.1; C.E.V. Buxton, 12.3; R.C. Bourne, 10.0 (stroke, steers)

Ht: bt Thames RC, 2 lths, 7m 45s

Final: bt Mainzer Ruder-Verein, Germany, not rowed out, 7m 52s

1920 Rev S.E. Swann, 11.7 (bow, steers); R.S. Shove, 12.5; A.A. Swann, 11.13; G.L. Thomson, 11.9 (stroke)

Ht: lost to Thames RC ¼ lth, 8m 38s

1921 H.O.C. Boret, 12.0 (bow, steers); J.H. Simpson, 12.5; Hon J.W.H. Fremantle, 12.2; P.H.G.S. Hartley, 11.5 (stroke)

Ht: lost to Magdalen College, Oxford, 3 lths, 7m 32s

1922 Hon J.W.H. Fremantle, 12.4 (bow, steers); D.T. Raikes, 13.11; A.B. Ritchie, 13.3; E.D. Horsfall, 12.7 (stroke)

Ht: lost to Grasshopper Club, Zurich, Switzerland, 2 lths, 8m 21s

1924 G.E.G. Gadsden, 11.7 (bow); R.S.C. Lucas, 13.6; G.O. Nickalls, 12.13 (steers); A.V. Campbell, 11.3 (stroke)

Ht: bt Brasenose College, Oxford, ¾ lth, 9m 0s
Final: lost to Third Trinity, Cambridge, 3 lths, 8m 37s

1925 K.N. Craig, 12.2 (bow); H.O.C. Boret, 12.8; G.O. Nickalls, 12.13 (steers); R.S.C. Lucas, 13.8 (stroke)

Ht: bt London RC, easily, 8m 7s
Final: lost to Third Trinity, Cambridge, 2 lths, 7m 27s (record)

1926 G.E.G. Gadsden, 11.2 (bow); C.R.M. Eley, 11.5; G.O. Nickalls, 12.9 (steers); H.O.C. Boret, 12.11 (stroke)

Ht: bt London RC, easily, 8m 0s
Final: lost to Thames RC, easily, 7m 34s

1927 K.N. Craig, 12.8 (bow); H.O.C. Boret, 12.12; G.O. Nickalls, 12.12 (steers); E.C. Hamilton-Russell, 11.7 (stroke)

Ht: bt Christ Church, Oxford, 1¼ lths, 8m 24s
Final: lost to Thames RC, 2 lths, 8m 1s

1928 K.N. Craig, 12.9 (bow, steers); G.A. Block, 12.4; L.V. Bevan, 13.2; J.S. Herbert, 11.5 (stroke)

Ht: lost to London RC, 2½ lths, 8m 16s

1930 J.C. Holcroft, 12.8 (bow); R. Beesly, 12.10; M.H. Warriner, 13.13; T.E. Letchworth, 12.6 (stroke, steers)

Ht: bt Selwyn College, Cambridge, easily, 8m 47s
Final: lost to London RC, 1½ lths, 7m 34s

1933 G.I.F. Thompson, 11.4 (bow); J.M. Couchman, 12.7; W.D.C. Erskine-Crum, 12.3 (steers); R.W.G. Holdsworth, 11.10 (stroke)

Ht: bt Thames RC, ⅓ lth, 7m 36s
Ht: lost to London RC, 1¾ lths, 8m 20s

1936 A.D. Kingsford, 11.13 (bow); T.G. Askwith, 11.13; D.J. Wilson, 12.12; W.G.R.M. Laurie, 13.4 (stroke)

Ht: bt Pembroke College, Cambridge, 1 lth, 8m 3s
Ht: bt Thames RC, 2½ lths, 7m 50s
Final: lost to Zurich RC, Switzerland, 2 lths, 7m 50s

1937 P.H. Gaskell, 12.0 (bow, steers); J.M. Couchman, 12.11; J.C. Cherry, 13.10; J.D. Sturrock, 14.6 (stroke)

Final: bt Thames RC, 1 lth, 8m 32s

1938 J.H.T. Wilson, 12.12 (bow); J. Turnbull, 13.8; J.C. Cherry, 13.2 (steers); W.G.R.M. Laurie, 13.1 (stroke)

Ht: bt Magdalen College, Oxford, 3 lths, 8m 4s
Ht: bt London RC, 4 lths, 7m 47s
Final: bt Trinity College, Oxford, easily, 7m 33s

1946 J.F. Burgess, 12.9 (bow); R.M.A. Bourne, 11.6; P. Bradley, 12.7; N.J. Bradley, 14.10 (stroke, steers)

Ht: bt Trinity Hall, Cambridge, 3 lths, 8m 54s
Ht: bt Thames RC, ½ lth, 7m 57s
Final: bt Oriel College, Oxford, 2½ lths, 7m 48s

1947 A.S.F. Butcher, 12.4 (bow, steers); H.W. Mason, 11.8; P. Bradley, 12.10; G.C. Richardson, 12.11 (stroke)

Ht: lost to Thames RC, 2 lths, 8m 1s

1948 P.N. Brodie, 11.6 (bow, steers); J.R.W. Gleave, 12.4; P. Bradley, 12.6; A.J.R. Purssell, 11.7 (stroke)

Ht: bt London RC, 3 lths, 7m 51s
Ht: lost to Thames RC, 1¼ lths, 7m 42s

1949 J.R.L. Carstairs, 12.11 (bow); J.R.W. Gleave, 12.9; W.A.D. Windham, 13.3; P. Bradley, 12.12 (stroke, steers)

Ht: lost to Trinity College, Oxford, 3½ lths, 7m 21s

1950 J.R.L. Carstairs, 12.4 (bow); P. Bradley, 12.13; E.A.P. Bircher, 13.3; R.D. Burnell, 14.4 (stroke, steers)

Ht: bt London RC, easily, 8m 8s
Ht: bt Trinity College, Oxford, 1½ lths, 7m 53s
Final: lost to Hellerup Roklubb, Denmark, 4 lths, 8m 3s

1951 H.C.I. Bywater, 11.11 (bow, steers); M.E.O'Brien, 13.2; P.T. Pulman, 12.3; D.M. Jennens, 12.1 (stroke)

Ht: bt Magdalen College, Oxford, 1½ lths, 8m 6s
Ht: bt London RC, 1¼ lths, 7m 57s
Final: lost to Thames RC, 1½ lths, 7m 53s

1953 D.D. Macklin, 11.6 (bow, steers); C.G.V. Davidge 12.2; W.A.D. Windham, 12.6; R.M.S. Gubbins, 11.0 (stroke)

Ht: bt London RC, 4 lths, 7m 20s
Final: bt First and Third Trinity, Cambridge, ¾ lth, 7m 25s

1954 E.O.G. Pain, 11.10 (bow, steers); D.A.T. Leadley, 13.1; W.A.D. Windham, 12.10; C.G.V. Davidge, 12.1 (stroke)

Ht: lost to Kobenhavns Roklubb, Denmark, 2 lths, 7m 48s

1955 J.A. Gobbo, 12.7 (bow); J.G. McLeod, 11.8; R.H. Carnegie, 13.9; C.G.V. Davidge, 12.1 (stroke, steers)

Ht: bt RC Thalwil, Switzerland, 1½ lths, 8m 15s
Final: lost to Club Krylia Sovetov, USSR, 3 lths, 7m 40s

1956 R.H. Carnegie, 13.9 (bow); D.A.T. Leadley, 12.8; S.G.D. Tozer, 13.9 (steers); C.G.V. Davidge (stroke)

Ht: lost to Thames RC, 2½ lths, 7m 45s

1957 I.W. Welsh, 13.5 (bow); J.F. Hall-Craggs, 13.3; S.G.D. Tozer, 13.9 (steers); A.C.F. Thomson, 12.5 (stroke)

Ht: lost to Club Krylia Sovetov, USSR, 2 lths, 7m 17s

1960 R.I.L. Howland, 12.11 (bow, steers); J.B. Cocking, 12.8; J.F. Hewitt, 12.6; D.A.T. Leadley, 12.6 (stroke)

Ht: lost to Belvoir RC, Zurich, Switzerland, easily, 7m 21s

1964 J.R. Chester, 12.12 (bow, steers); A.T. Lindsay, 13.0 J.C.D. Sherratt, 12.10; D.C.R. Edwards, 12.12 (stroke)

Ht: bt Molesey BC, 1⅔ lths, 7m 39s
Final: lost to Tideway Scullers School, easily, 7m 11s

1965 D.W.G. Calder, 12.11 (bow, steers); W. Howkins, 13.6; D.F. Legget, 12.6; A.D.J. Nielsen, 12.5 (stroke)

Ht: lost to Nautilus RC, 1¾ lths, 7m 11s

1973 (Leander/Kingston RC/Wallingford RC): A.E.J. Richardson (WRC); 13.1 (bow); R.J. Ayling (KRC), 14.10; C.J. Dalley, 14.2; P.S. Bramfitt, 13.1 (stroke, steers)

Ht: bt Sydney RC, Australia, foul, no time taken
Ht: lost to University of London, 2 lths, 7m 3s

1974 (Leander/Tideway Scullers/Univ. of London): E.M.R. Wells (TSc) 13.7 (bow, steers); S.C. Irving, 14.0; G.M.A. Proffitt (TSc), 13.0; A.A. Bayles (UL), 13.7 (stroke)

Final: lost to Dynamo Club, USSR, easily, 7m 12s

1984 (Kingston/Leander): A. Genziani (KRC) 14.7 (bow); P.C. Wensley (KRC), 14.7; T.F. Mossop (KRC), 14.8; C.J. Jones, 14.0 (stroke). (Steersman not recorded)

Ht: bt Northeastern University RA, USA, 3 lths, 7m 24s

Ht: lost to Nottinghamshire County RA and Tyne RC), 1½ lths, 6m 44s (record)

1988 M.A.H. Buckingham, 14.8 (bow); S.M.P. Peel, 14.0; S.N. Berrisford, 15.6; P. Mulkerrins, 14.1 (stroke). (Steersman not recorded)

Final: bt Penn Athletic Association, USA, easily, 6m 44s

1990 (Star/Leander 'A'/Thames Tradesman's); M.P. Cross (TT) 14.5 (bow); P.R. Mulkerrins (Star), 13.3; M.C. Pinsent, 14.12; T.J.C. Foster (Star), 13.10 (stroke). (Steersman not recorded)

Star (Star/Leander 'B'/Univ. of London): J.P. Ormerod, 14.9 (bow); D.R. Gillard, 14.7; S. O'Brien (Star), 16.8 (steers); A.R. Cassidy (UL), 13.8 (stroke)

Ht: Star/Leander 'A' bt Tideway Scullers School, easily, 7m 21s

Final: Star/Leander 'A' bt Star/Leander 'B'/Univ. of London, 4¾ lths, 7m 16s

1991 N.J. Clarry, 12.10 (bow, steers); D.R. Gillard, 14.9; K.St A. Allen, 13.8; F.B. Hunt-Davis, 14.3 (stroke)

(Leander/Molesey): J.L. Garrett, 14.7 (bow, steers); G.B. Stewart, 15.13; J.D.C. Walker, 13.10; G.M.P. Searle (MBC), 15.8 (stroke)

Final: Leander/Molesey bt Leander, 2 lths, 6m 55s

1992 J. Morris, 13.6 (bow); J.G. Michels, 13.2 (steers); B. Mavra, 14.8; K.K. Poole, 13.4 (stroke)

Ht: lost to Nottinghamshire County RA, 1¾ lths, 6m 50s

1993 (Leander/Univ. of London): R.J. Obholzer (UL), 14.6 (bow); R.H. Manners, 15.3; S.G. Redgrave, 16.9 (steers); F.B. Hunt-Davis, 15.1 (stroke)

Ht: bt Nautilus RC, 1 lth, 6m 45s

Ht: bt Ur-Kirolak, Spain, 2¼ lths, 7m 13s

Final: bt RC Hansa Dortmund, Germany, ⅔ lth, 6m 44s

PRINCE PHILIP CHALLENGE CUP

1965 D.C. Spencer, 13.4 (bow); H.W. Howell, 14.3; W. Fink, 13.3; E.S. Trippe, 13.8 (stroke); Hon M.J. Leigh, 9.0 (cox)

Ht: bt Tabor Academy, USA, 4 lths, 7m 48s

Ht: bt Hollingworth Lake RC, easily, 7m 30s

Ht: bt Thames RC, 1¾ lths, 7m 16s (equals record)

Final: bt Tideway Scullers School, ½ lth, 7m 3s (record)

1971 P.D.P. Angier, 12.1 (bow); C.M.C. Preston, 13.2; N.D.C. Tee, 11.10; J.C. Yallop, 13.12 (stroke); J.A. Easton, 9.7 (cox)

Ht: bt Tabor Academy, USA, easily, 8m 4s

Final: lost to London RC/University of London, 1⅔ lths, 8m 8s

1972 P.T. Summers, 13.10 (bow); R.C. Lester, 14.3; C.J. Dalley, 13.11; R.M. Winckless, 13.10 (stroke); S.G.G. Salt, 8.1 (cox)

Ht: lost to St Catharine's RC, Canada, 1¼ lths, 7m 34s

1973 (Leander/Univ of London): C.P. Etherington, 12.12 (bow); A.A. Bayles (UL), 13.8; H.P. Matheson, 14.1; R.C. Lester, 14.0 (stroke); P.J. Sweeney (TSc) 8.1 (cox)

Ht: bt Trud Club, Moscow, USSR, 6 feet, 7m 4s

Ht: lost to Northeastern University RA, USA, ¾ lth, 7m 0s (equals record)

1974 C.P. Etherington, 13.8 (bow); R.J. Ayling, 15.4; G.A.S. Locke, 13.13; C.R.D. McDougall, 13.3 (stroke); D. Tchang, 8.4 (cox)

Ht: lost to Lady Margaret BC/1st and 3rd Trinity BC, Cambridge, 2⅓ lths, 7m 59s

1976 P.S. Gregory, 14.11 (bow); W.W. Woodward-Fisher, 13.7; D.B. King, 13.12; G.A. Rankine, 14.1 (stroke);

R.C. Lee, 8.0 (cox)

Ht: bt Choate School, USA, easily, 7m 58s

Final: scratched

1986 P.A.J. Wright, 14.5 (bow); S. Turner, 14.4; S.N. Berrisford, 14.11; R.J. Stephens, 14.1 (stroke); P. Johnstone, 8.13 (cox)

Ht: lost to AZS Szczecin and AZS Wroclaw, Poland, ¾ lth, 7m 44s

1990 D.C. Spencer, 12.12 (bow); H.W. Howell, 15.1; W.R. Fink, 13.6; E.S. Trippe, 14.11 (stroke); P.J. Sweeney, 8.9 (cox)

Ht: lost to RC Hansa Dortmund, West Germany, ½ lth, 8m 34s

1991 (Leander/Star): P.R. Mulkerrins (S), 13.7 (bow); N.J. Burfitt, 13.13; T.G. Dillon, 14.10; S.N. Berrisford, 15.7 (stroke); A.C. Ellison, 7.12 (cox)

Ht: bt Blood Street Sculls, USA, ¾ lth, 8m 41s

Final: bt Dinamo Vilnius, Lithuania, USSR, 2⅔ lths, 7m 20s

1992 H.F.W. Worden, 14.3 (bow); D.J. Luke, 15.2; P.A.J. Bridge, 14.0; P.R. Rudaz, 15.2 (stroke); N. Chugani, 8.0 (cox)

Ht: bt Molesey BC/Reading University, not rowed out, 7m 1s

Final: bt Tideway Scullers School, 3 lths, 6m 49s (record)

1993 (Leander/Molesey): J.D.C. Walker (MBC), 14.2 (bow); C.A. Maclennan, 13.5; G.B. Stewart (MBC), 15.10; T.G. Dillon, 15.5 (stroke); A.C. Ellison, 7.12 (cox)

Ht: bt Tideway Scullers School, 2¾ lths, 7m 28s

Ht: bt Cambridge University/Goldie BC, 3 lths, 7m 20s

Final: bt Molesey BC/University of London, 1½ lths, 7m 10s

1994 J.G. Michels, 13.5 (bow); C.A. Maclennan, 13.12; H.C.A. Mills, 14.4; R.F. Morrison, 17.8 (stroke); A.C. Ellison, 7.12 (cox)

Ht: bt Oxford University/Trident RC, South Africa, 2 lths, 7m 11s

Final: lost to Nottinghamshire County RA, ⅔ lth, 6m 59s

1995 'A': J.G. Michels, 13.5 (bow); L.S.T. Reed, 14.11; S.G. Redgrave, 16.0; M.C. Pinsent, 16.0 (stroke); N. Chugani, 8.4 (cox)

'B': R.F. Morrison, 16.13 (bow); G.R. Pooley, 13.11; R.H. Manners, 15.3; C.A. Maclennan, 14.0 (stroke); G.G.P. Herbert, 8.9 (cox)

Final: 'A' bt 'B', 4 lths, 6m 44s (record)

THE QUEEN MOTHER CHALLENGE CUP

1985 (Leander/Quintin): I.B. Lloyd, 14.5 (bow); J.A. Kerr (QBC), 13.0; J.A. Green (QBC), 13.1; G.A. Mulcahy (QBC), 14.1 (stroke)

Ht: lost to Tideway Scullers, 1⅔ lths, 7m 17s

1987 I.B. Lloyd, 14.4 (bow); G. Baldock, 13.11; G.A. Mulcahy, 14.0; C. Guppy, 13.9 (stroke)

Ht: lost to Ridley BC, Canada, easily, 6m 40s

1989 I.B. Lloyd, 14.9 (bow); C. Guppy, 13.0; H.E.D. Trotter, 13.8; G.A. Mulcahy, 14.6 (stroke)

Ht: lost to Tideway Scullers, ⅓ lth, 7m 22s

1990 (Leander/Tideway Scullers/Kingston RC): C.J. Andrews (KRC), 13.9 (bow); O.W. Hall-Craggs (TSc), 13.2; J.R. Garman, 14.4; H.E.D. Trotter, 13.9 (stroke)

Ht: bt Upper Thames RC & Marlow RC, easily, 7m 3s

Ht: bt Emanuel & Windsor Boys' Schools, 3¼ lths, 7m 04s

Ht: lost to Danmarks RR, Denmark, 2½ lths, 6m 50s

1991 (Leander/Tideway Scullers): G. Walters (TSc), 14.4 (bow); O.W, Hall-Craggs (TSc), 13.1; J.R. Garman, 13.10; H.E.D. Trotter, 13.3 (stroke)

Ht: bt Henley RC, 2¾ lths, 6m 50s

Ht: bt Scottish Argonauts, 3⅔ lths, 7m 16s

Ht: bt Upper Thames RC 'A', easily, 7m 8s

Final: bt NCRA & London RC, easily, 7m 5s

1994 G.J. Lovett, 14,0 (bow); M.A. Brown, 14.6; A. Story, 17.0; H.R. Floyd, 13.12 (stroke)

Ht: bt Kingston RC, 2½ lths, 6m 59s

Ht: bt City of Oxford RC & Marlow RC, 3¾ lths, 6m 46s

Ht: lost to London RC 'A', 1 lth, 6m 46s

1995 C.G. Bullas, 13.3 (bow); B. Mavra, 14.9; S.W.L. Cottle (IC), 13.2; G.C.S. Smith, 12.5 (stroke)

Ht: bt Rob Roy BC, 1¼ lths, 6m 49s

Ht: lost to Tideway Scullers 'B', 1 lth, 6m 38s

1996 (Imperial Coll/Leander) G.C.S. Smith, 12.7 (bow); A.F. Warnock (IC) 13.12; S.W.L. Cottle (IC), 14.8; T.C. Gale (IC) 13.7 (stroke)

Ht: bt Castle Semple RC, 2¾ lths, 7m 1s

Ht: lost to Ratzeburger RC, Germany, 1½ lths, 6m 38s

SILVER WHERRIES

1847 T. Pollock (Cambridge Subscription Rooms) (bow); T.H. Fellows (stroke)

Ht: beat H.S. and J. Polehampton (Pembroke Coll, Oxford), easily, 10m 0s

Final: lost to W.S. Falls and W. Coulthard (St George's Club, London) on a foul

THE SILVER GOBLETS AND NICKALLS CHALLENGE CUP
(the latter added in 1895)

1850 C.L. Vaughan (Oriel Coll, Oxford) (bow); T.H. Fellows (stroke)
Final: lost to J.J. Hornby and J.W. Chitty (Oxford), easily

1851 W. Woodbridge (bow); T.H. Fellows (stroke)
Final: 1, J. Aitken (Exeter Coll, Oxford) and J.W. Chitty (Balliol Coll, Oxford); 2, J.E. Clarke (Wadham Coll, Oxford) and C.L. Vaughan (Oriel Coll, Oxford); 3, Woodbridge and Fellows

1866 J.G. Chambers (bow); R.A. Kinglake (stroke)
Final: 1, E.L. Corrie and W.B. Woodgate (Kingston RC); 2, A. Kemble and M.S. Foster (New Coll, Oxford); 3, Chambers and Kinglake, easily, 9m 23s

1875 C.W. Benson (bow); H.E. Rhodes (stroke)
Ht: lost to A. de L. Long and F.S. Gulston (London RC), 1½ lths, no time taken

1888 D.H. McLean (bow); S.D. Muttlebury (stroke)
Final: lost to N.P. Symonds (CUBC) and E. Buck (OUBC), not rowed out

1891 Lord Ampthill (bow); G. Nickalls (stroke)
Ht: bt A.M. Hutchinson and F.E.C. Clark (Thames RC) ½ lth, 9m 7s
Ht: bt F.E. and P.A.N. Thorn (London RC), 1 lth, 9m 6s
Final: bt F. Wilkinson and W.A.L. Fletcher (OUBC) 1 foot, 8m 36s

1892 F.E. Robeson (bow); G. Nickalls (stroke)
Ht: lost to V. Nickalls and W.A.L. Fletcher (OUBC), 2¼ lths, 9m 28s

1893 W.F.C. Holland (bow); J.A. Ford (stroke)
Ht: lost to V. Nickalls and W.A.L. Fletcher (OUBC), 3 lths, 8m 16s

1896 W.F.C. Holland (bow); J.A. Ford (stroke)
Ht: lost to V and G. Nickalls (London RC), easily, 9m 38s

1897 E.R. Balfour (bow); G. Nickalls (stroke)
Ht: bt W.E. Crum and G.O.C. Edwards (New Coll, Oxford), not rowed out, 9m 10s
Ht: bt H.G. Gold and R. Carr (Magdalen Coll, Oxford), easily, 8m 35s
Final: bt A.S. Ball and W.J. Fernie (Trinity Hall, Cambridge), not rowed out, 8m 59s

1899 C.K. Philips (bow); H.W.M. Willis (stroke)
Ht: bt H.A. Game and G.H. Brown (1st Trinity, Cambridge), 1 lth, 8m 36s
Final: bt G.E. Orme and D. Pennington (St George's Hosp), 1¼ lths, 8m 49s

1905 R.B. Etherington-Smith, 12.9 (bow); G. Nickalls, 12.12 (stroke)
Ht: lost to R.H. Nelson and P.H. Thomas (3rd Trinity, Cambridge), 2½ lths, 8m 34s

1906 A.K. Graham, 10.11 (bow); F.S. Kelly, 12.0 (stroke)
Ht: bt S.R. Wells and C. Franklin (Bedford RC), easily, 9m 0s
Ht: lost to B.C. Johnstone and R.V. Powell (3rd Trinity, Cambridge), 1 lth, 8m 15s (equals record)

1907 B.C. Johnstone, 12.12 (bow); R.V. Powell, 12.6 (stroke)
Final: bt J. Beresford and K. Vernon (Thames RC), easily, 8m 52s

1909 B.C. Johnstone, 12.11 (bow); E.G. Williams, 13.0 (stroke)

Ht: bt G.S. Johnston and J.H.E.V. Millington-Drake (Vikings Club), 2½ lths, 8m 58s

Ht: bt B.M. Arnold and S. Fairbairn (Jesus Coll, Cambridge), easily, 9m 9s

Final: bt J. Beresford and K. Vernon (Thames RC), 3 lths, 8m 30s

1910 J.S. Burn, 11.9 (bow); G.L. Thomson, 12.4 (stroke)

Ht: bt G.W.H. Walker and G.C. Drinkwater (Wadham Coll, Oxford), 3 lths, 9m 12s

Final: bt A. Wielsma and B.H. Croon (De Amstel RC, Amsterdam, ¾ lth, 8m 45s

1911 J.S. Burn, 12.3 (bow); G.L. Thomson, 12.2 (stroke)

Ht: lost to L.J. Cadbury and F.E. Hellyer (1st Trinity, Cambridge), 1 lth, 8m 43s

1923 G.O. Nickalls, 12.2 (bow); H.B. Playford, 13.7 (stroke)

Ht: bt T.C. Osborne and H.K. Wadams (Evesham RC), ¾ lth, 8m 26s

Ht: bt K.N. Craig and T.D.A. Collet (Pembroke Coll, Cambridge), easily, 8m 28s

Final: lost to W.F. Godden and R.E. Eason (Trinity Coll, Oxford), 5 feet, 8m 12s

1924 G.O. Nickalls, 12.13 (bow); R.S.C. Lucas, 13.6 (stroke)

Ht: lost to G.K. Hampshire and W. Philipps (Magdalen Coll, Oxford); not rowed out, 12m 0s

1925 G.O. Nickalls, 12.13 (bow); R.S.C. Lucas, 13.8 (stroke)

Final: lost to R.E. Morrison and E.C. Hamilton (3rd Trinity, Cambridge), 4 lths, 8m 17s

1926 G.O. Nickalls, 12.9 (bow); A.D.B. Pearson, 13.11 (stroke)

Ht: bt W. Rathbone and J.D.W. Thomson (Christ Church and University Coll, Oxford), easily, 8m 49s

Final: lost to H.R. Carver and E.C. Hamilton-Russell (3rd Trinity, Cambridge), 1¼ lths, 8m 36s

1927 G.O. Nickalls, 12.12 (bow); H.O.C. Boret, 12.12 (stroke)

Ht: bt T.W. Shaw and E.C.T. Edwards (Christ Church, Oxford), ½ lth, 9m 9s

Ht: bt G.E.G. Gadsden and A.G. Wansbrough (Eton Vikings), easily, 9m 2s

Final: lost to R.A. Nisbet and T.N.O'Brien (London RC), 1¾ lths, 9m 23s

1930 J.C. Holcroft, 12.8 (bow); T.E. Letchworth, 12.6 (stroke)

Ht: lost to W.A. Prideaux and H.R.N. Rickett (3rd Trinity, Cambridge), 2 lths, 8m 42s

1935 J.H.T. Wilson, 12.5 (bow); W.G.R.M. Laurie, 13.9 (stroke)

Ht: bt T.S and E.F. Bigland (Royal Chester RC), 2 lths, 8m 50s

Ht: scratched

1937 D.M.de R. Winser, 12.0 (bow); H.M. Young, 13.3 (stroke)

Ht: lost to D.G. Kingsford and G.M. Lewis (London RC), 1 lth, 9m 5s

1938 W.G.R.M. Laurie, 13.1 (bow); J.H.T. Wilson, 12.12 (stroke)

Ht: bt P.G and J.G. Rose (Burton Leander RC), easily, 9m 9s
Ht: bt E.W. Wingate and W.D. Baddeley (Vesta RC), easily, 8m 44s
Ht: bt G. Huse and G.C.C. Pepys (Oriel Coll, Oxford), 2 lths, 8m 8s
Final: bt E.F and T.S. Bigland (Royal Chester RC), easily, 8m 8s

1946 J.F. Burgess, 12.9 (bow); C.G. Burgess, 12.9 (stroke)

Ht: bt H.W.T. Beckett and J.B. Godber (Bedford RC), easily, 10m 39s
Ht: bt J.W. Lezica and A.R. Esperon (Club Nacional de Regatas, Uruguay), 4 lths, 8m 56s
Final: bt O. Secher and P. Paerregaard (Dansk Forening for Rosport, Denmark), not rowed out, 8m 47s

1948 W.G.R.M. Laurie, 12.13 (bow); J.H.T. Wilson, 12.7 (stroke)

Ht: bt J.A. Crosse and D.C. Lennon (King's Coll and LMBC, Cambridge), 2½ lths, 8m 25s
Ht: bt J.R.W. Gleave and D.G. Jamieson (Radcliffe Infirmary BC), easily, 8m 42s
Final: bt E.R. Bromley and F.S. Grace (Mosman RC, NSW, Australia), 3 lths, 8m 30s

1955 J.A. Gobbo, 12.7 (bow); C.G.V. Davidge, 12.1 (stroke)

Ht: bt H. Kocerka and B. Poniatowski (AZS Bydgoszcz, Poland), 4 lths, 8m 38s
Ht: bt A.M. Clay and B.G.R. Evans (Marlow RC), 2 lths, 9m 0s
Final: lost to I.Buldakov and V.Ivanov (Club Khimik, USSR), 4 lths, 8m 30s

1957 D.A.T. Leadley, 12.8 (bow); C.G.V. Davidge, 12.9 (stroke)

Ht: bt D.C. Sperling and L.B. McCagg (Cambridge BC, USA), easily, 8m 19s
Ht: bt M. Plaksin and S. Soldatov (Club Krasnoe Znamia, USSR), easily, 7m 53s
Final: bt J. Kloimstein and A. Sageder (EKuRV, Donau, Austria), ⅓ lth, 8m 17s

1958 D.A.T. Leadley, 12.8 (bow); C.G.V. Davidge, 12.9 (stroke)

Ht: bt I. Buldakov and V. Ivanov (Trud Club, Moscow, USSR), 2½ lths, 8m 7s
Final: bt R. Streuli and G. Kottmann (Belvoir RC, Zurich, Switzerland), 3½ lths, 8m 4s

1962 J.M.S. Lecky, 13.7 (bow); H.B. Budd, 14.11 (stroke)

S.C.H. Douglas-Mann, 12.1 (bow); S.C. Rand, 12.3 (stroke)

Ht: Lecky and Budd bt Hon R.A. Napier and A.J. Collier (LMBC, Cambridge), easily, 7m 54s
Ht: Lecky and Budd bt Douglas-Mann and Rand, 1¾ lths, 7m 49s (record)
Ht: Lecky and Budd lost to W. Neuss and K.G. Jordan (RC Nassovia Hochst 1881, W Germany), 3¾ lths, 7m 59s

1963 C.G.V. Davidge, 12.8 (bow); S.A. Mackenzie, 14.6 (stroke)

Ht: bt V. Lehtelä and T. Pitkänen (Valkeakosken Vesiveikot, Finland) ¾ lth, 8m 45s
Ht: bt J.W. Fryer and H.H. Scurfield (Norwich Union), easily, 8m 57s
Ht: bt A.G. Lane (Vesta RC) and D.W. Parry (Walton RC), 1½ lths, 9m 5s
Final: bt J.B. and T.K. Amlong (Vesper BC, USA), 4 lths, 7m 55s

1964 J.R. Kiely, 13.12 (bow); J.M.S. Lecky, 13.7 (stroke)

S.C.H. Douglas-Mann, 12.5 (bow); S.C. Rand, 12.6 (stroke)

M.J.W. Hall, 12.5 (bow); Hon. R.A. Napier, 12.11 (stroke)

J.Y. Scarlett, 12.11 (bow); D.C. Rutherford, 12.0 (stroke)

Ht: Kiely and Lecky bt J.S. Edmonds and P.A. Johnson (Potomac BC, USA), 1⅓ lths, 7m 48s (record)

Ht: Scarlett and Rutherford bt N.C. Bonsor and R.C.T. Mead (Keble Coll, Oxford), ½ lth, 8m 12s

Ht: Hall and Napier bt T.J. Reid and D. Molesworth (Whakatane RC, New Zealand), 4 lths, 8m 23s

Ht: Kiely and Lecky bt M.J. Theaker and P.J. Phillips (Derby RC), 4 lths, 8m 21s

Ht: Douglas-Mann and Rand bt Scarlett and Rutherford, 1¼ lths, 8m 18s

Ht: Hall and Napier bt M.A. Spracklen and B.G.R. Evans (Marlow RC), 2¾ lths, 8m 21s

Ht: Kiely and Lecky bt Douglas-Mann and Rand, 3½ lths, 7m 52s

Final: Kiely and Lecky bt Hall and Napier, 2 lths, 7m 53s

1965 S.C.H. Douglas-Mann, 12.3 (bow); S.C. Rand, 12.6 (stroke)

Ht: lost to R.J. Nicholson and R. Wait (Nottingham & Union RC), 2¾ lths, 7m 48s

M.J.W. Hall, 12.5 (bow); Hon. R.A. Napier, 12.11 (stroke)

Ht: bt C.H. and R.A.D. Freeman (Keble and Magdalen Colls Oxford), 4 feet, 7m 49s

Ht: lost to P. Gorny and G. Bergau (ASK Vorwaerts, Rostock, E. Germany), 4 lths, 7m 35s

1966 D.W.G. Calder, 13.6 (bow); J.W. Fraser, 14.0 (stroke)

Ht: bt P.R.F. Stanton and T.W. Key (Stratford-upon-Avon BC), easily, 8m 18s

Ht: lost to O. Paustian and P.E. Nielsen (Roklubben Skjold, Denmark), 4 lths, 8m 20s

1969 J.K. Mullard, 13.5 (bow); P.G. Saltmarsh, 13.9 (stroke)

Ht: bt G.W. Butler and M.G. Masson (Scottish Argonauts BC), easily, 8m 28s

Ht: lost to V. Bitterli and V. Fankhauser (See-Club Luzern, Switzerland), easily, 7m 58s

1971 G.A.S. Locke, 13.6 (bow); T.J. Crooks, 13.9 (stroke)

Ht: bt P.T. Summers and M.J. Hart (Corpus Christi Coll and Peterhouse, Cambridge), 1½ lths, 8m 15s

Ht: bt C.I. Blackwall and P.E. Harrison (London RC), not rowed out, no time taken

Ht: bt R. Symsyk and B. Denny (Don RC, Canada), 4 lths, 8m 10s

Final: bt C.J. Dalley and R.N. Winckless (Quintin BC), easily, 8m 7s

1972 A.C.D. Wiggin, 13.6 (bow); J.C. Pemberton, 12.11 (stroke)

Ht: bt D. Phillips and D. King (Nottingham Britannia RC), 3½ lths, 8m 39s

Ht: bt R.H.F. Metcalfe and J.R. Appleby (Durham ARC), easily, 8m 43s

Ht: lost to J. Broniec and A. Slusarski (KKW Bydgoszcz, Poland), easily, 8m 22s

1973 J.C. Pemberton, 13.4 (bow); P.T. Summers, 13.4 (stroke)

D.R. Payne, 12.10 (bow); D.R. Sawyier, 13.4 (stroke)

Ht: Payne and Sawyier bt Pemberton and Summers, 1½ lths, 8m 23s

Ht: Payne and Sawyier bt J. Machado and A. Albers (Santa Clara University RA, USA), easily, 7m 58s

Ht: Payne and Sawyier lost to M. Borchelt and R.T. Adams (Potomac BC, USA), easily, 7m 50s

1974 I.R. Bonsor, 12.13 (bow); M.H.G. Hayter, 12.8 (stroke)

Ht: lost to P.G.P. Stoddart and P.J. Marsden (OUBC), 4½ lths, 8m 46s

W.R. Fink, 13.12 (bow); C.I. Blackwall, 13.3 (stroke)

Ht: bt J.F. McQuattie and D. Gattey (Durham ARC and Durham Univ), easily, 8m 55s

Ht: lost to J. Macleod and A.N. Christie (LMBC, Cambridge), easily, 8m 51s

1975 G.A.S. Locke, 13.6 (bow); F.J. Smallbone (TTRC), 13.2 (stroke)

Ht: bt P.C. Johnson and R.C.R. Twallin (London RC), easily, 8m 6s

Ht: bt C.J.A.N. Money-Coutts and J.H. Clay (Eton Vikings), 2½ lths, 7m 40s

Ht: bt D. Tuffin and I. Knight (Molesey BC), 2¾ lths, 7m 54s

Final: lost to H.A. Droog and R.J. Luynenburg (ASR Nereus and RV De Where, Holland), ⅓ lth, 7m 36s

1979 A.C.D. Wiggin, 13.2 (bow); M.D.A. Carmichael, 12.9 (stroke)

Ht: bt J.P. Carababas and M.E. O'Brien (Detroit BC, USA), easily, 8m 14s

Ht: bt D. Clare and D.J. Burkitt (Newark RC), easily, 8m 15s

Ht: bt J.H. Clay and A. Whitwell (London and Thames Tradesmen's RCs), ¾ lth, 7m 57s

Final: bt J.W. Woodhouse and J.S. Palmer (CUBC), easily, 8m 10s

1980 A. Rankine (bow); J. Robson (stroke)

Ht: lost to A.M. Peach and E.R. Sims (Maidenhead RC), easily, 8m 33s

1982 I. Lloyd, 14.1 (bow); M.C.D. Carmichael, 13.3 (stroke)

Ht: lost to J. Macleod and A.N. Christie (London RC), 1¾ lths, 8m 12s

1984 P.C. Wensley (KRC), 14.7 (bow); C.J. Jones, 14.0 (stroke)

Ht: bt J.J. Purtill and M.E. Vannorsdall (Univ of Pennsylvania, USA), easily, 7m 53s

Ht: bt P.J. Hope and P.L. Reynolds (Kingston RC), 2⅓ lths, 7m 50s

Ht: lost to E.M.G. Pearson (CUBC) and C.D.M. Riches (Molesey BC), 2⅔ lths, 7m 37s

1986 A.J. Holmes, 14.7 (bow); S.G. Redgrave (Marlow RC), 15.10 (stroke)

Ht: bt J.P. Tucker and J.R. Cincotta (Univ of Wisconsin, USA), easily, 8m 9s

Ht: bt P.M. Brett and N.H.K. Smith (Aberdeen Univ), easily, 8m 44s

Ht: bt R.L.C. King and I.A. Stevens (Barclays Bank and Alton Blades RCs), easily, 8m 41s

Final: bt E.M.G. Pearson and C.D.M, Riches (Molesey BC), easily, 7m 39s

A.M. Peach, 12.9 (bow); C. Guppy, 12.7 (stroke)

Ht: bt A and J. Hooker (Marlow RC), 1 lth, 8m 11s

Ht: bt P. Dominey and M. Johnson (Thames RC), easily, 8m 49s

Ht: lost to Pearson and Riches, 4⅓ lths, 8m 19s

1987 A.J. Holmes, 14.2 (bow); S.G. Redgrave (Marlow RC), 15.10 (stroke)

Ht: bt T. Mills and K. Cameron (Harvard Univ, USA), easily, 8m 0s

Ht: bt J.M. Bohan and B.G. O'Hara (Iona Coll, USA), easily, 7m 18s (record)

Ht: bt M.T.C. Orr and C.D.M. Riches (Molesey BC), easily, 7m 39s

Final: bt Y and N. Pimenov (Dinamo Moscow, USSR), not rowed out, 7m 48s

1988 A.J. Holmes, 14.13 (bow); S.G. Redgrave, 15.11 (stroke)

Ht: bt P.C. Hovey and D.R. Radack (Union BC, USA), easily, 8m 35s

Ht: scratched

1989 S.N. Berrisford, 15.6 (bow); S.G. Redgrave, 15.11 (stroke)

C. Brooke-Partridge, 14.5 (bow); M.B. Partridge, 13.4 (stroke)

J.L. Garrett, 14.10 (bow); S.F. Hassan, 14.8 (stroke)

Ht: Berrisford and Redgrave bt C.H. Waumsley and M.J.S. Hackett (Gloucester RC), easily, 7m 59s

Ht: Brooke-Partridge and Partridge bt G.P.H. Johnson and T.J.P. Hine (Kingston RC), 4 lths, 7m 41s

Ht: Garrett and Hassan bt N.J. Howe and R.M.W. Williams (London RC), 1¼ lths, 7m 35s

Ht: Brooke-Partridge and Partridge lost to Y. and N. Pimenov (Dinamo, USSR), 3⅓ lths, 8m 2s

Berrisford and Redgrave bt Garrett and Hassan, 3¾ lths, 7m 50s

Ht: Berrisford and Redgrave bt Y. and N. Pimenov, 2¾ lths, 7m 27s

Final: Berrisford and Redgrave bt V. and G. Grabow (RC Witten, W. Germany), easily, 7m 9s (record)

1990 S.N. Berrisford, 15.6 (bow); S.G. Redgrave, 15.11 (stroke)

H.F.W. Worden, 13.11 (bow); J. Waller, 13.13 (stroke)

M.C. Pinsent, 14.12 (bow); P.R. Mulkerrins (Star), 13.3 (stroke)

Ht: Berrisford and Redgrave bt A.J. Major and T.W.J. Birtwistle (St Neots and Newark RCs), easily, 8m 5s

Ht: Pinsent and Mulkerrins (Star) bt D.S.M. Pinkney and C.T. Morley (Nottinghamshire County RA), 4½ lths, 8m 4s

Ht: Worden and Waller bt A.J. Cole and T.F. Eckersley (Kingston RC), 2½ lths, 8m 4s

Ht: Berrisford and Redgrave bt P.R. Kaye and J.D.M. Scrivener (Lea RC), 2 lths, 7m 51s

Ht: Pinsent and Mulkerrins (Star) bt Worden and Waller, easily, 8m 11s

Ht: Berrisford and Redgrave scratched

Ht: Pinsent and Mulkerrins (Star) lost to K.S. Sinzinger and H. Bauer (HK Linz, Austria), not rowed out, 7m 56s

1991 S.G. Redgrave, 16.0 (bow); M.C. Pinsent, 15.1 (stroke)

Ht: bt J. Billowes and W. Holford (Agecroft RC), 3½ lths, 7m 59s

Ht: bt M.T.C. Orr and C.D.M. Riches (Molesey BC), 5 lths, 7m 28s

Ht: bt J. Narmontas and S. Kucinskas (Dinamo Vilnus, Lithuania), easily, 8m 1s

Final: bt J. Robert and M. Bermudez (Natacio Banyoles, Spain), easily, 7m 38s

1992 P.P. Ashley-Carter, 13.2 (bow); A.P. Murray, 13.5 (stroke)

Ht: bt I.W. Hopkins and M.S. Chmiel (Tideway Scullers School), 1¾ lths, 7m 44s

Ht: bt G.G. Faultless and H.D.F. Hatton (UL/Tyrian Club), 3⅔ lths, 7m 57s

Ht: bt J.M. Michalitsianos and R.P. Metcalf (Lea RC), 2¼ lths, 7m 46s

Final: lost to D.R. Gillard and N.J. Clarry (Goldie BC), 3 lths, 7m 30s

1993 S.G. Redgrave, 1,9 (bow); M.C. Pinsent, 16.4 (stroke)

Ht: bt P.A and M.G. Murray (Cappoquin RC, Eire), 3 lths, 7m 46s

Ht: bt R. Walker and E. Moore (Sydney RC, Australia), ½ lths, 7m 51s

Ht: bt W.V. Weedon and M.S. Smith (Staines BC), 3¼ lths, 8m 15s

Final: bt W.M. Coventry and C.I. Clayton-Greene (Waikato RC, New Zealand), 1 lth, 7m 22s

1994 S.G. Redgrave, 16.10 (bow); M.C. Pinsent, 16.5 (stroke)

Ht: bt N.I. Aston and R.M. Woods (Royal Air Force RC), 2 lths, 8m 8s

Ht: bt D.E. Bangert and W.T.M. Mason (Goldie BC), 1 lth, 7m 24s

Ht: bt D. Kirchoff and H. Sennewald (Potsdam RG and RC Rostock, Germany), 2¼ lths, 7m 25s

Final: bt J. Van Driessche and L. Goiris (Gentse RSV, Belgium), 1¾ lths, 7m 22s

1995 S.G. Redgrave, 16.0 (bow); M.C. Pinsent, 16.0 (strke)

Ht: bt R.D. Sanders and R.X.K. McElroy (Newcastle RGS), 2¾ lths, 8m 10s

Ht: bt C. Korb and F. Fugel (RC Favorite Hammonia, Germany), 1½ lths, 7m 46s

Ht: bt D.R. Gillard and M.J.B. Kettle (Queen's Tower BC), easily, 6m 56s (record)

Final: bt R.D.T. Everington and M.B. Partridge (London RC and NCRA), 5 lths, 7m 18s

1996 R.J. Thorp, 13.5 (bow); A.P.L. Bizzell, 14.7 (stroke)

Ht: lost to D.B. Layton and K.S. Weller (Cambridge 99 RC), 3 lths, 8m 23s

THE DOUBLE SCULLS CHALLENGE CUP

1948 (Kingston/Leander): R.F. Winstone (KRC), 13.3 (bow); R.D. Burnell, 14.4 (stroke)

Ht: bt J. Edwards & R. Clarkson (Liverpool Victoria RC), 2¾ lths, 8m 20s

Ht: lost to B. Piessens & W.A. Collet (Belgian Royal Rowing Federation), 2 lths, 7m 54s

1949 (Maidenhead/Leander): B.H.T. Bushnell (MRC), 11.5 (bow); R.D. Burnell, 14.12 (stroke)

Ht: lost to E.W. Parsner & A. Larsen (DFDS RC, Denmark), 1 lth, 7m 27s

1951 P. Bradley, 12.13 (bow), R.D. Burnell, 14.9 (stroke)

Ht: bt J.B. Brown & K.W. Tinegate (Birmingham RC), 1¼ lths, 8m 11s

Ht: bt H. Wilke & W. Neuburger (RG Florsheim-Russelsheim, W. Germany, 3 lths, 8m 41s

Final: bt B.G. Davies & A.A.P. Kemp (Reading RC), 2 lths, 8m 41s

1959 C.G.V. Davidge, 12.9 (bow); S.A. Mackenzie, 13.10 (stroke)

Ht: bt G.W. Baker & M.A. Spracklen (Marlow RC), 2¼ lths, 7m 47s

Final: bt G.C. Justicz & N.J. Birkmyre (Birmingham RC and Ariel RC), 2¾ lths, 7m 55s

1962 G.C. Justicz, 12.5 (bow); N.J. Birkmyre, 13.10 (stroke)

Ht: bt O. Tjurin & B. Dubrovskiy (Trud Club, Leningrad, USSR, ¾ lth, 7m 19s

Final: bt D.N. Joyce & A. Maclehose (Exeter and Corpus Christi Colls, Oxford), easily, 7m 39s

1963 C.G.V. Davidge, 12.6 (bow); S.A. Mackenzie, 14.6 (stroke)

Ht: lost to M.B. Alwin & W van der Toght (RV Willem III and RV Skadi, Holland), easily, 7m 46s

1964 G.C. Justicz, 12.8; N.J. Birkmyre, 14.2 (stroke)

P.J. Webb, 10.10 (bow); A.V. Cooke, 12.2 (stroke)

Ht: Justicz & Birkmyre bt Webb & Cooke, ¼ lth, 7m 41s

Ht: Justicz & Birkmyre bt D. Molesworth & T.J. Reid (Whakatane RC, New Zealand), 2 lths, 7m 55s

Final: Justicz & Birkmyre bt H. Frederiksen & I.J. Kruse (Danske Studenters Roklub, Denmark), ¾ lth, 7m 32s

1965 G.C. Justicz, 13.2 (bow); N.J. Birkmyre, 14,0 (stroke)

N.P. Cooper, 12.12 (bow); R.N. Carpmael, 13.12 (stroke)

Ht: Cooper & Carpmael bt P.R. Hilditch & M.E. Gaylard (London RC), easily, 7m 29s

Ht: Justicz & Birkmyre lost to M. Studach & M. Burgin (Grasshopper Club, Zurich, Switzerland), 3 lths, 7m 20s

Ht: Cooper & Carpmael lost to M. Haake & J. Bruckhandler (TSC Berlin, E Germany), 3 lths, 7m 17s

1966 N.P. Cooper, 12.12 (bow); A.V. Cooke, 12.12 (stroke)

Ht: bt P.F. Islef & N.H. Secher (Danske Studenters Roklub, Denmark), 3½ lths, 7m 55s

Final: lost to M. Haake & J. Bruckhandler (TSC Berlin), 3¾ lths, 7m 20s

1972 P.G.R. Delafield, 14.0 (bow); T.J. Crooks, 14.0 (stroke)

Ht: bt H.A.E. Stheeman & R.B. Rakison (London RC), easily, 8m 6s

Ht: bt T.J.A. Bishop & G. Potts (Durham ARC), easily, 8m 10s

Final: bt L. Klecatsky & J.W. Dietz (New York Athletic Club), 1⅔ lths, 7m 24s

1973 (Leander/CUBC): M.J. Hart, 13.7 (bow); C.L. Baillieu, 13.5 (stroke)

Ht: bt T.J.A. Bishop & G. Potts (Durham ARC), easily, 7m 19s

Ht: G. Korschikov & J. Malischev (Dynamo Leningrad and Vodnik Khimki, USSR), 4 lths, 6m 59s (record)

Final: bt V. Isler & H. Ruckstuhl (See Clubs Stafa and Zurich, Switzerland), 4½ lths, 7m 11s

1975 M.J. Hart, 13.7 (bow); C.L. Baillieu, 13.5 (stroke)

Ht: bt M. Verlin & H. Killen (New York Athletic Club), 2 lths, 7m 16s

Ht: bt R.A. Prentice & M.S. Spencer (London RC & Argosies RC), easily, 7m 20s

Final: bt P. Levy & K.B. Gee (Weybridge RC and Molesey BC), easily, 7m 23s

1976 G.A.S. Locke, 13.9 (bow); P.S. Bramfitt, 13.5 (stroke)

Ht: bt A.N. Jelfs & J.A. Truswell (Abingdon RC), 1⅔ lths, 7m 24s

Ht: bt P.E. and S.M. Johnson (Newcastle Univ & Upper Thames RC), 2½ lths, 7m 45s

Ht: lost to R.A. Prentice & M.S. Spencer (London RC), 3 lths, 7m 35s

1977 M.J. Hart, 13.7 (bow); C.L. Baillieu, 13.5 (stroke)

Ht: bt P.W. Moore & D.A. Clift (Hollingworth Lake RC), easily, 8m 30s

Ht: bt A.M. Peach & E.R. Sims (Maidenhead RC), easily, 7m 43s

Final: bt R.G. Stone & C.R. Wood (Harvard Univ, USA), easily, 7m 20s

1978 M.J. Hart, 13.7 (bow); C.L. Baillieu, 13.5 (stroke)

Ht: bt J.L.M. Ferrara & D.L. Keefe (Potomac BC, USA), easily, 7m 42s

Ht: bt D. Topolski & I.J. Wilson (London RC and Thames Tradesmen's RC), easily, 7m 56s

Final: bt M.S. Spencer & R.A. Prentice (Poplar, Blackwall & District RC), easily, 7m 44s

1979 (Thames Tradesmen's/Leander): J. Clark, 14.4 (bow); C.L. Baillieu, 13.5 (stroke)

Ht: bt M. Cushway & P. Boosey (City Orient RC), easily, 7m 47s

Ht: bt D. Topolski & P. Barry (Tideway Scullers School), easily, 7m 53s

Final: bt A.C. Rudkin & I. Gold (Bewl Bridge RC and Poplar, Blackwall & District RC), easily, 7m 32s

1983 (Bewdley RC/Leander): J. Spencer-Jones, 13.1 (bow); C.L. Baillieu, 13.2 (stroke)

Ht: bt A.M. Cusack & I.W. Hopkins (Wallingford RC and Thames Tradesmen's RC), easily, 7m 47s

Ht: bt J. Dwan & F.J. Burwood (Poplar, Blackwall & District RC), easily, 7m 34s

Final: bt P. Johnson & N.A. Staite (Tees RC and Evesham RC), 3 lths, 7m 27s

1985 (Kingston/Leander): P. Clarke (KRC), 10.10, (bow); N.G. Spencer-Jones, 11.4 (stroke)

Ht: lost to J. Spencer-Jones & M.A.H. Buckingham (Bewdley RC and Marlow RC), 2½ lths, 7m 46s

1989 C. Skuse, 11.6 (bow); R.C. Luke, 11.8 (stroke)
J. Spencer-Jones, 13.5 (bow); M.A.H. Buckingham, 14.8 (stroke)
Ht: Skuse & Luke bt C.E. Clapp & B.J. Smith (Union BC, USA), 2⅔ lths, 7m 23s
Ht: Spencer-Jones & Buckingham lost to P. Luzek & I. Gruza (Dukla Praha, Czechoslovakia), 2 feet, 7m 5s
Ht: Skuse & Luke lost to R. Florijn & N. Rienks (Die Leythe and Okeanos, Holland), easily, 7m 32s

1990 I.R. Dryden, 13.6 (bow); R.C. Stanhope, 13.4 (stroke)
Ht: bt A.N. Graham & M.P. Burbanks (Molesey BC), 4 lths, 8m 20s
Ht: bt J.N. Hartland & N.P. Gardam (NCRA), 3 feet, 7m 50s
Ht: lost to M.B. Alloway & C.F. Williams (Tideway Scullers), 2½ lths, 8m 0s

1991 R.C. Luke, 12.1 (bow); C.J. Skuse, 12.2 (stroke)
Ht: bt M. Holmes & A. Pryde (Scottish Argonauts), 3½ lths, 7m 27
Ht: bt S.E. Winter & T.P. Dorrell (Stourport BC), easily, 7m 28s
Ht: bt D.C. Martinelli & A.D.J. Butt (Univ of London & London RC), 1 lth, 8m 0s
Final: lost to B. Eltang & H. Bang (Danske Studenters Roklub, Denmark, and Fana Roklubb, Norway), easily, 7m 32s

1992 C.J. Skuse, 11.3 (bow); R.C. Luke, 12.0 (stroke)
Ht: bt G.A. Annand & C.B. Pearsen (Queensland ARC, Australia), 2½ lths, 7m 29s
Ht: lost to D. Boddeke & J. van Bekkum (Delftsche SR Laga and Utrecht SR Triton, Holland), 1 lth, 7m 40s

1993 H.F.W. Worden, 14.6 (bow); P.R. Rudaz, 15.1 (stroke)
Ht: lost to I.W. Hopkins & M. Pollecutt (Molesey BC), ½ lth, 7m 19s

1994 M.J.A. McQuillan, 14.7 (bow); S.F. Trapmore, 13.12 (stroke)
Ht: lost to D.S. Whitelaw & A.M. Sinton (Kingston RC and NCRA), 4 lths, 7m 26s

1995 J.E. Cracknell, 14.8 (bow); R. Thatcher, 13.8 (stroke)
Ht: bt T.C. Scales & T.J. Stapleton (Peterborough City RC), easily, 7m 11s
Ht: bt E.M. Hausleitner & P.J. Vondra (Thames RC and London RC), easily, 7m 23s
Ht: lost to B. Jamieson & D.J. Gleeson (Augusta Training Centre, USA), ¾ lth, 6m 55s (record)

THE DIAMOND SCULLS

1846 T.H. Fellows
Ht: bt W.P. Cloves (3rd Trinity, Cambridge), not rowed out
Final: lost to E.G. Moon (Magdalen Coll, Oxford), easily
E.G. Peacock
Ht: lost to E.G. Moon on a foul

1865 T.J. Cocksedge
Ht: 1, E.B. Michell (Magdalen Coll, Oxford); 2, J. Rickaby (Brasenose Coll, Oxford); 3, T.J. Cocksedge, easily, 10m 7s

1866 H. Watney

Ht: lost to W.B. Woodgate (Kingston RC), easily, 10m 9s

J.G. Chambers

Ht: 1, W.G. Edwards (Christ Church, Oxford); 2, B. Walker (Corpus Christi Coll, Cambridge); 3, J.G. Chambers 3 lths, 10m 16s

1892 V. Nickalls

Ht: lost to J.J.K. Ooms (Neptunus RC, Amsterdam, Holland), easily, 9m 26s

1894 Hon R. Guinness

Ht: lost to G. Nickalls (Formosa BC), ¾ lth, 9m 8s

1895 Hon R. Guinness

Ht: bt E.A. Thompson (Argonaut RC, Toronto, Canada), easily, 9m 1s

Ht: bt R.K. Beaumont (Burton-on-Trent RC), easily, 9m 8s

Final: bt G. Nickalls, 1½ lths, 9m 11s

1896 Hon R. Guinness

Ht: bt H.T. Blackstaffe (Vesta RC), 2 lths, 9m 3s

Ht: bt V. Nickalls (London RC), 4 lths, 9m 19s

Final: bt R.K. Beaumont (Burton-on-Trent RC), 2 lths, 9m 35s

1901 W.C. Bond

Ht: lost to St G. Ashe (Thames RC), easily, 8m 58s

1902 R.B. Etherington-Smith

Ht: bt L.X.F. Prével (CN Nice, France), easily, 8m 43s

Ht: bt H.T. Blackstaffe (Vesta RC), 2¼ lths, 9m 1s

Ht: bt J. Beresford (Kensington RC), 2 lths, 8m 57s

Final: lost to F.S. Kelly (Balliol Coll, Oxford), 2½ lths, 8m 59s

1903 F.S. Kelly

Ht: bt C. Ernst (Wiking RC, Berlin), easily, 9m 19s

Ht: bt H.T. Blackstaffe (Vesta RC), easily, 8m 52s

Ht: bt A.H. Cloutte (London RC), easily, 8m 36s

Final: bt J. Beresford (Kensington RC), easily, 8m 41s

1905 F.S. Kelly, 12.1

Ht: bt G.H. Woodard (Christ Church, Oxford), easily, 8m 49s

Ht: bt T.D. Roberts (Christ Church, Oxford), 5 lths, 8m 40s

Ht: bt A.A. Stuart (London RC), easily, 8m 32s

Final: bt H.T. Blackstaffe (Vesta RC), easily, 8m 10s (record)

1907 D.C.R. Stuart, 11.2

Ht: bt D. Fitte (Vesta RC), ½ lth, 10m 2s

Ht: lost to A. McCulloch (University Coll, Oxford), easily, 9m 44s

R.V. Powell, 12.6

Ht: lost to A. McCulloch, easily, 9m 40s

1908 A. McCulloch, 12.5

Ht: bt J. de G. Edye (Auriol RC), easily, 8m 38s

Ht: bt C.W. Covell (Vesta RC), easily, 8m 36s

Final: bt A.A. Stuart (Kingston RC), easily, 8m 25s

1909 E.W. Powell, 11.6

Ht: lost to A.A. Stuart (Kingston RC), 2 lths, 9m 27s

1911 A. McCulloch, 12.4
Ht: bt C. McVilly (Derwent RC, Tasmania), 6 lths, 8m 54s
Ht: bt C.M. Stuart (Trinity Hall, Cambridge), 4 lths, 8m 31s
Ht: bt E.D.P. Pinks (London RC), ¼ lth, 8m 38s
Final: lost to E.W. Powell (Eton Vikings), not rowed out, 8m 49s

1921 D.H.L. Gollan, 13.4
Ht: bt L.A. Pattinson (Jesus Coll, Cambridge), easily, 8m 30s
Ht: lost to F.E. Eyken (Laga, Delft, Holland), easily, 9m 11s

1922 D.H.L. Gollan, 13.3
Ht: lost to J. Beresford, Jnr (Thames RC), easily, 9m 32s

1923 D.H.L. Gollan, 13.2
Ht: bt W.M. Hoover (Duluth BC, USA), ¾ lth, 8m 34s
Ht: bt R.S. Codman (Union BC, Boston, USA), easily, 8m 30s
Ht: bt H.A. Belyea (St John ARC, Canada), easily, 8m 11s
Final: lost to M.K. Morris (London RC), 1 lth, 8m 23s

1924 D.H.L. Gollan, 13.5
Ht: lost to J. Beresford, Jnr (Thames RC), 2½ lths, 10m 16s

S. Earl, 12.2
Ht: lost to J. Beresford, Jnr, not rowed out, no time taken

1925 D.H.L. Gollan, 13.3
Ht: bt L.H. Kent (Corpus Christi Coll, Oxford), easily, 8m 48s
Ht: bt M.P. Detton (SN de Nogent-sur-Marne, France), easily, 9m 0s
Final: lost to J. Beresford, Jnr (Thames RC), easily, 8m 28s

1926 D.H.L. Gollan, 13.7
Ht: lost to J. Beresford, Jnr (Thames RC), easily, 8m 32s

1928 T.D.A. Collet, 12.2
Ht: bt J.E. Hewens (Maidenhead RC), 1¾ lths, 9m 7s
Ht: lost to J. Wright (Argonaut RC, Canada), 2½ lths, 10m 6s

1929 T.D.A. Collet, 12.2
Ht: bt A.G.H. Willis (Pembroke Coll, Cambridge), 2 lths, 9m 3s
Ht: lost to F. Bradley (Pembroke Coll, Cambridge), 3 lths, 10m 30s

1930 T.D.A. Collet, 12.2
Ht: bt F. Gentry (Ibis RC), 1 lth, 9m 20s
Ht: bt D. Guye (London RC), 3 lths, 9m 59s
Ht: lost to J.S. Guest (Don RC, Canada), easily, 8m 42s

1932 T.A. Brocklebank, 11.1
Ht: lost to H. Buhtz (Berliner RC, Germany), not rowed out, 9m 31s

1938 R. Hope, 11.13
Ht: lost to T.H. Tyler (Thames RC), easily, 8m 58s

1946 R.D. Burnell, 14.0
Ht: bt B.H.T. Bushnell (Maidenhead RC), 1 lth, 8m 25s
Ht: lost to J. Sépheriades (SN de la Basse Seine, France), 4 lths, 10m 18s

1947 M.B. McNabb, 11.9
Ht: lost to B.H.T. Bushnell (Maidenhead RC), easily, 9m 19s

1948 A.D. Rowe, 12.9
Ht: bt D.G. Cooke (Exeter Coll, Oxford), easily, 8m 38s
Ht: lost to M.T. Wood (NSW Police, Australia), 1½ lths, 8m 10s

1950 A.D. Rowe, 12.12
: Ht: bt B. Piessens (Royal Belgian Rowing Federation), easily, 8m 49s
: Ht: bt E.M. Sturges (London RC), 3 lths, 8m 52s
: Ht: bt H.J. Renton (Magdalen Coll, Oxford), 1½ lths, 8m 41s
: Final: bt R.H. van Mesdag (Trinity Coll, Dublin), 3 lths, 9m 11s

1951 A.D. Rowe, 12.11
: Ht: lost to C.T. Neumeier (RV Willem III, Amsterdam, Holland), 3 lths, 8m 21s

1959 S.C. Rand, 12.8
: Ht: bt M.E. Gaylard (Imperial Coll), ½ lth, 8m 52s
: Ht: lost to H.L. Parker (Vesper BC, USA), ¾ lth, 8m 45s

1960 S.A. Mackenzie, 13.11
: S.C. Rand, 12.4
: Ht: Rand bt W.G. Beech (London RC), 2½ lths, 8m 6s
: Ht: Mackenzie bt R.N. Carpmael (London RC), easily, 8m 3s
: Ht: Rand bt D.F. Meineke (Durban RC, S. Africa), 4 lths, 8m 22s
: Ht: Mackenzie bt Rand, easily, 8m 23s
: Final: Mackenzie bt T. Kocerka (AZS Szczecin, Poland), ½ lth, 8m 3s

1961 S.C. Rand, 12.4
: Ht: bt K.R. Smith (Nottingham Univ), 4 feet, 8m 44s
: Ht: lost to O. Tjurin (Trud Club, Leningrad, USSR), 4 lths, 8m 29s

1962 S.A. Mackenzie, 14.1
: Ht: bt O.N. Tubbs (St Thomas's Hosp), easily, 8m 1s
: Ht: bt G. Kottmann (Belvoir RC, Switzerland), 1⅔ lths, 8m 21s
: Ht: bt E. Kubiak (Club Tryton, Poland), on a foul
: Final: bt W.L. Barry (Quintin BC), 3 lths, 8m 38s

1966 N.J. Birkmyre, 14.0
: Ht: lost to R.J. Hopley (Viking RC, S. Africa), 1¾ lths, 8m 33s

1967 A.V. Cooke, 12.11
: Ht: bt J.S. Pilgrim-Morris (RAF Bomber Command), 1½ lths, 8m 55s
: Ht: lost to J. Meissner (Amicitia RV, Mannheim, W Germany), easily, 9m 5s

M.J. Muir-Smith, 13.11
: Ht: lost to M.P. Watkinson (West End RC, New Zealand), 1¾ lths, 9m 45s

1968 A.V. Cooke, 12.11
: Ht: bt M.J. Cleal (Westminster Bank RC), 3⅓ lths, 8m 32s
: Ht: lost to P.A. Barry (Tideway Scullers School), 1 lth, 9m 42s

1969 T.J. Crooks, 14.1
: Ht: bt R.J. Hopley (Trident RC, S. Africa), easily, no time taken
: Ht: lost to W.P. Maher (Vesper BC, USA), 3¼ lths, 8m 25s

1972 P.D.P. Angier, 12.7
: Ht: lost to A. Timoschinin (WMF Moscow, USSR), not rowed out, 8m 49s

1973 T.J. Crooks, 14.0
Ht: bt S.G. Hoff (Norske Studenters Roklub, Norway) easily, 8m 46s
Ht: bt E.O. Hale (Lindisfarne RC, Australia), 2¾ lths, 8m 8s
Ht: lost to S. Drea (Neptune RC, Eire), 5 lths, 7m 55s

1977 T.J. Crooks, 13.10
Ht: bt I.K. Marriott (Abingdon RC), easily, 9m 35s
Ht: bt E.O. Hale (Sydney RC, Australia), 2¾ lths, 8m 32s
Final bt J.W. Dietz (New York Athletic Club, USA) 3⅔ lths, 8m 11s

1978 T.J. Crooks, 14.3
Ht: bt P.G. Cavalieri (Trident RC, S. Africa), easily, 8m 30s
Ht: bt D. Topolski (London RC), easily, 8m 24s
Final: bt H.P. Matheson (Thames Tradesmen's RC), easily, 8m 25s

1979 I. Lloyd, 14.6
Ht: bt I. Knight (Kingston RC), 2 lths, 8m 39s
Ht: lost to J.T. Ghoos (Antwerpse RV, Belgium), easily, 8m 55s

1981 C.L. Baillieu, 12.12
Ht: bt M. Knight (Nottingham & Union RC), easily, 9m 10s
Ht: bt D. Hamilton (Kingston RC, Canada), easily, 8m 37s
Ht: bt V. Nolte (RC Saar, W. Germany), easily, 8m 17s
Final: bt S.C. Howell (Univ of London), easily, 9m 38s

1982 C.L. Baillieu, 13.5
Ht: bt A.C. Rudkin (Bewl Bridge RC), easily, 8m 58s
Ht: bt A.V. Lovrich (Perth & Collegians RC, Australia), easily, 8m 24s
Final: bt A. Whitwell (Thames Tradesmen's RC), easily, 8m 18s

1984 C.L. Baillieu, 13.5
Ht: bt H.P. Matheson (NCRA), easily, 8m 0s
Ht: bt J.N. Melvin (London RC), 3½ lths, 8m 19s
Ht: bt P. Franke (Oceana RC, W. Germany), 4 lths, 8m 3s
Final: bt B. Eltang (Danske Studenten Roklub, Denmark), 4 lths, 7m 57s

1990 R.F.G. Henderson, 14.6
G.R. Pooley, 13.1
Ht: Henderson bt R.F. Redpath (Univ of London), easily, 8m 42s
Ht: Pooley bt J.T. McGowan (New York Athletic Club, USA), easily, 8m 20s
Ht: Henderson bt Pooley, 2½ lths, 8. 20s
Ht: Henderson bt W. van Belleghem (TR Bruges, Belgium), 1¾ lths, 8m 17s
Final: Henderson lost to E.F.M. Verdonk (Koru RC, New Zealand), ¾ lth, 8m 21s

1991 R.G.F. Henderson, 14.11
Ht: lost to P.M. Haining (NCRA), 2 lths, 7m 44s

1992 R.G.F. Henderson, 14.7

C.A. Maclennan, 14.3

Ht: Maclennan bt P.H. Ashmore (St Ives RC), easily, 7m 57s

Ht: Henderson bt S.R. Allpass (Thames RC), 3¾ lths, 7m 52s

Ht: Maclennan lost to S. Franke (RG Hansa Hamburg, Germany), ⅔ lth, 7m 50s

Ht: Henderson bt M.A. Hindery (Undine Barge Club, USA), easily, 8m 41s

Ht: Henderson bt S. Franke, easily, 8m 23s

Ht: Henderson bt F.M. Reininger (Fairmount RA, USA), ⅓ lth, 7m 44s

Final: Henderson bt P. Reedy (Melbourne Univ, Australia), 3 lths, 7m 44s

1994 G.R. Pooley, 13.10

Ht: bt I.G.P. Pritchard (Thames RC), easily, 8m 15s

Ht: lost to M.H. Hansen (Danmarks Rocenter, Denmark), 3½ lths, 7m 47s

1996 C.G. Bullas, 13.6

Ht: bt A. Van Den Broek (Castledore RC) 3 lths, 8m 53s

Ht: lost to A.R. Bihrer (Grasshopper Club, Zurich, Switzerland) 4 lths, 9m 19s

LADIES' CHALLENGE PLATE

1985 'A': A.M. Peach, 13.4 (bow); M.C.G. Chapman, 13.1; R.J. Stephens 13.1; J. Galliven, 13.5; P. Wright, 14.8; S.N. Berrisford, 15.5; S. Turner, 13.9; C.Guppy, 12.7 (stroke); G.A. Rees, 8.8 (cox)

Ht: bt Georgetown University RA, USA, 2 lths, 6m 46s

Ht: bt Molesey BC, 1½ lths, 6m 50s

Ht: bt Vesta RC, 1 lth, 6m 39s

Ht: bt Princeton University, USA, ⅔ lth, 6m 34s

Final: bt Garda Siochana BC, Eire, canvas, 6m 26s

'B': N. Rogers, 10.5 (bow); M. Richards, 11.2; R. Grant, 10.10; R.J. Spratley, 11.5; J. Mackay, 11.4; R. Ruff, 11.0; T.A. Sutherland, 11.0; B.J.S. Lovegrove, 11.2 (stroke); J.A. Sabater, 8.4 (cox)

Ht: bt Eliot House, USA, 3¼ lths, 6m 49s

Ht: lost to Harvard University, USA, 1¾ lths, 6m 47s

1987 S. Bell, 13.0 (bow); J. Richards, 13.0; T. Collerton, 13.12; J.B.L. Blunt, 12.12; K.J. Almand, 14.4; P.R. Rudaz, 14.10; H.E.D. Trotter, 13.13; P.M.G. Hubbard, 13.7 (stroke); S.M.C. Gruselle, 8.5 (cox)

Ht: bt City of Oxford RC, 4 lths, 6m 42s

Ht: lost to Tideway Scullers School, ¾ lth, 6m 24s

1988 H.E.D. Trotter, 14.5 (bow); R.C. Phelps, 13.12; C.P. Greenway, 16.3; I. Robinson, 15.2; J.R. Garman, 14.12; P.R. Rudaz, 14.8; R.J. Stephens, 13.10; K.J. Almand, 14.9 (stroke); G.G.P. Herbert, 7.10 (cox)

Ht: bt Harvard University, USA, 3/4 lths, 6m 39s

Ht: bt Florida Institute of Technology, USA, 4½ lths, 7m 3s

Ht: bt Tideway Scullers School, 1¾ lths, 6m 56s

Final: lost to Mercantile RC, Australia, 1 lth, 6m 23s (equals record)

1991 (Leander/Molesey): H.F.W. Worden, 13.8 (bow); D.J. Luke, 15.3; C.A. Maclennan, 14.1; R.H. Bartlett, 15.1; P.A.J. Bridge, 13.11; J. Waller, 14.3; M.W. Norton (MBC), 14.4; J.D. Hulls (MBC), 14.4 (stroke); N. Chugani, 8.6 (cox)

Ht: bt Cornell University, USA, ¾ lth, 6m 33s

Final: bt University of London/Oxford University, 1 lth, 6m 26s

1995 (Leander/Oxford Univ): J.R.W. Kawaja (O), 13.1 (bow); G.A. Rosengren (O), 14.1; M.J. Insley, 13.12; J.P. Purnell, 13.11; D.R.H. Clegg (O), 14.3; P.G. Rogers, 14.0; K.K. Poole (O), 13.7; J-I. Throndsen (O), 14.0; (stroke); T.G. Jackson, 8.3 (cox)

Ht: lost to Princeton University, USA, 1½ lths, 6m 20s

1996 H.W.F. Worden, 13.12 (bow); M.J. Insley, 14.0; T.C. Garbett, 14.2; T.E. Carson, 13.11; S.C. Powell, 15.3; P.R. Rudaz, 15.3; K.J. Almand, 14.11; M.B. Partridge, 12.2 (stroke); N. Chugani, 8.9 (cox)

Ht: bt Free Press BC 'B', easily, 7m 17s

Ht: bt RC Hansa Hamburg, Germany, 1 lth, 6m 16s

Ht: bt Nottinghamshire County RA, 1 lth, 6m 29s

Final: lost to Goldie BC, 3½ lths, 6m 23s

THAMES CHALLENGE CUP

1965 G.D. Rooker, 11.9 (bow); I.T. Grimble, 10.7; C.S. Powell, 14.3; J.S.B. McCowen, 13.0; J.S.P. Maynard, 14.1; N.R. Tumber, 13.0; A. Harris, 11.10; J.M. Wyatt, 12.3 (stroke); C.R.J. Woodhouse, 9.3 (cox)

Ht: lost to Pembroke College, Cambridge, ½ lth, 6m 46s

1966 C.R. Parry, 12.4 (bow); J.M.I. Hayter, 13.4; P.S.I. Allen, 14.6; J.S.P. Maynard, 14.5; J.M. Duncan, 14.1; C.S. Powell, 14.7; P.G. Saltmarsh, 13.3; S. Crooks, 12.7 (stroke); C.R.J. Woodhouse, 8.12 (cox)

Ht: lost to Molesey BC, ⅔ lth, 6m 53s

1968 C.R. Parry, 12.6 (bow); I.D. Morton, 11.4; R.J.S. Clarke, 12.11; G.C.D. Davidson, 12.11; T.M. Redfern, 12.11; T.J. Crooks, 13.8; N.D.C. Tee, 11.11; R.B. Crane, 11.6 (stroke); R.R. Burges, 8.9 (cox)

Ht: bt Furnivall SC, 3¼ lths, 7m 0s

Ht: bt Molesey BC, easily, 7m 21s

Ht: bt Scottish Argonauts BC, 2¾ lths, 8m 21s

Ht: bt Bedford RC, 1 lth, 8m 4s

Final: bt Cornell Univ, USA, 4 lth, 8m 8s

1969 S.F. Johnson, 12.0 (bow); P.D.P. Angier, 13.7; V.J. Pardhy, 12.7; J.C. Yallop, 14.3; G.A.S. Locke, 13.13; J.C. Pemberton, 13.1; C.M.C. Preston, 12.11; T.J. Bennett, 11.8 (stroke); J.A. Easton, 9.3 (cox)

Ht: bt Garda Siochana BC, Eire, 2⅓ lths, 6m 53s

Ht: bt Isis BC, 3⅔ lths, 7m 1s

Ht: bt Harvard University, USA, 2¼ lths, 6m 56s

Final: bt University of Pennsylvania, USA, 3 lths, 6m 43s

1970 S.A. Slee, 12.4 (bow); R.C. Lester, 13.2; A.C.D. Wiggin, 13.7; P.A. Fennessy, 12.6; C.M.C. Preston, 12.13; C.P. Etherington, 13.2; A.J. Allen, 12.12; C.P. Ellis, 12.11 (stroke); J.H. Newhouse, 9.1 (cox)

Ht: bt City Orient RC, easily, 7m 23s
Ht: bt St Mary's Hospital, London, 1¾ lths, 6m 52s
Ht: bt Yale University, USA, 2¼ lths, 7m 4s
Final: bt London RC, 1⅔ lths, 7m 1s

1971 N.M.L. Aitchison, 13.2 (bow); H.R. Jacobs, 13.0; A.C.D. Wiggin, 13.11; M.W. Trapp, 15.11; R.C. Edmondson, 13.3; C.P. Etherington, 13.4; P.S. Bramfitt, 12.11; S.W. Sadler, 12.6 (stroke); S.H. Martin, 8.11 (cox)

Ht: bt Vesta RC, easily, 7m 11s
Ht: bt Weybridge RC, 2¾ lths, 7m 10s
Ht: bt Tideway Scullers School, not rowed out, 7m 15s
Ht: lost to Kingston RC, 1 lths, 6 m. 56s

1973 J.G. Nelson-Edwards, 13.2 (bow); I. Wilson, 13.4; D.B. King, 14.4; N.C. Hardingham, 13.2; P.S. Plaisted, 14.7; G.S. Innes, 13.7; D.H. Carpenter, 11.3; D.G. Innes, 11.6 (stroke); S.E.G. Salt, 8.1 (cox)

Ht: bt Eliot House, USA, 1⅔ lths, 6m 57s
Ht: bt Norwich ARC, 2 lths, 6m 52s
Ht: lost to Garda Siochana BC, Eire, ¾ lth, 6m 40s

1974 D.B. King, 13.9 (bow); I.J. Wilson, 13.5; D.J.D. Tatton, 13.10; J.D. Randall, 14.10; P.S. Plaisted, 14.7; N.C. Hardingham, 14.4; P.S. Gregory, 14.12; D.G. Innes, 11.10 (stroke); R.C. Lee, 8.12 (cox)

Ht: bt ETuF, Essen, Germany, 1¾, 7m 17s
Ht: lost to Antwerp RC, Belgium, ⅔ lth, 7m 6s

1975 N.D. Whittaker, 11.12 (bow); C.G. Sayers, 12.7; D.H. Carpenter, 11.7; W.F. Riley, 13.7; W.G. Watkins, 12.10; O.C. Brocklebank, 12.9; N.J.D. Bull, 13.0; P.R. Taylor, 12.2 (stroke); P.W. Jenkinson, 8.0 (cox)

Ht: bt Barclay's Bank RC, easily, 6m 49s
Ht: bt Derby RC, 3½ lths, 6m 38s
Ht: bt Thames RC, 4 lths, 6m 47s
Ht: lost to Quintin BC, 1 lth, 6m 35s

1977 S.A. Vassallo, 12.7 (bow); I.R. Knight, 14.8; C.G. Sayers, 12.8; N.B. Rankov, 14.8; M.R. McGowan, 13.0; P.O. Langguth, 16.0; N.D. Whittaker, 12.2; E.D. Gate, 13.3 (stroke); P.W. Jenkinson, 8.9 (cox)

Ht: bt Bedford RC, easily, 7m 26s
Ht: bt Aberdeen University, easily, 7m 36s
Ht: bt St Catharine's RC, Canada, 3½ lths, 7m 3s
Final: lost to London RC, 1½ lths, 6m 47s

1978 N.D. Whittaker, 12.3 (bow); D.J. Crane, 12.8; C.G. Sayers, 12.11; J.M. Pritchard, 14.0; M.R. McGowan, 13.5; P.O. Langguth, 16.7; D.P. McDougall, 13.4; C.J. Jones, 11.13 (stroke); P.W. Jenkinson, 8.0 (cox)

Ht: bt Townmead RC, not rowed out, 7m 20s
Ht: bt Trinity College, Hartford, USA, 3½ lths, 6m 49s
Ht: bt Neptune RC, Eire, 1½ lths, 7m 3s
Ht: bt Potomac BC, USA, 1 lth, 6m 52s
Final: lost after re-row to London RC, 2 lths, 6m 54s

1979 R. Reilly, 13.0 (bow); D.R. Crockford, 13.1; A.J. Holmes, 13.13; P. Taylor, 13.5; C.G. Sayers, 12.10; J.M. Pritchard, 13.9; D.P. McDougall, 12.13; C.J. Jones, 12.12 (stroke); T.G. Johnson, 8.7 (cox)

Ht: bt Cambridge '99 RC, easily, 6m 59s

Ht: bt Garda Siochana, Eire, 4 lths, 6m 54s

Ht: bt Yale University, USA, easily, 5m 53s

Ht: bt Metropolitan RC, 2⅓ lths, 6m 53s
Final: bt London RC, 1¾ lths, 6m 49s

1981 F.W. Murison, 12.6 (bow); R.J. Spratley, 12.4; K.A. Reynolds, 12.6; D. Walter, 13.2; A.C. McLean, 13.0; P.W. Cross, 13.4; A.M. Peach, 12.12; J. Wilson, 12.6 (stroke); J. Diamond, 8.1 (cox)

Ht: bt Star Club, easily, 7m 25s

Ht: bt Kew Meadows BC, 3⅓ lths, 7m 23s

Ht: bt Thames RC, 3 lths, 6m 56s

Final: lost to Charles River RA, USA, 2⅓ lths, 7m 21s

1982 F.W. Murison, 13.0 (bow); K.A. Reynolds, 12.8; C.J. Perry, 13.4; J.D. Wilson, 12.3; C.R. Stevens, 12.11; D.R. Crockford, 13.9; A.H. Reynolds, 12.1; M.J. Diserens, 12.9 (stroke); T. Allen, 7.9 (cox)

Ht: bt University College, Galway, Eire, 3 lths, 6m 52s

Ht: bt Belfast RC, easily, 6m 49s

Ht: bt Henley RC, 1¾ lths, 6m 46s

Ht: lost to Goldie BC, ½ lth, 7m 1s

1984 'A': A.M. Peach, 13.3 (bow); B.J.S. Lovegrove, 12.3; S. Turner, 14.7; P.A.J. Wright, 14.0; R.J. Stephens, 13.0; S.N. Berrisford, 14.7; M.J. Gordon, 14.4; M.A.H. Buckingham, 13.7 (stroke); G.A. Rees, 8.12 (cox)

Ht: bt Lea RC 'B', 1¾ lths, 6m 23s (record)

Ht: bt Molesey BC, 2 lths, 6m 41s

Ht: bt Harvard University, USA, 1 lths, 6m 18s (record)

Ht: bt Nautilus Lightweight RC, 6 feet, 6m 34s

Final: lost to Cantabrigian RC, 2 lths, 6m 30s

'B': N. Rogers, 10.8 (bow); C. Hudson, 11.0; E. McMinn, 11.0; R.J. Spratley, 12.0; M. Williams, 10.10; R. Ruff, 10.12; T.A. Sutherland, 10.2; P. Burden, 11.1 (stroke); I. Barton, 8.6 (cox)

Ht: bt St Catharine's RC, Canada, ½ lth, 6m 26s

Ht: lost to Vesta RC, 1⅓ lths, 6m 40s

1990 G.B. Blanchard, 13.6 (bow); J. Wright, 13.8; C.A. Maclennan, 14.0; M.A.H. Buckingham, 15.4; P.M. Mant, 14.10; D.J. Luke, 15.2; R.A. Hull, 13.9; P.R. Rudaz, 14.7 (stroke); G.G.P. Herbert, 8.5 (cox)

Ht: bt Agecroft RC, 3 lths, 7m 1s

Ht: bt Thames Tradesmen's RC 'B', 2 lths, 6m 39s

Ht: bt Temple University, USA, ½ lth, 6m 36s

Ht: lost to Harvard University, USA, ⅔ lth, 6m 34s

THE WYFOLD CHALLENGE CUP

1961 J.M.G. Andrews, 12.2 (bow); J.F. Hall-Craggs, 12.1; R.L. Howard (steers), 13.13; M.J. Langton, 11.10 (stroke)

Ht: bt Quintin BC, easily, 7m 54s
Ht: bt Vesta RC, 3 lths, 7m 52s
Ht: lost to National Provincial Bank RC, easily, 7m 38s

1964 S.C. Farmer, 12.1 (bow); R.L.S. Fishlock, 11.8; M.J. Muir-Smith (steers), 13.6; D.C. Spencer, 13.0 (stroke)

Ht: lost to Leeds Univ, 1½ lths, 7m 30s

1966 C.A. Gore, 12.0 (bow, steers); M.I.M. Gardiner, 12.0; D.J. Macfarlane, 12.2; W.R.C. Lonsdale, 13.0 (stroke)

Ht: bt Royal Air Force, ½ lth, 7m 36s
Ht: bt Weybridge RC, ⅔ lths, 7m 37s
Ht: bt Nottingham Univ, ¼ lth, 7m 41s
Ht: lost to Norwich Union RC, 2¼ lths, 7m 51s

1967 C.R. Parry, 11.12 (bow, steers); F.N. Graham, 12.3; J.M.I. Hayter, 13.5; D.F. Legget, 12.12 (stroke)

Ht: bt Scottish Argonauts, 1 lth, 8m 5s
Ht: lost to Nautilus (Midlands), ⅔ lths, 7m 54s

1968 S.A. Slee, 11.7 (bow, steers); S.F. Jagger, 12.4; V. Pardhy, 12.2; A.C. Ingrey-Senn, 10.4 (stroke)

Ht: bt Eton Vikings Club, ¾ lths, 7m 35s
Ht: lost to Barclay's Bank RC, 3 feet, 8m 34s

1969 I.D. Morton, 11.1 (bow, steers); R.J.S. Clarke, 12.12; F.J.L. Dale, 13.0; N.D.C. Tee, 11.3 (stroke)

Ht: bt Univ of London, 4 lths, 7m 31s
Ht: bt Auriol RC, easily, 7m 33s
Ht: lost to Thames Tradesmen's RC, 1 lth, 7m 32s

1972 P.S. Bramfitt, 12.11 (bow, steers); C.P. Etherington, 12.12; N.D.C. Tee, 11.10; C.R.D. McDougall, 12.12 (stroke)

Ht: bt East Midlands Venturers, not rowed out, no time taken
Ht: bt Quintin BC, easily, 7m 49s
Ht: bt London RC, 3⅔ lths, 8m 0s
Ht: bt Kingston RC, 2⅔ lths, 7m 28s
Final: bt Trident RC, S. Africa, 2⅓ lths, 7m 25s

1974 D. Topolski, 10.9 (bow); C.M. Drury, 11.1; N.D.C. Tee, 10.9; G.F. Hall, 11.2 (stroke)

Ht: bt Poplar, Blackwall & District RC, 4½ lths, 7m 49s
Ht: bt Eton Vikings Club, 4 lts, 7m 50s
Ht: bt Potomac BC, USA, 3⅔ lths, 7m 51s
Ht: lost to Porcellian Club, USA, 1⅓ lths, 7m 37s

1975 P.S. Plaisted, 13.6 (bow); W.R. Woodward-Fisher, 13.4; D.B. King, 13.3; D.G. Innes, 11.10 (stroke)

Ht: bt Saxon BC, 2⅔ lths, 7m 30s
Ht: bt Kingston RC, ¾ lth, 7m 0s (record)
Ht: bt St Elmo RC, USA, 1⅓ lths, 7m 11s
Final: lost to Thames Tradesmen's RC, 1⅓ lth, 6m 57s (record)

1976 S.J. Clegg, 12.3 (bow); P. Cola Luca, 12.7; C.G. Sayers, 12.4; P.R. Taylor, 12.12 (stroke)

Ht: lost to University Coll and Hospital, 1¾ lths, 7m 6s

1978 P.R. Fisher, 13.0 (bow, steers); R.A. Gillespie, 12.10; M.A. Bramfitt, 15.7; J.F. McLean, 13.5 (stroke)

Ht: bt Kingston RC, 3 lths, 7m 49s
Ht: bt Harvard Univ, USA, 1¼ lths, 7m 31s
Ht: lost to Molesey BC, 3 lths, 7m 43s

1980 I.B. Lloyd, 14.4 (bow, steers); P.R. Taylor, 13.10; A.C. McLean, 13.1; D.W. Murray, 12.13 (stroke)

Ht: bt Thames Tradesmen's RC, easily, 7m 41s

Ht: bt Royal Hong Kong Yacht Club, easily, 7m 51s

Ht: bt Wallingford RC, 1⅔ lths, 7m 26s

Final: lost to Nottingham BC, 3⅓ lths, 7m 13s

1981 C.R. Stevens, 12.10 (bow, steers); S. Otter, 12.8; H.D.F. Hatton, 12.8; D. Skinner, 12.10 (stroke)

Ht: bt Maidenhead RC, easily, 8m 11s

Ht: bt Trident RC, S. Africa, easily, 7m 37s

Ht: bt Kew Meadows BC, 3¼ lths, 7m 33s

Final: lost to Hanlan BC, Canada, 1 lth, 7m 54s

1982 M.D. De'ath, 11.5 (bow); R.J. Spratley, 12.12; J.S. Mackay, 11.7; M.A. Holloway, 12.7 (stroke)

Ht: lost to Trident RC, S. Africa, 1¼ lths, 7m 36s

1983 D.R. Crockford, 13.4 (bow); C.J. Perry, 13.10; C.R. Stevens, 13.3; M.J. Diserens, 12.13 (stroke)

Ht: bt Thames RC, 1¾ lths, 7m 26s

Ht: bt Nottingham & Union RC, 2⅔ lths, 7m 55s

Ht: lost to Thames Tradesmen's RC, 1¼ lths, 7m 43s

1985 T.E.A. Collerton, 14.5 (bow, steers); S.D. Whitelaw, 12.0; B. Squires, 16.1; O.W. Hall-Craggs, 13.1 (stroke)

Ht: bt London RC 'C', 4 lths, 7m 14s

Ht: bt Molesey BC 'B', not rowed out, 7m 33s

Ht: lost to Lea RC 'B', ¾ lth, 7m 4s

1986 T.E.A. Collerton, 14.6 (bow); D.S. Whitelaw, 11.13; H.E.D. Trotter, 13.0; K.J. Almand, 13.5 (stroke)

Ht: bt London RC 'B', 1 lth, 7m 21s

Ht: bt Eton Excelsior RC, easily, 7m 41s

Ht: bt Belfast RC, 2 lths, 7m 20s

Ht: lost to Charles River RA, USA, 2 lths, 7m 17s

1987 J.A. Kerr, 13.12 (bow); H.C.B. Sayer, 12.10; S.C. Church, 14.0; D.S. Whitelaw, 13.5 (stroke)

Ht: lost to Boston RC, USA, 1¼ lths, 7m 19s

1988 R.J. Thorp, 13.9 (bow); G.B. Blanchard, 14.2; A.P.L. Bizzel, 14.11; R.J.A. Fane, 14.6 (stroke)

Ht: bt Upper Thames RC, 2½ lths, 7m 53s

Ht: bt Nottinghamshire County RA 'B', 2¾ lths, 7m 9s

Ht: lost to Nautilus RC, ½ lth, 7m 5s

1989 'A': T.J.C. Foster, 13.7 (bow); D.J. Luke, 15.0; P.R. Rudaz, 14.8; J.P. Ormerod, 13.9 (stroke)

'B': G.B. Blanchard, 14.2 (bow); R.J. Thorp, 13.9; K.St C. Allen, 13.0; R.J.A. Fane, 14.6 (stroke)

Ht: 'B' bt Nottingham & Union RC, 2⅔ lths, 7m 27s

Ht: 'A' bt Upper Thames RC 'A', easily, 7m 44s

Ht: 'B' bt Bewdley RC, 4¾ lths, 7m 2s

Ht: 'A' bt Marlow RC, 4⅔ lths, 7m 1s

Ht: 'B' bt Kingston RC, 4¼ lths, 7m 21s

Ht: 'A' bt Nautilus RC, 2¼ lths, 7m 9s

Ht: 'B' bt lost to Nottinghamshire County RA 'B', 1½ lths, 6m 54s

Ht: 'A' bt Fiat Avazione, Italy, 4¼ lths, 7m 21s

Final: 'A' bt Nottinghamshire County RA 'B', 1⅔ lths, 6m 32s (record)

1993 N.G.C. Smith, 13.2 (bow); H. Mills, 14.1; R. Thatcher, 13.12; J.P. Hodges, 11.13 (stroke)

Ht: bt Marlow RC, 3¾ lths, 7m 19s
Ht: bt London Welsh RC, 2½ lths, 7m 16s
Ht: bt Vesta RC, 4¾ lths, 7m 11s
Ht: bt Scottish Argonauts, 4½ lths, 7m 16s
Final: lost to London RC 'B', 4½ lths, 6m 55s

1995 R.J. Barrow, 11.13 (bow); T.T. Sullivan, 13.10; S.J. Fitchett, 13.2; A.J.G. Smee, 13.6 (stroke)

Ht: bt Royal Chester RC, 1¾ lths, 6m 54s
Ht: lost to Lea RC 'A', 2½ lths, 6m 57s

THE HENLEY PRIZE

1968 F.N. Graham, 12.6 (bow); R.C. Brereton, 12.4; R.S. Legget, 11.11; M.W. Trapp, 14.12 (stroke); G.K. Temple, 9.2 (cox)

Ht: bt Stratford-upon-Avon BC, 1¾ lths, 7m 45s
Ht: bt Burton Leander RC, 2½ lths, 8m 57s
Ht: lost to Crowland RC, 3 lths, 9m 41s

THE BRITANNIA CHALLENGE CUP

1969 R.C. Brereton, 12.8 (bow); R.C. Lester, 13.4; S.A. Slee, 12.2; G.J.O. Phillpotts, 11.4 (stroke), H.J. Twiss, 9.3 (cox)

Ht: bt Barclay's Bank RC, 1¾ lths, 7m 54s
Ht: bt Bewdley RC, 1⅔ lths, 7m 50s
Ht: bt Hereford RC, 1⅔ lths, 7m 47s
Ht: lost to Bedford RC, 1⅓ lths, 7m 50s

1975 D.J.D. Tatton, 12.5 (bow); J.D. Randall, 14.0; N.C. Hardingham, 13.2; P.S. Gregory, 14.0; R.C. Lee, 8.0 (cox)

Ht: bt Nottingham & Union RC, 3½ lths, 7m 34s
Ht: bt Hereford RC, 2 lths, 7m 17s
Ht: bt University Coll, Dublin, Eire, 1⅔ lths, 7m 20s
Final: bt Tideway Scullers, 2 lths, 7m 18s

1976 A.C. McLean, 12.12 (bow); P.L. Meaney, 13.1; P.S. Plaisted, 14.7; G.D. Gate, 13.2 (stroke); P.W. Jenkinson, 8.7 (cox)

Ht: bt Neptune RC, Eire, ⅔ lth, 7m 27s
Ht: bt City Orient RC, 1¾ lths, 7m 23s
Ht: lost to Wallingford Schools, ⅔ lth, 7m 30s

1978 I.R. Knight, 14.0 (bow); P.J. Hope, 13.0; G.J.E. Jack, 13.12; G.D. Gate, 13.4 (stroke) A.D. Shutes, 8.0 (cox)

Ht: lost to Kingston RC, 1 lth, 7m 40s

1980 D.R. Crockford, 13.2 (bow); P.S. Gregory, 14.7; A.J. Holmes, 14.5; C.J. Jones, 13.0 (stroke); T. Johnson, 8.6 (cox)

Ht: bt Henley RC, easily, 8m 2s
Ht: bt Vesta RC, 1 lth, 7m 37s
Ht: bt London RC, 2¾ lths, 7m 23s
Final: bt Wallingford School, 2¼ lths, 7m 24s

1981 G.R.N. Holland, 12.11 (bow); R.A.J. Gillespie, 13.2; S.P.W. Francis, 14.4; K.A. Reynolds, 12.11 (stroke); C. Scares, 8.6 (cox)

Ht: bt Northwich RC, 2½ lths, 8m 13s
Ht: bt Garda Siochana BC, Eire, easily, 8m 2s
Ht: lost to Saxon BC, 1⅔ lths, 7m 35s

1982 S.P.D. Tunney, 15.3 (bow); S.N. Berrisford, 14.4; A.G. Rankine, 15.4; D.A. Rankine, 14.1; K.D. Mentzell, 9,0 (cox)
Ht: bt Combined Services RC, 1¾ lths, 8m 5s
Ht: lost to Lea RC, 2⅔ lths, 7m 18s

1983 J.S. Mackay, 12.2 (bow); R.J. Spratley, 13.13; P. Webb, 12.13; J.D. Wilson, 12.12 (stroke); J. Baxter, 7.12 (cox)
Ht: lost to Molesey BC, 2 feet, no time taken

1987 A.N. Odell, 12.5 (bow); M.A. Frost, 13.6; D.J. Badcock, 13.4; P.A. Hamer, 13.11 (stroke) C.J. Jenkins (cox)
Ht: bt Sons of the Thames RC, 2⅓ lths, 7m 25s
Ht: lost to Garda Siochana BC, Eire, 2⅓ lths, 7m 21s

1988 P. Hammer, 14.4 (bow); D.J. Luke, 15.0; D.J. Badcock, 14.6; P. Hubbard, 14.1 (stroke) L. Pelz, 8.0 (cox)
Ht: bt Lea RC 'A' 1¾ lths, 7m 52s
Ht: lost to Walton RC, 1¼ lths, 7m 36s

1989 H.F.W. Worden, 14.4 (bow); M.V. Buckingham, 13.10; A.P.L. Bizzel, 14.11; J. Wright, 13.10 (stroke); G.G.P. Herbert, 7.10 (cox)
Ht: bt Walton RC, 2¼ lths, 7m 51s
Ht: bt Univ of Pennsylvania, USA, 1¼ lths, 7m 13s
Ht: bt Cork BC, Eire, 1 lth, 7m 32s
Ht: bt Harvard Univ, USA, ½ lth, 7m 10s
Final: bt Lea RC 'A', 2 lths, 6m 53s (record)

1993 D.R. Wilson, 14.1 (bow); R.F. Morrison, 16.10; F.G.J. Brown, 14.1; A.F. Murray, 14.1 (stroke); M. Watts, 8.4 (cox)
Ht: bt Bedford RC, 3 lths, 7m 1s
Ht: bt Tideway Scullers, 2 lths, 6m 58s
Ht: bt Nottingham & Union RC, easily, 7m 10s
Ht: lost to Goldie BC, 1 lth, 7.19

LEANDER RACES AT HENLEY, 1840–1996
(The results achieved by composite crews are shown in brackets)

	Total Races	Total Won	Total Lost
Grand	158	92 (+16)	44 (+6)
Stewards'	93	41 (+8)	40 (+4)
Prince Philip	24	10 (+6)	7 (+1)
Queen Mother	17	3 (+7)	3 (+4)
Silver Goblets	158	101 (+13)	40 (+3)
Double Sculls	63	36 (+10)	14 (+3)
Diamond Sculls	131	87	44
Ladies'	20	13 (+2)	4 (+1)
Thames	61	48	13
Wyfold	72	51	21
Britannia	38	28	10
TOTAL	835	572	263

LEANDER WINS AT HENLEY
(Wins by composite crews are shown by a bracketed asterisk, thus (*))

G:Grand, S:Stewards', PP:Prince Philip, QM:Queen Mother, SG:Silver Goblets, DS:Double Sculls, D:Diamond Sculls, L:Ladies', T:Thames, W:Wyfold, B:Britannia

	G	S	PP	QM	SG	DS	D	L	T	W	B
1840	*										
1845							*				
1849		*										
1875	*										
1880	*										
1891	*				*						
1892	*										
1893	*										
1894	*										
1895							*				
1896	*						*				
1897		*			*						
1898	*	*									
1899	*				*						
1900	*	*									
1901	*										
1903	*						*				
1904	*										
1905	*	*				*					
1906		*									
1907					*						
1908							*				
1909					*						
1910					*						
1913	*										
1914		*									
1922	*										
1924	*										
1925	*										
1926	*										
1929	*										
1932	*										
1934	*										
1937		*									
1938		*			*						
1946	*	*			*						
1948					*						
1949	*										

LEANDER WINS AT HENLEY

(Wins by composite crews are shown by a bracketed asterisk, thus (*))

	G	S	PP	QM	SG	DS	D	L	T	W	B
1950							*				
1951						*					
1952	*										
1953	*	*									
1957					*						
1958					*						
1959						*					
1960							*				
1962						*	*				
1963					*						
1964					*	*					
1965			*								
1968									*		
1969									*		
1970									*		
1971					*						
1972						*				*	
1973						*					
1975	(*)					*					*
1977						*	*				
1978						*	*				
1979					*	(*)			*		
1980											*
1981							*				
1982	(*)						*				
1983						(*)					
1984	(*)						*				
1985								*			
1986	(*)				(*)						
1987					(*)						
1988	(*)	*									
1989					*					*	*
1990		(*)									
1991	(*)	(*)	(*)	(*)	*			(*)			
1992		*					*				
1993		(*)	(*)		*						
1994						*					
1995			*		*						
Total	27	12	3	—	20	9	15	1	4	2	3
	(+6)	(+3)	(+2)	(+1)	(+2)	(+2)	—	(+1)	—	—	—

3

LEANDER MEMBERS IN OLYMPIC, WORLD, EUROPEAN AND COMMONWEALTH CHAMPIONSHIPS

The crews are shown in rowing order when a full club crew is represented. If members are rowing as part of a composite crew, only those members are listed and shown in alphabetical order. Again, an asterisk (*) indicates a composite crew.

1908 Olympic Games, Henley-on-Thames

Coxswainless Pairs (1st)
J.R.K. Fenning (bow), G.L. Thomson (stroke)

Single Sculls (2nd)
A. McCulloch

Coxswainlness Fours (2nd)
P.R. Filleul (bow), H.R. Barker, J.R.K. Fenning, G.L. Thomson (stroke)

Eights (1st)
A.C. Gladstone (bow), F.S. Kelly, B.C. Johnstone, G. Nickalls, C.D. Burnell, R.H. Sanderson, R.B. Etherington-Smith, H.C. Bucknall stroke), G.S. Maclagan (cox)

1912 Olympic Games, Stockholm

Eights (1st)
E.R. Burgess (bow), S.E. Swann, I.G. Wormald, E.D. Horsfall, J.A. Gillan, A.S. Garton, A.G. Kirby, P. Fleming (stroke), H.B. Wells (cox)

1920 Olympic Games, Antwerp

Eights (2nd)
S.E. Swann (bow), R.S. Shove, S. Earl, J.A. Campbell, W.E.C. James, R.S.C. Lucas, G.O. Nickalls, E.D. Horsfall (stroke), R.T. Johnstone (cox)

1932 Olympic Games, Los Angeles

Eights (4th)
D. Haig-Thomas (bow), K.M. Payne, T.G. Askwith, W.A.T. Sambell, C.J.S. Sergel, H.R.N. Rickett, D.H. McCowen, L. Luxton (stroke), J.M. Ranking (cox)

1936 Olympic Games, Berlin

Eights (4th)
A.D. Kingsford (bow), H.W. Mason, T.G. Askwith, D.G. Kingsford, M.P. Lonnon, J.M. Couchman, J.C. Cherry, W.G.R.M. Laurie (stroke), J.N. Duckworth (cox)

1948 Olympic Games, Henley-on-Thames

Double Sculls* (1st)
R.D. Burnell

Coxswainless Pairs (1st)
W.G.R.M. Laurie (bow), J.H.T. Wilson (stroke)

Single Sculls (unplaced)
A.D. Rowe

Eights (2nd)
A.P. Mellows (bow), D.J.C. Meyrick, C.B.M. Lloyd, P.M.O. Massey, E.A.P. Bircher, G.C. Richardson, M.C. Lapage, C.B.R. Barton (stroke), J.G. Dearlove (Thames RC) (cox)

1949 **European Championships, Amsterdam**
Double Sculls* (5th)
R.D. Burnell

1950 **British Empire Games, Auckland**
Single Sculls (2nd)
A.D. Rowe
Eights* (3rd)
P. Bradley, R.D. Burnell, P.A. de Giles, M.C. Lapage, W.A.D. Windham

1952 **Olympic Games, Helsinki**
Coxswainless Fours (4th)
H.H. Almond (bow), J.G.P. Crowden, J.S.M. Jones, G.A.H. Cadbury (stroke)
Eights (4th)
D.D. Macklin (bow), A.L. Macleod, N.B.M. Clack, R.F.A. Sharpley, E.J. Worlidge, C.B.M. Lloyd, W.A.D. Windham, D.M. Jennens (stroke), J.F.K. Hinde (cox)

1954 **European Championships, Amsterdam**
Coxswainless Pairs (3rd)
D.D. Macklin (bow), C.G.V. Davidge (stroke)

1956 **European Championships, Bled, Yugoslavia**
Coxswainless Pairs (unplaced)
D.A.T. Leadley (bow), C.G.V. Davidge (stroke)
Eights* (unplaced)
S.G.D. Tozer, J.F.K. Hinde (cox)

1956 **Olympic Games, Melbourne**
Eights* (unplaced)
C.G.V. Davidge, S.G.D. Tozer, J.F.K. Hinde (cox)

1957 **European Championships, Duisburg**
Coxswainless Pairs (1st)
D.A.T. Leadley (bow), C.G.V. Davidge (stroke)

1958 **European Championships, Poznan, Poland**
Coxswainless Pairs (4th)
D.A.T. Leadley (bow), C.G.V. Davidge (stroke)

1959 **European Championships, Macon, France**
Single Sculls (unplaced)
S.C. Rand

1960 **Olympic Games, Rome**
Single Sculls (unplaced)
S.C. Rand

1962 **World Championships, Lucerne**
Double Sculls (5th)
G.C. Justicz (bow), N.J. Birkmyre (stroke)
Single Sculls (2nd)
S.A. Mackenzie
British Empire and Commonwealth Games, Perth
Double Sculls (1st)
G.C. Justicz (bow), N.J. Birkmyre (stroke)

1963 **European Championships, Copenhagen**
Double Sculls (8th)
P.J. Webb (bow), A.V. Cooke (stroke)
Coxswainless Pairs (5th)
C.G.V. Davidge (bow), S.A. Mackenzie (stroke)

1964 **European Championships, Amsterdam**
Double Sculls (2nd)
P.J. Webb (bow), A.V. Cooke (stroke)

1964 **Olympic Games, Tokyo**
Double Sculls (7th)
P.J. Webb (bow), A.V. Cooke (stroke)

1965 **European Championships, Duisburg**
Double Sculls (8th)
N.P. Cooper (bow), S.A. Mackenzie (stroke)

1966 **World Championships, Bled, Yugoslavia**

Double Sculls (9th)
N.P. Cooper (bow), A.V. Cooke (stroke)

1969 **European Championships, Klagenfurt**

Coxswainless Pairs (14th)
J.K. Mullard (bow), P.G. Saltmarsh (stroke)

1971 **European Championships, Copenhagen**

Coxswainless Pairs (8th)
G.A.S. Locke (bow), T.J. Crooks (stroke)

1972 **Olympic Games, Munich**

Double Sculls (5th)
P.G.R. Delafield (bow), T.J. Crooks (stroke)

1973 **European Championships, Moscow**

Coxed Fours* (11th)
C.P. Etherington, R.C. Lester, H.P. Matheson

Double Sculls (3rd)
M.J. Hart (bow), C.L. Baillieu (stroke)

Coxswainless Pairs* (10th)
J.C. Yallop

Coxed Pairs (unplaced)
J.C. Pemberton (bow), P.T. Summers (stroke), R. Lee (cox)

1974 **World Championships, Lucerne**

Double Sculls (3rd)
M.J. Hart (bow), C.L. Baillieu (stroke)

Coxswainless Fours (unplaced)
C. McDougall (bow), S.G. Irving, C.P. Etherington, R.J. Ayling (stroke)

Eights* (2nd)
T.J. Crooks, H.P. Matheson, D.L. Maxwell, J.C. Yallop

1975 **World Championships, Nottingham**

Coxed Fours* (4th)
T.J. Crooks, R.C. Lester, H.P. Matheson

Double Sculls (3rd)
M.J. Hart (bow), C.L. Baillieu (stroke)

Coxswainless Fours* (4th)
J.C. Yallop

Quadruple Sculls* (6th)
M.H.G. Hayter

Eights* (9th)
S.G. Irving

1976 **Olympic Games, Montreal**

Double Sculls (2nd)
M.J. Hart (bow), C.L. Baillieu (stroke)

Quadruple Sculls* (9th)
T.J.A. Bishop, M.H.G. Hayter, J.A. Justice

Eights* (2nd)
T.J. Crooks, R.C. Lester, H.P. Matheson, D.L. Maxwell, J.C. Yallop

1977 **World Championships, Amsterdam**

Double Sculls (1st)
M.J. Hart (bow), C.L. Baillieu (stroke)

Single Sculls (4th)
T.J. Crooks

Quadruple Sculls* (7th)
M.D.A. Carmichael, A.C.D. Wiggin

Eights* (5th)
P.S. Gregory, G.A. Rankine, W.R. Woodward-Fisher, R. Lee (cox)

1978 **FISA Lightweight Championships, Amsterdam**

Single Sculls (10th)
P. Zeun

1978 **World Championships, Karapiro, New Zealand**
Double Sculls (2nd)
M.J. Hart (bow), C.L. Baillieu (stroke)
Single Sculls (11th)
T.J. Crooks
Quadruple Sculls* (10th)
M.D.A. Carmichael, A.C.D. Wiggin
Eights* (7th)
M.R. McGowan, G.A. Rankine, R. Lee (cox)

1978 **FISA Lightweight Championships, Copenhagen**
Eights* (1st)
P. Zeun

1979 **World Championships, Bled, Yugoslavia**
Double Sculls* (4th)
C.L. Baillieu
Coxswainless Pairs (4th)
A.C.D. Wiggin (bow), M.D.A. Carmichael (stroke)
Eights* (6th)
G.A. Rankine

1979 **FISA Lightweight Championships, Bled, Yugoslavia**
Eights* (5th)
D. Innes, P. Zeun, P. Jenkinson (cox)

1980 **Olympic Games, Moscow**
Coxed fours* (7th)
G.A. Rankine
Double Sculls* (4th)
C.L. Baillieu
Coxswainless Pairs (3rd)
A.C.D. Wiggin (bow), M.D.A. Carmichael (stroke)
Eights* (2nd)
D. McDougall, M.R. McGowan, J.M. Pritchard, M.A. Whitwell

1980 **FISA Lightweight Championships, Hazewinkel, Belgium**
Eights* (1st)
P. Zeun

1981 **World Championships, Munich**
Single Sculls (4th)
C.L. Baillieu
Eights* (2nd)
M.R. McGowan, J.M. Pritchard

1981 **FISA Lightweight Championships, Munich**
Eights* (unplaced)
P. Zeun

1982 **World Championships, Lucerne**
Single Sculls (6th)
C.L. Baillieu
Coxswainless Fours* (9th)
G.A. Rankine
Eights* (9th)
A.J. Holmes, D. McDougall, M.R. McGowan, J.M. Pritchard, R.C. Stanhope

1982 **FISA Lightweight Championships, Lucerne**
Coxswainless Fours* (unplaced)
P. Zeun

1983 **World Championships, Duisburg**
Double Sculls* (unplaced)
C.L. Baillieu

1984 **Olympic Games, Los Angeles**
Coxed Fours* (1st)
A.J. Holmes
Coxed Pairs* (8th)
A.M. Genziani
Eights* (5th)
D. McDougall, M.R. McGowan

1984 FISA Lightweight Championships, Montreal
Eights* (6th)
S.M. Jefferies (cox)

1985 World Championships, Hazewinkel, Belgium
Eights* (7th)
S.N. Berrisford

Lightweight Coxswainless Fours* (8th)
M. Williams

Lightweight Eights* (9th)
G.A. Rees (cox)

1986 World Championships, Nottingham
Coxed Pairs* (1st)
A.J. Holmes, P.J. Sweeney (cox)

1986 Commonwealth Games, Strathclyde
Coxed Fours* (1st)
A.J. Holmes

Coxless Pairs* (1st)
A.J. Holmes

1987 World Championships, Copenhagen
Coxed Fours* (5th)
J.M. Maxey, J.L. Garrett, H.V.O. Thomas (cox)

Coxswainless Pairs* (1st)
A.J. Holmes

Coxed Pairs* (2nd)
A.J. Holmes, P.J. Sweeney (cox)

Coxswainless Fours* (4th)
S.N. Berrisford

Eights* (9th)
T.G. Dillon, S. Turner

1988 Olympic Games, Seoul
Coxed Fours* (4th)
H.V.O. Thomas (cox)

Coxswainless Pairs (1st)
A.J. Holmes (bow), S.G. Redgrave (stroke)

Coxed Pairs (3rd)
A.J. Holmes (bow), S.G. Redgrave (stroke), P.J. Sweeney (cox)

Coxswainless Fours* (4th)
S.N. Berrisford, J.L. Garrett, P.K. Mulkerrins

Eights* (4th)
P.R.K. Beaumont, N.J. Burfitt, T.G. Dillon, S. Turner, R.C. Stanhope, S.M. Jefferies (cox)

1988 World Lightweight Championships, Milan
Eights* (8th)
M. Williams

1989 World Championships, Bled, Yugoslavia
Coxed Fours (3rd)
S. Turner (bow), G.B. Stewart, T.G. Dillon, M.C. Pinsent (stroke), H.V.O. Thomas (cox)

Coxswainless Pairs (2nd)
S.N. Berrisford (bow), S.G. Redgrave (stroke)

Coxed Pairs (5th)
S.N. Berrisford (bow), S.G. Redgrave (stroke), P.J. Sweeney (cox)

Coxswainless Fours (4th)
S.F. Hassan (bow), J.L. Garrett, N.J. Burfitt, P.R. Mulkerrins (stroke)

Quadruple Sculls* (unplaced)
R.C. Stanhope

Eights* (3rd)
T.J.C. Foster, R.C. Phelps, J.G. Singfield

Lightweight Double Sculls (7th)
R.C. Luke (bow), C.J. Skuse (stroke)

1990 World Championships, Tasmania

Coxed Fours* (4th)
T.G. Dillon, J.L. Garrett, R.C. Phelps, H.V.O. Thomas (cox)

Coxswainless Pairs (3rd)
M.C. Pinsent (bow), S.G. Redgrave (stroke)

Coxswainless Fours* (4th)
G.B. Stewart

Quadruple Sculls* (12th)
J.R. Garman, H.E.D. Trotter

Eights* (4th)
D.J. Luke

Lightweight Quadruple Sculls* (10th)
C.J. Skuse

1991 World Championships, Vienna

Coxed Fours* (4th)
S.N. Berrisford, N.J. Burfitt, T.G. Dillon, A.C. Ellison (cox)

Double Sculls (16th)
R.G.F. Henderson (bow), G.R. Pooley (stroke)

Coxswainless Pairs (1st)
S.G. Redgrave (bow), M.C. Pinsent (stroke)

Coxed Pairs* (10th)
J. Waller

Coxswainless Fours* (7th)
J.L. Garrett (bow), G.B. Stewart, J.D.C. Walker, J.E. Cracknell (stroke)

Eights* (3rd)
A.M. Obholzer, R.C. Phelps, R.C. Stanhope, G.G.P. Herbert (cox)

1992 Olympic Games, Barcelona

Coxed Fours* (9th)
S.N. Berrisford, N.J. Burfitt, T.G. Dillon, J. Deakin (cox)

Coxswainless Pairs (1st)
S.G. Redgrave (bow), M.C. Pinsent (stroke)

Coxed Pairs* (1st)
G.G.P. Herbert (cox)

Coxswainless Fours* (7th)
J.L. Garrett, S.F. Hassan, R.C. Stanhope

Quadruple Sculls* (13th)
G.R. Pooley

Eights* (6th)
F.B. Hunt-Davis, R.J. Obholzer, R.C. Phelps, S. Turner, J.D.C. Walker, A.C. Ellison (cox)

1993 World Championships, Roudnice, Czech Republic

Coxed Fours* (9th)
T.G. Dillon, C.A. Maclennan, A.C. Ellison (cox)

Coxswainless Pairs (1st)
S.G. Redgrave (bow), M.C. Pinsent (stroke)

Coxed Pairs* (1st)
G.G.P. Herbert (cox)

Coxswainless Fours* (5th)
F.B. Hunt-Davis, R.H. Manners

Quadruple Sculls* (14th)
G.R. Pooley

Eights* (6th)
H.V.O. Thomas (cox)

Lightweight Quadruple Sculls* (5th)
C.L.B. Long

1994 World Championships, Indianapolis

Coxed Fours* (10th)
R.F. Morrison

Coxswainless Pairs (1st)
S.G. Redgrave (bow), M.C. Pinsent (stroke)

Eights* (8th)
P.A.J. Bridge, F.B. Hunt-Davis, R.H. Manners, G.G.P. Herbert (cox)

1995 World Championships, Tampere, Finland

Coxed Fours* (7th)
C.A. Maclennan, R.F. Morrison, H. Bass (cox)

Double Sculls (10th)
J.E. Cracknell (bow), R. Thatcher (stroke)

Coxswainless Pairs (1st)
S.G. Redgrave (bow), M.C. Pinsent (stroke)

Eights* (6th)
P.A.J. Bridge, R. Hamilton, F.B. Hunt-Davis, A. Story, G.G.P. Herbert (cox)

Lightweight Quadruple Sculls* (10th)
S. Lee, C.L.B. Long

1996 Olympic Games, Atlanta

Double Sculls* (17)
J.E. Cracknell (bow), R. Thatcher (stroke)
(G.R. Pooley in heat and repechage)

Coxswainless Pairs (1st)
S.G. Redgrave (bow), M.C. Pinsent (stroke)

Eights* (8th)
P.A.J. Bridge, R. Hamilton, F.B. Hunt-Davis, A. Story, G.G.P. Herbert (cox)

1996 World Championships, Strathclyde

Lightweight Single Sculls (10th)
C.L.B. Long

LEANDER INTERNATIONAL REPRESENTATION

This list includes only those who were representing Leander when selected for international crews. It does not record international appearances by members of the Club who were representing other clubs or universities at the time.

The *Rowing Almanack* does not always give the clubs of international crews and while every effort has been made to trace these, I am aware that there may still be errors or omissions, for which I must apologise.

The FISA Lightweight Championships, inaugurated in 1974, were upgraded to World Championships only in 1985, but for simplicity I have recorded all lightweight appearances under World Championships.

O: Olympic Games: W: World Championships; E: European Championships (discontinued in 1973); CG: Commonwealth Games (includes former British Empire Games)

8+ = eights; 4– = coxswainless fours; 4+ = coxed fours; 4× = quadruple sculls; 2× = double sculls; 2– = coxswainless pairs; 2+ = coxed pairs; 1× = single sculls. Lwt = lightweight.

The two numerals that appear after the code letter (for example, O 8+:4) indicate that the member or his crew finished fourth in eights in the Olympic Games in the year in question.

H.H. Almond	1952 O 4–:4
T.G. Askwith	1932 O 8+:4; 1936 O 8+:4
R.J. Ayling	1974 W 4–:0
C.L. Baillieu	1973 E 2×:3; 1974 W 2×:3; 1975 W 2×:3; 1976 O 2×:2; 1977 W 2×:1; 1978 W 2×:2; 1979 W 2×:4; 1980 O 2×:4; 1981 W 1×:4; 1982 W 1×:6; 1983 W 2×:0
H.R. Barker	1908 O 4–:2
C.B.R. Barton	1948 O 8+:2
H. Bass	1995 W 4+:7
P.R.K. Beaumont	1988 O 8+:4
S.N. Berrisford	1985 W 8+:7; 1987 W 4–:4; 1988 O 4–:4; 1989 W 2–:2, 2+:5; 1991 W 4+:4; 1992 O 4+:9
E.A.P. Bircher	1948 O 8+:2
T.J.A. Bishop	1976 O 4+:9
P. Bradley	1950 CG 8+:3
P.A.J. Bridge	1994 W 8+:8; 1995 W 8+:6; 1996 O 8+:8
H.C. Bucknall	1908 O 8+:1
N.J. Burfitt	1988 O 8+:4; 1989 W 4–:4; 1991 W 4+:4; 1992 O 4+:9

E.R. Burgess	1912 O 8+:1
C.D. Burnell	1908 O 8+:1
R.D. Burnell	1948 O 2×:1; 1949 E 2×:5; 1950 CG 8+:3
G.A.H. Cadbury	1952 O 4–:4
J.A. Campbell	1920 O 8+:2
M.D.A. Carmichael	1977 W 4×:7; 1978 W 4×:10; 1979 W 2–:4; 1980 O 2–:3
J.C. Cherry	1936 O 8+:4
N.B.M. Clack	1952 O 8+:4
A.V. Cooke	1963 E 2×:8; 1964 E 2×:2, O 2×:7; 1965 E 2×:8; 1966 W 2×:9
N.P. Cooper	1965 E 2×:8; 1966 W 2×:9
J.M. Couchman	1936 O 8+:4
J.E. Cracknell	1991 W 4–:7; 1995 W 2×:10; 1996 O 2×:17
T.J. Crooks	1971 E 2–:8; 1972 O 2×:5; 1974 W 8+:2; 1975 W 4+:4; 1976 O 8+:2; 1977 W 1×:4; 1978 W 1×:11
J.G.P. Crowden	1952 O 4–:4
C.G.V. Davidge	1954 E 2–:3; 1956 E 2–:0, O 8+:0; 1957 E 2–:1; 1958 E 2–:4; 1963 E 2–:5
J. Deakin (cox)	1992 O 4+:9
P.G.R. Delafield	1972 O 2×:5
T.G. Dillon	1987 W 8+:9; 1988 O 8+:4; 1989 W 4+:3; 1990 W 4+:4; 1991 W 4+:4; 1992 O 4+:9; 1993 W 4+:9
J.N. Duckworth (cox)	1936 O 8+:4
S. Earl	1920 O 8+:2
A.C. Ellison (cox)	1991 W 4+:4; 1992 O 8+:6; 1993 W 4+:9
C.P. Etherington	1973 E 4+:11; 1974 W 4–:0
R.B. Etherington-Smith	1908 O 8+:1
J.R.K. Fenning	1908 O 2–:1, 4–:2
P.R. Filleul	1908 O 4–:2
P. Fleming	1912 O 8+:1
T.J.C. Foster	1989 W 8+:3
J.R. Garman	1990 W 4×:12
J.L. Garrett	1987 W 4+:5; 1988 O 4–:4; 1989 W 4–:4; 1990 W 4+:4; 1991 W 4–:7; 1992 O 4–:7
A.S. Garton	1912 O 8+:1
A.M. Genziani	1984 O 2+:8
P.A. de Giles	1950 OG 8+:3
J.A. Gillan	1912 O 8+:1

A.C. Gladstone	1908 O 8+:1
P.S. Gregory	1977 W 8+:5
D. Haig-Thomas	1932 O 8+:4
R. Hamilton	1995 W 8+:6; 1996 O 8+:8
M.J. Hart	1973 E 2×:3; 1974 W 2×:3; 1975 W 2×:3; 1976 O 2×:2; 1977 W 2×:1; 1978 W 2×:2
S.F. Hassan	1989 W 4–:4; 1992 O 4–:7
M.H.G. Hayter	1975 W 4×:6; 1976 O 4×:9
R.G.F. Henderson	1991 W 2×:16
G.G.P. Herbert (cox)	1991 W 8+:3; 1992 O 2+:1; 1993 W 2+:1; 1994 W 8+:8; 1995 W 8+:6; 1996 O 8+:8
J.F.K. Hinde (cox)	1952 O 8+:4; 1956 E 8+:0, O 8+:0
A.J. Holmes	1982 W 8+:9; 1984 O 4+:1; 1986 W 2+:1; OG 4+:1; 2–:1; 1987 W 2–:1, 2+:2; 1988 O 2–:1, 2+:3
E.D. Horsfall	1912 O 8+:1; 1920 O 8+:2
F.B. Hunt-Davis	1992 O 8+:6; 1993 W 4–:5; 1994 W 8+:8; 1995 W 8+:6; 1996 O 8+:8
D. Innes	1979 W lwt8+:5
S.G. Irving	1974 W 4+:0; 1975 W 8+:9
W.E.C. James	1920 O 8+:2
S.M. Jefferies (cox)	1984 W lwt8+:6; 1988 O 8+:4
P. Jenkinson (cox)	1979 W lwt 8+:6
D.M. Jennens	1952 O 8+:4
J.S.M. Jones	1952 O 4–:4
B.C. Johnstone	1908 O 8+:1
R.T. Johnstone (cox)	1920 O 8+:2
J.A. Justice	1976 O 4×:9
F.S. Kelly	1908 O 8+:1
A.D. Kingsford	1936 O 8+:4
D.G. Kingsford	1936 O 8+:4
A.G. Kirby	1912 O 8+:1
M.C. Lapage	1948 O 8+:2; 1950 CG 8+:3
W.G.R.M. Laurie	1936 O 8+:4; 1948 O 2–:1
D.A.T. Leadley	1956 E 2–:0; 1957 E 2–:1; 1958 E 2–:4
R. Lee (cox)	1973 E 2+:0; 1977 W 8+:5; 1978 W 8+:7
S. Lee	1995 W lwt4×:10
R.C. Lester	1973 E 4+:11; 1975 W 4+:4; 1976 O 8+:2

C.B.M. Lloyd	1948 O 8+:2; 1952 O 8+:4
G.A.S. Locke	1972 E 2–:8
C.L.B. Long	1993 W lwt4×:5; 1995 W lwt4×:10; 1996 W lwt 1×:10
M.P. Lonnon	1936 O 8+:4
R.S. Lucas	1920 O 8+:2
D.J. Luke	1990 W 8+:4
R.C. Luke	1989 W lwt2×:7
L. Luxton	1932 O 8+:4
S.A. Mackenzie	1962 W 1×:2; 1963 E 2–:5; 1965 E 2×:8
G.S. Maclagan (cox)	1908 O 8+:1
C.A. Maclennan	1993 W 4+:9; 1995 W 4+:7
A.L. Macleod	1952 O 8+:4
D.D. Macklin	1952 O 8+:4; 1954 E 2–:3
R.H. Manners	1993 W 4–:5; 1994 W8+:8
H.W. Mason	1936 O 8+:4
P.M.O. Massey	1948 O 8+:2
H.P. Matheson	1973 E 4+:4; 1974 W 8+:2; 1975 W 4+:4; 1976 O 8+:2
J.M. Maxey	1987 W 4+:5
D.L. Maxwell	1974 W 8+:2; 1976 O 8+:2
D.H.E. McCowen	1932 O 8+:4
A. McCulloch	1908 O 1×:2
C. McDougall	1974 W 4–:0
D. McDougall	1980 O 8+:2; 1982 W 8+:8; 1984 O 8+:5
M.R. McGowan	1978 W 8+:7; 1980 O 8+:2; 1981 W 8+:2; 1982 W 8+:9; 1984 O 8+:5
A.P. Mellows	1948 O 8+:2
D.J.C. Meyrick	1948 O 8+:2
R.F. Morrison	1994 W 4+:10; 1995 W 4+:7
P.K. Mulkerrins	1988 O 4–:4; 1989 W 4–:4
J.K. Mullard	1969 E 2–:14
G. Nickalls	1908 O 8+:1
G.O. Nickalls	1920 O 8+:2
A.M. Obholzer	1991 W 8+:3
R.J. Obholzer	1992 O 8+:6
K.M. Payne	1932 O 8+:4
J.C. Pemberton	1973 E 2+:0
R.C. Phelps	1989 W 8+:3; 1990 W 4+:4; 1991 W 8+:3; 1992 O 8+:6

M.C. Pinsent	1989 W 4+:3; 1990 W 2–:3; 1991 W 2–:1; 1992 O 2–:1; 1993 W 2–:1; 1994 W 2–:1; 1995 W 2–:1; 1996 O 2–:1
G.R. Pooley	1991 W 2×:16; 1992 O 4×:13; 1993 W 4×:14
J.M. Pritchard	1980 O 8+:2; 1981 W 8+:2; 1982 W 8+:9
S.C. Rand	1959 E 1×:0; 1960 O 1×:0
G.A. Rankine	1977 W 8+:5; 1978 W 8+:7; 1979 W 8+:6; 1980 O 4+:7; 1982 W 4–:5
J.M. Ranking	1932 O 8+:4
S.G. Redgrave	1988 O 2–:1, 2+:3; 1989 W 2–:2, 2+:5; 1990 W 2–:3; 1991 W 2–:1; 1992 O 2–:1; 1993 W 2–:1; 1994 W 2–:1; 1995 W 2–:1; 1996 O 2–:1
G.A. Rees (cox)	1985 W lwt8+:9; 1987 W lwt8+:7
G.C. Richardson	1948 O 8+:2
H.R.N. Rickett	1932 O 8+:4
A.D. Rowe	1948 O 1×:0; 1950 CG 1×:2
P.G. Saltmarsh	1969 E 2–:14
W.A.T. Sambell	1932 O 8+:4
R.H. Sanderson	1908 O 8+:1
C.J.S. Sergel	1932 O 8+:4
R.F.A. Sharpley	1952 O 8+:4
R.S. Shove	1920 O 8+:2
J.G. Singfield	1989 W 8+:3
C.J. Skuse	1989 W lwt2×:7; 1990 W lwt4×:10
R.C. Stanhope	1982 W 8+:9; 1988 O 8+:4; 1989 W 8+:3; 1991 W 4–:7; 1992 O 4–:7
G.B. Stewart	1989 W 4+:3; 1990 W 4–:4; 1991 W 4–:7
A. Story	1995 W 8+:8; 1996 O 8+:8
P.T. Summers	1973 E 2+:0
S.E. Swann	1912 O 8+:1; 1920 O 8+:2
P.J. Sweeney (cox)	1986 W 2+:1; 1987 W 2+:2; 1988 O 2+:3; 1989 W 2+:5
R. Thatcher	1995 W 2×:10; 1996 O 2×:17
H.V.O. Thomas (cox)	1987 W 4+:5; 1988 O 4+:4; 1989 W 4+:3; 1990 W 4+:4; 1993 W 8+:6
G.L. Thomson	1908 O 2–:1, 4–:2
S.G.D. Tozer	1956 E 8+:0, O 8+:0
H.E.D. Trotter	1990 W 4×:12
S. Turner	1987 W 8+:9; 1988 O 8+:4; 1989 W 4+:3; 1992 O 8+:6
J.D.C. Walker	1991 W 4–:7
J. Waller	1991 W 2+:10
P.J. Webb	1963 E 2×:8; 1964 E 2×:2, O 2×:7

H.B. Wells (cox)	1912 O 8+:1
A. Whitwell	1980 O 8+:2
A.C.W. Wiggin	1977 W 4×:7; 1978 W 4×:10; 1979 W 2–:4; 1980 O 2–:3
M. Williams	1985 W lwt4–:8; 1988 W lwt8+:8
J.H.T. Wilson	1948 O 2–:1
W.A.D. Windham	1950 OG 8+:3; 1952 O 8+:4
E.J. Worlidge	1952 O 8+:4
W.R. Woodward-Fisher	1977 W 8+:5
L.G. Wormald	1912 O 8+:1
J.C. Yallop	1973 E 2–:10; 1974 W 8+:2; 1975 W 4–:4; 1976 O 8+:2
P. Zeun	1977 W lwt1×:10; 1978 W lwt8+:1; 1979 W lwt8+:5; 1980 W lwt8+:1; 1981 W lwt8+:0; 1982 W lwt4–:0

INDEX

Index

A
Abbagnale, Carmine & Guiseppe, 164–5, 170, 173, 182, 188
Adam, Karl, 132
Adey, F.W., 41
Admiral, The, 36
Aegir, Groninger Studenten Roeiveerigen, Holland, 139, 143
Aitken, M., 178
Albert, Prince, 39, 41
Alwin, M.B., 135–6
Amateur Definition, 59, 81, 111, 198
Amateur Rowing Association, 67, 83, 100, 106, 111, 114, 116, 121, 125–6, 128, 130, 133, 136, 138, 141, 143–4, 158, 164, 170–71, 173, 175, 177, 184, 198
American Army Medical Corps, 114
Andrieux, M., 190, 192–4
Argonaut Club, 46, 53
Armstrong, B., 175
Arrow, The, 17, 24–5, 27, 46
Arrow Club, 14, 16–18
Askwith, T.G., 110, 122
Ayling, R.J., 147
Auckland Rowing Club, New Zealand, 135
Australian Institute for Sport, 166–7, 200

B
Badminton Library, 36
Baillieu, C.L., 145–7, 151, 157–8
Balfour, E.R., 74
Balliol College, Oxford, 51, 76
Banovic, M., 191
Barber, D., 189
Barcelona, Club de Remo, 124
Barclay's Bank, 98, 115
Barn Cottage Boat Club, 132–3, 137, 142
Barry, Bert, 116
Barry, Lou, 133
Barton, C.B.R., 116, 118
Bass, H., 191
Batten, Guin, 192, 194
Batten, Miriam, 179
Bauer, H., 176
Bayford, J.H., 24, 27–8
Beaumont, P.R.K., 166
Beckett, S., 44
Bedford Rowing Club, 139
Belgian International Championships, 161
Belgian Rowing Federation, 81
Belgians at Henley, 81–3
Bell's Life, 16–18, 22–30, 32–4, 37, 39, 42–6
— *Aquatic Register*, 18
Belson, D., 155–7

Beresford, J., Jnr, 109–10, 112, 116, 123, 182
Bergau, G., 138
Berlin 'Wiking' Ruder Club, Germany, 111
Berliner Ruder Club, Germany, 84, 107
Berrisford, S.N., 161–2, 171–8, 180, 190
Beveridge, J., 134
Bewdley Rowing Club, 147
Birkmyre, N.J., 134–5, 137, 142
Bishop, J.D., 24, 30, 37, 39, 41
Bishop's Walk, 21
Bishop's Yard, 21
Bisschop, V.de, 81
Blackfriars Bridge, 31, 34–5
Blanchard, G.B., 169
Bland, J.L., 159
Boat Race, The, 14, 26, 29, 39, 45, 68, 73, 82, 88, 92, 100, 105–6, 108, 114–6, 124–5, 129, 132, 138, 140, 159, 177, 186, 188
— Centenary History, 27
Boat Racing, 17
Border Regiment, The, 114
Boston, University, USA, 159
Boswell, T.A.G., 156–7
Bourne, R.C., 92–4
Bourne, R.M.A., 115
Bovill, W., 54–6
Bradley, N.J., 115–6
Brasenose College, Oxford, 36, 60, 64, 71
Brett, W.B., (Viscount Esher), 32–3
Brickwood, E.D., 17
Bridge, P.A.J., 179
British Columbia, University of, Canada, 149
British Empire Games, 112, 121–2, 128–9
British Olympic Association, 101, 193
British Petroleum, 153
Brown, Sue, 153
Bruce, S.M. (Viscount Bruce of Melbourne), 115, 127
Buckingham, M.A.H., 161
Budgett, R.G.M., 160, 180
Buldakov, Igor, 131
Bumpsted, T.B., 96
Burfitt, N.J., 166, 174, 180
Burgess, C.G., 116–7
Burgess, E.R., 92
Burgess, J.F., 116–7
Burkhard, U., 118
Burnell, C.D., ix, 77, 81–2, 88, 92, 115, 118, 142–, 170
Burnell, P.C.D., ix
Burnell, R.D., ix, 115–6, 118, 120–5, 141, 154, 157

Burnell, Rosalind, ix
Burrough, A., 113
Bushnell, B.H.T., 116, 118, 120
Buxton, M., 157

C
Cadbury, Sir Adrian, 125–6
Cairo Police Rowing Club, 144
California,
— University of, USA, 106–7, 118, 150
— University of, Berkeley, USA, 159
Cambridge University Boat Club, 14, 23, 27, 29–33, 39, 51, 55, 87–9, 106–7, 109, 113, 115–6, 124–5, 129, 140, 145, 161, 175, 187–8
— Subscription Rooms, 36–7, 39
Camoys, Lord, 36
Campbell, C., 41
Campbell, H., 34
Campbell, N., 162
Canadian Association of Amateur Oarsmen, 102
Canadian Henley, 84
Cane, W.W.H., 109
Cantabrigian Rowing Club, 161
Carmichael, M.D.A., 152, 158
Carr, F.C., 139
Centre Sportif des Forces de l'Armée Francaise, 130
Chapman, H., 41
Charles River Rowing Association, USA, 160–1
Chelsea Embankment, 35
Cherry, J.C., 110–14
Childe of Hale, The, 36
Christ Church, Oxford, 24, 43
Christ Church, The, 24
Chugani, N., 179
Chuter, Penny, 154, 158, 160–1, 170–1, 173, 175
Clare College, Cambridge, 124
Clark, J., 146, 158
Clayton–Greene, C., 186–7
Clift, D.A., 160
Clive, L., 107
Cliveden and Maidenhead Regatta, 44
Cologne Regatta, 177, 179, 192
Colquhoun, Sir Patrick, 17, 22, 41, 44–50, 55–6, 58
Colquhoun,
— Goblets, 18
— Sculls, 17
Commonwealth Games (formerly British Empire Games) 131, 135, 164
Complete Oarsman, The, 16
Conant, J.W., 41

Coni, P.R.C., 153-4, 156-8, 162, 178, 187
Cooke, Sir Theodore, 89
Cooke, A.V., 136-8
Coombes, R., 41
Cooper, N.P., 138
Cop, I., 178-9, 182, 187-8
Cork,
— Exhibition, 84
— International Regatta, 84, 161
Cornell University, USA, 72-3, 130, 135, 137, 139-40
Corsair, The, 25
Cottesloe, Lord, 127
Coventry, W., 186-7
Coward, Sir Noel, 82
Cracknell, J.E., 191-2, 194
Crescent Club, 41
Crick, J.L.M., 124
Crooks, T.J., 139, 143-5, 147, 151, 160
Cross, M.P., 160, 175-6, 189
Crowland Rowing Club, 139
Crum, W.E., 74

D
Daily Telegraph, The, ix, 166
Dalgleish, A., 39
Dalley, C.J., 144
Dartmouth College, USA, 143
Dartmouth Rowing Club, USA, 122
Davidge, C.G.V., 121-2, 129-32, 135-6, 142
Davis, C.M., 134
Delafield, P.G.R., 145
Delft,— Roeivereeniging de Delftsche Sport, Holland, 116
Dillon, T.G., 166, 174, 180
Dinamo Club, Moscow, 172, 178
Doggett, Thomas, 13, 15
Doggett's Coat and Badge, 13, 26, 34, 158
Dolphin Cutter Club, 33
Domesday Book, The, 13
Douglas-Mann, S.C.H., 131
Dreyfus, A., 109
Driessche, J.Van, 188
Drury, D.H., 139
Duckworth, J.N., 111
Duisburg, Regatta, 172, 177

E
Edgar, King, 13
Edinburgh, Prince Philip, Duke of, 126, 141
Edward VII, King, 84, 95
Edward VIII, King, 99
— as Prince of Wales, 95
Edwards, H.R.A., 107, 132, 136
Edwards-Moss, T.C., 60
Egan, T., 40
Eliot House, USA, 161
Elizabeth II, Queen, 126

— as Princess Elizabeth, 115
Ellison, A.C., 160
Eltang, B., 147, 162
Emanuel School, 139
Emerald, The, 25, 27
Emmanuel College, Cambridge, 84
Essen Regatta, 179, 182
Etherington, C.P., 157
Etherington-Smith, R.B., 82, 86, 88
Eton College, ix, 14, 24, 52, 55, 73, 99; Boating Book, 27; Etonian Club, 37; Monarch Boat Club, 14; Old Etonians, 14
Ettingshausen, C.Von, 182
European Championships, 81, 122; (1947) 121; (1949) 121; (1950) 122; (1951) 125; (1953) 127; (1954) 129-31; (1955) 130-4; (1956) 130; (1957) 131; (1958) 131; (1959) 132; (1960) 154; (1961) 134; (1963) 135-6; (1964) 137-8; (1965) 138; (1969) 143; (1971) 144; (1973) 145
European Union Championships, 190

F
Fairbairn, G.E., 89
Fairbairn, S., 84, 102, 105
— Bust, 177
Faibairnism, 97, 107, 109, 118
Fane, R.J.A., 169
Fédération Francaise des Sociétés d'Aviron (FFSA), 173
Fédération Internationale des Sociétés d'Aviron (FISA), 121, 138, 186-7, 197
— Championships for Juniors, 139
Fellows, H.W., 41, 45
Fellows, T.H., 41
Fenning, J.R.K., 89, 91-2
Fishmongers' Company, 13
Fisk, G.C., 125
Fleming, P., 92
Fletcher, W.A.L., 84, 86, 88, 95, 99-100
Flush Day, 50
Foster, T.J.C., 172, 174-6, 186
Foundation for Sport and the Arts, 200
Fox, T.A., 124-5
France Club, 188
Frankfurt Regatta, 111
Freckleton, Fiona, 179
Freemasons Tavern, 56
Fry's Magazine, 17
Funny Club, the, 14, 17, 23

G
Garda Siochana Boat Club, Dublin, 139, 162-3
Gardner, J.C., 71
Garrett, J.L., 154, 165, 172-4, 180
Garton, A.S., ix, 115
Garton, J.L., 154, 156

Gentlemen of Lyons, The, 17
Gentlemen of the Pearl Cutter, The, 17
George V, King, 92
George VI, King, 99, 126
George, R.D., 109
Georgetown University Rowing Association, USA, 162
Ghent, 81
— Club Nautique, 81-2, 86, 88-9
— Regatta, 161, 169, 172
— Royal Sport Nautique, 81, 84, 87-8
Gibbon, J.H., 83, 115
Giles, P.A.de, 125
Gillan, Sir Angus, 82
Gloucester, Prince Henry, Duke of, 99
Gloucester River Club, 30
Goiris, L., 188
Gold, Sir Harcourt, 73, 76-7, 82, 115, 126
Goldie Boat Club, 122, 125, 161, 187, 192
Goldie, C.J.D., 82
Goldie, J.H.D., 60, 66
Goldman, P., 21
Goolden, C., 46, 54-5
— Cup, 18, 46, 54
Gorny, P., 138
Grabow, Guido and Volker, 172
Graham, P., 189
Grainger, B.G., 175, 177
Granville, A.K.B., 32
Grenfell, W.H. (Lord Desborough), 83
Gridley, R.C.M.G., 96
Grimes, C.L., 132
Gröbler, J., 175-9, 184, 186-7, 189-91, 195
Guards Club, The, 14, 25
Gurdon, C., 62

H
Haig-Thomas, P., 115-6
Haining, P.M., 179, 187, 192
Hall-Craggs, J.F., 138
Hall-Craggs, O.W., 184
Hamburg,
— RC Favorite Hammonia, 81
— Regatta, 111
Hamilton, J.H., 105
Hampshire, G.K., 104-5
Hampshire, Susan, 105
Hanlan Boat Club, Canada, 161
Hansa Dortmund, Ruder Club, Germany, 172, 176, 178, 186-8, 191
Hansen, A. and F., 146, 162
Harriman, Averill, 114
Hart, M.J., 145-6, 151
Hartley, P.H.G.H.S., 98
Harvard University, USA, 93-5, 113, 122, 124, 132, 136-7, 139, 144, 147-8, 161-2
Hassan, S.F. 172-3
Hayter, M.H.G., 151

Index

Head of the River Race, The, 68, 116, 125, 145, 166, 175, 177, 179, 186, 188, 192
Hellerup Roklubb, Denmark, 122
Hellyer, F.E., 122
Henderson, R.G.F., 178, 180-2
Henley One-Day Regatta, 1945, 115
Henley Peace Regatta, 1919, 100
— Leander Cup, 100
Henley Royal Regatta, ix, xi, 14, 34, 52-3, 62-3, 100, 102, 111, 115, 153-4, 156
— Controversy over foreign entries, 1901, 83
— Records of, 41, 72, 104, 139
Henry, Prince of the Netherlands, 43
Herald, The, 34
Herbert, G.G.P., 170, 178, 180, 182, 184, 188, 192
Herne Club, The, 46
Hero and Leander (song), 13
Hill, R.D., ix, 145-6, 148
Hinde, J.F.K., 125, 130
Hodgson, A.B., 113
Hoeltzenbein, P., 182, 188-9
Holland, J., 193
Holme Pierrepont, National Water Sports Centre, 143, 148, 150, 152, 164, 179
Holmes, A.J., 160, 162, 164-5, 167, 170, 173
Holmes, C., 179
Home Countries International, 161
Honey & Archer, 24
Hornby, 31-2
Hornemann, W.F., 27, 42
Horsfall, E.D., 102
Houses of Parliament, 35
Howard, R.L., 132
Hulls, J.D., 176
Hunt & Chandler, 16
Hunt–Davis, F.B., 180, 186
Huntley, F.O.J., 82
Hutchinson, A.M., 71
Hylton–Smith, K., 21, 153
Hylton–Smith, R., 21

I
Ilex Club, 46
Imperial College, London, 98, 191
Isis Boat Club, 132, 139
Isler, U., 145
Ivanov, Viktor, 131
Ivanov, Vyacheslav, 135

J
Jackson, P.H., 112
Jackson's Oxford Chronicle, 40
Jaguar Cars, 158
Jahrling, H., 195, 200
Janousek, B., 143-5, 147-8, 151-2, 159, 160
Jefferies, S.M., 166

Jeffreys, G., 41
Jenkins, T.L., 41
Jennens, D.M., 124-5
Jerome, K., Jerome, 49
Jesus College, Cambridge, 93, 97, 104, 111, 113, 116, 130
John Cross, The, 36
Jones, C.J., 150
Julius, A.A., 41-2
Jung, T., 174, 177
Justicz, G.C., 134-5, 137, 142

K
Keller, T.H., 143
Kellner, U., 174, 177
Kelly, F.S., 84, 86, 95
Kelly, J.B. Jnr, 118, 122
Kelly, J.B. Snr, 118
Kent, C.W., 64, 71-2
Kent, Duke of, 99
Kiely, J.R., 137
Kilmorey, Lord, 37
King's College Club, 33
Kingsford, D.G., 111, 113
Kingston Head of the River Race, 190
Kingston Rowing Club, 58, 112, 116, 118, 144
Kirby, A.G., 95
Kirchoff, D., 188
Kolbe, P-M, 151
Kobenhavns Roklubb, Denmark, 129
Kocerka, T., 133, 135
Korschikov, G., 145
Kottman, G., 131
Krasnoe Znamia Club, USSR, 130
Krylia Sovetov Club, USSR, 129-30
Kubiak, E., 135
Kvik, Roforeningen, Denmark, 129

L
Laga, Studenten Roeivereening, Delft, Holland, 124
Lambeth, 17, 21-2, 36, 52
— Bridge, 27
— Palace, 21-2, 53
Landale, O., 71
Lang, I.M., 116
Larsen, A., 121
Laurie, W.G.R.M., 109-10, 112, 118-9, 152
Layton, J., 31-2, 42
Lea Rowing Club, 173
Leadley, D.A.T., 130-2, 142
Leander Club: Accounts, 22, 42; Cadet Scheme, 134, 138-9, 141-3, 151, 198; Coat and Badge, 18, 44, 46; Coat of Arms, 47; First Henley appearance, 36; Flag, 41; General Meetings, 57-8, 60, 66, 68, 70, 75, 95, 114, 154, 200; Henley clubhouse, xi, 60,

69-72, 94, 96, 98, 114-5, 141, 153-8, 200; HMS *Leander*, 98-9, 136; *The Leander*, 17, 24-5, 27; Membership, 41, 57, 63-4, 67, 75, 94, 97, 115, 153, 200; Minutes, 42, 45, 47, 51, 56, 97, 128, 135; Nook Enclosure, 70, 75; Origins, 16-18; Pink Hippo Club, 153; Putney boathouse, 58-9, 60, 78, 98, 115, 134; Private races, 17, 23-5, 27-33, 55; Rules, 41, 45, 57; Service crew, 100; Short History, ix, 39, 45, 50, 65, 141; Star and Arrow Club, 170; Subscriptions, 41, 46, 115, 155-158; Temple Island Enclosure, 65, 94; The Brilliants, 24-5, 32, 37, 40, 53, 60, 66, 92, 153, 178, 195, 197, 201; Trust, 154-6, 158, 200; University Qualification Rule, 66-67; White House Enclosure, 65, 94
Lecky, J.M.S., 137
Lees, M.A., 177, 184
Leetham Rowing Club, 116
Lehmann, R.C., 16, 39, 60, 62, 66, 86
Lehtelä, V., 135
Lester, R.C., 145, 147-8
Lincoln, Earl of, 14
Liverpool Cup, 37-8
Lloyd, C.B.M., 118, 124-5
Lloyd, I.B., 184, 199
Locke, G.A.S., 143-4
London,
— Bridge, 13, 15, 44
— Livery Companies and Guilds, 13, 16
London Old and New, 35
London Rowing Club, 52-5, 57-8, 68, 72, 76-8, 82, 92, 97, 105-7, 109-11, 133, 142, 149, 160-1
London Scullers' Club, 37, 41
London Society, 26
London, University of, Boat Club, 98, 133-5, 137, 149-50, 159-60, 166-7, 173, 175-6, 178, 186-7, 190, 192
Long, C.L.B., 197
Lonsdale, A.V., 56
Lowndes, J., 134
Lucas, R.S.C., 104-5
Lucerne, Rotsee Regatta, 143-6, 159-60, 162, 170, 173, 176, 180, 182, 187, 191-3
Luke, R.C., 173-4
Lyon & Co, 21
Lyon, W., 21-2, 27

M
Mackenzie, S.A., 132-6, 138
Macklin, D.D., 129
Maclagan, G.S., 77, 95
Maclennan, C.A., 180
Macleod, A.L., 125

Macon blades, 132
Magdalen College, Oxford, ix, 74, 84, 88–9, 92, 100, 104–5
Mainz Regatta, 109
Mainzer Ruder–Verein, 93–4
Malischev, Juri, 145
Mannheim Regatta, 192
Marlow
— Regatta, 132, 137, 139, 143–4, 150
— Rowing Club, 152, 160, 162, 166, 199
Mary, Queen, 92
Mason, H.W., 110, 115
Massey, P.M.O., 116, 125
Match des Seniors, 170, 174, 179, 187
Matheson, H.P., 147, 152
Mays–Smith, D.H., 142, 152
Maxey, J.M., 165
Maxwell, D.L., 147
McCulloch, A., 106
McDougall, D.F., 150, 158, 160
McGowan, M.R., 158–60
McLean, D.H., 66
Mellen, W.P., 102, 104–5
Mercantile Rowing Club, Melbourne, 167
Mesdag, R.H.van, 123
Meteor Club, 46
Metropolitan Regatta, 84, 168
Michels, J.G., 190
Milling, G., 128
Molesey Boat Club, 60, 132, 134, 137, 142, 161–2, 178–80, 186–8, 191–2
Mosman Rowing Club, Sydney, 134
Moto Guzzi, Canottieri, Italy, 134–5
Moynihan, Hon C.B., 158
Mulkerrins, P.R., 174–5
Mullard, J.K., 143

N
Napier, Hon R.A., 137
National Amateur Rowing Association, 116, 198
National Championships, 150–1, 159, 161, 170
National Lottery, ix, 200
Nautilus Club, 136, 144, 162
Naval Academy, USA, 129
Navy Sports Club, USSR, 133–4
Nereus, Amsterdamsche Studenten Roeivereeniging, Holland, 81
New College, Oxford, 68, 73–4, 92, 94
New Year's Honours, 164, 170, 186, 201
Newcastle-on-Tyne, 14
Nicholson, M.A., 114
Nickalls, G., 17, 71, 74, 84, 86, 88, 92, 94, 100, 102, 106, 188, 191
Nickalls, G.O., 100, 102, 104–6, 115, 127
Nickalls, T., 74, 188
Nickalls, V., 71, 74, 188
Nickolov, M., 152

Njord, Studenten Roeivereeniging, Leiden, Holland, 122, 124
Northumbrian Boat Club, 46
Norton, R.B., 132
Norwich Union Rowing Club, 139
Nottidge, J., 52
Nottingham International Regatta, 152, 171
Nottinghamshire County Rowing Association, 164, 172–4, 180, 189–90
Noulton, W., 28, 30, 33

O
Obholzer, A., 178
Obholzer, R.J., 180
O'Brien, Lord, 84
Olav, King, 126
Olympic Games, 100, 122–3, 125 – (1908, London) 87–92, 100; (1912, Stockholm) 92, 102; (1920, Antwerp) 100–2; (1924, Paris) 105; (1928, Amsterdam) 105–6; (1932, Los Angeles) 106–7; (1936, Berlin) 110–11; (1948, London) 74, 116–20; (1952, Helsinki) 123, 125; (1956, Melbourne) 130; (1960, Rome) 132–3; (1964, Tokyo) 136, 138; (1972, Munich) 144–5; (1976, Montreal) 145, 148; (1980, Moscow) 146, 158; (1984, Los Angeles) 147, 160; (1988, Seoul) 170; (1992, Barcelona) 182; (1996, Atlanta) 189, 193
Ooms, J.J.K., 81
Ormsund Roklub, Norway, 162
Orthodoxy, ix, 87, 97, 107, 109, 115–6, 118
Oxford University Boat Club, ix, 14, 23, 27–29, 39, 51, 159, 166, 173, 178, 186
— Radleian Club, 14

P
Page Trophy, 166, 177
Pain, E.O.G., 128
Pardhy, V., 139
Paris,
— International Regatta, 58–9
— Universal Exhibition, 58
Parish, J., 27, 30, 40, 42, 44
Parsner, E., 121
Payne, J., 82
Payne, K.M., 107, 109, 149, 155, 157
Pembroke College, Cambridge, 109–10, 115–6, 124, 138
Pennsylvania, University of, USA, 82–3, 130, 134, 139–40, 160–2, 167, 172
Peters, J.S., 199
Peterson, M., 193
Phelps, J., 34
Phelps, R.C., 174, 177–8, 180, 186

Philadelphia Gold Cup, 122
Phillips, W. (Lord Milford), 104–5
Piediluco, Paolo d'Aloja Memorial Regatta, 188
Pilgrim–Morris, J.S., 177
Pimenov, Nikolai and Yuri, 165, 172, 176, 178
Pinsent, M.C., 171, 174–80, 182–4, 186–95, 197, 200
Pitkänen, T., 135
Pitman, C.M., 16–7, 71, 86, 95, 100–4, 106, 114
Pitman, F.I., 99, 114
Playford, H.H., 52
Playford, H.M., 102
Pollock, C., 41
Pooley, G.R., 178–80, 194
Potomac Boat Club, USA, 149
Potter (Club Steward), 114
Princeton University, USA, 108–9, 162
Prior, 55
Pritchard, J.M., 150, 158–60

Q
Queen Bess, The, 36
Queen's Birthday Honours, 171
Quintin Boat Club, 110, 139, 144, 149

R
Radley College, 139
Railton, J.A.N., 136
Rand, S.C., 132–4
Randall, J.D., 156–7, 164
Ranelagh Regatta, 14
Rankine, G.A., 158
Ratzeburg, Regatta, 150, 162, 172
Ratzeburger Ruder Club, 132, 138
Reading
— Head of the River Race, 166
— Regatta, 139
— University Boat Club, 180
Red House, The, 22, 24, 31, 33
Redgrave, S.G., 152, 160, 162, 164–6, 170–80, 182–4, 186–95, 197, 200–1
Reed, L.S.T., 190
Reedy, P., 180, 182
Reininger, F.M., 180–1
Remenham Club, 94, 121, 137, 149
Renshaw, G., 22
Rentacrew, 177
Rew, C.H., 97, 123
Rickett, C.G., 142, 152
Rickett, H.R.N., ix, 98, 106–7, 125, 141–4
Ridley College, Canada, 162
Risso, E., 118
Rogers, R., 188, 191
Rolland, J-C., 190, 192–4
Rowe, A.D., 114, 118, 121–4
Rowe, G.D., 60–71, 73, 77, 94, 96, 99–100, 106

Index

Rowe, R.P.P., 71
Rowing Almanack, ix, 37, 64, 81, 84, 96, 101–3, 145, 148
Rowing (Badminton Library), 22
Rowing (magazine), 182
Royal Chester Rowing Club, 52–3
Royal, The Princess, 166
Royal Netherlands Yacht Club, 43
Royal Shrewsbury School, 115
Royal Thames Regatta, 39–40, 44, 46
Rubin, R., 132
Ruckstuhl, H.E., 145
Rufli, E., 109–10, 116

S
St John's College, Cambridge,
— Lady Margaret Boat Club, 122–4, 129
St John's College, Oxford, 41, 73
St Thomas's Hospital, 21, 35
Saltmarsh, P.G., 143
Salzgitter Regatta, 150
San Diego Training Centre, USA, 188, 191
Sanderson, R.H., 95
Savill, J., 113
Sayers, C.G., 150
Scott, R., 193–4
Scullers Head of the River Race, 146, 177, 179, 194
Sculling Championship of the Thames, 41
Scurfield, H.H., 132
Searle and Son, 21
Searle, G., 179–80, 182, 186, 188–9
Searle, J.W.C., 179–80, 182, 186, 188–9
Searle, Miss, 21–2
Sennewald, H., 188
Shark, The, 17
Shepheard, E.W., 41
Shiplake College, 139
Shove, R.S., 100
Singfield, J.G., 174, 189
Sinzinger, K.S., 176
Skuse, C., 173–4
Slater, 24
Smith, C.B., 164
Somville, O.de, 81
Spencer-Jones, J.L., 147, 162
Sporting Life – An Anthology of Sporting Prints, 21
Sporting Magazine, 24
Sports Aid Foundation, 198
Sports Council, 200
Spracklen, M.A., 160, 162, 164, 170–1, 175–6, 182, 188–9
Stangate, 21, 35, 57, 197
Stanhope, R.C., 159, 166, 178, 180
Star, The, 16
Star Club, Bedford, 175, 178

Star Club, The, 14, 16–18
Star and Garter Hotel, Putney, 22, 32, 53
Steward, H.A., 114–5
Steward, H.T., 16–7, 57, 59, 64, 70, 72, 77, 80, 88, 96
Stewart, G.B., 174, 180
Stuart, D.C.R., 87–8
Streppelhoff, T., 188–9
Streuli, R., 131
Sturrock, J., 111–2
Sunday Telegraph, The, 162
Sunday Times, The, ix
Sutherland, P.B.T., 114, 134, 138
Swann, S.E., 100
Sweeney, M.A., 187
Sweeney, P.J., 148, 162, 173–4, 176
Sydney Rowing Club, 92, 125, 132
Symonds, R.H.H., 123–5, 128, 130

T
Tanner, D.W., 173, 175
Taylor, Mat, 52, 55–6
Thames Club, 46
Thames National Regatta, 46
Thames Rowing Club, 68, 71–3, 92, 97–8, 102, 104–7, 109–12, 116, 118, 121, 124–5
Thames Tradesmen's Rowing Club, 146–9, 151, 159–60
Thames Unity Club of Lambeth, 46
Thatcher, R., 188, 191–2
Thomas, H.V.D., 165, 174
Thomson, G.L., 89, 91
Three Men in a Boat, 49
Three Towns Roddklubben, Sweden, 130
Tideway Scullers School, 133, 137–8, 142–5, 147, 149, 150–1, 180
Times, The, ix, 74, 122, 125
Timoshinin, A., 145
Tinné, C.E., 92
Tissot, J., 155, 158
Tjurin, O., 134
Togt, W.van der, 135–6
Tokyo Imperial University, 109–10
Toronto,
— Canadian National Exhibition, 102, 198
— Regatta, 102
— University, 102
Tottenham, C.R.W., 61
Tower, G.E., 93
Tozer, S.G.D., 93
Trident Rowing Club, South Africa, 149
Trinity College, Cambridge, 24, 37, 77
— First Trinity Boat Club, 58, 60, 76, 82, 106
— Second Trinity Boat Club, 43
— Third Trinity Boat Club, 68, 83–6
Trinity College, Dublin, 149
— Dublin University Boat Club, 84

Trinity College, Oxford, 121
Trinity Hall, Cambridge, 52, 68, 73, 116
Trinity, The, 125
Trud Club, USSR, 134, 137
Tukalov, Y., 128–9
Turn and Taxis, Prince Eric of, 94
Turner, S., 174, 180
Tyrian Boat Club, 159–60

U
Undine Barge Club, USA, 102
Union Boat Club, Boston, USA, 96, 109, 147–8
Union-Sportive Metropolitaine des Transports, Paris, 126–7
University College, Dublin, 149
University College, Oxford, 37, 58, 60, 84

V
Vaal Regatta, South Africa, 179
Vancouver Rowing Club, Canada, 129–30
Varese, Societa Canottieri, Italy, 124
Vauxhall, 23, 25, 27, 30
Verdon, P., 92
Vesper Boat Club, Philadelphia, USA, 84, 86, 135, 138, 148, 198
Vesta Rowing Club, 162
Veterans Head of the River Race, 177
Victoria Cup and Salver, 36–7
Victoria Embankment, 35
Victoria, Queen, 14, 22
Volante Club, 46
Vorwaerts, ASR, Rostock, Germany, 143

W
Wallace, S., 41
Wallingford,
— Rowing Club, 192
— Schools, 159
Walker, R., 189–91, 193
Wandle Club, 46, 52
Ward, W. Dudley, 82–3
Ward, Penelope Dudley, 82
Washington, University of, USA, 111, 159–60
Watermen and Lightermen, Company of, 13
Watermen, The (Opera), 13
Wearne, R., 189–91, 193
Webb, P.J., 136–8
Webber, H., 41
Weightman, D., 193–4
Westminster, 26–9, 33, 35, 55
— Bridge, 21, 23–4, 30
Westminster School, 14, 24, 30, 52, 54–5
— Isis Club, 14
Whipsnade Zoo, 136
Whitwell, A., 158–60, 164
Whitworth, A., 74
Wiggin, A.C.W., 152, 158–9

William Frederick, The, 25
Willoughby, 55
Wilson, J.H.T., 118–9
Winckless, R.N., 144
Windham, W.A.D., 121, 124
Wingfield Sculls, 15–7, 27, 36, 96, 116, 118, 146, 166, 170, 179, 194
Winser, D.M.de R., 109
Winstone, R.F., 118
Wissenschaft, SC, DHfK, Leipzig, Germany, 140
Wood, H., 41–2
Wood, M.T., 118, 122
Wood, T.L., 49, 55–6
Woodward–Fisher, W.R., 158
Worcester Boating Club, 30
World Championships, (1962) 135; (1970) 143; (1974) 145, 147; (1975) 145, 148; (1977) 146; (1978) 146, 152; (1979) 152; (1981) 147, 160; (1982) 147, 159; (1983) 147, 159; (1985) 162; (1986) 164; (1987) 165–6; (1989) 174; (1990) 176; (1991) 178–9, 189; (1993) 187; (1994) 189; (1995) 189, 192; (1996) 197
World Professional Sculling Championship, 36

Y
Yale University, USA, 73, 94, 130, 134, 159
Yallop, J.C., 147

Z
Zalgiris Viljnus, Club, Lithuania, 137–8, 176
Zurich, Ruder Club, 109–11, 113, 116
Zeveglj, D., 178–9, 182, 187–8